Internet Information Services (IIS) 7.0 Administrator's Pocket Consultant

William R. Stanek

PUBLISHED BY
Microsoft Press
A Division of Microsoft Corporation
One Microsoft Way
Redmond, Washington 98052-6399

Library of Congress Control Number: 2007939309

Printed and bound in the United States of America.

1 2 3 4 5 6 7 8 9   QWE   2 1 0 9 8 7

Distributed in Canada by H.B. Fenn and Company Ltd.

A CIP catalogue record for this book is available from the British Library.

Microsoft Press books are available through booksellers and distributors worldwide. For further information about international editions, contact your local Microsoft Corporation office or contact Microsoft Press International directly at fax (425) 936-7329. Visit our Web site at www.microsoft.com/mspress. Send comments to mspinput@microsoft.com.

Acquisitions Editor: Martin DelRe
Developmental Editor: Karen Szall
Project Editor: Maureen Zimmerman
Editorial Production: Interactive Composition Corporation
Technical Reviewer: Bob Hogan; Technical Review services provided by Content Master, a member of CM Group, Ltd.

Body Part No. X14-25665

To my wife and children for their love, their support, and their extraordinary ability to put up with the clackety-clackety of my keyboard.

Contents at a Glance

Table of Contents

What do you think of this book? We want to hear from you!

Microsoft is interested in hearing your feedback so we can continually improve our books and learning resources for you. To participate in a brief survey, please visit:

www.microsoft.com/learning/booksurvey

Acknowledgments

Writing *Internet Information Services (IIS) 7.0 Administrator's Pocket Consultant* was a lot of fun—and a lot of work. As I set out to write this book, my first goal was to determine what had changed between IIS 6 and IIS 7.0 and what new administration options were available. With any product, and especially with IIS 7.0, this meant doing a great deal of research to determine exactly how things work and a lot of digging into the configuration internals. Thankfully I'd already written many books on IIS, Web technologies, and Web publishing, so I had a starting point of reference for my research—but it was by no means a complete one.

When you start working with IIS 7.0, you'll see at once that this release is different from previous releases. What won't be readily apparent, however, is just how different IIS 7.0 is from its predecessors—and that's because many of the most significant changes to the product are under the surface. These changes affect the underlying architecture and not just the interfaces—and these changes were some of the hardest for me to research and write about.

Because pocket consultants are meant to be portable and readable—the kind of book you use to solve problems quickly and easily and get the job done wherever you might be—I had to carefully review my research to make sure I focused on the core of IIS 7.0 administration. The result is the book you hold in your hand, which I hope you'll agree is one of the best practical, portable guides to IIS 7.0.

It is gratifying to see techniques I've used time and again to solve problems put into a printed book so that others may benefit from them. But no man is an island, and this book couldn't have been written without help from some very special people. As I've stated in all my previous books with Microsoft Press, the team at Microsoft Press is top-notch. Throughout the writing process, Maureen Zimmerman was instrumental in helping me stay on track and getting the tools I needed to write this book. Maureen did a top-notch job managing the editorial process. Thanks also to Martin DelRe for believing in my work and shepherding it through production.

Unfortunately for the writer (but fortunately for readers), writing is only one part of the publishing process. Next came editing and author review. I must say, Microsoft Press has the most thorough editorial and technical review process I've seen anywhere—and I've written a lot of books for many different publishers. Bob Hogan was the technical editor for the book. Joel Rosenthal was the copy editor for the book. I want to thank both of them for their careful reviews. Bob and Joel are great to work with!

I also want to thank Lucinda, Jack, Karen, Denise, and everyone else at Microsoft who has helped me during this project. Hopefully, I haven't forgotten anyone but if I have, it was an oversight. *Honest.;-)*

Introduction

Welcome to *Internet Information Services (IIS) 7.0 Administrator's Pocket Consultant*. As the author of over 65 books, I've been writing professionally about Web publishing and Web servers since 1994. Over the years, I've written about many different Web server technologies and products, but my favorite has always been Internet Information Services (IIS). IIS provides the core services for hosting Web servers, Web applications, and Microsoft Windows SharePoint services. From top to bottom, IIS 7.0 is substantially different from earlier versions of IIS. For starters, the underlying configuration architecture for IIS has been completely reconstructed—IIS configuration architecture is now based entirely on Extensible Markup Language (XML) and XML schema.

Having written many top-selling Web publishing and XML books, I was able to bring a unique perspective to this book—the kind of perspective you can gain only after working with technologies for many years. You see, long before IIS 7.0 architecture was built on XML and related technologies, I was working with, researching, and writing about these technologies. The advantage for you, the reader, is that my solid understanding of these technologies allowed me to dig into the IIS configuration architecture and to provide a comprehensive roadmap to this architecture and the hundreds of related configuration settings in this book.

In addition, as you've probably noticed, there's more than enough information about IIS 7.0 on the Web and in other printed books. There are tutorials, reference sites, discussion groups, and more to help make it easier to use IIS 7.0. However, the advantage to reading this book instead is that all the information you need to learn IIS 7.0 is organized in one place and presented in a straightforward and orderly fashion. This book has everything you need to customize IIS installations, master IIS configuration, and maintain IIS servers.

In this book, I teach you how features work, why they work the way they work, and how to customize them to meet your needs. You'll also learn why you may want to use certain features and when to use other features to resolve any issues you are having. In addition, this book provides tips, best practices, and examples of how to optimize IIS 7.0 to meet your needs. This book won't just teach you how to configure IIS—it'll teach you how to squeeze every last bit of power out of the application and how to make the most of the features and options included in IIS 7.0.

Also, unlike many other books on the subject, this book doesn't focus on a specific user level. This isn't a lightweight, beginners-only book. Regardless of whether you are a novice administrator or a seasoned professional, many of the concepts in this book will be valuable to you. And you'll be able to apply them to your IIS server installations.

Who Is This Book For?

Internet Information Services (IIS) 7.0 Administrator's Pocket Consultant covers core services for hosting Web servers, Web applications, and Windows SharePoint services. The book is designed for:

- Current Microsoft Web administrators and developers

- Administrators and developers of intranets and extranets

- Administrators and developers migrating to Microsoft Web-based solutions

- Programmers, engineers, and quality assurance personnel who manage internal or test servers running any of these services

To pack in as much information as possible, I assume that you already have basic networking skills and a basic understanding of Web servers. With this in mind, I don't devote entire chapters to understanding the World Wide Web, Web services, or Web servers. I do, however, cover configuration, enterprise-wide server management, performance tuning, optimization, automation, and much more.

I also assume that you're fairly familiar with the standard Windows user interface and that if you plan to use the scripting techniques outlined in the book, you know scripting. If you need help learning Windows or scripting, you should read other resources (many of which are available from Microsoft Press and the Microsoft Web site as well).

How This Book Is Organized

Rome wasn't built in a day, and this book wasn't intended to be read in a day, a week, or even 21 days. Ideally, you'll read this book at your own pace, a little each day, as you work your way through all the features IIS has to offer. This book is organized into four parts with 14 chapters and a comprehensive reference in an appendix. The chapters are arranged in a logical order, taking you from planning and deployment tasks to configuration and maintenance tasks.

Speed and ease of reference are essential parts of this hands-on guide. This book has an expanded table of contents and an extensive index to help you find answers to problems quickly. Many other quick reference features have been added to the book as well, including quick step-by-step instructions, lists, tables with fast facts, and extensive cross-references.

As with all the books in the Pocket Consultant series, *Internet Information Services (IIS) 7.0 Administrator's Pocket Consultant* is designed to be a concise and easy-to-use resource for managing Web servers running IIS. This book is the readable resource guide that you'll want on your desktop at all times, as it covers everything you'll need to perform core Web administration tasks. Because the focus is on giving you maximum value in a pocket-sized guide, you don't have to wade through hundreds of pages of extraneous information to find what you're looking for. Instead, you'll find exactly what you need to get the job done.

In short, this book is designed to be the one resource you can turn to whenever you have questions regarding Web server administration. To this end, the book zeroes in on daily administration procedures, frequently used tasks, documented examples, and options that are representative while not necessarily inclusive. One of the key goals I had when writing this book is to keep the content so concise that the book remains compact and easy to navigate, while ensuring that it is packed with as much information as possible. Thus, rather than a hefty 1,000-page tome or a lightweight 100-page quick reference, you get a valuable resource guide that can help you quickly and easily perform common tasks, solve problems, and implement advanced IIS techniques, such as failed request tracing, handler mapping, customized Hypertext Transfer Protocol (HTTP) redirection, and integrated request processing.

Conventions Used in This Book

I've used a variety of elements to help keep the text clear and easy to follow. You'll find code terms and listings in monospace type, except when I tell you to actually type a command. In that case, the command appears in **bold** type. When I introduce and define a new term, I put it in *italics*.

Other conventions include:

- **Note**   Provides additional details on a particular point that needs emphasis.
- **Tip**   Offers helpful hints or additional information.
- **Caution**   Warns you when there are potential problems you should look out for.
- **More Info**   Points to more information on the subject.
- **Real World**   Provides real-world advice when discussing advanced topics.
- **Best Practice**   Examines the best technique to use when working with advanced configuration and administration concepts.

I truly hope you find that *Internet Information Services (IIS) 7.0 Administrator's Pocket Consultant* provides everything you need to perform the essential administrative tasks on IIS servers as quickly and efficiently as possible. You are welcome to send your thoughts to me at *williamstanek@aol.com*.

Other Resources

No single magic bullet exists for learning everything you'll ever need to know about IIS. While some books claim to be all-in-one guides, there's simply no way one book can do it all. With this in mind, I hope you'll use this book as it is intended to be used: as a concise and easy-to-use resource.

Your current knowledge will largely determine your success with this or any other IIS resource or book. As you encounter new topics, take the time to practice what you've learned and read about. Seek out further information as necessary to get the practical hands-on know-how and knowledge you need.

Throughout your studies, I recommend that you regularly visit Microsoft's IIS site (*http://www.iis.net*) and Microsoft's support site (*http://support.microsoft.com*) to stay current with the latest changes in the software. To help you get the most out of this book, there's a corresponding Web site at *http://www.williamstanek.com/iis* which contains information about IIS, updates to the book, and updated information about IIS.

Support

Every effort has been made to ensure the accuracy of this book. Microsoft Press provides corrections for its books at the following address:

http://www.microsoft.com/mspress/support

If you have comments, questions, or ideas about this book, please send them to Microsoft Press using either of the following methods:

Postal Mail:

Microsoft Press
Attn: *Internet Information Services (IIS) 7.0 Administrator's Pocket Consultant* Editor
One Microsoft Way
Redmond, WA 98052-6399

E-mail:

MSPINPUT@MICROSOFT.COM

Chapter 1
IIS 7.0 Administration Overview

Let's start with the bad news right up front: Internet Information Services (IIS) 7.0 isn't what you think it is. Although IIS 7.0 *is* the latest release of Internet Information Services, it *isn't* what it seems. IIS does look a lot like its predecessors, but this is deceiving because under the surface, the architecture is completely different. So much has changed, in fact, that perhaps it might have been better if Microsoft had given IIS 7.0 a new product name. That way you'd know that IIS 7.0 was completely different from its predecessors, allowing you to start with a fresh perspective and a reasonable expectation of having to learn a whole new bag of tricks. Seasoned IIS pros also are going to have to unlearn some old tricks; and that's not only going to be difficult, it might be the single biggest obstacle to mastering IIS 7.0.

IIS 7.0 provides the core services for hosting Web servers, Web applications, and Microsoft Windows SharePoint Services. Throughout this book, I'll refer to administration of IIS, Web applications, and Windows SharePoint Services as *Microsoft Web administration* or simply *Web administration*. As you get started with Microsoft Web administration, you should concentrate on these key areas:

- What's new or changed in IIS 7.0

- How IIS 7.0 configuration schema and global configuration architecture are used

- How IIS 7.0 works with your hardware

- How IIS works with Windows-based operating systems

- Which administration tools are available

- Which administration techniques you can use to manage and maintain IIS

Working with IIS 7.0: What You Need to Know Right Now

Microsoft fully integrated Microsoft ASP.NET and the Microsoft .NET Framework into IIS 7.0. Unlike IIS 6, IIS 7.0 takes ASP.NET and the .NET Framework to the next level by integrating the ASP.NET runtime extensibility model with the core server architecture, allowing developers to fully extend the core server architecture by using ASP.NET and the .NET Framework. This tighter integration makes it possible to use existing ASP.NET features such as .NET Roles, Session Management, Output Caching, and Forms Authentication with all types of content.

IIS 7.0 has generalized the Hypertext Transfer Protocol (HTTP) process activation model that IIS 6 introduced with application pools and made it available for all protocols through an independent service called the Windows Process Activation Service, and developers can use Windows Communication Foundation (WCF) protocol adapters to take advantage of the capabilities of this service. You also should know up front that IIS 7.0 includes a metabase compatibility component that allows your existing scripts and applications to continue running but does not use a metabase to store configuration information. Instead of a metabase, IIS 7.0 uses a distributed configuration system with global and application-specific configuration files that are based on a customizable set of Extensible Markup Language (XML) schema files. These XML schema files define the configuration elements and attributes in addition to valid values for those elements and attributes, providing you precise control over exactly how you can configure and use IIS.

Microsoft built the configuration system around the concept of modules. *Modules* are standalone components that provide the core feature set of an IIS server. Microsoft ships more than 40 independent modules with IIS 7.0. Either these modules are IIS 7.0–native modules that use a Win32 DLL or IIS 7.0–managed modules that use a .NET Framework Class Library contained within an assembly. Because all server features are contained within modules, you can modify the available features easily by adding, removing, or replacing a server's modules. Further, by optimizing the installed modules based on the way an IIS server is used, you can enhance security by reducing the attack surface area and improve performance by reducing the resources required to run the core services.

> **Note**   Because modules are such an important part of IIS 7.0, you'll find much discussion about them and how they are used in this book. Chapter 2, "Deploying IIS 7.0 in the Enterprise," introduces all the available native and managed modules. Chapter 5, "Managing Global IIS Configuration," details how to install and manage modules. The appendix, "Comprehensive IIS 7.0 Module and Schema Reference," provides a complete guide to using modules and schemas.

IIS 7.0 is more secure than IIS 6 because of built-in request filtering and rules-based Uniform Resource Locator (URL) authorization support. You can configure request filtering to reject suspicious requests by scanning URLs sent to a server and filtering out unwanted requests. You can configure URL authorization rules to require logon and allow or deny access to specific URLs based on user names, .NET roles, and HTTP request methods. To make it easier to resolve problems with the server and Web applications, IIS 7.0 includes new features for diagnostics, real-time request reviewing, and error reporting. These features allow you to:

- View the current running state of the server.

- Trace failed requests through the core server architecture.

- Obtain detailed error information to pinpoint the source of a problem.

IIS 7.0 has many other new and enhanced features, but few are as important as the new set of administration tools, including new graphical, command-line, and scripting administration tools. The new graphical administration tool uses a browser-like interface and adds features for delegated administration, remote administration over Secure HTTP (HTTPS), and extensibility through custom user interface components. The new command-line administration tool makes it possible to perform most configuration tasks with a single line of command text. With ASP.NET, you can manage IIS configuration through the .NET Framework by using the Microsoft.Web.Administrators application programming interface (API). With scripting, you can manage IIS configuration through the IIS 7.0 Windows Management Instrumentation (WMI) provider.

Because of the many changes, much of what you know about IIS is obsolete or irrelevant. But there's a light at the end of the tunnel—well, it's more like a freight train coming right at you—but it's there. The changes in IIS 7.0 are well worth the time and effort you'll spend learning the new architecture and the new techniques required to manage Web servers. Our dependence on ASP.NET and the .NET Framework will only grow over time, and the more you learn about the heart of the .NET architecture—IIS 7.0—the better prepared you'll be for now and for the future.

With IIS 7.0, key components that were a part of previous IIS releases are no longer available or work in different ways than they did before. Because IIS 7.0 does not use a metabase, applications designed for IIS 6 will not run on IIS 7.0 without special actions being taken. To run IIS 6 applications, you must install the IIS 6 compatibility and metabase feature. To manage IIS 6 applications and features, you must install IIS 6 Manager, IIS 6 scripting tools, and IIS 6 WMI compatibility. Additionally, IIS 7.0 does not include Post Office Protocol version 3 (POP3) or Simple Mail Transfer Protocol (SMTP) services. With IIS 7.0, you can send e-mail messages from a Web application by using the SMTP E-mail component of ASP.NET.

IIS Manager is the graphical user interface (GUI) for managing both local and remote installations of IIS 7.0. To use IIS Manager to manage an IIS server remotely, Web Management Service (WMSVC) must be installed and started on the IIS server you want to manage remotely. WMSVC is also required when IIS site or application administrators want to manage features over which they've been delegated control.

The Web Management Service provides a hostable Web core that acts as a standalone Web server for remote administration. After you install and start WMSVC on an IIS server, it listens on port 8172 on all unassigned IP addresses for four specific types of requests:

- **Login Requests**   IIS Manager sends login requests to WMSVC to initiate connections. On the hostable Web core, login requests are handled by Login.axd. The authentication type is either NT LAN Manager (NTLM) or Basic, depending on what you select when you are prompted to provide credentials in the connection dialog box.

- **Code Download Requests** If login is successful, WMSVC returns a list of user interface (UI) modules for the connection. Each IIS Manager page corresponds to a specific UI module. If there's a module that IIS Manager doesn't have, it will request to download the module binaries. Code download requests are handled by Download.axd.

- **Management Service Requests** After a connection is established, your interactions with IIS Manager cause management service requests. Management service requests direct module services in WMSVC to read or write configuration data, runtime state, and providers on the server. Management service requests are handled by Service.axd.

- **Ping Requests** Ping requests are made from within the WMSVC service to the hostable Web core. Ping requests are made by Ping.axd to ensure that the hostable Web core continues to be responsive.

The Web Management Service stores a limited set of editable configuration values in the registry. Each time the service is started, the Web configuration files are regenerated in the following directory: *%SystemRoot%*\ServiceProfiles\LocalService \AppData\Local\Temp\WMSvc. To enhance security, WMSVC requires SSL (HTTPS) for all connections. This ensures that data passed between the remote IIS Manager client and WMSVC is secure. Additionally, WMSVC runs as Local Service with a reduced permission set and a locked down configuration. This ensures that only the minimal set of required modules are loaded when the hostable Web core starts. See Chapter 3, "Core IIS 7.0 Administration," for more information.

Note *%SystemRoot%* refers to the SystemRoot environment variable. The Windows operating system has many environment variables, which are used to refer to user- and system-specific values. Often, I'll refer to environment variables in this book using this syntax: *%VariableName%*.

Introducing IIS 7.0 Configuration Architecture

You can use IIS 7.0 to publish information on intranets, extranets, and the Internet. Because today's Web sites use related features, such as ISAPI filters, ASP, ASP.NET, CGI, and the .NET Framework, IIS bundles these features as part of a comprehensive offering. What you need to know right now about IIS 7.0 is how IIS 7.0 uses the configuration schema and its global configuration system. In Chapter 2, you'll learn about the available setup features and the related configuration modules.

IIS 7.0 Configuration Schema

Unlike IIS 6, in which the main configuration information is stored in metabase files, IIS 7.0 has a unified configuration system for storing server, site, and application settings. You can manage these settings by using an included set of managed code, scripting APIs, and management tools. You can also manage these settings by directly editing the configuration files themselves. Direct editing of configuration files is possible because the files use XML and are written in plain-language text files based on a predefined set of XML schema files.

Note   IIS 7.0 always takes the master state for configuration from the configuration files. This is a dramatic change from IIS 6, in which the master state was taken from the in-memory configuration database, which was flushed periodically to disk.

Using the XML schema to specify the configuration settings ensures that the related configuration files are well-structured XML, which is easy to modify and maintain. Because configuration values are stored using easy-to-understand text strings and values, they are easy to work with. By examining the schema itself, you can determine the exact set of acceptable values for any configuration option. IIS shares the same schema with ASP.NET configuration, ensuring that configuration settings for ASP.NET applications are just as easy to manage and maintain.

On an IIS server, schema files are stored in the *%SystemRoot%*\System32\Inetsrv \Config\Schema directory. The four standard schema files are:

- **IIS_schema.xml**   This file provides the IIS configuration schema.

- **ASPNET_schema.xml**   This file provides the ASP.NET configuration schema.

- **FX_schema.xml**   This file provides the .NET Framework configuration schema (providing features beyond what the ASP.NET schema offers).

- **rscaext.xml**   This file provides the Runtime Status and Control API (RSCA) configuration schema, providing dynamic properties for obtaining detailed runtime data.

IIS reads in the schema files automatically during startup of the application pools. The IIS schema file is the master schema file. Within the IIS schema file, you'll find configuration sections for each major feature of IIS, from application pooling to failed request tracing. The ASP.NET schema file builds on and extends the master schema with specific configuration sections for ASP.NET. Within the ASP.NET schema file, you'll find configuration sections for everything from anonymous identification to output cache settings. The FX schema file builds on and extends the ASP.NET schema file. Within the FX schema file, you'll find configuration settings for application settings, connection strings, date-time serialization, and more.

Whereas configuration sections are also grouped together for easier management, section groups do not have schema definitions. If you want to extend the configuration features and options available in IIS, you can do this by extending the XML schema. You extend the schema by following these basic steps:

1. Specify the desired configuration properties and the necessary section container in an XML schema file.

2. Place the schema file in the *%SystemRoot%*\System32\Inetsrv\Config\Schema directory.

3. Reference the new section in IIS 7.0's global configuration file.

The basic syntax for a schema file is as follows:

```
<!-
The text within this section is a comment. It is standard
practice to provide introductory details in the comments at the
beginning of the schema file.
-->
<configSchema>
    <sectionSchema name="configSection1">
    </sectionSchema>
    <sectionSchema name="configSection2">
    </sectionSchema>
    <sectionSchema name="configSection3">
    </sectionSchema>
</configSchema>
```

As an administrator or developer, you don't necessarily need to be able to read and interpret XML schemas to succeed. However, because having a basic understanding of schemas is helpful, I'll introduce the essentials. Within schema files, configuration settings are organized into sets of related features called *schema sections*. The schema for a configuration section is defined in a <sectionSchema> XML element. For example, the features related to the HTTP listener in IIS are defined with a schema section named system.applicationHost/listenerAdapters. In the IIS_schema.xml file, this section is defined as follows:

```
<sectionSchema name="system.applicationHost/listenerAdapters">
 <collection addElement="add" >
  <attribute name="name" type="string" required="true" isUniqueKey="true" />
  <attribute name="identity" type="string" />
  <attribute name="protocolManagerDll" type="string" />
  <attribute name="protocolManagerDllInitFunction" type="string" />
 </collection>
</sectionSchema>
```

This schema definition states that the system.applicationHost/listenerAdapters element can contain a collection of add elements with the following attributes:

- **name**   A unique string that is a required part of the add element.

- **identity**   An identity string that is an optional part of the add element.

- **protocolManagerDll**   A string that identifies the protocol manager DLL.

- **protocolManagerDllInitFunction**   A string that identifies the initialization function for the protocol manager DLL.

An attribute of an element is either optional or required. If the attribute definition states required="true" as with the name attribute, the attribute is required and must be provided when you are using the related element. Otherwise, the attribute is considered optional and does not need to be provided when you are using the related element. In addition to being required, attributes can have other enforced conditions, including:

- **isUniqueKey**   If set to true, the related value must be unique.

- **encrypted**   If set to true, the related value is expected to be encrypted.

With some attributes, you'll see default values and possibly an enumerated list of the acceptable string values and their related internal values. In the following example, the identityType attribute has a default value of NetworkService and a list of other possible values:

```
<attribute name="identityType" type="enum" defaultValue="NetworkService">
  <enum name="LocalSystem" value="0"/>
  <enum name="LocalService" value="1"/>
  <enum name="NetworkService" value="2"/>
  <enum name="SpecificUser" value="3"/>
</attribute>
```

The friendly name of a value is provided to make the value easier to work with. The actual value used by IIS is provided in the related value definition. For example, if you set identityType to LocalService, the actual configuration value used internally by IIS is 2.

As a standard rule, you cannot use enumerated values in combination with each other. Because of this, the identityType attribute can have only one possible value. In contrast, attributes can have flags, which can be used together to form combinations of values. In the following example, the logEventOnRecycle attribute uses flags and has a default set of flags that are used in combination with each other:

```
<attribute name="logEventOnRecycle" type="flags" defaultValue="Time,
Memory, PrivateMemory">
  <flag name="Time" value="1"/>
  <flag name="Requests" value="2"/>
  <flag name="Schedule" value="4"/>
  <flag name="Memory" value="8"/>
  <flag name="IsapiUnhealthy" value="16"/>
  <flag name="OnDemand" value="32"/>
  <flag name="ConfigChange" value="64"/>
  <flag name="PrivateMemory" value="128"/>
</attribute>
```

Again, the friendly name is provided to make the value easier to work with. The actual value used by IIS is the sum of the combined flag values. With a setting of "Time, Requests, Schedule," the logEventOnRecycle attribute is set to 7 (1+2+4=7).

Attribute values can also have validation. IIS performs validation of attribute values when parsing the XML and when calling the related API. Table 1-1 provides an overview of the validators you'll see in schemas.

Table 1-1   Summary of Attribute Validation Types in an IIS XML Schema

Validation Type	Validation Parameter	Validation Fails If...
validationType= "applicationPoolName"	validationParameter=""	A validated value contains these characters: |<>&\"
validationType= "integerRange"	validationParameter= "<minimum>, <maximum>[,exclude]"	A validated value is outside [inside] range, in integers.
validationType= "nonEmptyString"	validationParameter=""	A validated value has a string value that is not set.
validationType= "siteName"	validationParameter=""	A validated value contains these characters: /\.?
validationType= "timeSpanRange"	validationParameter= "<minimum>,<maximum>, <granularity> [,exclude]"	A validated value is outside [inside] range, in seconds.
validationType= "requireTrimmedString"	validationParameter=""	A validated value has white space at start or end of value.

IIS 7.0 Global Configuration System

IIS uses a global configuration system that is difficult to understand at first but gets easier and easier to understand once you've worked with it awhile. Because there's no sense trying to ease into this, I'll dive right in. If you'll hang with me for a few pages, I'll get you through the roughest parts and zero in on exactly what you need to know—I promise.

IIS configuration settings are stored in configuration files that together set the running configuration of IIS and related components. One way to think of a configuration file is as a container for the settings you apply and their related values. You can apply multiple configuration files to a single server and the applications it is running. Generally, you manage configuration files at the .NET Framework root level, the server root level, and the various levels of a server's Web content directories. A server's Web content directories include the root directory of the server itself, the root directories of configured Web sites, and any subdirectories within Web sites. The root levels and the various levels of a server's Web content directories can be described as containers for the settings you apply and their values. If you know a bit about object-oriented programming, you might expect the concepts of parent-child relationship and inheritance to apply—and you'd be right.

Through inheritance, a setting applied at a parent level becomes the default for other levels of the configuration hierarchy. Essentially, this means that a setting applied at a parent level is passed down to a child level by default. For example, if you apply a setting at the server root level, the setting is inherited by all Web sites on the server and by all the content directories within those sites.

The order of inheritance is as follows:

```
.NET Framework root → server root → Web Site root →
top-level directory → subdirectory
```

This means that the settings for the current .NET Framework root are passed down to IIS, the settings for IIS are passed down to Web sites, and the settings for Web sites are passed down to content directories and subdirectories. As you might expect, you can override inheritance. To do this, you specifically assign a setting for a child level that contradicts a setting for a parent. As long as overriding a setting is allowed (that is, overriding isn't blocked), the child level's setting will be applied appropriately. To learn more about overriding and blocking, see Chapter 5.

When working with the configuration files, keep the following in mind:

- The .NET Framework root IIS applies depends on the current running version of ASP.NET and the .NET Framework. The default configuration files for the .NET Framework root are Machine.config and Web.config, which are stored in the *%SystemRoot%*\Microsoft.net\Framework*Version*\Config\Machine.config directory. Machine.config sets the global defaults for the .NET Framework settings in addition to some ASP.NET settings. Web.config sets the rest of the global defaults for ASP.NET. See Chapter 8, "Running IIS Applications," and Chapter 9, "Managing Applications, Application Pools, and Worker Processes," for more information about configuring the .NET Framework and ASP.NET.

- The default configuration file for the server root is ApplicationHost.config, which is stored in the *%SystemRoot%*\System32\Inetsrv\Config directory. This file controls the global configuration of IIS. See Chapter 5 for more information about configuring IIS servers.

- The default configuration file for a Web site root is Web.config. This file is stored in the root directory of the Web site to which it applies and controls the behavior for the Web site. See Chapters 8 and 9 for more information about configuring IIS applications.

- The default configuration file for a top-level content directory or a content subdirectory is Web.config. This file is stored in the content directory to which it applies and controls the behavior of that level of the content hierarchy and downwards. See Chapter 6 for more information about configuring content directories.

In some cases, you may want a .config file to include some other .config file. This can be done by using the configSource attribute to refer to the .config file containing the settings you want to use. Currently, the referenced .config file must reside in the same directory as the original .config file. Note that this behavior may change to allow .config files in other directories to be used. To see how this works, consider the following example from the ApplicationHost.config file:

```
<?xml version="1.0" encoding="UTF-8"?>
<!-- applicationHost.config -->
<configuration>
 <system.webServer>
  <httpErrors>
   <error statusCode="401" prefixLanguageFilePath="%SystemDrive%\
inetpub\custerr" path="401.htm" />
   <error statusCode="403" prefixLanguageFilePath="%SystemDrive%\
inetpub\custerr" path="403.htm" />
   <error statusCode="404" prefixLanguageFilePath="%SystemDrive%\
inetpub\custerr" path="404.htm" />
   <error statusCode="405" prefixLanguageFilePath="%SystemDrive%\
inetpub\custerr" path="405.htm" />
   <error statusCode="406" prefixLanguageFilePath="%SystemDrive%\
inetpub\custerr" path="406.htm" />
   <error statusCode="412" prefixLanguageFilePath="%SystemDrive%\
inetpub\custerr" path="412.htm" />
   <error statusCode="500" prefixLanguageFilePath="%SystemDrive%\
inetpub\custerr" path="500.htm" />
   <error statusCode="501" prefixLanguageFilePath="%SystemDrive%\
inetpub\custerr" path="501.htm" />
   <error statusCode="502" prefixLanguageFilePath="%SystemDrive%\
inetpub\custerr" path="502.htm" />
  </httpErrors>
 </system.webServer>
</configuration>
```

In this example, error elements specify how certain types of HTTP error status codes should be handled. If you wanted to customize the error handling for a server, you might want to extend or modify the default values in a separate .config file and then reference the .config file in ApplicationHost.config. To do this, you would update the ApplicationHost.config file to point to the additional .config file. An example follows.

```
<?xml version="1.0" encoding="UTF-8"?>
<!-- applicationHost.config -->
<configuration>
 <system.webServer>
  <httpErrors configSource=errorMode.config />
</configuration>
```

You would then create the errorMode.config file and store it in the same directory as the ApplicationHost.config file. The following is an example of the contents of the errorMode.config file:

```
<?xml version="1.0" encoding="UTF-8"?>
<!-- errorMode.config -->
```

```
<configuration>
 <system.webServer>
 <httpErrors>
 <error statusCode="401" prefixLanguageFilePath="%SystemDrive%\inetpub\
custerr" path="401.htm" />
 <error statusCode="403" prefixLanguageFilePath="%SystemDrive%\inetpub\
custerr" path="403.htm" />
 <error statusCode="404" prefixLanguageFilePath="%SystemDrive%\inetpub\
custerr" path="404.htm" />
 <error statusCode="405" prefixLanguageFilePath="%SystemDrive%\inetpub\
custerr" path="405.htm" />
 <error statusCode="406" prefixLanguageFilePath="%SystemDrive%\inetpub\
custerr" path="406.htm" />
 <error statusCode="412" prefixLanguageFilePath="%SystemDrive%\inetpub\
custerr" path="412.htm" />
 <error statusCode="500" prefixLanguageFilePath="%SystemDrive%\inetpub\
custerr" path="500.htm" />
 <error statusCode="501" prefixLanguageFilePath="%SystemDrive%\inetpub\
custerr" path="501.htm" />
 <error statusCode="502" prefixLanguageFilePath="%SystemDrive%\inetpub\
custerr" path="502.htm" />
   </httpErrors>
   </system.webServer>
</configuration>
```

When you make these or other types of changes in configuration files, you don't need to worry about restarting IIS or related services. IIS automatically picks up the changes and uses them. In these examples, you'll note that we're working with the system.webServer section of the configuration file. As per the schema definition files, all settings are defined within specific configuration sections. Although sections cannot be nested, a section can exist within a section group, and that section group can in turn be contained in a parent section group. A section group is simply a container of logically related sections.

In ApplicationHost.config, section groups and individual sections are defined in the configSections element. The configSections element controls the registration of sections. Every section belongs to one section group. By default, ApplicationHost.config contains these section groups:

- **system.applicationHost**   Defines the following sections: applicationPools, configHistory, customMetadata, listenerAdapters, log, sites, and webLimits.

- **system.webServer**   Defines the following sections: asp, caching, cgi, defaultDocument, directoryBrowse, globalModules, handlers, httpCompression, httpErrors, httpLogging, httpProtocol, httpRedirect, httpTracing, isapiFilters, modules, odbcLogging, serverRuntime, serverSideInclude, staticContent, urlCompression, and validation. Includes the security and tracing subgroups.

- **system.webServer.security**   A subgroup of system.webServer that defines the following sections: access, applicationDependencies, authorization, ipSecurity, isapiCgiRestriction, and requestFiltering. Includes the authentication subgroup.

- **system.webServer.security.authentication**   A subgroup of system.webServer .security that defines the following sections: anonymousAuthentication, basicAuthentication, clientCertificateMappingAuthentication, digestAuthentication, iisClientCertificateMappingAuthentication, and windowsAuthentication.

- **system.webServer.security.tracing**   A subgroup of system.webServer.security that defines the traceFailedRequests and traceProviderDefinitions sections.

In ApplicationHost.config, section groups and individual sections are defined as follows:

```
<configSections>
 <sectionGroup name="system.applicationHost">
  <section name="applicationPools" allowDefinition="AppHostOnly"
overrideModeDefault="Deny" />
  <section name="configHistory" allowDefinition="AppHostOnly"
overrideModeDefault="Deny" />
  <section name="customMetadata" allowDefinition="AppHostOnly"
overrideModeDefault="Deny" />
  <section name="listenerAdapters" allowDefinition="AppHostOnly"
overrideModeDefault="Deny" />
  <section name="log" allowDefinition="AppHostOnly"
overrideModeDefault="Deny" />
  <section name="sites" allowDefinition="AppHostOnly"
overrideModeDefault="Deny" />
  <section name="webLimits" allowDefinition="AppHostOnly"
overrideModeDefault="Deny" />
 </sectionGroup>
 <sectionGroup name="system.webServer">
 ...
 </sectionGroup>
</configSections>
```

In Machine.config, you'll also find definitions for section groups and individual sections. These are similar to those used in ApplicationHost.config but are used for configuring the .NET Framework and some ASP.NET settings. When working with either .config file, keep in mind that a section is the basic unit of deployment, locking, searching, and containment for configuration settings. Every section has a name attribute and optional allowDefinition and overrideModeDefault attributes. The name attribute sets the unique section name. The allowDefinition attribute specifies the level at which the section can be set:

- **Everywhere**   The section can be set in any configuration file including directories mapped to virtual directories that are not application roots, and their subdirectories.

- **MachineOnly**   The section can be set only in ApplicationHost.config or Machine.config. Because this is the default setting, a section that doesn't have an allowDefinition attribute uses this setting automatically.

- **MachineToWebRoot**   The section can be set only in the .NET Framework root's Machine.config or Web.config file, or in ApplicationHost.config.

- **MachineToApplication**   The section can be set only in the .NET Framework root's Machine.config or Web.config file, in ApplicationHost.config, or in Web.config files for application root directories.

- **AppHostOnly**   The section can be set only in Web.config files for application root directories.

The OverrideModeDefault attribute sets the default lockdown state of a section. Essentially, this means that it controls whether a section is locked down to the level in which it is defined or can be overridden by lower levels of the configuration hierarchy. If this attribute is not set, the default value is Allow. With Allow, lower level configuration files can override the settings of the related section. With Deny, lower level configuration files cannot override the settings of the related section. As discussed in Chapter 5, you'll typically use location tags to lock or unlock sections for specific Web sites or applications.

Because the complete configuration settings of a server and its related sites and applications are stored in the configuration files, you easily can back up or duplicate a server's configuration. Backing up a server's configuration is a simple matter of creating a copy of the configuration files. Similarly, duplicating a server's configuration on another server is a simple matter of copying the source configuration files to the correct locations on another server.

IIS 7.0 and Your Hardware

Before you deploy IIS 7.0, you should carefully plan the server architecture. As part of your planning, you need to look closely at pre-installation requirements and the hardware you will use. IIS 7.0 is no longer the simple solution for hosting Web sites that it once was. It now provides the core infrastructure for hosting Web servers, Web applications, and Windows SharePoint Services.

Guidelines for choosing hardware for Internet servers are much different from those for choosing other types of servers. A Web hosting provider might host multiple sites on the same computer and might also have service level agreements that determine the level of availability and performance required. On the other hand, a busy e-commerce site might have a dedicated Web server or even multiple load-balanced servers. Given that Internet servers are used in a wide variety of circumstances and might be either shared or dedicated, here are some guidelines for choosing server hardware:

- **Memory**   The amount of random access memory (RAM) that's required depends on many factors, including the requirements of other services, the size of frequently accessed content files, and the RAM requirements of the Web applications. In most installations, I recommend that you use at least 1 gigabyte (GB) of RAM. High-volume servers should have a minimum of 2 to 4 GB of RAM. More

RAM will allow more files to be cached, reducing disk requests. For all IIS installations, the operating system paging file size should at least equal the amount of RAM on the server.

Note Don't forget that as you add physical memory, virtual paging to disk grows as well. With this in mind, you might want to ensure that the Pagefile.sys file is on the appropriate disk drive, one that has adequate space for the page file to grow, along with providing optimal input/output (I/O) performance.

More Info For detailed information on memory management and performance tuning, see Chapter 12, "Performance Tuning, Monitoring, and Tracing."

- **CPU** The CPU processes the instructions received by the computer. The clock speed of the CPU and the size of the data bus determine how quickly information moves among the CPU, RAM, and system buses. Static content, such as HTML and images, place very little burden on the processor, and standard recommended configurations should suffice. Faster clock speeds and multiple processors increase the performance scalability of a Web server, particularly for sites that rely on dynamic content. 32-bit versions of Windows run on Intel x86 or compatible hardware. 64-bit versions of Windows run on the x64 family of processors from AMD and Intel, including AMD64 and Intel Extended Memory 64 Technology (Intel EM64T). IIS provides solid benchmark performance on Intel Xeon, AMD Opteron, and AMD Athlon processors. Any of these CPUs provide good starting points for the typical IIS server. You can achieve significant performance improvements with a large processor cache. Look closely at the L1, L2, and L3 cache options available—a larger cache can yield much better performance overall.

- **SMP** IIS supports symmetric multiprocessors (SMPs) and can use additional processors to improve performance. If the system is running only IIS and doesn't handle dynamic content or encryption, a single processor might suffice. You should always use multiple processors if IIS is running alongside other services, such as Microsoft SQL Server or Microsoft Exchange Server.

- **Disk drives** The amount of data storage capacity you need depends entirely on the size of content files and the number of sites supported. You need enough disk space to store all your data plus workspace, system files, and virtual memory. I/O throughput is just as important as drive capacity. However, disk I/O is rarely a bottleneck for Web sites on the public Internet—generally, bandwidth limits throughput. High-bandwidth sites should consider hardware-based redundant array of independent disks (RAID) solutions using copper or fiber channel–based small computer system interface (SCSI) devices.

- **Data protection**   Unless you can tolerate hours of downtime, you should add protection against unexpected drive failures by using RAID. Hardware RAID implementations are always preferred over software RAID implementations. RAID 0 (disk striping without parity) offers optimal read/write performance, but if a drive fails, IIS won't be able to continue operation until the drive is replaced and its contents are restored from backup. Because of this, RAID 0 isn't the recommended choice. RAID 1 (disk mirroring) creates duplicate copies of data on separate physical drives, allowing the server to remain operational when a drive fails, and even while the RAID controller rebuilds a replacement drive in a failed mirror. RAID 5 (disk striping with parity) offers good protection against single-drive failure but has poor write performance. Keep in mind that if you've configured redundant load-balanced servers, you might not need RAID. With load balancing, the additional servers might offer the necessary fault tolerance.

- **UPS**   Sudden power loss and power spikes can seriously damage hardware. To prevent this, get an uninterruptible power supply (UPS). A properly configured UPS system allows the operating system to automatically shut down the server gracefully in the event of a power outage, and it's also important in maintaining system integrity when the server uses write-back caching controllers that do not have on-board battery backups. Professional hosting providers often offer UPS systems that can maintain power indefinitely during extended power outages.

If you follow these hardware guidelines, you'll be well on your way to success with IIS.

IIS 7.0 Editions and Windows

IIS 7.0 is available for both desktop and server editions of Windows. On Windows Vista, IIS 7.0 offers Web administrators and Web developers a complete platform for building and testing dynamic Web sites and Web applications. IIS 7.0 running on Windows Vista also enables process activation, process management, and the necessary HTTP infrastructure for creating WCF–based applications.

As discussed further in Chapter 2, the way IIS 7.0 works on Windows Vista depends on the edition of Windows Vista you are using. On Windows Vista Starter and Home Basic editions, IIS 7.0 cannot be used to host Web sites, Web applications, or Windows SharePoint Services. On these editions, a limited set of IIS features are available, such as Windows Activation Service components that are used to enable WCF-based applications. Users who install WCF-based applications will not need to install these components. The necessary components are installed automatically by WCF. With these editions, the simultaneous request execution limit for IIS is three, meaning that an application or a group of running applications could make up to three simultaneous requests for Web content through the installed IIS components.

On Windows Vista Home Premium, most of the IIS 7.0 features required for Web site development are available. The available features should allow most casual or hobbyist administrators and developers to build and test dynamic Web sites and Web applications. Many advanced features are missing, however, including advanced authentication components, advanced logging components, and FTP server components. As with Starter and Home Basic editions of Windows Vista, the simultaneous request execution limit for IIS is three for Windows Vista Home Premium, meaning you or running applications could make up to three simultaneous requests for Web content through the installed IIS components.

For Windows Vista Business, Enterprise, and Ultimate editions, all IIS 7.0 features are available. This means that professional Web administrators and Web developers have everything necessary to design, build, and test Web sites and Web applications. The simultaneous request execution limit is ten for these editions of Windows Vista, meaning you or running applications could make up to ten simultaneous requests for Web content through the installed IIS components.

With server editions of Windows, you can use IIS to host Web servers, Web applications, and Windows SharePoint Services. All features of IIS 7.0 are available on all editions of Windows Server 2008. On Windows Server operating systems, IIS 7.0 has no request execution limit. This means that an unlimited number of simultaneous requests can be made to the IIS 7.0 server core.

Web Administration Tools and Techniques

Web administrators will find that there are many ways to manage Web and application servers. The key administration tools and techniques are covered in the following sections.

Managing Resources by Using Key Administration Tools

Many tools are available for managing Web resources. Key tools you'll use are shown in Table 1-2. Most of these tools are available on the Administrative Tools menu. Click Start and choose All Programs, Administrative Tools, and then the tool you want to use. You can use all the tools listed in the table to manage local and remote resources. For example, if you connect to a new computer in IIS Manager, you can manage all its sites and services remotely from your system.

Table 1-2 Quick Reference for Key Web Administration Tools

Administration Tool	Purpose
Active Directory Users and Computers	Manages domain user, group, and computer accounts.
Computer Management	Manages services, storage, and applications. The Services And Applications node provides quick access to Indexing Service catalogs and IIS sites and servers.

Table 1-2   Quick Reference for Key Web Administration Tools

Administration Tool	Purpose
Data Sources (ODBC)	Configures and manages Open Database Connectivity (ODBC) data sources and drivers. Data sources link Web front ends with database back ends.
DNS	Public Internet sites must have fully qualified domain names (FQDNs) to resolve properly in browsers. Use the Domain Name System (DNS) administrative snap-in to manage the DNS configuration of your Windows DNS servers.
Event Viewer	Allows you to view and manages events and system logs. If you keep track of system events, you'll know when problems occur.
Internet Information Services (IIS) 6.0 Manager	Manages Web and application server resources that were designed for IIS 6. This tool is included for backward compatibility only.
Internet Information Services (IIS) Manager	Manages Web and application server resources that were designed for IIS 7.0.
Web Management Service (WMSVC)	Allows you to use the IIS Manager to manage Web and application server resources on remote servers.
Reliability and Performance Monitor	Tracks system reliability and performance allowing you to pinpoint performance problems.
Services	Views service information, starts and stops system services, and configures service logons and automated recoveries.

When you add services to a server, the tools needed to manage those services are automatically installed. If you want to manage these servers remotely, you might not have these tools installed on your workstation. In that case, you need to install the administration tools on the workstation you're using.

Web Administration Techniques

Web administrators have many options for managing IIS. The key administration tools are:

- IIS Manager (InetMgr.exe)

- IIS Administration objects made available through the IIS 7.0 WMI provider

- IIS command-line administration tool (AppCmd.exe)

IIS Manager provides the standard administration interface for IIS. To start IIS Manager, click Start and choose All Programs, Administrative Tools, and then Internet Information Services (IIS) Manager. When started, IIS Manager displays the Start page shown in Figure 1-1 and automatically connects to the local IIS installation, if it's available. On the Start page, you have the following options:

- **Connect to localhost** Connects you to the IIS installation on the local computer

- **Connect to a server** Allows you to connect to a remote server

- **Connect to a site** Allows you to connect to a specific Web site on a designated Web server

- **Connect to an application** Allows you to connect to a specific Web application on a designated site and server

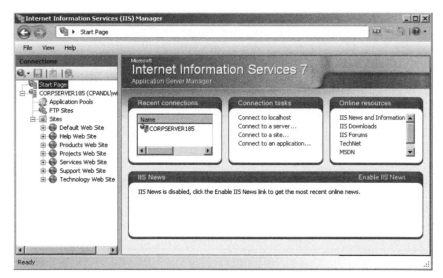

Figure 1-1 You can access servers, sites, and applications by using IIS Manager.

As discussed previously, remote access to an IIS server is controlled by the WMSVC. When you install and start WMSVC on an IIS server, it listens on port 8172 on all unassigned IP addresses and allows remote connections from authorized user accounts. You can connect to a remote server by following these steps:

1. In Internet Information Services (IIS) Manager, click Start Page in the console tree and then click Connect To A Server. This starts the Connect To A Server wizard.

2. Type or select the server name in the Server Name box. For a server on the Internet, type the FQDN of the server, such as www.adatum.com. For a server on the local network, type the computer name, such as WEBSVR87. Port 80 is the default port for connections. As necessary, you can provide the port to which you

want to connect. For example, if you want to connect to the server on port 8080, you would follow the server name by :8080, such as WEBSVR87:8080.

3. After you type the server name (and optionally the port number), click Next. IIS Manager will then try to use your current user credentials to log on to the server. If this fails, you'll need to provide the appropriate credentials on the presented Provide Credentials page before clicking Next to continue. Click Finish to complete the connection.

Tip   If IIS Manager displays a connection error stating that the remote server is not accepting connections, you'll need to log on locally or through remote desktop. Once logged on, check to ensure the Management Service is started and configured properly. For more information, see the "Enabling and Configuring Remote Administration" section of Chapter 3.

You can connect to a specific Web site on a designated server by following these steps:

1. In Internet Information Services (IIS) Manager, click Start Page in the console tree and then click Connect To A Site. This starts the Connect To A Site Wizard.

2. Type or select the server name in the Server Name box, such as TESTSVR22. In the Site Name box, type or select the name of the Web site to which you want to connect, such as Default Web Site.

3. Click Next. IIS Manager will then try to use your current user credentials to log on to the server. If this fails, you'll need to provide the appropriate credentials on the presented Provide Credentials page before clicking Next to continue. Click Finish to complete the connection.

You can connect to a specific application on a designated site and server by following these steps:

1. In Internet Information Services (IIS) Manager, click Start Page in the console tree and then click Connect To An Application. This starts the Connect To An Application Wizard.

2. Type or select the server name in the Server Name box, such as TESTSVR22. In the Site Name box, type or select the name of the Web site to which you want to connect, such as Default Web Site.

3. In the Application Name box, type or select the relative path of the Web application to which you want to connect, such as /MyApplication or /Apps/Myapp.

4. Click Next. IIS Manager will then try to use your current user credentials to log on to the server. If this fails, you'll need to provide the appropriate credentials on the presented Provide Credentials page before clicking Next to continue. Click Finish to complete the connection.

As Figure 1-2 shows, IIS Manager has been completely redesigned for IIS 7.0. Instead of being a snap-in for the Microsoft Management Console, IIS Manager is now a stand-alone application with a browser-like interface. Once you connect to a server, site, or application, IIS Manager automatically connects to these installations upon startup. You can change this behavior by disconnecting from the remote server while in IIS Manager. See Chapter 3 for more information on using IIS Manager.

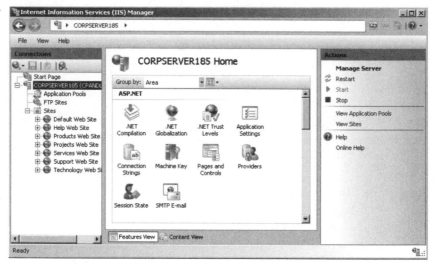

Figure 1-2   IIS Manager has a completely redesigned interface in IIS 7.0.

IIS 7.0 introduces the concept of delegated administration. With *delegated administration*, a machine administrator can delegate administrative control safely and securely. Delegated administration allows different levels of the configuration hierarchy to be managed by other users, such as site administrators or application developers. In a standard configuration, the default delegation state limits write access to most config-uration settings to machine administrators only, and you must explicitly modify the delegation settings to grant write access to others. You'll learn more about IIS security and delegation in Chapter 10, "Managing Web Server Security."

IIS Manager and other graphical tools provide just about everything you need to work with IIS 7.0. Still, there are times when you might want to work from the command line, especially if you want to automate installation or administration tasks. To help you with all your command-line needs, IIS 7.0 includes the IIS command-line administration tool (AppCmd.exe). AppCmd.exe is located in the *%SystemRoot%*\System32\Inetsrv directory. By default, this directory is not in your command path. Because of this, you'll need either to add this directory to the default path or change to this directory each time you want to use this tool. Add this directory temporarily to your default path by typing the following at an elevated command prompt:

```
path %PATH%;%SystemRoot%\System32\inetsrv
```

Then add this directory permanently to your default path by typing the following at an elevated command prompt:

```
setx PATH %PATH%;%SystemRoot%\System32\inetsrv
```

Note You use Path to temporarily update the command path for the current window. You use SETX PATH to permanently update the command path for future command windows.

Table 1-3 provides a summary of the core set of administration objects for the IIS command-line administration tool.

Table 1-3 Administration Objects for the IIS Command-Line Administration Tool

Object Type	Description	Related Commands
APP	Allows you to create and manage Web application settings by using related list, set, add, and delete commands	list, set, add, and delete
APPPOOL	Allows you to create and manage application pools by using related list, set, add, delete, start, stop, and recycle commands	list, set, add, delete, start, stop, and recycle
BACKUP	Allows you to create and manage backups of your server configuration by using list, add, delete, and restore commands	list, add, delete, and restore
CONFIG	Allows you to manage general configuration settings by using related list, set, search, lock, unlock, clear, reset, and migrate commands	list, set, search, lock, unlock, clear, reset, and migrate
MODULE	Allows you to manage IIS modules by using related list, set, add, delete, install, and uninstall commands	list, set, add, delete, install, and uninstall
REQUEST	Allows you to list current HTTP requests by using a related list command	list
SITE	Allows you to create and manage virtual sites by using related list, set, add, delete, start, and stop commands	list, set, add, delete, start, and stop
TRACE	Allows you to manage failed request tracing by using related list, configure, and inspect commands	list, configure, and inspect
VDIR	Allows you to create and manage virtual directory settings by using related list, set, add, and delete commands	list, set, add, and delete
WP	Allows you to list running worker processes by using a related list command	list

The basics of working with the IIS command-line administration tool are straightforward. Most administration objects support these basic commands:

- **ADD**   Creates a new object with the properties you specify.

- **DELETE**   Deletes the object you specify.

- **LIST**   Displays a list of related objects. Optionally, you can specify a unique object to list, or you can type one or more parameters to match against object properties.

- **SET**   Sets parameters on the object specified.

Some objects support other commands, including:

- **RECYCLE**   Recycles the object you specify by deleting it and then re-creating it

- **START**   Starts the object you specify if it is stopped

- **STOP**   Stops the object you specify if it is started or otherwise active

To type commands, use the following basic syntax:

```
appcmd Command <Object-type>
```

where *Command* is the action to perform, such as list, add, or delete, and Object-type is the object on which you want to perform the action, such as app, site, or vdir. Following this, if you wanted to list the configured sites on a server, you could type the following command at an elevated command prompt:

```
appcmd list site
```

Because the IIS command-line administration tool will also accept plural forms of object names, such as apps, sites, or vdirs, you could also use:

```
appcmd list sites
```

In either case, the resulting output is a list of all configured sites on the server with their related properties, such as:

```
SITE "Default Web Site" (id:1,bindings:http/*:80:,state:Started)
```

You'll find a comprehensive discussion of using the IIS command-line administration tool in Chapter 4, "Managing IIS 7.0 from the Command Line." In addition, you will see examples of using this tool throughout the book.

Chapter 2
Deploying IIS 7.0 in the Enterprise

Before you deploy Internet Information Services (IIS) 7.0, you should carefully plan the machine and administration architecture. As part of your planning, you need to look closely at the protocols and roles IIS will use and modify both server hardware and technology infrastructure accordingly to meet the requirements of these roles on a per-machine basis. Your early success with IIS 7.0 will largely depend on your understanding of the ways you can use the software and in your ability to deploy it to support these roles.

IIS 7.0 Protocols

TCP/IP is a protocol suite consisting of Transmission Control Protocol (TCP) and Internet Protocol (IP). TCP/IP is required for internetwork communications and for accessing the Internet. Whereas TCP operates at the transport layer and is a connection-oriented protocol designed for reliable end-to-end communications, IP operates at the network layer and is an internetworking protocol used to route packets of data over a network.

IIS 7.0 uses protocols that build on TCP/IP, including:

- Hypertext Transfer Protocol (HTTP)
- Secure Sockets Layer (SSL)
- File Transfer Protocol (FTP)
- Simple Mail Transfer Protocol (SMTP)

HTTP and SSL

As you probably already know, HTTP is an application-layer protocol that makes it possible to publish static and dynamic content on a server so that it can be viewed in client applications, such as Microsoft Windows Internet Explorer. Publishing a Web document is a simple matter of making the document available in the appropriate directory on an HTTP server and assigning the appropriate permissions so that an HTTP client application can access the document. An HTTP session works like this:

1. The HTTP client application uses TCP to establish a connection to the HTTP server. The default (well-known) port used for HTTP connections is TCP port 80. You can configure servers to use other ports as well. For example, TCP port 8080 is a popular alternative to TCP port 80 for sites that are meant to have limited access.

2. After connecting to the server, the HTTP client application requests a Web page or other resource from the server. In the client application, users specify the pages or resources they want to access by using a Web address, otherwise known as a Uniform Resource Locator (URL).

3. The server responds to the request by sending the client the request resource and any other related files, such as images, that you've inserted into the requested resource. If you've enabled the HTTP Keep-Alive feature on the server, the TCP connection between the client and server remains open to speed up the transfer process for subsequent client requests. Otherwise, the TCP connection between the client and server is closed and the client must establish a new connection for subsequent transfer requests.

That in a nutshell is essentially how HTTP works. The protocol is meant to be simple yet dynamic, and it is the basis upon which the World Wide Web is built.

With HTTP, you can configure access to documents so that anyone can access a document or so that documents can be accessed only by authorized individuals. To allow anyone to access a document, you configure the document security so that clients can use Anonymous authentication. With Anonymous authentication, the HTTP server logs on the user automatically using a guest account, such as IUSR. To require authorization to access a document, configure the document security to require authentication using one of the available authentication mechanisms, such as Basic authentication, which requires a user to type a user name and password.

You can use Secure Sockets Layer (SSL) to enable Hypertext Transfer Protocol Secure (HTTPS) transfers. SSL is an Internet protocol used to encrypt authentication information and data transfers passed between HTTP clients and HTTP servers. With SSL, HTTP clients connect to Web pages using URLs that begin with *https://*. The *https* prefix tells the HTTP client to try to establish a connection using SSL. The default port used with secure connections is TCP port 443 rather than TCP port 80. See Chapter 10, "Managing Web Server Security," for more information on SSL.

FTP

FTP is an application-layer protocol that makes it possible for client applications to retrieve files from or transfer files to remote servers. FTP predates HTTP, and its usage is in decline as compared to HTTP. With FTP, you can publish a file so that a client can download it by making the file available in the appropriate directory on an FTP server and assigning the appropriate permissions so that an FTP client application can access the document. To upload a file to an FTP server, you must grant an FTP client application permission to log on to the server and access directories used for uploading files.

An FTP session works like this:

1. The FTP client application uses TCP to establish a connection to the FTP server. The default (well-known) port used for FTP connections is TCP port 21. FTP servers listen on this port for client connection requests. After the client and server establish a connection, the server randomly assigns the client a TCP port number above 1023. This initial TCP connection (with port 21 for the server and a random port for the client) is then used for transmission of FTP control information, such as commands sent from the client to the server and response codes returned by the server to the client.

2. The client then issues an FTP command to the server on TCP port 21. Standard FTP commands include GET for downloading a file, CD for changing directories, PUT for uploading files, and BIN for switching to binary mode.

3. When the client initiates a data transfer with the server, the server opens a second TCP connection with the client for the data transfer. This connection uses TCP port 20 on the server and a randomly assigned TCP port above 1023 on the client. After the data transfer is complete, the second connection goes in a wait state until the client initiates another data transfer or the connection times out.

That in a nutshell is how FTP works. As you can see, FTP is a bit clunkier than HTTP, but it is still fairly simple.

Real World   What sets FTP and HTTP apart is primarily the way you transfer files. FTP transfers files as either standard text or encoded binaries. HTTP has the capability to communicate the file format to the client, and this capability allows the client to determine how to handle the file. If the client can handle the file format directly, it renders the file for display. If the client has a configured helper application, such as with PDF documents, the client can call the helper application and let it render the file for display within the client window. The component that makes it possible for HTTP clients and servers to determine file format is their support for the Multipurpose Internet Mail Extensions (MIME) protocol. Using the MIME protocol, an HTTP server identifies each file with its corresponding MIME type. For example, an HTML document has the MIME type text/html, and a GIF image has the MIME type image/gif.

With FTP, you can allow anonymous downloads and uploads in addition to restricted downloads and uploads. To allow anyone to access a file, configure directory security so that clients can use Anonymous authentication. With Anonymous authentication, the FTP server logs the user on automatically using a guest account and allows the anonymous user to download or upload files as appropriate. To require authorization to log on and access a directory, configure directory security to require authentication using one of the available authentication mechanisms, such as Basic authentication, which requires a user to type a user name and password prior to logging on and downloading or uploading files.

SMTP

SMTP is an application-layer protocol that makes it possible for client applications to send e-mail messages to servers and for servers to send e-mail messages to other servers. A related protocol for retrieving messages from a server is Post Office Protocol version 3 (POP3). In IIS 6, full implementations of Simple Mail Transfer Protocol (SMTP) and Post Office Protocol version 3 (POP3) are included. IIS 7.0 does not include SMTP or POP3 services.

With IIS 7.0, a Web application can send e-mail on behalf of a user by using the SMTP E-mail component of Microsoft ASP.NET. An SMTP session initiated by a Web application works like this:

1. The Web application generates an e-mail message in response to something a user has done.

2. The System.Net.Mail API (a component of ASP.NET) delivers the email to an online SMTP server or stores the message on disk where it is stored for later delivery.

3. When sending mail to an SMTP server, the IIS server uses TCP port 25 to establish the connection. SMTP can be running on the local machine or on a different machine.

That is essentially how SMTP is used by Web applications. Microsoft doesn't provide other e-mail features as a part of IIS. However, a separate SMTP Server component is included as an optional feature that you can install on a computer running a Windows Server operating system.

IIS 7.0 Roles

You can deploy IIS on both desktop and server platforms. On desktop platforms, you can use IIS 7.0 for designing, building, and testing dynamic Web sites and Web applications. On server platforms, IIS 7.0 can have several different roles:

- **Application server**   Application servers host distributed applications built using ASP.NET, Enterprise Services Network Support, and Microsoft .NET Framework 3.0. You can deploy application servers with or without Web Server (IIS) support. When you deploy an application server without Web Server (IIS) support, you configure application services through the application server core APIs and by adding or removing role services. Because the server lacks IIS configuration and administration components, you won't have any of the common IIS features and won't be able to configure the server by using IIS 7.0 modules, and you can't manage the server by using IIS 7.0 administration tools. To avoid these limitations, you should install the application server with Web Server (IIS) support. You'll then be able to use IIS features to better manage the application server installation.

- **Web server**   Web servers use the services bundled in IIS 7.0 to host Web sites and Web applications. Web sites hosted on a Web server can have both static content and dynamic content. You can build Web applications hosted on a Web server by using ASP.NET and .NET Framework 3.0. When you deploy a Web Server, you can manage the server configuration by using IIS 7.0 modules and administration tools.

- **Microsoft Windows SharePoint Services server**   Computers running Windows SharePoint Services enable team collaboration by connecting people and information. A SharePoint Services server is essentially a Web server running a full installation of IIS and using managed applications that provide the necessary collaboration functionality. When you deploy SharePoint Services, you can manage the server by using IIS 7.0 modules and administration tools in addition to several SharePoint-specific tools, including SharePoint Central Administration and the SharePoint Products and Technologies Configuration Wizard.

Table 2-1 organizes the 75 configuration features available for the three server roles into 14 general categories. Each entry for a particular configuration feature has one of the following values:

- **Available**   Indicates a feature that is available for selection during installation. You can add available features as necessary to optimize the configuration of your server.

- **Default**   Indicates a feature that is selected for installation by default. Although you may be able to deselect default features during setup, you should not do this in most cases because it could adversely affect the server performance or necessary core functionality.

- **Included**   Indicates an included but unlisted feature that is part of the IIS server core. With application servers, these features are included only when you choose to install Web Server (IIS) support. With Web Server and SharePoint Services Server, these features are included automatically.

- **Not Installed**   Indicates an available feature that is not installed as part of the standard setup. With Web and SharePoint Services servers, you can configure these features after installation by enabling the related modules. With application servers, these features are configurable after installation only when you choose to install Web Server (IIS) support or modify the role services associated with an installed Web server role.

- **Required**   Indicates a feature that is required in order to install the server role. Setup selects required features automatically during installation.

- **N/A**   Indicates a feature that is not applicable or available for a particular server role.

- **Web Common**   Indicates a feature installed by default as part of the common Web Server (IIS) features of an application server.

- **WPASS Required**   Indicates an application server feature required for Windows Process Activation Service Support.

Table 2-1   Configuration Features for Application and Web Servers and Computers Running SharePoint Services

Feature	Application Server	Web Server	SharePoint Services
.NET Framework 3.0			
.NET Framework 3.0	Required	Available	Required
Application Server Support			
Application Server Foundation	Default	N/A	N/A
COM+ Network Access	Available	N/A	N/A
TCP Port Sharing	WPASS Required	N/A	N/A
Web Server (IIS) Support	Available	N/A	N/A
Application Development Features			
.NET Extensibility	Web Common; WPASS Required	Available	Required
ASP	Available	Available	Available
ASP.NET	Web Common	Available	Required
CGI	Available	Available	Available
ISAPI Extensions	Web Common	Available	Required
ISAPI Filters	Web Common	Available	Required
Server-Side Includes	Available	Available	Available
Common HTTP Features			
Default Document	Web Common	Default	Required
Directory Browsing	Web Common	Default	Required
HTTP Errors	Web Common	Default	Required
HTTP Redirection	Web Common	Available	Available
Static Content	Web Common	Default	Required

Table 2-1   Configuration Features for Application and Web Servers and Computers Running SharePoint Services

Feature	Application Server	Web Server	SharePoint Services
Distributed Transaction Support			
Incoming Remote Transaction Support	Available	N/A	N/A
Outgoing Remote Transaction Support	Available	N/A	N/A
WS-Atomic Transaction Support	Available	N/A	N/A
Extended Features			
File Cache	Not Installed	Not Installed	Not Installed
Managed Engine	Not Installed	Not Installed	Not Installed
Token Cache	Not Installed	Not Installed	Not Installed
HTTP Trace	Not Installed	Not Installed	Not Installed
URI Cache	Not Installed	Not Installed	Not Installed
FTP Publishing Service			
FTP Management Console	Not Installed	Available	Not Installed
FTP Server	Not Installed	Available	Not Installed
Health and Diagnostics Features			
Custom Logging	Not Installed	Available	Not Installed
HTTP Logging	Web Common	Default	Required
Logging Tools	Web Common	Available	Required
ODBC Logging	Not Installed	Available	Not Installed
Request Monitor	Web Common	Default	Required
Tracing	Web Common	Available	Required
IIS Server Core			
Anonymous Authentication	Included	Included	Included
Configuration Validation	Included	Included	Included
HTTP Cache	Included	Included	Included
Protocol Support	Included	Included	Included

Table 2-1 Configuration Features for Application and Web Servers and Computers Running SharePoint Services

Feature	Application Server	Web Server	SharePoint Services
Performance Features			
Dynamic Content Compression	Web Common	Available	Required
Static Content Compression	Web Common	Default	Required
Security Features			
Basic Authentication	Web Common	Available	Required
Client Certificate Mapping Authentication	Web Common	Available	Available
Digest Authentication	Web Common	Available	Required
IIS Client Certificate Mapping Authentication	Web Common	Available	Available
IP and Domain Restrictions	Web Common	Available	Available
Request Filtering	Web Common; WPASS Required	Default	Available
URL Authorization	Web Common	Available	Available
Windows Authentication	Web Common	Available	Required
Web Management Tools			
IIS Management Console	Default	Default	Required
IIS Management Scripts and Tools	Web Common	Available	Not Installed
IIS Management Service	Web Common	Available	Not Installed
IIS 6 Management Compatibility	Not Installed	Available	Required
IIS Metabase Compatibility	Not Installed	Available	Required
IIS 6 WMI Compatibility	Not Installed	Available	Not Installed

Table 2-1   Configuration Features for Application and Web Servers and Computers Running SharePoint Services

Feature	Application Server	Web Server	SharePoint Services
IIS 6 Scripting Tools	Not Installed	Available	Not Installed
IIS 6 Management Console	Not Installed	Available	Not Installed
Windows Activation Service			
.NET Environment	Required	Available	Required
Configuration APIs	Required	Required	Required
Process Model	Required	Required	Required
Windows Process Activation Service Support			
HTTP Activation	WPASS Required	N/A	N/A
MSMQ Activation	WPASS Required	N/A	N/A
Named Pipes Activation	Available	N/A	N/A
TCP Activation	Available	N/A	N/A
Windows Process Activation Service Support (Additional)			
Message Queuing Server	WPASS Required	N/A	N/A
Non-HTTP Activation	WPASS Required	N/A	N/A
Windows SharePoint Services Support			
SharePoint Applications	N/A	N/A	Default
SharePoint Management Tools	N/A	N/A	Default

When configuring application servers, Web servers, and SharePoint Services, it is important to understand exactly what comprises the .NET Framework 3.0. The Microsoft .NET Framework 3.0 is a managed code programming model for Windows. It combines the power of the .NET Framework 2.0 with four new technologies:

- **Windows CardSpace (WCS)**   A suite of .NET technologies for managing digital identities. Windows CardSpace supports any digital identity system and gives users consistent control of their digital identities. A digital identity can be as simple as an e-mail address and password used to log on to a Web site, or it can include a user's full contact and logon information. Client applications display each digital identity as an information card. Each card contains information about a particular digital identity, including what provider to contact to acquire a security token for the identity. By selecting a card and sending it to a provider such as Amazon or Yahoo!, users can validate their identity and log on to the service offered by the site.

- **Windows Communication Foundation (WCF)**   A suite of .NET technologies for building and running connected systems. WCF supports a broad array of distributed systems capabilities to provide secure, reliable, and transacted messaging along with interoperability. Servers establish distributed communications through service endpoints. Service endpoints have an endpoint address, a binding that specifies how the endpoint can communicate, and a contract description that details what an endpoint communicates.

- **Windows Presentation Foundation (WPF)**   A suite of .NET technologies for building applications with attractive and effective user interfaces. WPF supports tight integration of application user interfaces, documents, and media content, allowing developers to create a unified interface for all types of documents and media. This means that applications can use the same interface for displaying forms, controls, fixed-format documents, on-screen documents, 2D images, 3D images, video, and audio.

- **Windows Workflow Foundation (WF)**   A suite of .NET technologies for building workflow-enabled applications on Windows. WF provides a rules engine that allows for the declarative modeling of units of application logic within the scope of an overall business process. What this means is that developers can use WF to model and implement the necessary programming logic for a business process from start to finish.

To support applications written for IIS 6, you can deploy IIS 7.0 with IIS 6 compatibility enabled. If you have existing IIS 6 server installations, you can also install the IIS 6 Management Compatibility tools to support remote administration of these server installations. You also can deploy IIS 7.0 to support remote administration. You can use both desktop and server platforms for remote administration of other IIS servers in addition to the sites and applications configured on these servers. For remote administration of an IIS server, you must enable the Web Management Service (WMSVC) on the server you want to manage remotely. Then install the Web management tools on the machine you want to use for remote administration.

Navigating the IIS 7.0 Role Services and Features

As discussed previously, you can deploy IIS 7.0 running on a computer running Windows Server 2008 to support three specific roles: application server, Web server, and Windows SharePoint Services server. You can deploy IIS 7.0 running on a Windows desktop to support designing, building, and testing sites and applications. The components used to support these roles are referred to as either role services or features, depending on which user interface you are working with. In the sections that follow, I discuss each of the server roles and the related role services.

Role Services for Application Servers

You use application servers running on Windows Server 2008 editions to host distributed applications built by using ASP.NET, Enterprise Services, and WCF. Figure 2-1 provides an overview of the related services for application servers.

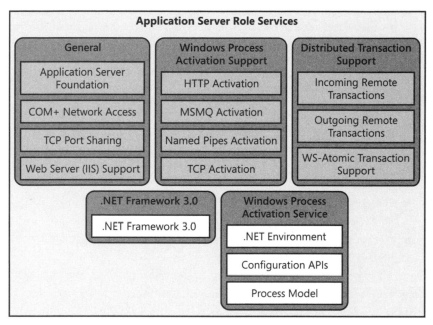

Figure 2-1   Role services for application servers.

When you install an application server, only the Application Server Core and Enterprise Services Network Access services are included as standard core features. In addition to the standard core features, you must install the .NET Framework 3.0 components and the Windows Activation Service components. Other components are optional and should be installed based on the specific requirements of the distributed applications you are hosting.

Application servers can use the following general-purpose role services:

- **Application Server Foundation**   Provides the core application server functionality through these .NET Framework 3.0 technologies: Windows CardSpace, WCF, WPF, and WF. These technologies allow you to deliver managed-code applications that model business processes.

- **COM+ Network Access** Enables application servers to invoke applications remotely over the network. Applications being invoked must have been built using Enterprise Services and provide support for hosting COM+ components.

- **TCP Port Sharing** Allows multiple applications to share a single TCP port. By using this feature, many Web applications can coexist on the same server in separate, isolated processes while sharing the network infrastructure required for sending and receiving data over TCP ports.

- **Web Server (IIS) Support** Allows the application server to host Web sites with both static and dynamic content. The Web sites support the standard IIS server extensions and allow you to create Web pages containing dynamic content. This allows an application server to host an internal or external Web site or provide an environment for developers to create Web applications. See Table 2-2 for a complete list of IIS features installed by default when you select this feature.

The Windows Process Activation Service supports distributed Web-based applications that use different protocols to transfer information. You can use the following related components:

- **.NET Environment** Installs the .NET Environment for use with managed code activation.

- **Configuration APIs** Installs the managed code APIs that allow you to configure the process model.

- **Process Model** Installs a process model for developing and running applications.

Windows Process Activation Service Support enables the application server to invoke applications remotely over a network by using protocols such as HTTP, Microsoft Message Queuing (MSMQ), named pipes, and TCP. This allows applications to start and stop dynamically in response to incoming requests, resulting in improved performance and enhanced manageability. To specify which protocols an application server can use with Windows Process Activation, you can use the following related role services:

- **HTTP Activation** Supports process activation over HTTP. This is the standard activation method used by most Web applications. Applications that support HTTP Activation can start and stop dynamically in response to requests that arrive via HTTP. With HTTP, the application and the computers with which it communicates need to be online to pass active communications back and forth without the need for queuing requests.

- **Message Queuing Activation** Supports process activation over Microsoft Message Queue (MSMQ). This activation method is used when the application server runs distributed messaging applications. Applications that support MSMQ Activation and message queuing can start and stop dynamically in response to requests that arrive via MSMQ. With message queuing, source applications send messages to queues, where they are stored temporarily until target applications retrieve them. This queuing technique allows applications to communicate across different types of networks and with computers that may be offline.

- **Named Pipes Activation**   Supports process activation over named pipes. Applications that support Named Pipes Activation can start and stop dynamically in response to requests that arrive via named pipes. You use this activation method when Web applications communicate with older versions of the Windows operating system. A *named pipe* is a portion of memory that one process can use to pass information to another process such that the output from one process is the input of the other process. Named pipes have standard network addresses such as \\.\Pipe\Sql\Query, which a process can reference on a local machine or a remote machine. The Named Pipes protocol is used primarily for local or remote connections by applications written for Microsoft Windows NT, Windows 98, and earlier versions of Windows.

- **TCP Activation**   Supports process activation over TCP. Applications that support TCP Activation can start and stop dynamically in response to requests that arrive via TCP. With TCP, the application and the computers with which it communicates need to be online so they can pass active communications back and forth without the need for queuing requests.

When using Windows Process Activation Support, these additional roles services may be required:

- **Non-HTTP Activation**   Provides non-HTTP activation support using any of the following: MSMQ, named pipes, and TCP. IIS installs this feature as a WCF Activation component.

- **Message Queuing Server**   Provides the necessary server functions for message queuing.

Tip   Each of the Windows Process Activation Support features has a related set of required role services. With HTTP Activation, all the features listed as Web Common in Table 2-1 are required. With Message Queuing Activation, Message Queuing Server and Non-HTTP Activation are required. With TCP Activation and Named Pipes Activation, Non-HTTP Activation is required.

When applications communicate with each other, they may need to perform various types of transactions, such as queries to retrieve data stored in a database or a data submission to update data stored in a database. When the application server hosts the database or needs to query a single database to complete a transaction, transactions are fairly straightforward. Things get complex fast, though, when you are working with multiple databases hosted on multiple computers. A transaction that involves multiple databases hosted on multiple computers is referred to as a *distributed transaction*. With distributed transactions, you need a way to guarantee that all the data you need is either retrieved or submitted as appropriate, and this is where Distributed Transactions support comes into the picture. Distributed Transactions support provides services that help ensure that distributed transactions are successfully completed.

To enable Distributed Transactions support on an application server, you can use the following related role services:

- **Incoming Remote Transactions**   Provides distributed transaction support to help ensure that incoming remote transactions are successfully completed

- **Outgoing Remote Transactions**   Provides distributed transaction support to help ensure that outgoing remote transactions are successfully completed

- **WS-Atomic Transactions**   Provides distributed transaction support for applications that use two-phase commit transactions with Simple Object Access Protocol (SOAP)–based exchanges. SOAP-based exchanges contain text-based commands that are formatted with XML. If you plan to use SOAP for two-phase commit transactions, you'll also need to set and configure HTTP endpoints.

Real World   WS-Atomic Transactions use SSL to encrypt network traffic when communicating with clients. To use SSL, you must install a server authentication certificate suitable for SSL encryption on the WS-AT site in IIS. If you obtain a certificate from a certificate authority (CA), you can import the certificate as part of the setup process. For small-scale and test environments, you also have the option of creating a self-signed certificate during setup. The drawback of this type of certificate is that you must install it manually on clients.

In your deployment planning, there is a distinct advantage to deploying an application server with Web Server support. When you deploy an application server with Web Server support, you can configure application services using the APIs provided by ASP.NET and the .NET Framework. Because the server includes IIS configuration and administration components, you'll have all of the common IIS features available and will be able to configure the server by using the IIS 7.0 modules and the IIS 7.0 administration tools.

Role Services for Windows Desktops and Web Servers

Web servers running on Windows Vista desktop editions or on Windows Server 2008 editions can host Web sites and Web applications. Figure 2-2 provides an overview of the related role services for Web servers.

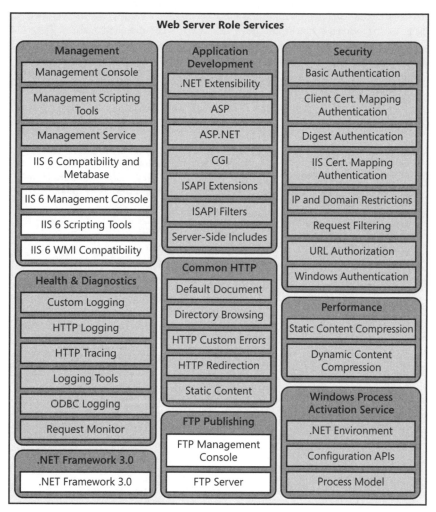

Figure 2-2   Role services for Web servers.

As summarized in Table 2-1, when you install a Web server, several configuration features are installed automatically as part of the server core, and other features are installed by default (if applicable for the operating system version you are using). These features represent core internal components in addition to the recommended minimum and required components for managing a Web server and publishing a Web site. In most installations of IIS 7.0, you will want to install additional features based on the specific requirements of the Web sites and Web applications the server is hosting.

As discussed in Chapter 1, "IIS 7.0 Administration Overview," Windows Server editions and Windows Vista editions have different sets of supported features. Table 2-2 provides a feature comparison based on Windows version and edition. The table also lists the related request limitations of Windows versions and editions. Because Windows Server editions have no request limitations, you can use them in live production environments. Because Windows Vista editions have severe request limitations, they are best suited for individual administrator or developer use and use in test and development environments.

Table 2-2   Feature Comparison Based on Windows Version and Edition

Feature	Windows Server 2008	Windows Vista Business & Ultimate	Windows Vista Home Premium	Windows Vista Home Basic
IIS Server Core				
Anonymous Authentication	Included	Included	Included	N/A
Configuration Validation	Included	Included	Included	N/A
HTTP Cache	Included	Included	Included	N/A
Protocol Support	Included	Included	Included	N/A
Common HTTP Features				
Default Document	Default	Default	Default	N/A
Directory Browsing	Default	Default	Default	N/A
HTTP Errors	Default	Default	Default	Default
HTTP Redirection	Available	Available	Available	Available
Static Content	Default	Default	Default	N/A
Application Development Features				
.NET Extensibility	Available	Available	Available	Available
ASP	Available	Available	Available	N/A
ASP.NET	Available	Available	Available	N/A
CGI	Available	Available	Available	N/A
ISAPI Extensions	Available	Available	Available	N/A
ISAPI Filters	Available	Available	Available	N/A

Table 2-2   Feature Comparison Based on Windows Version and Edition

Feature	Windows Server 2008	Windows Vista Business & Ultimate	Windows Vista Home Premium	Windows Vista Home Basic
Server-Side Includes	Available	Available	Available	N/A
Health and Diagnostics Features				
Custom Logging	Available	Available	Available	N/A
HTTP Logging	Default	Default	Default	Default
Logging Tools	Available	Available	Available	Available
ODBC Logging	Available	Available	N/A	N/A
Request Monitor	Default	Default	Default	Default
Tracing	Available	Available	Available	Available
Security Features				
Basic Authentication	Available	Available	Available	N/A
Client Certificate Mapping Authentication	Available	Available	N/A	N/A
Digest Authentication	Available	Available	N/A	N/A
IIS Client Certificate Mapping Authentication	Available	Available	N/A	N/A
IP and Domain Restrictions	Available	Available	Available	Available
Request Filtering	Default	Available	Available	Available
URL Authorization	Available	Available	Available	Available
Windows Authentication	Available	Available	N/A	N/A
Performance Features				
Static Content Compression	Default	Default	Default	N/A

Table 2-2   Feature Comparison Based on Windows Version and Edition

Feature	Windows Server 2008	Windows Vista Business & Ultimate	Windows Vista Home Premium	Windows Vista Home Basic
Dynamic Content Compression	Available	Available	Available	Available
Web Management Tools				
IIS Management Console	Default	Default	Default	N/A
IIS Management Scripts and Tools	Available	Available	Available	Available
IIS Management Service	Available	Available	Available	N/A
IIS 6 Management Compatibility	Available	Available	Available	Available
IIS Metabase compatibility	Available	Available	Available	Available
IIS 6 WMI Compatibility	Available	Available	Available	N/A
IIS 6 Scripting Tools	Available	Available	Available	N/A
IIS 6 Management Console	Available	Available	Available	N/A
FTP Publishing Service				
FTP Management Console	Available	Available	N/A	N/A
FTP Server	Available	Available	N/A	N/A
Windows Activation Service				
.NET Environment	Available	Available	Available	Available
Configuration APIs	Default	Available	Available	Available
Process Model	Default	Default	Default	Default
Limitations				
Request Execution Limit	Unlimited	10	3	3

As the table shows, many different features are available with Web servers. I'll discuss each of the features I haven't previously discussed in this section, and you'll also find detailed information on these features in appropriate chapters throughout this book. In the appendix, "Comprehensive IIS 7.0 Module and Schema Reference," you'll also find a detailed description of features with related configuration modules.

The IIS Server Core features provide the foundation functions for IIS. You can use these features as follows:

- **Anonymous Authentication**   Supports anonymous access to a server. With anonymous access, any user can access content without having to provide credentials. Each server has to have at least one authentication mechanism configured, and this is the default mechanism.

- **Configuration Validation**   Validates the configuration of a server and its applications. If someone improperly configures a server or application, IIS 7.0 generates errors that can help detect and diagnose the problem.

- **HTTP Cache**   Improves performance by returning a processed copy of a requested Web page from cache, resulting in reduced overhead on the server and faster response times. IIS 7.0 supports several levels of caching including output caching in user mode and output caching in kernel mode. When you enable kernel-mode caching, cached responses are served from the kernel rather than from IIS user mode, giving IIS an extra boost in performance and increasing the number of requests IIS can process.

- **Protocol Support**   Provides support for common protocols used by Web servers, including HTTP keep-alives, custom headers, and redirect headers. *HTTP keep-alives* allows clients to maintain open connections with servers, which speeds up the request process once a client has established a connection with a server. *Custom headers* and *redirect headers* allow you to optimize the way IIS works to support advanced features of the HTTP 1.1 specification.

The Common HTTP features install the common services required for serving Web content. You can use these features as follows:

- **Default Document**   Supports displaying of default documents. When you've enabled this feature and a user enters a request with a trailing '/,' such as http://www.adatum.com/, IIS can redirect the request to the default document for the Web server or directory. For best performance, you should list the default document you use the most first and reduce the overall list of default documents to only those necessary.

- **Directory Browsing**   Supports directory browsing functionality. When you've enabled default documents but there is no current default document, IIS can use this feature to generate a listing of the contents of the specified directory. If you haven't enabled the default document or directory browsing features, and a client requests a directory-level URL, IIS returns an empty response.

- **HTTP Errors**   Supports custom error and detailed error notification. When you enable this feature and the server encounters an error, the server can return a customer error page to all clients regardless of location, a detailed error message to all clients regardless of location, or a detailed error for local clients and a custom error page for remote clients. IIS displays a custom error page based on the type of HTTP error that occurred.

- **HTTP Redirection**   Supports redirection of HTTP requests to send users from an old site to a new site. In the default configuration for redirection, all requests for files in the old location are mapped automatically to files in the new location you specify. You can customize this behavior in several ways.

- **Static Content**   Supports static Web content, such as HTML documents and GIF or JPEG images. The staticContent/mimeMap configuration collection in the applicationHost.config file determines the list of file extensions supported.

Note   Each of these common features has a related IIS 7.0 native module that Setup installs and activates when you select the feature. For the exact mapping of common features to their corresponding native modules, see the appendix. You'll learn more about working with these features in Chapter 5, "Managing Global IIS Configuration."

The Application Development features install the features required for developing and hosting Web applications. You can use these features as follows:

- **.NET Extensibility**   Enables a Web server to host .NET Framework applications and provides the necessary functionality for IIS integration with ASP.NET and the .NET Framework. When you are working with managed modules, you must also enable the Managed Engine. The *Managed Engine* is the actual server component that performs the integration functions.

- **ASP**   Enables a Web server to host classic Active Server Pages (ASP) applications. Web pages that use ASP are considered to be dynamic because IIS generates them at request time. To use ASP, you must also use ISAPI Extensions.

- **ASP.NET**   Enables a Web server to host ASP.NET applications. Web pages that use ASP.NET are considered to be dynamic because they are generated at request time. To use ASP.NET, you must also use .NET Extensibility, ISAPI Extensions and ISAPI Filters.

- **CGI**   Enables a Web server to host Common Gateway Interface (CGI) executables. CGI describes how executables specified in Web addresses, also known as *gateway scripts*, pass information to Web servers. By default, IIS handles all files with the .exe extension as CGI scripts.

- **ISAPI Extensions**   Allows ISAPI Extensions to handle client requests. In the IIS server core, several components rely on handlers that are based on ISAPI Extensions, including ASP and ASP.NET. By default, IIS handles all files with the .dll extension as ISAPI Extensions.

- **ISAPI Filters**   Allows ISAPI Filters to modify Web server behavior. IIS uses ISAPI Filters to provide additional functionality. When you select ASP.NET as part of the initial setup, Setup configures an ASP.NET filter to provide this functionality. In applicationHost.config, each version of ASP.NET installed on the Web server must have a filter definition that identifies the version and path to the related filter.

- **Server-Side Includes**   Allows a Web server to parse files with Server-Side Includes (SSI). SSI is a technology that allows IIS to insert data into a document when a client requests it. When this feature is enabled, files with the .stm, .shtm, and .shtml extension are parsed to see if they have includes that should be substituted for actual values. If this feature is disabled, IIS handles .stm, .shtm, and .shtml files as static content, resulting in the actual include command being returned in the request.

Health and Diagnostics features enable you to monitor your servers, sites, and applications and to diagnose problems if they occur. You can use these features as follows:

- **Custom Logging**   Enables support for custom logging. Typically, custom logging uses the ILogPlugin interface of the Component Object Model (COM). Rather than using this feature, Microsoft recommends that you create a managed module and subscribe to the RQ_LOG_REQUEST notification.

- **HTTP Logging**   Enables support for logging Web site activity. You can configure IIS 7.0 to use one log file per server or one log file per site. Use per-server logging when you want all Web sites running on a server to write log data to a single log file. Use per-site logging when you want to track access separately for each site on a server.

- **Logging Tools**   Allows you to manage server activity logs and automate common logging tasks using scripts.

- **ODBC Logging**   Enables support for logging Web site activity to ODBC-compliant databases. In IIS 7.0, ODBC logging is implemented as a type of custom logging.

- **Request Monitor**   Allows you to view details on currently executing requests, the run state of a Web site or the currently executing application domains, and more.

- **Tracing**   Supports tracing of failed requests. Another type of tracing that you can enable after configuration is HTTP tracing, which allows you to trace events and warnings to their sources through the IIS server core.

Security features make it possible to control access to a server and its content. You can use these features as follows:

- **Basic Authentication**   Requires a user to provide a valid user name and password to access content. All browsers support this authentication mechanism, but they transmit the password without encryption, making it possible for a malicious individual to intercept the password as the browser is transmitting it. If you want to require Basic Authentication for a site or directory, you should disable Anonymous Authentication for the site or directory.

■ **Client Certificate Mapping Authentication** Maps client certificates to Active Directory accounts for the purposes of authentication. When you enable certificate mapping, this feature performs the necessary Active Directory certificate mapping for authentication of authorized clients.

■ **Digest Authentication** Uses a Windows domain controller to authenticate user requests for content. Digest Authentication can be used through firewalls and proxies.

■ **IIS Client Certificate Mapping Authentication** Maps SSL client certificates to a Windows account for authentication. With this method of authentication, user credentials and mapping rules are stored within the IIS configuration store.

■ **IP and Domain Restrictions** Allows you to grant or deny access to a server by IP address, network ID, or domain. Granting access allows a computer to make requests for resources but doesn't necessarily allow users to work with resources. If you require authentication, users still need to authenticate themselves. Denying access to resources prevents a computer from accessing those resources, meaning that denied users can't access resources even if they could have authenticated themselves.

■ **Request Filtering** Allows you to reject suspicious requests by scanning URLs sent to a server and filtering out unwanted requests. By default, IIS blocks requests for file extensions that could be misused and also blocks browsing of critical code segments.

■ **URL Authorization** Supports authorization based on configuration rules. This allows you to require logon and to allow or deny access to specific URLs based on user names, .NET roles, and HTTP request method.

■ **Windows Authentication** Supports Windows-based authentication using NTLM, Kerberos, or both. You'll use Windows Authentication primarily in internal networks.

For enhancing performance, IIS supports both static compression and dynamic compression. With static compression, IIS performs an in-memory compression of static content upon first request and then saves the compressed results to disk for subsequent use. With dynamic content, IIS performs in-memory compression every time a client requests dynamic content. IIS must compress dynamic content every time it is requested because dynamic content changes.

When you are trying to improve server performance and interoperability, don't overlook the value of these extended features:

- **File Cache**   Caches file handles for files opened by the server engine and related server modules. If IIS does not cache file handles, IIS has to open the files for every request, which can result in performance loss.

- **Managed Engine**   Enables IIS integration with the ASP.NET runtime engine. When you do not configure this feature, ASP.NET integration also is disabled, and no managed modules or ASP.NET handlers will be called when pooled applications run in Integrated mode.

- **Token Cache**   Caches Windows security tokens for password based authentication schemes, including Anonymous Authentication, Basic Authentication, and Digest Authentication. Once IIS has cached a user's security token, IIS can use the cached security token for subsequent requests by that user. If you disable or remove this feature, a user must be logged on for every request, which can result in multiple logon user calls that could substantially reduce overall performance.

- **HTTP Trace**   Supports request tracing for whenever a client requests one of the traced URLs. The way IIS handles tracing for a particular file is determined by the trace rules that you create.

- **URI Cache**   Caches the Uniform Resource Identifier (URI)–specific server state, such as configuration details. When you enable this feature, the server will read configuration information only for the first request for a particular URI. For subsequent requests, the server will use the cached information if the configuration does not change.

You use Web management tools for administration and can divide the available tools into two general categories: those required for managing IIS 7.0 and those required for backward compatibility with IIS 6. You can use the related setup features as follows:

- **IIS Management Console**   Installs the Internet Information Services (IIS) Manager, the primary management tool for working with IIS 7.0.

- **IIS Management Scripts and Tools**   Installs the IIS command line administration tool and related features for managing Web servers from the command prompt.

- **IIS Management Service**   Installs the Web Management Service (WMSVC), which provides a hostable Web core that acts as a standalone Web server for remote administration.

- **IIS Metabase Compatibility**   Provides the necessary functionality for backward compatibility with servers running IIS 6 Web sites by installing a component that translates IIS 6 metabase changes to the IIS 7.0 configuration store.

- **IIS 6 WMI Compatibility**   Provides the necessary functionality for scripting servers running IIS 6 Web sites by installing the IIS 6 Windows Management Instrumentation (WMI) scripting interfaces.

- **IIS 6 Scripting Tools**   Provides the necessary functionality for scripting servers running IIS 6 Web sites by installing the IIS 6 Scripting Tools.

- **IIS 6 Management Console**   Installs the Internet Information Services (IIS) 6.0 Manager, which is required to remotely manage servers running IIS 6 sites and to manage FTP servers for IIS 6.

Role Services for Servers Running SharePoint Services

You use servers running Windows SharePoint Services to enable team collaboration by connecting people and information. A server running SharePoint Services is essentially a Web server running a full installation of IIS and using managed applications that provide the necessary collaboration functionality. When you deploy SharePoint Services on a server, you can manage the server by using IIS 7.0 modules and administration tools and several SharePoint-specific tools, including SharePoint Central Administration and the SharePoint Products And Technologies Configuration Wizard. After installation, both management tools will be available on the Administrative Tools menu.

On a SharePoint site, you can host lists and libraries. A *list* is a collection of information on a site that you share with team members, including announcements, contacts, discussion boards, tasks, and team calendars. A *library* is a location on a site where you can create, store, and manage the files used by a team. SharePoint sites can host Web pages in addition to lists and libraries, and your Web pages can use static content, dynamic content, or both.

In your deployment planning for servers running SharePoint Services, you must consider several additional issues including the additional security and connectivity requirements that may be necessary for team collaboration. You'll want to ensure that you carefully protect access to a server running SharePoint Services. You'll also want to ensure that team members can access the server from remote locations as appropriate for the potential sensitivity of the information they are sharing.

As part of your planning, you'll need to consider the additional workload produced by SharePoint applications running on the server in addition to resources used by user connections. Windows SharePoint Services has a number of standard applications that run on a server running SharePoint Services, and these applications place an additional burden on the server's physical resources. Each user connection to a server will place an additional workload on the server, as will the requests and modifications users make.

Setting Up IIS 7.0

The way you set up IIS 7.0 depends on the role and operating system you are using. As discussed previously, you can configure IIS 7.0 to support one of three server roles: application server, Web server, and server running SharePoint Services. You can also configure IIS 7.0 as part of a desktop installation. I discuss deploying IIS 7.0 in each of these situations in the sections that follow.

Installing Application Servers

You can install an application server with or without Web server support by following these steps:

1. Start Server Manager by clicking the Server Manager icon on the Quick Launch toolbar or by clicking Start, Administrative Tools, Server Manager.

2. In Server Manager, select the Roles node in the left pane, and then, under Roles Summary, click Add Roles. This starts the Add Roles Wizard. If the wizard displays the Before You Begin page, read the Welcome page, and then click Next. You can avoid seeing the Welcome page the next time you start this wizard by selecting the Do Not Show Me This Page Again check box before clicking Next.

3. On the Select Server Roles page, select the Application Server role. You'll then see the Add Features Required For Application Server dialog box. This dialog box lists the features that are required in order to install an application server. Click Add Required Features to close the dialog box and add the .NET Framework 3.0 components and the Windows Process Activation Service components to the application server installation.

4. When you are deploying an application server with Web Server support, you can elect to accept the default common Web features or configure the exact features you'd like to use. If you have not installed Web Server (IIS) components previously and want to select the Web server (IIS) components for installation, select Web Server (IIS), and then click Next twice. Otherwise, just click Next twice to continue.

5. You should now see the Select Role Services page. If not previously installed, select Web Server (IIS) Support to install the application server with Web server support in the standard default configuration. You'll then see a dialog box listing the additional required roles. After you review the required roles, click Add Required Role Services to close the dialog box.

   Note   The required roles are the same as those listed in Table 2-1 as Web Common. I recommend selecting Web Server (IIS) Support if the application server will host Web sites or Web services. This will ensure that Setup selects the required Web Common features by default, and this will be helpful later in the setup process.

6. Select other role services to install as appropriate, and then click Next. If you select a role service with additional required features, you'll see a dialog box listing the additional required roles. After you review the required roles, click Add Required Role Services to close the dialog box.

7. If you selected the WS-Atomic Transactions feature, you'll see the Choose A Certificate For SSL Encryption page next. You have the following options:

   ❑ **Choose An Existing Certificate For SSL Encryption** Select this option if you previously obtained a certificate from a certification authority (CA) and want to install it for use with the WS-AT site that Setup will configure on the server. If you've previously imported certificates using the Certificate snap-in or the Import Certificate Wizard, you'll see a list of available certificates, and you can click the certificate you want to use. Otherwise, click Import to start the Certificate Import Wizard, and then follow the prompts to import the certificate.

   ❑ **Create A Self-Signed Certificate For SSL Encryption** Select this option if you are using WS-Atomic transactions with a limited number of clients or for testing/development purposes and want to create and then automatically install a self-signing certificate for use with the WS-AT site that Setup will configure on the server. You will need to install the same certificate manually on all clients that need to be able to authenticate with the server.

   ❑ **Choose A Certificate For SSL Encryption Later** Select this option if you haven't obtained a certificate from a CA yet but plan to later. When you choose this option, IIS disables SSL on the WS-AT site until you import the certificate, as discussed in Chapter 10.

8. If you selected Web Server (IIS) on the Select Server Roles page, as discussed in Step 5, click Next twice to display the Select Role Services page for Web server features. You can then select the Web server features to install. In most cases, you'll want to select additional features rather than trying to remove features. When selecting or clearing role services, keep the following in mind before you click Next to continue:

   ❑ If you select a role service with additional required features, you'll see a dialog box listing the additional required roles. After you review the required roles, click Add Required Role Services to accept the additions and close the dialog box. If you click Cancel instead, Setup clears the feature you previously selected.

   ❑ If you try to remove a role service that is required based on a previous selection, you'll see a warning prompt about dependent services that Setup must also remove. In most cases, you'll want to click Cancel to preserve the previous selection. If you click Remove Dependent Role Services, Setup will remove the previously selected dependent services, which could cause the Web server to not function as expected

9. Click Next. On the Confirm Installation Selections page, click the Print, E-mail, Or Save This Information link to generate an installation report and display it in Windows Internet Explorer. You can then use standard Windows Internet Explorer features to print or save the report. After you've reviewed the installation options and saved them as necessary, click Install to begin the installation process.

10. When Setup finishes installing the application server with the features you've selected, you'll see the Installation Results page. Review the installation details to ensure that all phases of the installation completed successfully. If any portion of the installation failed, note the reason for the failure, and then use these trouble-shooting techniques:

   a. Click the Print, E-mail, Or Save The Installation Report link to create or update the installation report and display it in Windows Internet Explorer.

   b. Scroll down to the bottom of the installation report in Windows Internet Explorer, and then click Full Log (For Troubleshooting Only) to display the Server Manager log in Notepad.

   c. In Notepad, press Ctrl+F, type the current date in the appropriate format for your language settings, such as 2007-08-30, and then click Find Next. Notepad will then move through the log to the first Setup entry from the current date.

   d. Review the Server Manager entries for installation problems, and take corrective actions as appropriate.

Installing Web Servers

You can install a Web server by following these steps:

1. Start the Server Manager by clicking the Server Manager icon on the Quick Launch toolbar or by clicking Start, Administrative Tools, Server Manager.

2. In Server Manager, select the Roles node in the left pane and then, under Roles Summary, click Add Roles. This starts the Add Roles Wizard. If the wizard displays the Before You Begin page, read the Welcome page, and then click Next. You can avoid seeing the Welcome page the next time you start this wizard by selecting the Do Not Show Me This Page Again check box before clicking Next.

3. On the Select Server Roles page, select the Web Server (IIS) role. You'll then see the Add Features Required For Web Server dialog box. This dialog box lists the features that are required to install a Web server. Click Add Required Features to close the dialog box and add the Windows Activation Service components to the Web server installation. Click Next twice to continue.

4. On the Select Role Services page, Setup selects the core set of standard features by default. When selecting or clearing role services, keep the following in mind before you click Next to continue:

   ❑ If you select a role service with additional required features, you'll see a dialog box listing the additional required roles. After you review the required roles, click Add Required Role Services to accept the additions and close the dialog box. If you click Cancel instead, Setup will clear the feature you previously selected.

   ❑ If you try to remove a role service that is required based on a previous selection, you'll see a warning prompt about dependent services that Setup must also remove. In most cases, you'll want to click Cancel to preserve the previous selection. If you click Remove Dependent Role Services, Setup will also remove the previously selected dependent services, which could cause the Web server to not function as expected.

5. Click Next. On the Confirm Installation Options page, click the Print, E-mail, Or Save This Information link to generate an installation report and display it in Windows Internet Explorer. You can then use standard Windows Internet Explorer features to print or save the report. After you've reviewed the installation options and saved them as necessary, click Install to begin the installation process.

6. When Setup finishes installing the application server with the features you've selected, you'll see the Installation Results page. Review the installation details to ensure that all phases of the installation completed successfully. If any portion of the installation failed, note the reason for the failure and then use these trouble-shooting techniques:

   a. Click the Print, E-mail, Or Save The Installation Report link to create or update the installation report and display it in Windows Internet Explorer.

   b. Scroll down to the bottom of the installation report in Windows Internet Explorer and then click Full Log (For Troubleshooting Only) to display the Server Manager log in Notepad.

   c. In Notepad, press Ctrl+F, type the current date in the appropriate format for your language settings, such as 2007-08-30, and then click Find Next. Notepad will then move through the log to the first Setup entry from the current date.

   d. Review the Server Manager entries for installation problems and take corrective actions as appropriate.

Installing Windows SharePoint Services

Windows SharePoint Services uses one of two distinctly different configurations: independent server configuration and dependent load-balanced configuration. With an independent server configuration, you install Windows SharePoint Services on a single server that has its own database for storing application and user information. With a dependent load-balanced configuration, you install SharePoint Services on a computer as part of a Web farm where all servers share a Microsoft SQL Server 2000 or SQL Server 2005 database. Although both types of installations are configured using a similar initial setup process, if you want to connect to the SQL Server database and use load balancing, you must configure a server that is part of a Web farm.

> **Note**   Windows SharePoint Services 2008 is a supplement to the Windows Server 2008 operating system. As such, Windows SharePoint Services 2008 is not included in Windows Server 2008 and must be installed separately. Once you've downloaded the installer packages from Microsoft and double-clicked each one to install it, you can configure this role using Server Manager, as discussed in this section. However, because SharePoint is a supplement, the wizard pages and related setup options may be different.

You can install Windows SharePoint Services on a computer by following these steps:

1. Start Server Manager by clicking the Server Manager icon on the Quick Launch toolbar or by clicking Start, Administrative Tools, Server Manager.

2. In Server Manager, select the Roles node in the left pane, and then, under Roles Summary, click Add Roles. This starts the Add Roles Wizard. If Setup displays the Before You Begin page, read the Welcome page and then click Next. You can avoid seeing the Welcome page the next time you start this wizard by selecting the Do Not Show Me This Page Again check box before clicking Next.

3. On the Select Server Roles page, select the Windows SharePoint Services role. You'll then see the Add Role Services And Features Required For Windows Share-Point Services dialog box. As listed previously in Table 2-1, this dialog box lists the features that are required in order to install SharePoint Services. Click Add Required Features to close the dialog box and add the Web Server (IIS), Windows Activation Service, and .NET Framework 3.0 components to the Share-Point installation. Click Next.

4. Read the introduction to Windows SharePoint Services. As necessary, click the links provided to learn more about the features offered with Windows SharePoint Services. Click Next when you are ready to continue.

5. On the Select Configuration Type page, choose the type of installation. If you are deploying a single-server solution, select Install Only On This Server and then click Next. If you are deploying a server that is part of a Web farm, select Install As Part Of A Server Farm, and then click Next.

6. Although individual SharePoint sites can use different languages, the administration site for Windows SharePoint Services can use only the language chosen during Setup, and you cannot change this language later. On the Select The Language For The Administration Site page, use the selection drop-down list provided to choose the desired language for the administration site, such as English, German, or Korean, and then click Next.

7. If you are installing a single-server configuration of Windows SharePoint Services, on the Specify E-mail Settings page, configure the default e-mail settings that SharePoint will use to send e-mail notifications to administrators. You can use the options provided as follows:

   ❑ **Outbound SMTP Server**   Sets the fully qualified domain name of the e-mail server that will send notifications to administrators, such as mail.adatum.com.

   ❑ **From E-mail Address**   Sets the e-mail address that will appear in the From field of notification messages, such as wss-admin@adatum.com.

   ❑ **Reply-To E-mail Address**   Sets the reply-to e-mail address for notification messages, such as wss-incoming@adatum.com.

8. If you have not previously installed Web Server (IIS), click Next twice to display the Select Role Services page for Web server features. You can then select the Web server features to install. In most cases, you'll want to select additional features rather than trying to remove features. When selecting or clearing role services, keep the following in mind before you click Next to continue:

   ❑ If you select a role service with additional required features, you'll see a dialog box listing the additional required roles. After you review the required roles, click Add Required Role Services to accept the additions and close the dialog box. If you click Cancel instead, Setup will clear the feature you previously selected.

   ❑ If you try to remove a role service that is required based on a previous selection, you'll see a warning prompt about dependent services that Setup must also remove. In most cases, you'll want to click Cancel to preserve the previous selection. If you click Remove Dependent Role Services, Setup will also remove the previously selected dependent services, which could cause the Web server to not function as expected.

9. On the Confirm Installation Selections page, click the Print, E-mail, Or Save This Information link to generate an installation report and display it in Windows Internet Explorer. You can then use standard Windows Internet Explorer features to print or save the report. After you've reviewed the installation options and saved them as necessary, click Install to begin the installation process.

10. If you are setting up a server that is part of a Web farm, you must configure a connection to the shared SQL Server database and perform other preliminary setup tasks by using the Windows SharePoint Services Central Administration tool.

11. When Setup finishes installing the application server with the features you've selected, you'll see the Installation Results page. Review the installation details to ensure that all phases of the installation completed successfully. If any portion of the installation failed, note the reason for the failure and then use these trouble-shooting techniques:

    a. Click the Print, E-mail, Or Save The Installation Report link to create or update the installation report and display it in Windows Internet Explorer.

    b. Scroll down to the bottom of the installation report in Windows Internet Explorer and then click Full Log (For Troubleshooting Only) to display the Server Manager log in Notepad.

    c. In Notepad, press Ctrl+F, type the current date in the appropriate format for your language settings, such as 2007-08-30, and then click Find Next. Notepad will then move through the log to the first Setup entry from the current date.

    d. Review the Server Manager entries for installation problems and take corrective actions as appropriate.

Adding or Removing Web Server Features on Windows Vista

In earlier versions of Windows, you use Add/Remove Windows Components in the Add or Remove Programs application to add or remove operating system components. In Windows Vista, you configure operating system components as Windows features that you can turn on or off rather than add or remove.

You can configure Web server features on a computer running Windows Vista by completing these steps:

1. Click Start, and then click Control Panel.

2. In Control Panel, click Programs.

3. Under Programs And Features, click Turn Windows Features On Or Off. This displays the Windows Features dialog box.

4. You'll find Windows features for Web servers under the following nodes:

    ❑ **Internet Information Services/FTP Publishing Service**   Includes the FTP Management Console and the FTP Server

    ❑ **Internet Information Services/Web Management Tools**   Includes the IIS 6 Management and IIS 7.0 Management components

❑ **Internet Information Services/World Wide Web Services** Includes the Application Development, Common HTTP, Health and Diagnostics, Performance, and Security features

❑ **Microsoft .NET Framework 3.0** Includes the XPS View and the HTTP Activation and Non-HTTP Activation components for WCF

❑ **Microsoft Message Queue (MSMQ) Server** Includes the MSMQ Core server components in addition to support and integration components for message queuing

❑ **Windows Process Activation Service** Includes the .NET Environment, Configuration APIs, and Process Model

To turn features on, select feature check boxes. To turn features off, clear feature check boxes. As you select features, Windows Vista selects any required related features automatically without a warning prompt.

5. When you click OK, Windows Vista reconfigures components as appropriate for any changes you've made. You may need your original installation media.

Managing Installed Roles and Role Services

When you are working with Web and application servers and servers running Share-Point Services, Server Manager is the primary tool you'll use to manage roles and role services. Not only can you use Server Manager to add or remove roles and role services, you can also use Server Manager to view the configuration details and status for roles and roles services.

Viewing Configured Roles and Role Services

On Windows Server, Server Manager lists roles you've installed when you select the Roles node in the left pane. As Figure 2-3 shows, the main view of the Roles node displays a Roles Summary section that lists the number of roles and the names of the roles installed. When there are error-related events for a particular server role, Server Manager displays a warning icon to the left of the role name.

In the Roles window, the name of the role is a clickable link that accesses the related role details. The role details provide the following:

■ Summary information about the status of related system services. If applicable, Server Manager lists the number of related services that are running or stopped, such as "System Services: 3 Running, 2 Stopped."

■ Summary information about events the related services and components have generated in the last 24 hours, including details on whether any errors have occurred, such as "Events: 1 error(s), 6 warning(s), 2 informational in the last 24 hours."

■ Summary information about the role services installed including the number of role services installed and the installed or not installed status of each individual role service that you can use with the role.

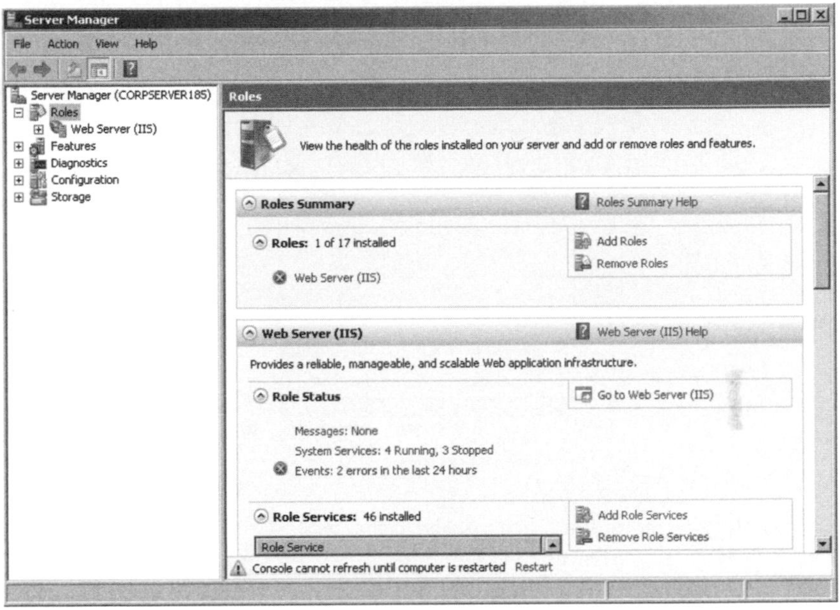

Figure 2-3   View the status details for installed roles.

Tip   By default, Server Manager refreshes the details once an hour. You can refresh the details manually by selecting Refresh on the Action menu. If you want to set a different default refresh interval, click Configure Refresh at the bottom of the Summary window, use the options provided to set a new refresh interval, and then click OK.

In Server Manager's main window, if you click a role under Roles Summary or click the Go To Manage Roles link under Roles Summary section or click a role under Roles Summary, Server Manager displays expanded summary details on the events and services for the related role. As shown in Figure 2-4, Server Manager lists all events in the last 24 hours. If you click an event and then click View Event Properties, you can get detailed information about the event. Additionally, Server Manager provides details regarding the system services used by the role and their status. You can manage a service by clicking it and then clicking the related Stop, Start, or Restart links provided. In many cases, if a service isn't running as you think it should, you can click Restart to resolve the issue by stopping and then starting the service.

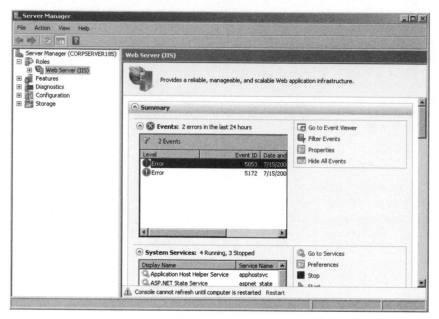

Figure 2-4   View recent events and manage system services.

Adding or Removing Roles on Servers

When you select the Roles node in Server Manager, the Roles Summary pane section details on the current roles that you've installed. In the Roles Summary section, you'll find options for adding and removing roles. You can add a role as discussed previously in the "Setting Up IIS 7.0" section of this chapter. The roles you can remove depend on the type of server. The roles are as follows:

- On application servers, you can remove the application server role, the Web server role, or both.

- On a Web server, you can remove the Web server role.

- On a server computer running SharePoint Services, you can remove the Windows SharePoint Services role or both the Windows SharePoint Services role and the Web server role.

You can remove a server role by completing the following steps:

1. Start Server Manager by clicking the Server Manager icon on the Quick Launch toolbar or by clicking Start, Administrative Tools, Server Manager.

2. In Server Manager, select the Roles node in the left pane, and then click Remove Roles. This starts the Remove Roles Wizard. If Setup displays the Before You

Begin page, read the Welcome page and then click Next. You can avoid seeing the Welcome page the next time you start this wizard by selecting the Do Not Show Me This Page Again check box before clicking Next.

3. On the Remove Server Roles page, clear the check box for the role you want to remove, and then click Next. If you try to remove a role that another role depends on, you'll see a warning prompt stating that you cannot remove the role unless you also remove the other role as well. If you click Remove Dependent Role Services, Setup will remove both roles.

4. On the Confirm Removal Selections page, review the related role services that Setup will remove based on your previous selections, and then click Remove.

5. When Setup finishes modifying the server configuration, you'll see the Removal Results page. Review the modification details to ensure that all phases of the removal process completed successfully. If any portion of the removal process failed, note the reason for the failure and then use the previously discussed troubleshooting techniques to help resolve the problem.

Viewing and Modifying Role Services on Servers

In Server Manager, you can view the role services configured for a role by selecting Roles in the left pane and then scrolling down to the Role Services section for the role you want to work with. In the details section, you'll find a list of role services that you can install in addition to their current Installed or Not Installed status. You can manage role services for application servers and Web servers by using the Add Role Services and Remove Role Services functions provided for the related role details entry. The Windows SharePoint Services role, however, does not have individual role services that you can manage in this way. With a server computer running Share-Point Services, you can modify the Web server role or remove only the Windows SharePoint Services role.

You can add role services by completing the following steps:

1. Start Server Manager by clicking the Server Manager icon on the Quick Launch toolbar or by clicking Start, Administrative Tools, Server Manager.

2. In Server Manager, select the Roles node in the left pane, and then scroll down until you see the Roles Services section for the role you want to manage. In the Roles Services section for the role, click Add Role Services. This starts the Add Role Services Wizard.

3. On the Select Role Services page, Setup makes the currently selected roles unavailable so that you cannot select them. To add a role, select it in the Role Services list. When you are finished selecting roles to add, click Next, and then click Install.

You can remove role services by completing the following steps:

1. Start Server Manager by clicking the Server Manager icon on the Quick Launch toolbar or by clicking Start, Administrative Tools, Server Manager.

2. In Server Manager, select the Roles node in the left pane and then scroll down until you see the Roles Services section for the role you want to manage. In the Roles Services section for the role, click Remove Role Services. This starts the Remove Role Services Wizard.

3. On the Select Role Services page, Setup selects the currently installed roles. To remove a role, clear the related check box. When you are finished selecting roles to remove, click Next, and then click Remove.

Chapter 3
Core IIS 7.0 Administration

Core Internet Information Services (IIS) administration tasks revolve around connecting to servers, managing services, and configuring remote administration. In IIS 7.0, you connect to individual servers and manage their IIS components through the IIS Manager whether you are working with a local server or a remote server. To perform most administration tasks with sites and servers, you'll need to log in to the IIS server using an account that has administrator privileges.

Working with IIS and URLs

To retrieve files from IIS servers, clients must know three things: the server's address, where on the server the file is located, and which protocol to use to access and retrieve the file. Normally, this information is specified as a Uniform Resource Locator (URL). URLs provide a uniform way of identifying resources that are available. The basic mechanism that makes URLs so versatile is their standard naming scheme.

URL schemes name the protocol the client will use to access and transfer the file. Clients use the name of the protocol to determine the format for the information that follows the protocol name. The protocol name is generally followed by a colon and two forward slashes. The information after the double slash marks follows a format that depends on the protocol type referenced in the URL. Here are two general formats:

protocol://hostname:port/path_to_resource

protocol://username:password@hostname:port/ path_to_resource

Host name information used in URLs identifies the address to a host and is broken down into two or more parts separated by periods. The periods are used to separate domain information from the host name. Common domain names for Web servers begin with *www*, such as *www.microsoft.com*, which identifies the Microsoft WWW server in the commercial domain. Domains you can specify in your URLs include:

- **com**   Commercial sites
- **edu**   Education sites
- **gov**   Nonmilitary government sites
- **mil**   Military sites
- **net**   Network sites
- **org**   Organizational sites

Port information used in URLs identifies the port number to be used for the connection. Generally, you don't have to specify port numbers in your URLs unless the connection will be made to a port other than the default. Port 80 is the default port for HTTP. If you request a URL on a server using the URL *http://www.microsoft.com/docs/my-yoyo.htm*, port 80 is assumed to be the default port value. On the other hand, if you wanted to make a connection to port 8080, you'd need to type in the port value, such as *http://www.microsoft.com:8080/docs/my-yoyo.htm*.

Port values that fall between zero and 1023, referred to as *well-known ports*, are reserved for specific data type uses on the Internet. Port values between 1024 and 49151 are considered *registered ports*, and those between 49152 and 65535 are considered *dynamic ports*.

The final part of a URL is the path to the resource. This path generally follows the directory structure from the server's home directory to the resource specified in the URL.

URLs for FTP can also contain a user name and password. User name and password information allows users to log in to an FTP server using a specific user account. For example, the following URL establishes a connection to the Microsoft FTP server and logs on using a named account, such as *ftp://sysadmin:rad$4@ftp.microsoft.com /public/download.doc*.

In this instance, the account logon is *sysadmin*, the password is *rad$4*, the server is *ftp.microsoft.com*, and the requested resource is *public/download.doc*.

If a connection is made to an FTP server without specifying the user name and password, you can configure the server to assume that the user wants to establish an anonymous session. In this case the following default values are assumed: *anonymous* for user name and the user's e-mail address as the password.

URLs can use uppercase and lowercase letters, the numerals 0–9, and a few special characters, including:

- Asterisks (*)
- Dollar signs ($)
- Exclamation points (!)
- Hyphens (-)
- Parentheses (left and right)
- Periods (.)
- Plus signs (+)
- Single quotation marks (')
- Underscores (_)

You're limited to these characters because other characters used in URLs have specific meanings, as shown in Table 3-1.

Table 3-1   Reserved Characters in URLs

Character	Meaning
:	The colon is a separator that separates the protocol from the rest of the URL scheme; separates the host name from the port number; and separates the user name from the password.
//	The double slash marks indicate that the protocol uses the format defined by the Common Internet Scheme Syntax (see RFC 1738 for more information).
/	The slash is a separator and is used to separate the path from the host name and port. The slash is also used to denote the directory path to the resource named in the URL.
~	The tilde is generally used at the beginning of the path to indicate that the resource is in the specified user's public Hypertext Markup Language (HTML) directory.
%	Identifies an escape code. Escape codes are used to specify special characters in URLs that otherwise have a special meaning or aren't allowed.
@	The at symbol is used to separate user name and/or password information from the host name in the URL.
?	The question mark is used in the URL path to specify the beginning of a query string. Query strings are passed to Common Gateway Interface (CGI) scripts. All the information following the question mark is data the user submitted and isn't interpreted as part of the file path.
+	The plus sign is used in query strings as a placeholder between words. Instead of using spaces to separate words that the user has entered in the query, the browser substitutes the plus sign.
=	The equal sign is used in query strings to separate the key assigned by the publisher from the value entered by the user.
&	The ampersand is used in query strings to separate multiple sets of keys and values.
^	The caret is reserved for future use.
{}	Braces are reserved for future use.
[]	Brackets are reserved for future use.

To make URLs even more versatile, you can use escape codes to specify characters in URLs that are either reserved or otherwise not allowed. Escape codes have two components: a percent sign and a numeric value. The percent sign identifies the start of an escape code. The number following the percent sign identifies the character being escaped. The escape code for a space is a percent sign followed by the number

20 (%20). To refer to a file called "my party hat.htm," for example, you could use this escape code in a URL such as this one:

http://www.microsoft.com/docs/my%20party%20hat.htm

Understanding the Core IIS Architecture

You can think of IIS as a layer over the operating system where, in most cases, you might need to perform an operating system–level task before you perform an IIS task. Web sites, Web applications, and virtual directories are the core building blocks of IIS servers. Every IIS server installation has these core building blocks. As you set out to work with IIS servers and these basic building blocks, you'll also want to consider what access and administrative controls are available.

Working with Web Sites

You can use a single IIS server to host multiple Web sites. Web sites are containers that have their own configuration information, which includes one or more unique bindings. A Web site binding is a combination of an Internet Protocol (IP) address, port number, and optional host headers on which HTTP.sys listens for requests. Many Web sites have two bindings: one for standard requests and one for secure requests. For example, you could configure a Web site to listen for standard HTTP requests on IP address 192.168.10.52 and TCP port 80. If you've also configured the server for Secure Sockets Layer (SSL), you also could configure a Web site to listen for Secure HTTP (HTTPS) requests on IP address 192.168.10.52 and TCP port 443.

When you install IIS on a server, Setup creates a default Web site and configures the bindings for this site so that HTTP.sys listens for requests on TCP port 80 for all IP addresses you've configured on the server. Thus if the server has multiple IP addresses, HTTP.sys would accept requests from any of these IP addresses, provided that the requests are made on TCP port 80. Increasingly, modern Web sites use host headers. *Host headers* allow you to assign multiple host names to the same IP address and TCP port combination. Here, IIS uses the host name passed in the HTTP header to determine the site that a client is requesting. For example, a single server could use host headers to host *catalog.adatum.com*, *sales.adatum.com*, and *www.adatum.com* on IP address 192.168.15.68 and TCP port 80.

Working with Web Applications and Virtual Directories

IIS handles every incoming request to a Web site within the context of a Web application. A Web application is a software program that delivers Web content to users over HTTP or HTTPS. Each Web site has a default Web application and one or more additional Web applications associated with it. The default Web application handles incoming requests that you haven't assigned to other Web applications. Additional Web applications handle incoming requests that specifically reference the application.

Each Web application must have a root virtual directory associated with it. The root virtual directory sets the application name and maps the application to the physical directory that contains the application's content. Typically, the default Web application is associated with the root virtual directory of the Web site and any additional virtual directories you've created but haven't mapped to other applications. Following this, in the default configuration, the default applications handles an incoming request for the / directory of a Web site in addition to other named virtual directories, such as /images or /data. IIS maps references to /, /images, /data, or other virtual directories to the physical directory that contains the related content. For the / directory of the default Web site, the default physical directory is *%SystemRoot%*/Inetpub/Wwwroot.

When you create a Web application, the application's name sets the name of the root virtual directory. Therefore, if you create a Web application called Sales, the related root virtual directory is called Sales, and this virtual directory in turn maps to the physical directory that contains the application's content, such as *%SystemRoot%*/Inetpub/Wwwroot/Sales.

Controlling Access to Servers, Sites, and Applications

By default, IIS is configured to allow anyone to anonymously access the Web sites and applications configured on an IIS server. You can control access to Web sites and Web applications by requiring users to authenticate themselves. As discussed in Chapter 10, "Managing Web Server Security," IIS supports a number of authentication methods for Web sites, including Basic authentication, Digest authentication, Client Certificate authentication, and Windows authentication. When working with Microsoft ASP.NET and Web applications, you also can use ASP.NET impersonation and Forms authentication.

Regardless of the authentication techniques you use, however, Windows Server 2008 permissions ultimately determine if users can access files and directories. Before users can access files and directories, you must ensure that the appropriate users and groups have access at the operating system level. After you set operating system–level permissions, you must set IIS-specific security permissions as discussed in Chapter 10.

As an administrator, you can manage the configuration of IIS from the command prompt or within IIS Manager. For administration of Web servers, Web sites, and Web applications using the command line, Windows Management Instrumentation (WMI), or direct editing of the configuration files, you must have write permissions on the target configuration files. For administration of Web servers, Web sites, and Web applications using IIS Manager, IIS 7.0 specifies three administrative roles:

- **Web server administrator**   A *Web server administrator* is a top-level administrator who has complete control over an IIS server and can delegate administration of features to Web site administrators and Web application administrators. A Web server administrator is a member of the Administrators group on the local server or a domain administrator group in the domain of which the server is a member.

- **Web site administrator**   A *Web site administrator* is an administrator who has been delegated control of a specific Web site and any applications related to that Web site. A Web site administrator can delegate control of a Web application to a Web application administrator.

- **Web application administrator**   A *Web application administrator* is an administrator who has been delegated control of a specific Web application. A Web site administrator can delegate control of a Web application to a Web application administrator.

The settings that administrators can configure depend on their administrative role on a particular server. Table 3-2 summarizes the areas of administration for each administrative role.

Table 3-2   Areas of Administration for Administrative Roles

Administrator Area	Web Server Administrator	Web Site Administrator	Web Application Administrator
Web server	Yes, no restrictions	No server-level permissions	No server-level permissions
Web sites on a Web server	Yes, no restrictions	Yes, for site delegated	No site-level permissions
Web applications on a Web site	Yes, no restrictions	Yes, within delegated sites	Yes, for delegated applications
Virtual directories used by sites and applications	Yes, no restrictions	Yes, within delegated sites	Yes, for delegated applications
Physical directories used by sites and applications	Yes, no restrictions	Yes, within delegated sites	Yes, for delegated applications
Files in virtual and physical directories	Yes, no restrictions	Yes, for site delegated	No site-level permissions
Designate Web application administrators	Yes, no restrictions	Yes, within delegated sites	Yes, for delegated applications

Understanding the Services and Processing Architecture

A strong understanding of the services and processing architecture used by IIS 7.0 is essential to your success as an administrator. As you'll see in this section, IIS 7.0 is very different from its predecessors, and the differences you'll learn about mean that you manage core IIS 7.0 features in fundamentally different ways. Although this section provides an initial discussion of applications and application pools, IIS applications and application pools are discussed in detail in Chapter 8, "Running IIS Applications."

Essential IIS Services and Processes

Windows services and processes are other areas where Windows and IIS are tightly integrated. Table 3-3 provides a summary of key services that IIS uses or depends on. Note that the services available on a particular IIS server depend on its configuration. Still, this is the core set of services that you'll find on most IIS servers.

As the table shows, the World Wide Web Publishing Service and Windows Process Activation Service provide the essential services for IIS 7.0. Management of the Web service and Web applications is internalized. The Web Administration Service component of the Web Service Host is used to manage the service itself. Worker processes are used to control applications, and no Internet Server Application Programming Interface (ISAPI) applications run within the IIS process context.

IIS Worker Process Isolation Mode

Worker Process isolation mode is the standard processing mode for Web sites and Web applications. This mode allows sites and applications to:

- Recycle worker threads
- Monitor process health
- Use advanced application pooling configurations
- Take advantage of other IIS 7.0 features

The World Wide Web Publishing Service and Windows Process Activation Service provide the essential services for IIS 7.0. From a high level, the standard IIS 7.0 operating mode works as depicted in Figure 3-1. Service Host processes control all Web resources running on a server. Starting, pausing, or stopping the World Wide Web Publishing Service affects all Web sites on the server. It doesn't directly affect the Service Host. Instead, Windows Server uses an intermediary to control the Service Host for you. For non-Web services, this intermediary is the Inetmgr.exe process. A single instance of Inetmgr.exe is used to manage Web sites and Web applications.

Management of the Web service and Web applications is internalized. The Web Administration Service component of the Web Service Host is used to manage the service itself. Worker processes are used to control applications, and no ISAPI applications run within the IIS process context.

Table 3-3   Essential IIS Services

Display Name	Service Name	Description	Default Startup Type	Log On As	Default Recovery	Dependencies
Application Host Helper Service	Appho-stsvc	Provides configuration history services and app pool account mapping for file and directory access locking.	Automatic	Local System	Restart the service	None
ASP.NET State Service	aspnet_state	Provides support for out-of-process session state management for ASP.NET. Out-of-process state management ensures that the session state is preserved when an application's worker process is recycled. IIS uses this service only when you set the Session State mode to State Server or SQL Server. Otherwise, IIS does not use this service.	Manual	Network Service	Restart the service	None
FTP Publishing Service	MSFTP-SVC	Provides services for transferring files by using FTP. If the server isn't configured as an FTP server, the server doesn't need to run this service. In a standard installation of IIS 7.0, when you install FTP, this service is, by default, configured for manual startup only.	Manual	Local System	Take no action	IIS Admin Service
IIS Admin Service	IISAD-MIN	Allows administration of IIS 6.0–related features, including the metabase. If the server doesn't need backward compatibility, the server doesn't need to run this service.	Automatic	Local System	Run iisreset.exe	HTTP, RPC, Security Accounts Manager
Web Management Service	WMSVC	Enables remote and delegated management of IIS using IIS Manager. If a server is locked down so it can be accessed locally only, the server doesn't need to run this service.	Automatic	Local Service	Restart the service	HTTP
Windows Process Activation Service	WAS	Provides essential features for messaging applications and the Microsoft .NET Framework, including process activation, resource management, and health management. This service is essential for IIS.	Automatic	Local System	Run iisre-set.exe	RPC
World Wide Web Publishing Service	W3SVC	Provides essential services for transferring files by using HTTP and administration through the IIS Manager. This service is essential for IIS.	Automatic	Local System	Take no action	HTTP, Windows Process Activation Service

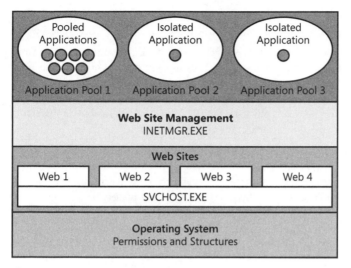

Figure 3-1   A conceptual view of the standard operating mode for IIS 7.0.

Worker processes are used in several ways:

- **Single worker process—single application**   Here a single worker process running in its own context (isolated) handles requests for a single application as well as instances of any ISAPI extensions and filters the application's need. The application is the only one assigned to the related application pool.

- **Single worker process—multiple applications**   Here, a single worker process running in its own context (isolated) handles requests for multiple applications assigned to the same application pool as well as instances of any ISAPI extensions and filters the applications' needs.

- **Multiple worker processes—single application**   Here, multiple worker processes running in their own context (isolated) share responsibility for handling requests for a single application as well as instances of any ISAPI extensions and filters the application's needs. The application is the only one in the related application pool.

- **Multiple worker processes—multiple applications**   Here, multiple worker processes running in their own context (isolated) share responsibility for handling requests for multiple applications assigned to the same application pool as well as instances of any ISAPI extensions and filters the applications' needs.

The standard operating mode ensures that all sites run within an application context and have an associated application pool. The default application pool is DefaultAppPool. You can also assign sites and applications to custom application pools.

Each application or site in an application pool can have one or more worker processes associated with it. The worker processes handle requests for the site or application.

You can configure application pools to manage worker processes in many ways. You can configure automatic recycling of worker threads based on a set of criteria such as when the process has been running for a certain amount of time or uses a specific amount of memory. You can also have IIS monitor the health of worker threads and take actions to recover automatically from failure. These features might eliminate or reduce your dependence on third-party monitoring tools or services.

You can also create a Web garden in which you configure multiple worker processes to handle the workload. Applications configured using this technique are more responsive, more scalable, and less prone to failure. Why? A Hypertext Transfer Protocol (HTTP) listener, called Http.sys, listens for incoming requests and places them in the appropriate application pool request queue. When a request is placed in the queue, an available worker process assigned to the application can take the request and begin processing it. Idle worker processes handle requests in first-in, first-out (FIFO) order.

Worker processes can also be started on demand. If there are unallocated worker processes and no current idle worker processes, IIS can start a new worker process to handle the request. In this way, resources aren't allocated until they're needed, and IIS can handle many more sites than it could if all processes were allocated on startup.

Understanding and Using IIS Applications

You can configure Web sites to run several different types of applications, including:

- Common Gateway Interface (CGI) programs.
- Internet Server Application Programming Interface (ISAPI) applications.
- ASP.NET applications using managed code.

CGI describes how programs specified in Web addresses, also known as *gateway scripts*, pass information to Web servers. Gateway scripts pass information to servers through environment variables that capture user input in forms in addition to information about users submitting information. In IIS 7.0, standard CGI is implemented through the CgiModule and multi-threaded CGI is implemented through the FastCgiModule. The CgiModule has a managed handler that specifies that all files with the .exe extension are to be handled as CGI programs.

The way CGI programs are handled is determined by the way you've configured the CGI feature within IIS. By default, CGI is disabled. When you enable CGI, the CgiModule is the default handler for .exe programs. You can modify the handler configuration for .exe programs to use the FastCgiModule. This configuration is useful if you've installed the PHP Hypertext Preprocessor (PHP) on your IIS server and want to use it. Once you've configured the server to use FastCgi for .exe programs, you should add handler mappings for PHP-related file extensions and configure these mappings so that they use the PHP executable, such as Php-cgi.exe. For example, you could add mappings for *.php and *.php5. Your IIS server would then process files with the .PHP and .PHP5 extensions through Php-cgi.exe.

In IIS 7.0, ISAPI is implemented using two modules, IsapiModule and IsapiFilterModule. The IsapiModule makes it possible to use ISAPI applications and ISAPI extensions. In the IIS server core, several components rely on handlers that are based on ISAPI extensions, including ASP and ASP.NET. The IsapiModule has a managed handler that specifies that all files with the .dll extension are to be handled as ISAPI extensions. If you remove this module, ISAPI extensions mapped as handlers or explicitly called as ISAPI extensions won't work anymore.

IIS uses ISAPI filters to provide additional functionality. If you selected ASP.NET during initial configuration, an ASP.NET filter is configured to provide classic functionality through aspnet_filter.dll, an ISAPI filter. For classic ASP.NET functionality, each version of ASP.NET installed on a Web server must have a filter definition that identifies the version and path to the related filter. After you install new versions of ASP.NET, you can add definitions for the related filter.

ISAPI and CGI restrictions control the allowed ISAPI and CGI functionality on a server. When you want to use an ISAPI or CGI application, you must specifically allow the related DLL or EXE to run.

Understanding and Using ASP.NET Applications

When you are working with ASP.NET, it is important to consider the managed pipeline mode you will use. IIS 7.0 supports two modes for processing requests to ASP.NET applications:

- Classic

- Integrated

Classic pipeline mode, depicted in Figure 3-2, is the standard processing mode used with IIS 6.0. If a managed Web application runs in an application pool with classic mode, IIS processes the requests in an application pool by using separate processing pipelines for IIS and ISAPI. This means that requests for ASP.NET applications are processed in multiple stages like this:

1. The incoming HTTP request is received through the IIS core.

2. The request is processed through ISAPI.

3. The request is processed through ASP.NET.

4. The request passes back through ISAPI.

5. The request passes back through the IIS core where the HTTP response finally is delivered.

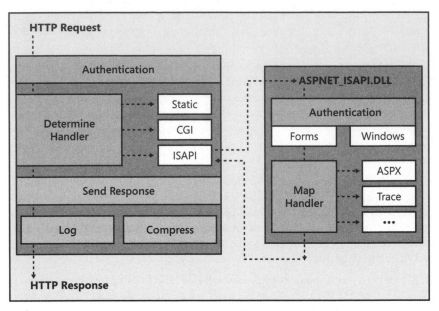

Figure 3-2   Here is a conceptual view of classic ASP.NET processing.

Integrated pipeline mode, depicted in Figure 3-3, is a dynamic processing mode that can be used with IIS 7.0. If a managed Web application runs in an application pool with integrated mode, IIS processes the requests in an application pool by using an integrated processing pipeline for IIS and ASP.NET. This means that requests for ASP.NET applications are processed directly like this:

1. The incoming HTTP request is received through the IIS core and ASP.NET.

2. The appropriate handler executes the request and delivers the HTTP response.

From an administrator perspective, applications running in classic pipeline mode can appear to be less responsive than their integrated counterparts. From an application developer perspective, classic pipeline mode has two key limitations. First, services provided by ASP.NET modules and applications are not available to non-ASP.NET requests. Second, ASP.NET modules are unable to affect certain parts of IIS request processing that occurred before and after the ASP.NET execution path.

With an integrated pipeline, all native IIS modules and managed modules can process incoming requests at any stage. This enables services provided by managed modules to be used for requests to pages created using static content, ASP.NET, PHP, and more. Direct integration makes it possible for developers to write custom authentication modules, to create modules that modify request headers before other components process the request, and more.

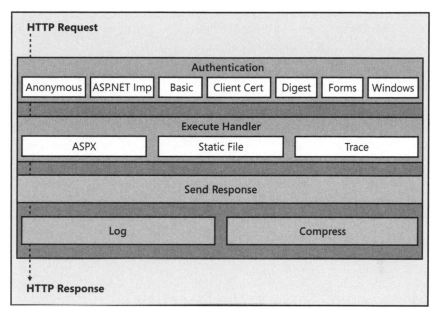

Figure 3-3   A conceptual view of integrated ASP.NET processing.

When working with the integrated pipeline mode, it is important to keep in mind that in this mode ASP.NET does not rely on the ISAPI or ISAPI Extension modules. Because of this, the running of an integrated ASP.NET application is not affected by the ISAPI CGI restriction list. The ISAPI CGI restriction list applies only to ISAPI and CGI applications (which includes ASP.NET classic applications). For integrated mode to work properly, you must specify handler mappings for all custom file types.

Further, many applications written for classic pipeline mode will need to be migrated to run properly in integrated pipeline mode. The good news is that the Configuration Validation module, included as a part of the server core, can automatically detect an application that requires migration and return an error message stating that the application must be migrated. You can migrate applications by using Appcmd.exe (general-purpose IIS command-line administration tool). Any migration error reported by IIS typically contains the necessary command for migrating the application. To use this command to migrate an application automatically, right-click the command-prompt icon and choose Run As Administrator. You then can migrate an application manually by running the following command at the elevated command prompt:

```
appcmd migrate config AppPath
```

where *AppPath* is the virtual path of the application. The virtual path contains the name of the associated Web site and application. For example, if an application named

SalesApp was configured on the Default Web Site and needed to be migrated, you could do this by running the following command:

appcmd migrate config "Default Web Site/SalesApp"

When AppCmd finishes migrating the application, the application will run in both classic and integrated modes.

> **Real World**   Although IIS notifies you initially about applications that you need to migrate, IIS will not notify you about migration problems if you subsequently change the application code so that it uses a configuration that is not compatible with integrated mode. In this case, you may find that the application doesn't run or doesn't work as expected, and you'll need to migrate the application manually from a command prompt. If you don't want to see migration error messages, modify the validation element in the application's Web.config file so that its validateIntegrated-ModeConfiguration attribute is set to false, such as:
>
> <system.webServer>
> <validation validateIntegratedModeConfiguration="false" />
> </system.webServer>

Managing IIS Servers: The Essentials

When you installed IIS 7.0, you had the opportunity to install the IIS management tools. The standard administration tool for IIS 7.0 is Internet Information Server (IIS) Manager. The standard administration tool for IIS 6.0 is Internet Information Services (IIS) 6.0 Manager.

Using Internet Information Services (IIS) Manager

You can access Internet Information Services (IIS) Manager by clicking Start and choosing Administrative Tools and then Internet Information Services (IIS) Manager. IIS Manager automatically connects to the local IIS installation (if available). Using the choices available when you select the Start Page node, you can connect to one or more remote servers, sites, and applications as discussed in Chapter 1, "IIS 7.0 Administration Overview." Each additional computer, site, or application to which you connect will have a separate node that you can use to manage its resources.

> **Real World**   Firewalls and proxy servers might affect your ability to connect to systems at remote locations. If you need to connect regularly to servers through firewalls or proxies, you'll need to consider the administration techniques you might want to use and then consult your company's network or security administrator to determine what steps need to be taken to allow those administration techniques. Typically, the network/security administrator will have to open TCP or UDP ports to allow remote communication between your computer or network and the remote computer or network. Each type of tool you want to use might require you to open different ports. By default, the Web Management Service (WMSVC) running on an IIS server listens on TCP port 8172. Because any administrator can easily change the

default listen port, you may need to check the current configuration by logging on locally or checking your organization's configuration policy documentation. Be sure to provide the connection port when setting the server name. For example, to connect to www.adatum.com on TCP port 8175, you'd type the server name as **www.adatum.com:8175**.

The node level you select determines what IIS Manager displays in the right pane. When you select a server node in the left pane, the right pane displays the core administration tasks as shown in Figure 3-4. By default, IIS Manager groups the tasks into three areas:

- **ASP.NET**   Includes tasks related to managing ASP.NET and the .NET Framework

- **IIS**   Includes tasks related to managing sites and applications

- **Management**   Includes tasks related to configuring administrative roles, delegation, and remote administration

Figure 3-4   Use IIS Manager to manage Web servers, sites, and applications.

Using the Group By drop-down list, you can select Category to group by category or No Grouping to list the tasks in alphabetical order. The categories are similar to the ones used during Setup and include Application Development, Health And Diagnostics, HTTP Features, Performance, Security, and Server Components. The Views button, to the right of the Group By drop-down list, allows you to control how the tasks are listed. The views available are:

- **Details**   Lists tasks with a small icon, task name, and summary description

- **Icon**   Lists tasks with the task name under a large icon

- **Tiles**   Lists tasks with a large icon to the left of the task name

- **List**   Lists tasks with a small icon to the left of the task name

When you expand a server node by double-clicking it, you'll see the following additional nodes as well. Application Pools allows you to view and manage the application pools on the server. When you select the Application Pools node, you'll see a list of application pools by name, status, and other key statistics. Sites allows you to view and manage the Web sites on the server. When you select the Sites node, you'll see a list of Web sites on the server organized by name, ID, status, binding, and local directory path. When you expand the Sites node by double-clicking it, you'll see the sites on the server.

> **Note**   In Figure 3-4, there's also a node for FTP sites. The availability of this node and the way this node works depends on whether you are using classic FTP or nextgen FTP. I'll refer to FTP as originally implemented in IIS 7 for Windows Vista and early releases of Windows Server 2008 as "classic FTP." Classic FTP runs within the context of IIS 6. This means classic FTP uses IIS 6 compatibility mode and requires IIS 6 compatibility features, such as the IIS Manager console for IIS 6 and the IIS 6 metabase. The "nextgen" FTP server for IIS 7, included in all other releases of Windows Server 2008, is fully integrated with IIS 7 and includes enhanced features, such as FTP publishing points.

When you select the node for a specific site, you'll see a list of the site's top-level applications and virtual directories. Selecting the node for an application or virtual directory allows you to manage the configuration at that level.

Enabling and Configuring Remote Administration

The Web Management Service (WMSVC) enables remote and delegated management of IIS through IIS Manager. This means that you must configure and enable the Web Management Service before you can remotely manage a server and before delegated users can perform administration tasks.

You can configure the Web Management Service by completing these steps:

1. Start IIS Manager. In the left pane, select the icon for the computer you want to work with. If the computer isn't shown, connect to it as discussed previously, and then select it.

2. When you group by Area, the Management Service feature is listed under Management. Select the Management Service feature and then in the Actions

pane, click Open Feature. This displays the Management Service pane as shown in Figure 3-5.

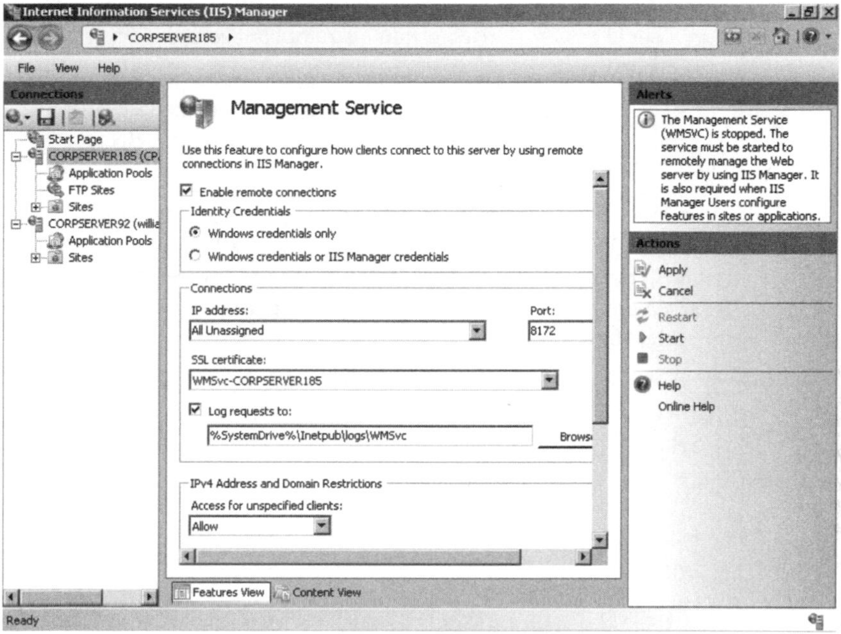

Figure 3-5 Configure options for remote and delegated administration.

3. If the Web Management Service is started, you must stop it before you can configure its properties. Click Stop.

4. If you want to allow local management and local delegated administration only, clear the Enable Remote Connections check box. Otherwise, select this check box to allow remote administration.

5. Under Identity Credentials, use one of the following options to determine the permitted credentials:

   ❑ **Windows Credentials Only** Choose this option to restrict remote access for administration to those individuals with Windows administrator accounts.

   ❑ **Windows Credentials Or IIS Manager Credentials** Choose this option to allow remote access for administration to those individuals with Windows administrator accounts or IIS Manager accounts.

6. Under Connections, use the IP Address drop-down list to select the IP addresses on which the server will listen for remote connections. You can select a specific

IP address to allow connections on that IP address only or All Unassigned to allow connections on any configured IP address.

7. Under Connections, in the Port box, type the TCP port number on which the server should listen for remote administrator connections. The default port is TCP port 8172.

8. All remote administration activities are encrypted automatically using SSL. Under Connections, in the SSL Certificate drop-down list, select the certificate the server should use for encryption.

9. All remote administration activities are logged automatically to the %SystemDrive%\Inetpup\logs\WMSvc directory on the IIS server. To use a different directory, click Browse, and then use the Browse For Folder dialog box to select the new logging location. To disable remote administration logging, clear the Log Requests To check box.

10. By default, any client with an IPv4 address can connect to the Web server. To restrict access to clients with specific IP addresses, set Access For Unspecified Clients to Deny and then add allowed clients using the Allow option.

11. Click Start to run the Web Management Service with the updated configuration.

You can start, stop, or restart the Web Management Service by completing these steps:

1. Start the IIS Manager. In the left pane, select the icon for the computer you want to work with. If the computer isn't shown, connect to it as discussed previously, and then select it.

2. When you group by Area, the Management Service feature is listed under Management. Select the Management Service feature and then in the Actions pane, click Open Feature.

3. In the Actions pane, you can do one of the following:

   ❑ Select Start to start the Web Management Service.

   ❑ Select Stop to stop the Web Management Service.

   ❑ Select Restart to stop and then start the Web Management Service as necessary to ensure that the service and all related processes are recycled for troubleshooting.

Starting, Stopping, and Restarting All Internet Services

With classic FTP servers and IIS 6.0 servers, Window Server uses the Inetinfo.exe process to manage all Internet Information Services. Inetinfo is able to do this because it tracks all IIS resources running on a computer and can issue commands to these resources. As an administrator, you can control Inetinfo through IIS 6.0 Manager or the Iisreset.exe command-line utility. If you use either feature, all services on an IIS 6 server are started, stopped, or restarted as appropriate. When you use either technique on an IIS 7.0 server, the following services are started, stopped, or restarted:

- FTP Publishing Service

- IIS Admin Service

- Windows Process Activation Service

- World Wide Web Publishing Service

On an IIS 7.0 server, the following services are not started, stopped, or restarted:

- Application Host Helper Service

- ASP.NET State Service (ensures that out-of-process state is maintained)

- Web Management Service (ensures that remote administration capabilities are enabled)

Tip   On an IIS 7.0 server, by default, FTP Publishing Service is configured for manual startup only. Because of this, if you use IIS 6.0 Manager or iisreset to start or restart Internet services, FTP Publishing Service will not be started. To ensure that FTP Publishing Service is started or restarted, you must set the startup type to Automatic.

You can use the Iisreset.exe command-line utility to start, stop, and restart IIS services. To start any IIS services that are stopped on the local computer, type the following command:

iisreset /start

To stop all IIS services that are running, paused, or in an unknown state on the local computer, type the following command:

iisreset /stop

To stop and then restart IIS services on the local computer, type the following command:

iisreset /restart

You can also control IIS services on remote computers. To do this, use the following syntax:

iisreset *computername command*

such as:

iisreset engsvr01 /restart

With the Restart Internet Services command (Iisreset), the sequence of tasks is important to understand. This command performs the following tasks:

1. Stops Internet Information Services running on the computer.

2. Attempts to resolve potential problems with runaway processes or hung applications by stopping all related processes.

3. Starts IIS services and then starts DLL Hosts as necessary.

Table 3-4 provides a listing of all switches for the Iisreset.exe command-line utility. Rebooting computers is covered in the section of this chapter titled "Rebooting IIS Servers."

Table 3-4   IISRESET Switch Functions

Switch	Function
/DISABLE	Disables restarting of IIS services on the local system.
/ENABLE	Enables restarting of IIS services on the local system.
/NOFORCE	Doesn't forcefully terminate IIS services if attempting to stop them gracefully fails.
/REBOOT	Reboots the local or designated remote computer.
/REBOOTONERROR	Reboots the computer if an error occurs when starting, stopping, or restarting IIS services.
/RESTART	Stops and then restart all IIS services. Attempts to resolve potential problems with runaway processes or hung applications.
/START	Starts all IIS services that are stopped.
/STATUS	Displays the status of all IIS services.
/STOP	Stops all IIS services that are running, paused, or in an unknown state.
/TIMEOUT:*val*	Specifies the time-out value (in seconds) to wait for a successful stop of IIS services. On expiration of this time-out, the computer can be rebooted if the /REBOOTONERROR parameter is specified. With /STOP and /RESTART, an error is issued. The default value is 20 seconds for restart, 60 seconds for stop, and 0 seconds for reboot.

Managing Individual Resources in IIS Manager

Sites and virtual servers that use the same IIS services can be controlled individually or as a group. You can control individual sites and virtual servers much as you do other server resources. For example, if you're changing the configuration of a site or performing other maintenance tasks, you might need to stop the site, make the changes, and then restart it. When a site is stopped, the site doesn't accept connections from users and can't be used.

In IIS Manager, you can start, stop, or restart all Web sites published on a server by following these steps:

1. Start IIS Manager.

2. In the left pane, select the icon for the computer you want to work with. If the computer isn't shown, connect to it as discussed previously, and then select it.

3. In the Actions pane, you can do one of the following:

    ❑ Select Start to start the World Wide Web Publishing Service and make all Web sites on the server available.

    ❑ Select Stop to stop the World Wide Web Publishing Service and make all Web sites on the server unavailable.

    ❑ Select Restart to stop and then start the World Wide Web Publishing Service as necessary to ensure that the service and all related processes are recycled for troubleshooting.

In IIS Manager, you can start, stop, or restart an individual Web site by following these steps:

1. Start IIS Manager.

2. In the left pane, expand the node for the computer you want to work with. If the computer isn't shown, connect to it as discussed previously, and then expand the computer node.

3. With the Sites node selected in the left pane, in the Name list, click the Web site you want to work with.

4. In the Actions pane under Manage Web Site, select Start, Stop, or Restart to start, stop, or restart the selected Web site.

Rebooting IIS Servers

Using the Iisreset.exe utility, you can reboot local and remote computers. To use this feature, you must have installed IIS on the computer and you must be a member of a group that has the appropriate user rights. To reboot a local system, you must have the right to shut down the system. To reboot a remote system, you must have the right to force shutdown from a remote system. You should reboot an IIS server only if the Restart IIS procedure fails.

To reboot a computer by using Iisreset.exe, type the following command:

iisreset *computername* /**reboot**

such as in the following example:

iisreset engsvr01 /reboot

If users are working on files or performing other tasks that need to be exited gracefully, you should set a time-out value for services and processes to be stopped. By default, the time-out is zero seconds, which forces immediate shutdown and tells Windows Server 2008 not to wait for services to be shut down gracefully. You could set a time-out value of 60 seconds when rebooting engsvr01 as follows:

iisreset engsvr01 /reboot /timeout:60

Managing IIS Services

Each IIS server in the organization relies on a set of services for publishing pages, transferring files, and more. To manage IIS services, you can use the Services node in either the Server Manager or the Computer Management console. With Server Manager you can manage only local server installations but have additional options for working with server features and roles. With Computer Management, you can work with both local and remote servers.

Chapter 2 discusses techniques for working with Server Manager, so this chapter focuses on Computer Management. You can start Computer Management by doing the following:

1. Click Start, Administrative Tools, and then Computer Management.

2. If you want to connect to a remote computer, right-click Computer Management in the console tree and on the shortcut menu, select Connect To Another Computer. You can now choose the IIS server whose services you want to manage.

3. Expand the Services And Applications node by clicking the plus sign (+) next to it, and then choose Services.

Figure 3-6 shows the Services view in the Computer Management console.

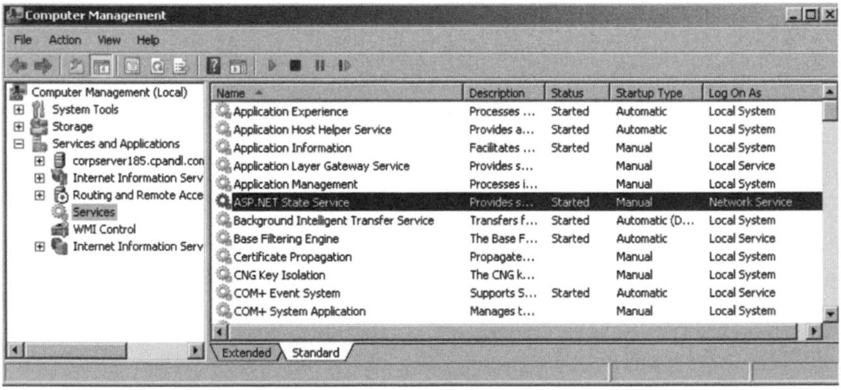

Figure 3-6   Use the Services node to manage IIS services.

The key fields of this dialog box are used as follows:

- **Name**   The name of the service.

- **Description**   A short description of the service and its purpose.

- **Status**   The status of the service as Started, Paused, or Stopped. (Stopped is indicated by a blank space.)

- **Startup Type**   The startup setting for the service.

> **Note**   Automatic services are started when the system boots up. Manual services are started by users or other services. Disabled services are turned off and can't be started.

- **Log On As**   The account the service logs on as. The default in most cases is the local system account.

Starting, Stopping, and Pausing IIS Services

As an administrator, you'll often have to start, stop, or pause IIS services. You manage IIS services through the Computer Management console or through the Services console. When you manage IIS services at this level, you're controlling all sites or virtual servers that use the service. For example, if a computer publishes three Web sites and you stop the World Wide Web Publishing Service, all three Web sites are stopped and are inaccessible.

To start, stop, or pause services in the Computer Management console, follow these steps:

1. In the left pane, right-click Computer Management in the console tree and on the shortcut menu, select Connect to Another Computer. You can now choose the IIS server whose services you want to manage.

2. Expand the Services And Applications node by clicking the plus sign (+) next to it, and then choose Services.

3. In the right pane, right-click the service you want to manipulate, and then select Start, Stop, or Pause as appropriate. You can also choose Restart to have Windows stop and then start the service after a brief pause. In addition, if you pause a service, you can select Resume to resume normal operation.

> **Tip**   When services that are set to start automatically fail to do so, the status area is blank, and you'll usually receive notification in a dialog box. Service failures can also be logged to the system's event logs. In Windows Server 2008, you can configure actions to handle service failures automatically. For example, you could have Windows Server 2008 attempt to restart the service for you. For details, see the section of this chapter titled "Configuring Service Recovery."

Configuring Service Startup

Most IIS services are configured to start automatically, and normally they shouldn't be configured with another startup setting. That said, if you're troubleshooting a problem, you might want a service to start manually. You might also want to disable a service so that its related virtual servers don't start. For example, if you move an FTP server to a new server, you might want to disable the FTP Publishing service on the original IIS server. In this way the FTP Publishing service isn't used, but you could turn it on if you need to (without your having to reinstall FTP support).

> **Tip**   With IIS 7.0, it is important to note that two important services are configured for manual startup: ASP.NET State Service and FTP Publishing Service. If a server uses out-of-state processing, you'll want to enable ASP.NET State Service for automatic startup. If a server uses FTP, you'll want to enable FTP Publishing Service.

You configure service startup as follows:

1. In the left pane of the Computer Management console, connect to the IIS server whose services you want to manage.

2. Expand the Services And Applications node by clicking the plus sign (+) next to it, and then choose Services.

3. In the right-hand pane, right-click the service you want to configure, and then choose Properties.

4. On the General tab, choose a startup type in the Startup Type drop-down list as shown in Figure 3-7. Select Automatic to start the service when the system boots up. Select Automatic (Delayed Start) to delay the start until other automatic services are started. Select Manual to allow the service to be started manually. Select Disabled to turn off the service.

5. Click OK.

Configuring Service Recovery

You can configure Windows services to take specific actions when a service fails. For example, you could attempt to restart the service or reboot the server. To configure recovery options for a service, follow these steps:

1. In the left pane of the Computer Management console, connect to the computer whose services you want to manage.

2. Expand the Services And Applications node by clicking the plus sign (+) next to it, and then choose Services.

3. In the right pane, right-click the service you want to configure, and then choose Properties.

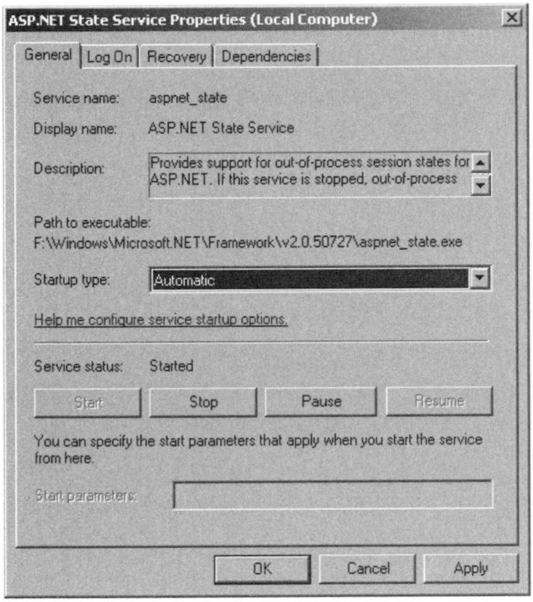

Figure 3-7   For troubleshooting, you might want to change the service startup type.

4. Select the Recovery tab, shown in Figure 3-8. You can now configure recovery choices for the first, second, and subsequent recovery attempts. The available choices are:

   ❑ Take No Action

   ❑ Restart The Service

   ❑ Run A Program

   ❑ Restart The Computer

5. Configure other settings based on your previously selected recovery settings. If you elected to restart the service, you'll need to specify the restart delay. After stopping the service, Windows waits for the specified delay before trying to start the service. In most cases a delay of 1–2 minutes should be sufficient.

6. Click OK.

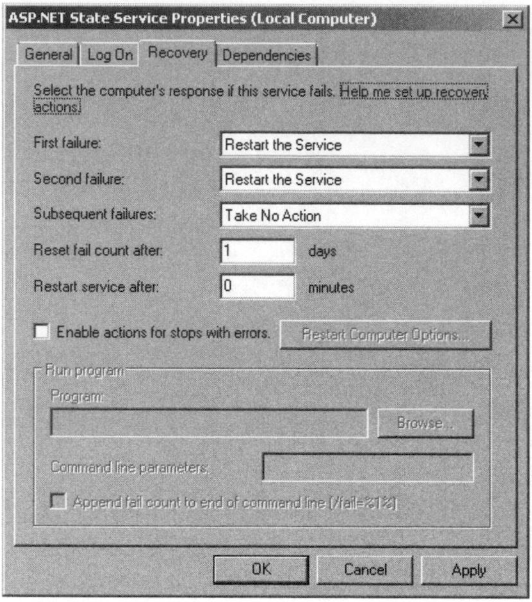

Figure 3-8   You can configure services to recover automatically in case of failure.

When you configure recovery options for critical services, you *might* want Windows to try to restart the service on the first and second attempts and then reboot the server on the third attempt.

Chapter 4

Managing IIS 7.0 from the Command Line

Internet Information Services (IIS) 7.0 introduces the IIS Command-line Administration Tool (AppCmd.exe) to complement the expanding role of IIS administrators and developers. AppCmd provides an extensible command-line environment for IIS 7.0 that builds on the existing framework provided by Microsoft .NET Framework 3.0. When you install IIS 7.0 on a server or desktop computer running Windows Vista, Setup installs AppCmd when you select the IIS Management Scripts and Tools role service. Another command-line environment you can use to work with IIS is Microsoft Windows PowerShell. On the Microsoft Web site, Windows PowerShell is available as a free download for computers running Windows Vista and is an installable feature in Windows Server 2008, through Server Manager. Once you install Windows Power-Shell, you can use its capabilities to configure and manage IIS.

Using the Windows PowerShell

Anyone with a UNIX background is probably familiar with the concept of a command shell. Most UNIX-based operating systems have several full-featured command shells available, including Korn shell (KSH), C shell (CSH), and Bourne Shell (SH). Although Microsoft Windows operating systems have always had a command-line environment, they've lacked a full-featured command shell, and this is where Windows PowerShell comes into the picture.

Introducing the Windows PowerShell

Not unlike the less-sophisticated Windows command prompt, the UNIX command shells operate by executing built-in commands, external commands, and command-line utilities and then returning the results in an output stream as text. The output stream can be manipulated in various ways, including redirecting the output stream so that it can be used as input for another command. This process of redirecting one command's output to another command's input is called *piping*, and it is a widely used shell-scripting technique.

The C Shell is one of the more sophisticated UNIX shells. In many respects, C Shell is a marriage of some of the best features of the C programming language and a full-featured UNIX shell environment. The Windows PowerShell takes the idea of a full-featured command shell built on a programming language a step further. It does this by implementing a scripting language based on Microsoft C# and an object model based on the .NET Framework.

Basing the scripting language for Windows PowerShell on C# ensures that the scripting language can be easily understood by current C# developers and also allows new developers to advance to C#. Using an object model based on the .NET Framework allows the Windows PowerShell to pass complete objects and all their properties as output from one command to another. The ability to redirect objects is extremely powerful and allows for a much more dynamic manipulation of a result set. For example, not only can you get the name of a particular user, but you also can get the entire related user object. You can then manipulate the properties of this user object as necessary by referring to the properties you want to work with by name.

Running and Using Windows PowerShell

Windows PowerShell is installed using the Add Features Wizard. After you use the Add Features Wizard to add the Windows PowerShell, Windows PowerShell is located in the *%SystemRoot%*\System32\WindowsPowerShell*Version* directory, where *Version* is the version of PowerShell that is installed. An example of this would be *%System-Root%*\System32\WindowsPowerShell\v2.0. You can run Windows PowerShell by completing the following steps:

1. Click Start, click All Programs, and then click Accessories.

2. Start an elevated command prompt by right-clicking Command Prompt, and then selecting Run As Administrator.

3. In the Command Prompt window, type **powershell** at the command prompt or run a script that invokes Windows PowerShell. To exit Windows PowerShell, type **exit**.

You can also invoke Windows PowerShell from the Windows PowerShell program group. (Each version of Windows PowerShell installed has a different program group.) Do this by performing the following steps:

1. Click Start, All Programs.

2. Click the program group for the version of Windows PowerShell you want to start.

3. Click Windows PowerShell.

Usually, when the shell starts, you will see a message similar to the following:

```
Windows PowerShell
Copyright (C) 2006 Microsoft Corporation. All rights reserved.
```

You can disable this message by starting the shell with the –nologo parameter, like so:

powershell –nologo

For a complete list of PowerShell parameters, type **powershell -?**.

Regardless of how you start the shell, you know you are using the Windows PowerShell because the command prompt title bar changes to Command Prompt–powershell, and the current path is preceded by PS. When the shell starts, user and system profiles are run to set up the environment. The following is a list and description of the profile files run, in the order of their execution:

1. *%AllUsersProfile%*\My Documents\WindowsPowerShell\Microsoft.PowerShell_profile.ps1

   A system-wide profile executed for all users. This profile is used by the system administrator to configure common settings for the Windows PowerShell.

2. *%UserProfile%*\My Documents\WindowsPowerShell\Microsoft.PowerShell_profile.ps1

   A user-specific profile for the logged on user. This profile is used by the current user to configure specific user settings for the Windows PowerShell.

You can start Windows PowerShell without loading profiles by using the –noprofile parameter, like so:

powershell -noprofile

The first time you start Windows PowerShell, you typically see a message indicating that scripts are disabled and that none of the listed profiles is executed. This is the default secure configuration for the Windows PowerShell. To enable scripts for execution, type the following command at the PowerShell prompt:

set-executionpolicy allsigned

This command sets the execution policy to require all scripts to have a trusted signature to execute. For a less restrictive environment, you can run the following command:

set-executionpolicy remotesigned

This command sets the execution policy so that scripts downloaded from the Web execute only if they are signed by a trusted source. To work in an unrestricted environment, you can run the following command:

set-executionpolicy unrestricted

This command sets the execution policy to run scripts regardless of whether they have a digital signature.

Running and Using Cmdlets

Windows PowerShell introduces the concept of a cmdlet (pronounced "command let"). A *cmdlet* is the smallest unit of functionality in the Windows PowerShell. You can think of a cmdlet as a built-in command. Rather than being highly complex, most cmdlets are quite simple and have a small set of associated properties.

You use cmdlets the same way you use any other commands and utilities. Cmdlet names are not case-sensitive. This means that you can use a combination of both uppercase and lowercase characters. After starting the Windows PowerShell, you can type the name of the cmdlet at the prompt and it will run in much the same way as a command-line command.

For ease of reference, cmdlets are named using verb-noun pairs. As Table 4-1 shows, the verb tells you what the cmdlet does in general. The noun tells you what specifically the cmdlet works with. For example, the get-variable cmdlet gets a named Windows PowerShell environment variable and returns its value. If you don't specify which variable to get as a parameter, get-variable returns a list of all Windows PowerShell environment variables and their values.

Table 4-1   Common Verbs Associated with Cmdlets and Their Meanings

Cmdlet Verb	Usage
New-	Creates a new instance of an item or object
Remove-	Removes an instance of an item or object
Set-	Modifies specific settings of an object
Get-	Queries a specific object or a subset of a type of object

You can work with cmdlets in two ways:

- Executing commands directly at the shell prompt
- Running commands from within scripts

You can enter any command or cmdlet you can run at the Windows PowerShell command prompt into a script by copying the related command text to a file and saving the file with the .ps1 extension. You can then run the script in the same way you would any other command or cmdlet.

Note Windows PowerShell also includes a rich scripting language and allows the use of standard language constructs for looping, conditional execution, flow control, and variable assignment. Discussion of these features is beyond the scope of this book. A good resource is *Microsoft Windows PowerShell Step By Step* (Microsoft Press, 2007).

From the Windows command-line environment or a batch script, you can execute Windows PowerShell cmdlets with the -command parameter. Typically when you do this, you will also want to suppress the Windows PowerShell logo and stop execution of profiles. After doing this, you could type the following command at a command prompt or insert it into a .bat script:

powershell −nologo −noprofile −command get-service

Finally, when you are working with Windows PowerShell, it is important to remember that the current directory may not be part of the environment path. Because of this, you may need to use ".\" when you run a script in the current directory, such as:

.*runtasks*

Running and Using Other Commands and Utilities

Because Windows PowerShell runs within the context of the Windows command prompt, you can run all Windows command-line commands, utilities, and graphical applications from within the Windows PowerShell. However, it is important to remember that the Windows PowerShell interpreter parses all commands before passing off the command to the command prompt environment. If the Windows PowerShell has a like-named command or a like-named alias for a command, this command is executed rather than the expected Windows command. (See the "Using Cmdlet Aliases" section later in this chapter for more information on aliases.)

PowerShell commands and programs not used in Windows must reside in a directory that is part of the PATH environment variable. If the item is found in the path, it is run. The PATH variable also controls where the Windows PowerShell looks for applications, utilities, and scripts. In Windows PowerShell, you can work with Windows environment variables by using $env. If you want to view the current settings for the PATH environment variable, type **$env:*path***. If you want to add a directory to this variable, you can use the following syntax:

$env:path += ";*DirectoryPathToAdd*"

where *DirectoryPathToAdd* is the directory path you want to add to the path, such as:

$env:path += ";C:\Scripts"

To have this directory added to the path every time you start the Windows PowerShell, you can add the command line as an entry in your profile. Keep in mind that cmdlets are like built-in commands rather than stand-alone executables. Because of this, they are not affected by the PATH environment variable.

Working with Cmdlets

Cmdlets provide the basic foundation for working with a computer from within the Windows PowerShell. Although there are many different cmdlets for many different uses, cmdlets all have common features. I'll examine these common features in this section.

Using Windows PowerShell Cmdlets

At the Windows PowerShell prompt, you can get a complete list of available cmdlets by typing **help ***. To get help documentation on a specific cmdlet, type **help** followed by the cmdlet name, such as:

help get-variable

Table 4-2 provides a list of cmdlets you'll use commonly for administration. Although there are many other available cmdlets, these are the ones you're likely to use the most.

Table 4-2   Cmdlets Commonly Used for Administration

Cmdlet Name	Description
ConvertFrom-SecureString	Exports a secure string to a safe format
ConvertTo-SecureString	Creates a secure string from a normal string
Get-Alias	Returns alias names for cmdlets
Get-AuthenticodeSignature	Gets the signature object associated with a file
Get-Credential	Gets a credential object based on a password
Get-Date	Gets the current date and time
Get-EventLog	Gets the log data from the Windows log files
Get-ExecutionPolicy	Gets the effective execution policy for the current shell
Get-Host	Gets host information
Get-Location	Displays the current location
Get-PSDrive	Gets the drive information for the specified PS drive
Get-Service	Gets a list of services
Import-Alias	Imports an alias list from a file
New-Alias	Creates a new cmdlet-alias pairing
New-Service	Creates a new service
Push-Location	Pushes a location to the stack
Read-Host	Reads a line of input from the host console
Restart-Service	Restarts a stopped service
Resume-Service	Resumes a suspended service
Set-Alias	Maps an alias to a cmdlet
Set-AuthenticodeSignature	Places an Authenticode signature in a script or other file
Set-Date	Sets the system date and time on the host system
Set-ExecutionPolicy	Sets the execution policy for the current shell
Set-Location	Sets the current working location to a specified location
Set-Service	Makes and sets changes to the properties of a service
Start-Service	Starts a stopped service
Start-Sleep	Suspends shell or script activity for the specified period
Stop-Service	Stops a running service
Suspend-Service	Suspends a running service
Write-Output	Writes an object to the pipeline

Using Cmdlet Parameters

All cmdlet parameters are designated with an initial hyphen (-). To reduce the amount of typing required, some parameters are position-sensitive such that you can sometimes pass parameters in a specific order without having to specify the parameter name. For example, with get-service, you aren't required to specify the -Name parameter; you can type simply:

Get-service *ServiceName*

where *ServiceName* is the name of the service you want to examine, such as:

Get-service W3SVC

This command line returns the status of the World Wide Web Publishing Service. Because you can use wildcards, such as *, with name values, you can also type **get-service w*** to return the status of all services that start with W, including Web Management Service, Windows Process Activation Service, and World Wide Web Publishing Service.

All cmdlets support the common set of parameters listed in Table 4-3. However, for you to use these parameters, you must run the cmdlet in such a way that these parameters are returned as part of the result set.

Table 4-3   Common Cmdlet Parameters

Parameter Name	Description
-Confirm	Pauses processes and requires the user to acknowledge the action before continuing. Remove- and Disable- cmdlets have this parameter.
-Debug	Provides programming-level debugging information about the operation.
-ErrorAction	Controls the command behavior when an error occurs.
-ErrorVariable	Sets the name of the variable (in addition to the standard error) in which to place objects for which an error has occurred.
-OutBuffer	Sets the output buffer for the cmdlet.
-OutVariable	Sets the name of the variable in which to place output objects.
-Verbose	Provides detailed information about the operation.
-WhatIf	Allows the user to view what would happen if a cmdlet were run with a specific set of parameters. Remove- and Disable- cmdlets have this parameter.

Understanding Cmdlet Errors

When you work with cmdlets, you'll encounter two standard types of errors:

- **Terminating errors**   Errors that halt execution

- **Nonterminating errors**   Errors that cause error output to be returned but do not halt execution

With both types of errors, you'll typically see error text that can help you resolve the problem that caused it. For example, an expected file might be missing or you may not have sufficient permissions to perform a specified task.

Using Cmdlet Aliases

For ease of use, Windows PowerShell lets you create aliases for cmdlets. An *alias* is an abbreviation for a cmdlet that acts as a shortcut for executing the cmdlet. For example, you can use the alias **gsv** instead of the cmdlet name **get-service**.

Table 4-4 provides a list of commonly used default aliases. Although there are many other aliases, these are the ones you'll use most frequently.

Table 4-4   Commonly Used Cmdlet Aliases

Alias	Cmdlet
clear, cls	Clear-Host
Diff	Compare-Object
cp, copy	Copy-Item
Epal	Export-Alias
Epcsv	Export-Csv
foreach	ForEach-Object
fl	Format-List
ft	Format-Table
fw	Format-Wide
gal	Get-Alias
ls, dir	Get-ChildItem
gcm	Get-Command
cat, type	Get-Content
h, history	Get-History
gl, pwd	Get-Location
gps, ps	Get-Process
gsv	Get-Service
gv	Get-Variable
group	Group-Object
ipal	Import-Alias
ipcsv	Import-Csv
r	Invoke-History

Table 4-4   Commonly Used Cmdlet Aliases

Alias	Cmdlet
ni	New-Item
mount	New-PSDrive
nv	New-Variable
rd, rm, rmdir, del, erase	Remove-Item
rv	Remove-Variable
sal	Set-Alias
sl, cd, chdir	Set-Location
sv, set	Set-Variable
sort	Sort-Object
sasv	Start-Service
sleep	Start-Sleep
spps, kill	Stop-Process
spsv	Stop-Service
write, echo	Write-Output

You can create additional aliases using the Set-Alias cmdlet. The syntax is:

Set-alias *aliasName cmdletName*

where *aliasName* is the alias you want to use and *cmdletName* is the cmdlet for which you are creating an alias. The following example creates a "go" alias for the get-process cmdlet:

Set-alias go get-process

To use your custom aliases whenever you work with Windows PowerShell, type the related command line in your profile.

Using Cmdlets with IIS

Using cmdlets with IIS is a simple matter of running cmdlets in a way that affects the IIS installation. For example, you can use the Get-Service, Start-Service, Pause-Service, Resume-Service, and Stop-Service cmdlets to manage the services used by IIS. New Windows PowerShell cmdlets that are specific to IIS also will become available periodically for your use in managing IIS servers. As these cmdlets become available, you'll be able to install them through server updates or by downloading and installation an installer program.

Although the shared configuration feature of IIS 7 is much more efficient, Windows PowerShell could be used to help you deploy the same IIS configuration to multiple servers. Listing 4-1 provides the source code and examples for doing this.

Listing 4-1 Deploying IIS with Windows PowerShell

Listing for ServerList.txt
```
WebServer84
WebServer92
WebServer76
WebServer15
```

Listing for FileList.txt
```
C:\windows\microsoft.net\framework\v2.0.50727\config\machine.config
C:\windows\microsoft.net\framework\v2.0.50727\config\web.config
C:\windows\System32\inetsrv\config\applicationHost.config
C:\inetpub\wwwroot\web.config
C:\inetpub\wwwroot\SalesApp\web.config
C:\inetpub\wwwroot\SupportApp\web.config
```

DeployServers.ps1
```
############################################################
# sourceComputer sets the source computer for the deployment.
# This scripts looks for two text files in the same directory:
# ServerList.txt sets the list of servers for the deployment.
# FileList.txt sets the list of files to copy.
############################################################

$sourceComputer = "WebServer95"
$serverList = get-content '.\ServerList.txt'
$filesToCopy = get-content '.\FileList.txt'

foreach ($targetComputer in $serverList)
{
    foreach ($file in $filesToCopy)
    {
        $sourcePath = "\\" + (join-path $sourceComputer $file)
        $targetPath  = "\\" + (join-path $targetComputer $file)
        write-host -for this "$targetComputer : Copying files from
$sourcePath"

        copy-item $sourcePath $targetPath -recurse -force
    }
}
```

This listing uses three source files that you've placed in the same directory:

- **ServerList.txt** contains a list of servers to which you want to copy configuration files and for which you have full administrator privileges.

- **FileList.txt** contains a list of configuration files you want to copy from the source according to the full file paths listed.

- **DeployServers.ps1** contains the script that you will execute to deploy the configuration to the previously listed servers. In this script, the $source-Computer variable sets the name of the source server for the deployment.

Before you use these files you should update them and test them in a development environment. If you update these files for your environment and then execute Deploy-Servers.ps1 from a Windows PowerShell command line, you will copy the configuration files from your source server to the designated target servers. The script uses the get-content cmdlet to read computer names from the ServerList.text file and configuration files from the FileList.text file. The outer foreach loop iterates through each computer name stored in the server list, storing each name into the $targetComputer variable in turn. The inner loop iterates through each file name in the file list, storing each name in the $file variable in turn. Next, the join-path cmdlet is used to concatenate strings to produce complete source and destination paths. Finally, the copy-item cmdlet is used to perform the copy actions, whereas the -recurse parameter will copy all subdirectories (if necessary) and the -force parameter causes existing files to be overwritten.

Using the IIS Command-Line Administration Tool

The IIS command line administration tool (AppCmd.exe) is a command-line management interface built on .NET Framework 3.0. You use AppCmd to manage most aspects of IIS configuration that you would otherwise manage in IIS Manager. This means that you can typically use either tool to configure IIS 7.0.

Running and Using the IIS Command Line Administration Tool

After you've installed the IIS Management Scripts and Tools role service as discussed in Chapter 2, "Deploying IIS 7.0 in the Enterprise," you can use AppCmd to manage the configuration of an IIS server from the command line. AppCmd is located in the *%SystemRoot%*\System32\Inetsrv directory. Because this directory is not in your command path by default, you should add this directory to your command path. Once you've done so, you can run AppCmd by completing the following steps:

1. Click Start, click All Programs, and then click Accessories.

2. Start an elevated command prompt. On the Accessories menu, right-click Command Prompt, and then select Run As Administrator.

3. In the Command Prompt window, type the necessary command text, or run a script that invokes AppCmd.

Because AppCmd is an extension of .NET Framework, a specific set of management objects are available for your use. As Table 4-5 shows, these objects are identified by .NET Framework class IDs. Each object class has an instance name and an alias. For example, *DefaultSiteObjectClass*, which is used to configure the properties of Web sites, is assigned the instance name *site* and the alias *sites*. This allows you to reference *DefaultSiteObjectClass* using either *site* or *sites* in the command text. The actions (commands) you can perform on an object are defined as a list of verb names that are passed through to the object. For *DefaultSiteObject*, the related actions you can perform are List, Set, Add, Delete, Start, and Stop.

Table 4-5   IIS Management Objects

Object Name	Object Class ID	Object Alias	Object Actions
App	*DefaultAppObject*	Apps	List, Set, Add, and Delete
Apppool	*DefaultAppPoolObject*	Apppools	List, Set, Add, Delete, Start, Stop, and Recycle
Backup	*DefaultBackupObject*	Backups	List, Add, Delete, and Restore
Config	*DefaultConfigObject*	Configs	List, Set, Search, Lock, Unlock, Clear, Reset, and Migrate
Vdir	*DefaultDirObject*	Vdirs	List, Set, Add, and Delete
Module	*DefaultModuleObject*	Modules	List, Set, Add, Delete, Install, and Uninstall
Request	*DefaultRequestObject*	Requests	List
Site	*DefaultSiteObject*	Sites	List, Set, Add, Delete, Start, and Stop
Trace	*DefaultTraceObject*	Traces	List, Configure, and Inspect
Wp	*DefaultWorkerProcessObject*	Wps	List

AppCmd has a helper file called Appcmd.xml. This file, written in XML, helps the command-line tool when you are working with .NET Framework objects, actions, and aliases. As the following example shows, entries in Appcmd.xml are organized according to management objects and the related actions:

```
<appcmd>
    <object name="site" alias="sites" classId="DefaultSiteObject" >
        <verb name="list" classId="DefaultSiteObject" />
        <verb name="set" classId="DefaultSiteObject" />
        <verb name="add" classId="DefaultSiteObject" />
        <verb name="delete" classId="DefaultSiteObject" />
        <verb name="start" classId="DefaultSiteObject" />
```

```
    <verb name="stop" classId="DefaultSiteObject" />
  </object>
. . .
  <object name="trace" alias="traces" classId="DefaultTraceObject" >
    <verb name="list" classId="DefaultTraceObject"  />
    <verb name="configure" classId="DefaultTraceObject"  />
    <verb name="inspect" classId="DefaultTraceObject"  />
  </object>
</appcmd>
```

Although this is an important file for AppCmd's internal use, it is not one you can or should modify. In fact, if you modify this file, AppCmd may not be able to initialize objects properly according to their class IDs, which will cause AppCmd to fail to run.

Working with the IIS Command Line Administration Tool

When you are working with AppCmd, you can get help information on available commands:

- To view a list of management objects and general parameters, type **appcmd** at the command prompt.

- To view actions related to a specific management object, type **appcmd** *Object-Name* /? where *ObjectName* is the name of the management object you want to examine, such as **appcmd trace** /?.

- To view the syntax for an action used with a particular object, type **appcmd** *Action ObjectName* /? where *Action* is the action to perform and *ObjectName* is the name of the management object on which you want to perform the action, such as **appcmd configure trace** /?.

When you work with AppCmd, you'll find that just about every command accepts parameters and specific parameter values that qualify what you want to work with. These parameters and parameter values correspond to attributes and attribute values assigned in IIS configuration files. Further, most commands require that you specify the name of the configuration feature or property you are working with. Typically, you can specify the name in a relative way, such as **"Default Web Site"** when referring to a Web site or **"Default Web Site/SalesApp"**. You can also specify a name in a literal way by referring to the exact type of name you are working with, such as / **site.name="Default Web Site"** when referring to a Web site or /**app.name="Default Web Site/SalesApp"**. To see more clearly how this works, consider the following syntax example:

```
appcmd add module [[/module.name:] "ModuleName"]
[/app.name: "AppPath"]
```

In this syntax example, the brackets tell you that /module.name: is optional. Thus, you could specify the module name using either of the following syntaxes:

appcmd add module "*CustModule*"

or

appcmd add module /module.name:"*CustModule*"

Typically, a command that accepts a name-related parameter has it as its first parameter, allowing you to specify the name with or without the literal reference. When configuration features or properties have names in addition to aliases, you can specify either value as the identity. Although quotation marks around parameter values are optional in most cases, you should use them in most instances. This will ensure that you include quotation marks when they are mandatory, such as when a name value contains spaces. For example, you can list properties related to the default Web site by running the following command:

appcmd list site "Default Web Site"

But the same code, without the quotation marks but with the same syntax otherwise (that is, appcmd list site Default Web Site), generates a syntax error.

With List commands, you can typically return an object set containing all related items simply by omitting the name. For example, if you type **appcmd list site** at the command prompt without specifying an identity, you get a list of all sites on the server.

Working with IIS Commands

You use IIS commands to manage the configuration of your IIS servers. These commands work with objects matching a specific set of criteria. The sections that follow provide an overview of the available commands with their most commonly used syntaxes.

Using Configuration Management Commands

Several configuration management commands are provided. These commands, along with their syntaxes, follow:

- **AppCmd List Config**   Lists configuration sections from the server level by default or at a specified configuration level.

```
appcmd list config ["ConfigPath"] [/section:SectionName]
[/parameter1:value1 ...]
```

■ **AppCmd Set Config**   Modifies a configuration section at the server level by default or at a specified configuration level.

```
appcmd set config ["ConfigPath"] /section:SectionName
[/parameter1:value1 ...]
```

■ **AppCmd Search Config**   Searches the configuration file(s) at or below the server level or at by default or below a specified level for definitions of the specified configuration settings.

```
appcmd search config ["ConfigPath"] [/section:SectionName]
[/parameter1:value1 ...]
```

■ **AppCmd Lock Config**   Locks the specified configuration section at the server level or at a specified level so it cannot be overridden at a lower level.

```
appcmd lock config ["ConfigPath"] /section:SectionName
[/parameter1:value1 ...]
```

■ **AppCmd Unlock Config**   Unlocks the specified configuration section at the server level by default or at a specified level so it can be overridden at a lower level.

```
appcmd unlock config ["ConfigPath"] /section:SectionName
[/parameter1:value1 ...]
```

■ **AppCmd Clear Config**   Clears and optionally deletes the specified configuration section at the server level by default or at a specified level.

```
appcmd clear config ["ConfigPath"] /section:SectionName
[/parameter1:value1 ...] [/delete]
```

■ **AppCmd Reset Config**   Resets the specified configuration section at the server level by default or at a specified level to its default configuration state.

```
appcmd reset config ["ConfigPath"] /section:SectionName
[/parameter1:value1 ...]
```

- **AppCmd Migrate Config** Migrates the configuration features of a legacy server so that the server can use new server features. You can optionally clear the original configuration after migration and recurse through lower configuration levels to ensure that all lower levels are also migrated.

```
appcmd migrate config ["ConfigPath"] [/section:SectionName]
[/clear] [/recurse]
```

Using Module Management Commands

Several module management commands are provided. These commands, along with their syntaxes, follow:

- **AppCmd List Module** Returns a list of modules enabled for a specified application or having specific module attributes.

```
appcmd list module [[/module.name:]"ModuleName"]
[/app.name:"AppPath"]
```

- **AppCmd Set Module** Sets the properties of a specified module.

```
appcmd set module [[/module.name:]"ModuleName"]
[/app.name:"AppPath"] [/parameter1:value1 ...]
```

- **AppCmd Add Module** Enables a new managed module or an installed native module with the specified settings.

```
appcmd add module /name:"ModuleName" [/app.name:"AppPath"]
[/parameter1:value1 ...]
```

- **AppCmd Delete Module** Disables a module by removing it from the enabled list.

```
appcmd delete module [[/module.name:]"ModuleName"]
[/app.name:"AppPath"]
```

- **AppCmd Install Module**   Installs a native module. By default, modules are also added to the enabled list.

```
appcmd install module /name:"ModuleName" /image:PathToDLL
[/add:true|false]
```

- **AppCmd Uninstall Module**   Uninstalls the specified native module. By default modules are also removed from the enabled list.

```
appcmd uninstall module [/module.name:]"ModuleName"
[/remove:true|false]
```

Using Site Management Commands

You can manage Web sites and their configurations by using the following commands and command-line syntaxes:

- **AppCmd List Site**   Lists virtual sites on a server.

```
appcmd list site [[/site.name:]SiteNameOrURL]
[/parameter1:value1 ...]
```

- **AppCmd Set Site**   Configures a virtual site on a server.

```
appcmd set site [/site.name:]SiteNameOrURL
[/parameter1:value1 ...]
```

- **AppCmd Add Site**   Adds a new virtual site on a server.

```
appcmd add site /name:Name /id:ID /bindings:UrlAndPort
/physicalPath:Path
```

Note   Technically, bindings and physicalPath are optional, but a site won't work until you provide these parameters. Adding the physical path is what allows IIS to create the root virtual directory and root application for the site.

- **AppCmd Delete Site** Deletes a virtual site on a server.

```
appcmd delete [/site.name:]site SiteNameOrURL
```

- **AppCmd Start Site** Starts a virtual site on a server.

```
appcmd start site [/site.name:]SiteNameOrURL
```

- **AppCmd Stop Site** Stops a virtual site on a server.

```
appcmd stop site [/site.name:]SiteNameOrURL
```

Using Application Pool Management Commands

You can manage application pools and their configurations by using the following commands and command-line syntaxes:

- **AppCmd List Apppool** Lists the application pools on a server.

```
appcmd list apppool [[/apppool.name:]"AppPoolName"]
[/parameter1:value1 ...]
```

- **AppCmd Set Apppool** Sets the properties of an application pool on a server.

```
appcmd set apppool [/apppool.name:]"AppPoolName"
[/managedRuntimeVersion:"Version"]
[/managedPipelineMode: Integrated|Classic]
[/queueLength:"queueLength"] [/autoStart:true|false]
```

- **AppCmd Add Apppool** Creates an application pool on a server.

```
appcmd add apppool /name:"AppPoolName"
[/managedRuntimeVersion:"Version"]
[/managedPipelineMode: Integrated|Classic]
[/queueLength:"queueLength"] [/autoStart:true|false]
```

- **AppCmd Delete Apppool**   Deletes an application pool from a server.

```
appcmd delete apppool [[/apppool.name:]"AppPoolName"]
```

- **AppCmd Start Apppool**   Starts an application pool on a server.

```
appcmd start apppool [[/apppool.name:]"AppPoolName"] [/wait]
[/timeout:WaitTimeMilliseconds]
```

- **AppCmd Stop Apppool**   Stops an application pool on a server.

```
appcmd stop apppool [[/apppool.name:]"AppPoolName"] [/wait]
[/timeout:WaitTimeMilliseconds]
```

- **AppCmd Recycle Apppool**   Recycles the worker processes of an application pool on a server.

```
appcmd recycle apppool [[/apppool.name:]"AppPoolName"]
[/parameter1:value1 ...]
```

Using Application Management Commands

You can manage applications and their configurations by using the following commands and command-line syntaxes:

- **AppCmd List App**   Lists the properties of all applications or a specific application on a server.

```
appcmd list app [[/app.name:]AppNameOrURL]
[/site.name:"SiteName"] [/apppool.name:"AppPoolName"]
[/path: "VirtualPath"] [/parameter1:value1 ...]
```

- **AppCmd Set App**   Sets the properties of an application on a server.

```
appcmd set app [/app.name:]AppNameOrURL [/parameter1:value1 ...]
```

- **AppCmd Add App**   Creates an application on a server.

```
appcmd add [/app.name:]app /site.name: "ParentSiteName"
/path: "VirtualPath" /physicalPath: "Path"
```

> **Note**   Technically, physicalPath is optional, but an application won't work until you provide this parameter. Adding the physical path is what allows IIS to create the root virtual directory and map it to the virtual path you provide.

- **AppCmd Delete App**   Deletes an application on a server.

```
appcmd delete [/app.name:]app AppNameOrURL
```

Using Virtual Directory Management Commands

You can manage virtual directories and their configurations by using the following commands and command-line syntaxes:

- **AppCmd List Vdir**   Lists the virtual directories or properties of a specific virtual directory on a server.

```
appcmd list vdir [[/vdir.name:]"VdirNameOrUrl"]
[/app.name:"ParentAppName"] [/path: "VirtualPath"]
[/parameter1:value1 ...]
```

- **AppCmd Set Vdir**   Sets the properties of a specific virtual directory on a server.

```
appcmd set vdir [[/vdir.name:]"VdirNameOrUrl"]
[/physicalPath:Path] [/logonMethod:Method] [/userName:User]
[/password:Password]
```

- **AppCmd Add Vdir**   Creates a virtual directory on a server.

```
appcmd add vdir /app.name:"ParentAppName" /path: "VirtualPath"
[/physicalPath: "Path"] [/logonMethod:Method]
[/userName:User] [/password:Password]
```

■ **AppCmd Delete Vdir**   Deletes a virtual directory on a server.

```
appcmd delete vdir [[/vdir.name:]"VdirNameOrUrl"]
```

Using Utility Commands

Several general-purpose utility commands are provided. These commands, along with their syntaxes, follow:

■ **AppCmd List Wp**   Lists the worker processes currently running on a server.

```
appcmd list wp [[/process.name:]"ProcessID"]
[/wp.name: "ProcessID"] [/apppool.name: "AppPoolName"]
```

■ **AppCmd List Request**   Lists the requests currently executing on a server. Optionally finds requests that have been executing for longer than a specified time in milliseconds.

```
appcmd list request [[/process.name:]"ProcessID"]
[/request.name: "ProcessID"] [/site.name:"SiteName"]
[/wp.name:"WpName"] [/apppool.name:"AppPoolName"]
[/elapsed:Milliseconds]
```

■ **AppCmd List Backup**   Lists the configuration backups or a specified configuration backup on a server.

```
appcmd list backup [/backup.name:]"BackupName"]
```

■ **AppCmd Add Backup**   Creates a configuration backup on a server.

```
appcmd add backup [/name:"BackupName"]
```

■ **AppCmd Delete Backup**   Deletes a configuration backup on a server.

```
appcmd delete backup [/backup.name:]"BackupName"
```

■ **AppCmd Restore Backup** Restores a configuration backup, overwriting the current system state. By default, AppCmd stops the server before performing the restore.

```
appcmd restore backup [/backup.name:]"BackupName"
[/stop:true|false]
```

■ **AppCmd List Trace** Lists the failed requests logs for a site, a worker process, or with the specified log attributes.

```
appcmd list trace [/trace.name:]"TraceName"
[/site.name:"SiteName"] [/wp.name: "WorkerProcessName"]
[/verb:Verb] [/statuscode:StatusCode]
```

■ **AppCmd Configure Trace** Configures failed request tracing for a server or site.

```
appcmd configure trace ["SiteName"] [/enablesite | /disablesite]
[/enable | /disable] [/path:Path]
[/areas:TraceProvider1/Area1, TraceProvider1/Area2,…]
[/verbosity]
[/timeTaken: "ExecuteTime"] [/statuscodes: "code1,code2,..."]
```

■ **AppCmd Inspect Trace** Displays trace events logged on a server.

```
appcmd inspect trace [/trace.name:]"TraceName"
[/event.name:"EventName"]
[/level:VerbosityLevel]
```

Chapter 5
Managing Global IIS Configuration

Managing a server's global configuration is a key part of Web site management and optimization. Web site properties identify the site, set its configuration values, and determine where and how documents are accessed. You can manage a server's global configuration at several levels:

- As global defaults
- As site defaults
- As application or directory defaults

You set global defaults at the Web server level, and all Web sites and applications on the server can inherit them. You set individual defaults at the Web site level, and they apply only to the selected Web site. You set application and directory defaults at the directory level, and they apply only to the selected application or directory. Unlike in Internet Information Services (IIS) 6.0, changes you make to the configuration are applied automatically and you do not need to restart servers, sites, or applications to apply configuration changes.

Understanding Configuration Levels and Global Configuration

You use global properties to set default property values for new Web sites and applications created on a server. Anytime you change global properties, existing Web sites and applications will also inherit the changes. In most cases, the new settings are applied automatically without having to restart server processes. In other cases, when a configuration is locked or restricted, the changes are inherited only if you unlock or unrestrict the configuration.

Table 5-1 provides a summary of all standard administrative features according to the level at which they can be configured. When you are configuring IIS features, it is important to keep in mind the inheritance hierarchy. As discussed in Chapter 1, "IIS 7.0 Administration Overview," settings you assign in a higher level of the hierarchy are inherited by the lower levels of the hierarchy. The server node represents the top of the hierarchy, followed by the site node, the top-level application/virtual directory nodes within a site, the virtual directory nodes within applications or other virtual directories, and so on.

Table 5-1   IIS Features According to the Configuration Level

Feature	Description	Server Level	Site Level	Application Level
.NET Compilation	Allows you to configure batch, behavior, and assembly properties for compiling managed code	Yes	Yes	Yes
.NET Globalization	Allows you to configure language and encoding properties for managed code	Yes	Yes	Yes
.NET Profile	Allows you to configure the information that will be stored on a per-user basis in a .NET Profile	No	Yes	Yes
.NET Roles	Allows you to configure user groups for use with Membership Users and Forms authentication	No	Yes	Yes
.NET Trust Levels	Allows you to set the trust level for managed modules, handlers, and applications	Yes	Yes	Yes
.NET Users	Allows you to configure users who belong to .NET Roles and who use Forms authentication	No	Yes	Yes
Application Settings	Allows you to configure name and value pairs for managed code use at run time	Yes	Yes	Yes
ASP	Allows you to configure properties for ASP applications	Yes	Yes	Yes
Authentication	Allows you to view and manage authentication modes	Yes	Yes	Yes
Authorization Rules	Allows you to specify rules for authorizing users to access applications	Yes	Yes	Yes
CGI	Allows you to configure properties for CGI programs	Yes	Yes	Yes
Compression	Allows you to configure and manage the way static compression and dynamic compression are used	Yes	Yes	Yes
Connection Strings	Allows you to configure strings that Web sites and applications can use to connect to data sources	Yes	Yes	Yes
Default Document	Allows you to configure default files to return when clients do not specify a file in a request	Yes	Yes	Yes

Table 5-1   IIS Features According to the Configuration Level

Feature	Description	Server Level	Site Level	Application Level
Directory Browsing	Allows you to configure information to display in a directory listing	Yes	Yes	Yes
Error Pages	Allows you to configure custom error pages to return when errors occur	Yes	Yes	Yes
Failed Request Tracing	Allows you to configure logging of failed request traces	Yes	Yes	Yes
Feature Delegation	Allows you to configure the default delegation state for features in IIS Manager	Yes	No	No
Handler Mappings	Allows you to configure resources that handle responses for specific request types	Yes	Yes	Yes
HTTP Redirect	Allows you to configure rules for redirecting incoming requests to another file or URL	Yes	Yes	Yes
HTTP Response Headers	Allows you to configure HTTP headers that are added to responses from the Web server	Yes	Yes	Yes
IIS Manager Permissions	Allows you to configure permissions for users who can manage Web sites and applications	No	Yes	Yes
IIS Manager Users	Allows you to designate and manage Web site and Web application administrators	Yes	No	No
IP and Domain Restrictions	Allows you to restrict or grant access to Web content based on IP addresses or domain names	Yes	Yes	Yes
ISAPI and CGI Restrictions	Allows you to restrict or enable specific ISAPI and CGI extensions on the Web server	Yes	No	No
ISAPI Filters	Allows you to configure ISAPI filters that modify IIS functionality	Yes	Yes	No
Logging	Allows you to configure how IIS logs requests on the Web server	Yes	Yes	Yes
Machine Key	Allows you to configure encryption, validation, and decryption settings for managed application services	Yes	Yes	Yes

Table 5-1 IIS Features According to the Configuration Level

Feature	Description	Server Level	Site Level	Application Level
Management Service	Allows you to configure IIS Manager for delegated and remote administration	Yes	No	No
MIME Types	Allows you to configure extensions and associated content types that are served as static files	Yes	Yes	Yes
Modules	Allows you to configure native and managed modules that process requests on the Web server	Yes	Yes	Yes
Output Caching Rules	Allows you to configure rules for caching served content in the output cache	Yes	Yes	Yes
Pages and Controls	Allows you to configure properties for pages and controls in Microsoft ASP.NET applications	Yes	Yes	Yes
Providers	Allows you to configure providers for provider-based application services, including those used with .NET Roles, .NET Users, and .NET Profiles	Yes	Yes	Yes
Server Certificates	Allows you to create and manage certificates for Web sites that use Secure Sockets Layer (SSL)	Yes	No	No
Session State	Allows you to configure session state settings and Forms authentication cookie settings	Yes	Yes	Yes
SMTP E-mail	Allows you to configure e-mail address and delivery options to send e-mail messages from Web applications	Yes	Yes	Yes
SSL Settings	Allows you to specify requirements for SSL and client certificates	No	Yes	Yes
Worker Processes	Allows you to view information about worker processes and currently executing requests	Yes	No	No

In IIS Manager, you can access the global Web server configuration level by clicking the node for the computer you want to work with in the left pane and then double-clicking the configuration task you want to work with. Alternately, you can click the task to select it and then click Open Feature in the Actions pane.

In the IIS configuration files, the <configSections> element defines configuration sections by using <section> elements. A *configuration section* is the basic unit of deployment and locking for a server's configuration properties. You use the *allowDefinition* attribute of the related <section> element to specify the level or levels where the related properties of the section can be set.

Table 5-2 shows the acceptable values for the *allowDefinition* attribute. By assigning one of these values to a configuration section, you can specify the number or levels at which the configuration can be controlled. *MachineOnly* is the default setting. You can use *MachineOnly* to specify that a configuration section can be managed using the Microsoft .NET Framework root and server root configuration files.

Table 5-2   Attributes for Controlling Configuration Sections

Attribute Value	.NET Framework Level	Server Level	Site Level	Application Level	Virtual Directory Level
Everywhere	Yes	Yes	Yes	Yes	Yes
MachineOnly	Yes	Yes	No	No	No
MachineToWebRoot	Yes	Yes	Yes	No	No
MachineToApplication	Yes	Yes	Yes	Yes	No
AppHostOnly	No	No	No	Yes	No

The *OverrideModeDefault* attribute controls whether a section is locked down to the level in which it is defined or can be overridden. You can set this attribute to one of two acceptable values—either *Allow* or *Deny*—or leave the attribute without a value. If you leave the attribute without a value or set it to *Allow*, lower-level configuration files can override the settings of the related section. Otherwise, overriding settings is not allowed. For example, you can use *MachineOnly* to specify that a configuration section can be managed using the .NET Framework root and server root configuration files. If you also set *OverrideModeDefault* to *Allow*, any settings configured at the .NET Framework level can be overridden by settings at the server root level. However, if you set *OverrideModeDefault* to *Deny*, settings configured at the .NET Framework level cannot be overridden by settings at the server root level.

You manage configuration locking by editing the configuration files or by using the IIS Command -line Administration Tool. In the configuration files, individual section elements are typed like this:

```
<section name="asp" overrideModeDefault="Deny" />
<section name="isapiCgiRestriction" allowDefinition="AppHostOnly"
overrideModeDefault="Deny" />
```

In this example, the asp section uses the default *allowDefinition* of *MachineOnly*, and *isapiCgiRestriction* uses the *allowDefinition* of *AppHostOnly*. To change the way these sections are used, you can directly edit the related attribute values, such as shown in the following example:

```
<section name="asp" allowDefinition="MachineToApplication"
overrideModeDefault="Allow" />
<section name="isapiCgiRestriction" allowDefinition="AppHostOnly"
overrideModeDefault="Allow" />
```

Note   Because IIS 7.0 also allows you to use location locking, it is easy to confuse global configuration locking and location locking. With *global configuration locking*, you specify the permitted levels at which configuration settings can be managed. With *location locking*, you lock or unlock a specific configuration section at a specific configuration level. You'll learn more about location locking in the "Managing Configuration Sections" section of this chapter.

Managing Configuration Sections

You can manage configuration sections and control the way they are used by IIS at any configuration level. This means that you can control the usage of configuration sections for an entire server, individual sites, individual applications, and individual virtual directories. Although you can manage locking by editing the configuration files, the easiest way to view and work with configuration sections is to use the IIS Command-line Administration Tool.

Working with Configuration Sections

Each configuration section in the applicationHost.config file has an *OverrideModeDefault* attribute that controls whether a section is locked down to the level in which it is defined or can be overridden at lower levels of the configuration hierarchy. As discussed previously in the chapter in the section "Understanding Configuration Levels and Global Configuration," you can either allow or deny override. If you allow overriding the server level configuration, you can then use location locking to lock or unlock specific configuration sections at specific configuration levels. To understand this concept better, consider the following example:

You want to allow each site on a server to use a different set of default documents but do not want individual applications within sites to be able to use different sets of default documents. With this in mind, you allow the default document settings to be overridden in the applicationHost.config file as shown here:

```
<sectionGroup name="system.webServer">
    <section name="defaultDocument" overrideModeDefault="Allow" />
</sectionGroup>
```

You then lock the default document settings at the site level for each site on the server using location locking. The related entries in the Web.config file for each site are shown here:

```
<configuration>
 <location path="" overrideMode="Deny">
  <system.webServer>
   <defaultDocument>
    <files />
   </defaultDocument>
  </system.webServer>
 </location>
</configuration>
```

The default document settings are now locked at the site level. Because of this, you can manage the document settings at the site level but cannot manage the document settings for individual applications or virtual directories. In fact, if you access the Default Document feature for an application in IIS Manager, you will find that the Apply and Cancel actions are dimmed, so they cannot be selected. You also won't be able to configure the features by using AppCmd. In both instances, you should also see an error message stating that the configuration section cannot be used at this path because it is locked.

Note With configuration locking, it is important to remember that locking controls configuration through IIS Manager and AppCmd only. If someone has write access to the site-level directory on the server, he or she could edit the site's Web.config file and remove any restrictions you've enforced.

Determining Settings for a Configuration Section

By using the IIS Command-line Administration Tool, you can determine the settings for a configuration section in several different ways. You can use the List Config command to determine the exact settings being applied or inherited for any configuration section at any level of the configuration hierarchy. Sample 5-1 provides the syntax and usage. The ConfigPath is the application path for the configuration level you want to examine. The ConfigPath for the default Web site is "Default Web Site/".

Sample 5-1 List Config Syntax and Usage

Syntax
```
appcmd list config ["ConfigPath"] [/section:SectionName]
[/parameter1:value1 ...]
```
Usage
```
appcmd list config "Default Web Site/SalesApp"

appcmd list config /section:defaultDocument
```

Example Output

```
c:\appcmd list config "Default Web Site/SalesApp"
/section:defaultDocument

<system.webServer>
  <defaultDocument enabled="true">
    <files>
      <add value="Default.htm" />
      <add value="Default.asp" />
      <add value="index.htm" />
      <add value="index.html" />
      <add value="iisstart.htm" />
      <add value="default.aspx" />
    </files>
  </defaultDocument>
</system.webServer>
```

You can use the Search Config command to search the configuration files to determine exactly where unique settings are being applied on an IIS server. If you type **appcmd search config** without providing any additional parameters, you'll get a list of the server, site, and application paths where configuration files have been created. Other ways to use Search Config are to specify a starting configuration path from which to begin the search or to specify a configuration section to determine the locations where it is uniquely configured. You can also search for configuration sections by name and enabled or disabled state.

Sample 5-2 provides the syntax and usage for Search Config. Based on the example output, the configuration section was configured in three locations: application-Host.config, the default Web site's Web.config, and the Sales application/virtual directory's Web.config.

Sample 5-2 Search Config Syntax and Usage

Syntax
```
appcmd search config ["ConfigPath"] [/section:SectionName]
[/parameter1:value1 ...]
```
Usage
```
appcmd search config

appcmd search config "Default Web Site/"

appcmd search config "Default Web Site/" /section:defaultDocument

appcmd search config "Default Web Site/" /section:defaultDocument
/enabled

appcmd search config "Default Web Site/" /section:defaultDocument
/enabled:true
```

Example Output

```
c:\appcmd search config
CONFIGSEARCH "MACHINE/WEBROOT/APPHOST"
CONFIGSEARCH "MACHINE/WEBROOT/APPHOST/Default Web Site"
CONFIGSEARCH "MACHINE/WEBROOT/APPHOST/Default Web Site/SalesApp"
CONFIGSEARCH "MACHINE/WEBROOT/APPHOST/Default Web Site/Sales"

c:\appcmd search config /section:defaultDocument
CONFIGSEARCH "MACHINE/WEBROOT/APPHOST"
CONFIGSEARCH "MACHINE/WEBROOT/APPHOST/Default Web Site"
CONFIGSEARCH "MACHINE/WEBROOT/APPHOST/Default Web Site/Sales"
```

Modifying Settings for a Configuration Section

By using the IIS Command-line Administration Tool, you can run the Set Config command to modify the settings of a configuration section at the server level by default or at a specified configuration level. Sample 5-3 provides the syntax and usage for Set Config. The sample also provides examples for adding entries to a collection element. Here, entries are added to the files collection associated with the defaultDocument configuration section.

Sample 5-3   Set Config Syntax and Usage

Syntax
```
appcmd set config ["ConfigPath"] /section:SectionName
[/parameter1:value1 ...]
```
Usage
```
appcmd set config /section:defaultDocument /enabled:true

appcmd set config "Default Web Site/SalesApp"
/section:defaultDocument /enabled:true
```
Usage for Adding an Entry to a Named Collection
```
appcmd set config /section:defaultDocument
/+files.[value="main.html"]
```
Usage for Inserting an Entry at a Specific Location
```
appcmd set config /section:defaultDocument
/+files.[@start,value='main.html']

appcmd set config /section:defaultDocument
/+files.[@end,value='main.html']

appcmd set config /section:defaultDocument
/+files.[@2,value='main.html']
```
Usage for Removing an Entry from a Named Collection
```
appcmd set config /section:defaultDocument
/-files.[value='main.html']

appcmd set config /section:defaultDocument /-files.[@2]
```

Locking and Unlocking Configuration Sections

By using the IIS Command-line Administration Tool, you can run the Lock Config command to lock a configuration section. By default, the configuration is locked at the server level, but you can also specify a specific configuration level to lock. Locking the configuration at a specific level prevents the related settings from being overridden at a lower level of the configuration hierarchy.

Sample 5-4 provides the syntax and usage for Lock Config. When you use Lock Config, AppCmd creates the necessary location lock for you so that you don't have to type the related markup manually.

Sample 5-4   Lock Config Syntax and Usage

Syntax
```
appcmd lock config ["ConfigPath"] /section:SectionName
```
Usage
```
appcmd lock config "Default Web Site/" /section:defaultDocument
```

By using the IIS Command-line Administration Tool, you can run the Unlock Config command to unlock a configuration section. By default, the configuration is unlocked at the server level, but you can also specify a specific configuration level to unlock. Unlocking the configuration at a specific level allows the related settings to be overridden at a lower level of the configuration hierarchy.

Sample 5-5 provides the syntax and usage for Unlock Config. When you use Unlock Config, AppCmd removes a previously set location lock so that you don't have to remove the related markup manually.

Sample 5-5   Unlock Config Syntax and Usage

Syntax
```
appcmd unlock config ["ConfigPath"] /section:SectionName
[/parameter1:value1 ...]
```
Usage
```
appcmd unlock config "Default Web Site/" /section:defaultDocument
```

Clearing and Resetting Configuration Sections

By using the IIS Command-line Administration Tool, you can run the Clear Config command to clear and optionally delete a specified configuration section. By default, the configuration is cleared at the server level, but you can also specify a specific configuration level to clear. Clearing the configuration at a specific level allows inherited settings from a parent level to be used at that level and at lower levels of the configuration hierarchy. Sample 5-6 provides the syntax and usage for Clear Config.

Sample 5-6   Clear Config Syntax and Usage

Syntax
```
appcmd clear config ["ConfigPath"] /section:SectionName [/delete]
```
Usage
```
appcmd clear config "Default Web Site/" /section:defaultDocument

appcmd clear config "Default Web Site/" /section:defaultDocument
/delete
```

By using the IIS Command-line Administration Tool, you can run the Reset Config command to reset a specified configuration section to its default configuration state. By default, the configuration is reset at the server level, but you can also specify a specific configuration level to reset. Sample 5-7 provides the syntax and usage for Reset Config.

Sample 5-7   Reset Config Syntax and Usage

Syntax
```
appcmd reset config ["ConfigPath"] /section:SectionName
```
Usage
```
appcmd reset config /section:defaultDocument
```

Extending IIS with Modules

IIS supports native modules that use a Win32 DLL and managed modules that use a .NET Framework Class Library contained within an assembly. The configuration tasks available in IIS Manager depend on the role services and modules you've installed and enabled on your IIS 7.0 server.

With IIS 7.0, installing and enabling modules are two separate processes. To use native modules, you must install and enable them. To use managed modules, however, you need only to enable them. As discussed in Chapter 2, "Deploying IIS 7.0 in the Enterprise," you can add or remove role services, and when you do this, you install or uninstall related modules. Installing a module through a related role service registers the module so that it can be used with IIS. In many but not all cases, this also configures and enables the related IIS module automatically.

By adding or removing role services on a server, you make modules and their related DLLs available for use on a server. After you've added the appropriate role services to a server, you may also want to manage modules through the configuration files and the administration tools. The key reasons to do this are to:

- Manage the level at which modules are available

- Manage module-specific properties

In the sections that follow, I discuss how you can control modules and their related handlers through the configuration files. To ensure a better understanding of IIS configuration architecture, you should read and review this section even if you do not plan to edit the configuration files manually.

Controlling Native Modules through the Configuration Files

You can manage native modules at the server, site, application, and virtual directory level. Because of inheritance, settings you assign at a higher level of the configuration hierarchy are inherited automatically by lower levels of the configuration hierarchy. In the <globalModules> section of the configuration files, native modules you've installed are identified by their name and DLL image, such as:

```
<globalModules>
<add name="DefaultDocumentModule"
 image="%windir%\system32\inetsrv\defdoc.dll" />
<add name="DirectoryListingModule"
 image="%windir%\system32\inetsrv\dirlist.dll" />
 . . .
</globalModules>
```

In the <modules> section of the configuration files, native modules you've enabled are identified by their name, such as:

```
<modules>
 <add name="DefaultDocumentModule" />
 <add name="DirectoryListingModule" />
 <add name="StaticFileModule" />
 ...
</modules>
```

You can uninstall native modules by removing the corresponding entry from the <globalModules> and <modules> sections of the appropriate configuration file. For example, if you remove the <globalModules> and <modules>entries for Directory-ListingModule from the applicationHost.config file, you uninstall this module for the server and all lower configuration levels.

Rather than uninstalling native modules, you may want to disable them at a specific level of the configuration hierarchy and then enable them only where they should be used. For example, if you want a module to be used only with designated applications, you can leave the corresponding entry in the <globalModules> section and remove the corresponding entry from the<modules> sections of the application-Host.config file. Then in the Web.config files for the applications that should be able to use the module, you add an entry for the module in the <modules> section to allow the application to use the module.

Controlling Managed Modules through the Configuration Files

Like native modules, you can control managed modules at the server, site, application, and virtual directory level. Because of inheritance, settings you assign at a higher level of the configuration hierarchy are inherited automatically by lower levels of the configuration hierarchy.

Unlike native modules, managed modules do not need to be installed before you can enable them for use. In the <modules> section of the configuration files, managed modules you've enabled are identified by their name and associated .NET type, such as:

```
<modules>
 <add name="Profile" type="System.Web.Profile.ProfileModule"
preCondition="managedHandler" />
 <add name="UrlMappingsModule" type="System.Web.UrlMappingsModule"
preCondition="managedHandler" />
</modules>
```

As the example also shows, all managed modules also have a precondition that stipulates that they must use a managed handler by default. Preconditions on managed modules provide conditional logic that controls the way Web content is handled. If you remove the managedHandler precondition from a managed module, IIS will also apply the module to content that is not served by managed handlers. For example, the Forms authentication module has a managedHandler precondition and is therefore called only when ASP.NET content, such as .aspx pages, are requested. If an .html page is requested, the Forms authentication is not called. However, if you want to protect all Web content with Forms authentication, you can do so by removing the managed-Handler precondition from the Forms authentication module entry in the configuration files.

You can also enable all managed modules to run for all requests in your applications by setting runAllManagedModulesForAllRequests property in the <modules> section to true as shown in the following example:

```
<modules runAllManagedModulesForAllRequests="true" />
```

When you set the runAllManagedModulesForAllRequests property to true, the managedHandler precondition has no effect and IIS runs all managed modules for all requests.

You can disable managed modules by removing the corresponding entry from the <modules> section of the appropriate configuration file. For example, if you remove the <modules> entry for the OutputCache module from the applicationHost.config file, you disable this module for the server and all lower configuration levels. If you want a managed module to be used only with designated applications, you can add an entry for the module in the <modules> section of the application's Web.config file.

Controlling Managed Handlers through the Configuration Files

IIS processes all requests for Web content based on the type of content as determined by the file extension of the requested resource. Specifically, the file extension requested by a user tells IIS which handler to use to process the request. Each type of content has a specific handler that is identified in a handler mapping. This allows IIS 7.0 to use handler mappings to automatically select the appropriate set of handlers for a particular type of file.

Using preconditions, IIS 7.0 takes handler mapping a step further than do earlier versions of IIS. Handler preconditions ensure that IIS uses only handlers that are compatible with the runtime version of the .NET Framework and operating mode being used by the application pool processing a request. Handler mappings are configured at the server level during setup, and you'll find handler mappings in the <handlers> section of the applicationHost.config file. Here is an example:

```
<system.webServer>
 <handlers accessPolicy="Read, Script">
  <add name="AssemblyResourceLoader-
Integrated" path="WebResource.axd" verb="GET,DEBUG" type="System.Web.Handl
ers.AssemblyResourceLoader" preCondition="integratedMode" />
  <add name="PageHandlerFactory-
Integrated" path="*.aspx" verb="GET,HEAD,POST,DEBUG" type="System.Web.UI.P
ageHandlerFactory" preCondition="integratedMode" />    <add name="AXD-
ISAPI-2.0" path="*.axd" verb="GET,HEAD,POST,DEBUG" modules="IsapiModule"
scriptProcessor="%windir%\Microsoft.NET\Framework\v2.0.50727\aspnet_isapi.
dll" preCondition="classicMode,runtimeVersionv2.0,bitness32" responseBuffe
rLimit="0" />
 </handlers>
</system.webServer>
```

The preconditions assigned to a handler control the way the handler works. The standard types of preconditions are as follows:

- **Mode**   Applications running on a server running IIS 7.0 can use Classic mode or Integrated mode. With the Mode precondition, components that need to run in a particular operating mode can be marked to load only in worker processes that have this operating mode. This is important because setting the operating mode is an application pool property in IIS 7.0, and IIS worker processes use this property to determine how to process requests. Use classicMode to ensure that the handler is loaded only by the IIS core for application pools that are running in Classic mode. Use integratedMode to ensure that the handler is loaded only by the IIS core for application pools that are running in Integrated mode.

- **Runtime Version**   IIS can support different versions of the .NET Framework side by side. However, currently only one version of the .NET Framework can be loaded in a worker process at a time. With the Runtime Version precondition, you can mark components so that they are used only when a worker process loads a particular version of the .NET Framework. This is important because setting the version of the .NET Framework is an application pool property in IIS 7.0 and IIS worker processes use this property to preload the appropriate version of the .NET Framework on startup. Use runtimeVersion1.1 to ensure that the handler is loaded by the IIS core only for application pools that are using .NET Framework Version 1.1. Use runtimeVersion2.0 to ensure that the handler is loaded by the IIS core only for application pools that are using .NET Framework Version 2.0.

■ **Bitness**   64-bit processors are becoming the new standard in server computing. As 64-bit processors are gradually being favored over 32-bit processors, more and more software is being written for 64-bit operating systems. To ensure compatibility, computers running 64-bit versions of Windows Server 2008 provide a 32-bit execution environment on top of the 64-bit execution environment. IIS 7.0 takes advantage of this and allows you to run 32-bit and 64-bit worker processes side by side. To ensure that IIS loads DLLs with the right bitness into a worker process, you must set the correct Bitness precondition. Use bitness32 for DLLs that are designed for 32-bit operating systems. Use bitness64 for DLLs that are designed for 64-bit operating systems.

Thus, if a handler has the following precondition assignment:

```
preCondition="classicMode,runtimeVersionv2.0,bitness32"
```

IIS uses the handler only when the application pool processing a request is using Classic operating mode, .NET Framework Version 2.0, and a 32-bit execution environment.

In the applicationHost.config file, the <handlers> section also sets the global access policy for managed handlers. Access policy, set using the *accessPolicy* attribute of the <handlers> section, determines whether handlers that require Read, Script or Execute permission can run. Required access, set using the *requireAccess* attribute of the add element, specifies the type of access a handler requires.

With *accessPolicy*, the type of access can be set as:

■ **Read**   Allows handlers that require Read access to run. With a Read access policy, IIS processes files as static content, which does not allow IIS to process any scripts contained in files.

■ **Script**   Allows handlers that require Script access to run. With a Script access policy, IIS processes files as dynamic content, which allows IIS to process any scripts contained in files.

■ **Execute**   Allows handlers that require Execute access to run. With an Execute access policy, IIS allows files being requested to be directly executed, such as would be necessary to execute unmapped ISAPI extensions.

The following example shows how *accessPolicy* and *requireAccess* are used in configuration files:

```
<system.webServer>
 <handlers accessPolicy="Read, Script">
  <add name="ISAPI-dll" path="*.dll" verb="*" modules="IsapiModule"
resourceType="File" requireAccess="Execute" />
 . . .
 </handlers>
 </system.webServer>
```

This means that only handlers that require Read or Script access will execute. IIS will not run any handler that requires Execute access. If IIS receives a request for an unmapped ISAPI extension, IIS will generate a runtime error. If you wanted to allow Execute access, you would need to change the access policy as shown in this example:

```
<handlers accessPolicy="Read, Script, Execute">
 . . .
 </handlers>
```

You should change access policy to allow execute permissions only if this is a requirement for your server environment. Otherwise, you'll want to set access policy so that only Script and Read permissions are allowed. If you wanted to prevent IIS from handling dynamic content, you could set Read access policy as shown in the following example:

```
<handlers accessPolicy="Read">
 . . .
 </handlers>
```

This means that only handlers that require Read access will execute. IIS will not run any handler that requires Execute or Script access. If IIS receives a request for dynamic content, such as an .aspx page or an unmapped ISAPI extension, IIS will generate a runtime error.

Using the Configuration and Schema Files to Install Non-Standard Extension Modules

As additional modules become available from Microsoft or other sources, you'll be able to download, install, and enable them to extend the functionality of your IIS servers. You should never install a new module without first thoroughly testing it in a development environment to determine the possible impact. Once you've rigorously tested the module and your servers to ensure that there are no adverse effects, you should also test various configurations and uninstall procedures to ensure that the module can be configured as expected and uninstalled cleanly.

Once they are approved by Microsoft, most modules are made available at the IIS Web site (*http://www.iis.net*). Once you've downloaded an extension module, you should be able to install and enable it easily. The general steps for installing and enabling a module will be similar to the following:

1. Unzip the compressed files in the download by right-clicking the Zip file and then selecting Extract All.

2. In the Extract Compressed (Zipped) Folders dialog box, click Extract to accept the default folder location for the files. Alternately, click Browse, and then use the Select A Destination dialog box to select a destination folder for the files you are extracting. Then click OK.

3. Review the module's ReadMe file or other documentation and then run the module's Setup program.

The module's Setup program should perform some or all of the following configuration tasks:

1. Stop IIS services, if necessary.

2. Copy any necessary schema files to the *%SystemRoot%*\System32\Inetsrv \Config\Schema directory. IIS reads in the schema files in this directory automatically during startup of the application pools.

3. Copy the module DLL to the *%SystemRoot%*\System32\Inetsrv directory. This allows IIS to execute the DLL.

4. Create the appropriate entries in the <moduleProviders> and <modules> sections of the administration schema file so that the module is available for management. The administration schema file (Administration.xml) controls the management interface available in IIS Manager and is located in the *%SystemRoot%*\System32\Inetsrv\Config\Schema directory.

5. Create the appropriate entries in the <globalModules> and <modules> sections of the applicationHost.config file so that the module is installed and enabled. The entry in the <globalModules> section maps to the DLL in the %SystemRoot%\System32\Inetsrv directory.

6. If you later register programs for use with the module, you'll create handler mappings in the <handlers> section of the applicationHost.config file to allow the programs to be used for processing requests based on specific file extensions.

7. Start IIS services, if the services were previously stopped.

If the module you are installing doesn't have a setup program, you must perform similar procedures manually to ensure that the module is properly configured. You can learn more about an extension module by examining its schema file. The named attributes in the schema file represent properties that you can set to optimize the module behavior. Each attribute also should have details on the associated values for each property. You'll need to refer to the module documentation to determine how the module is used.

Managing Modules

You can manage modules and control the way they are used by IIS at any configuration level. This means that you can configure module usage for an entire server, individual sites, individual applications, and individual virtual directories. The easiest way to view and work with IIS modules is to use IIS Manager or the IIS Command-line Administration Tool.

Viewing Installed Native and Managed Modules

In IIS Manager, you can view the modules that are installed and enabled by completing the following steps:

1. Start IIS Manager. Navigate to the level of the configuration hierarchy you want to manage. To view global configuration details, select the computer name in the left pane. To view site or application details, expand nodes as necessary until you can select the site, application, or virtual directory you want to work with.

2. When you group by area, the Modules feature is listed under IIS. Double-click the Modules feature. This displays the Modules page as shown in Figure 5-1.

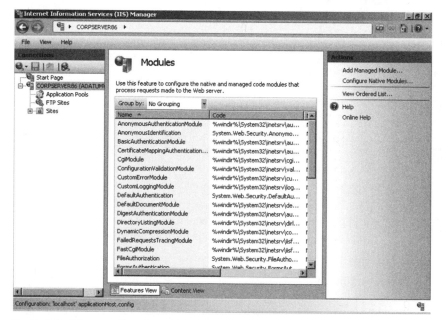

Figure 5-1 View or edit native and managed code modules.

3. On the Modules page, you can use the Group By drop-down list to group module entries in several different ways. You can group by:

- ❏ **Entry Type**   Groups modules according to whether they have local definitions or inherited definitions. Modules that are enabled at that level are listed under Local. Modules that are enabled at a higher level are listed under Inherited.

- ❏ **Module Type**   Groups modules according to whether they are native or managed modules. Native modules are listed under Native Modules. Managed modules are listed under Managed Modules.

By using the IIS Command-line Administration Tool, you can view the local and inherited modules enabled at a specific configuration level by running the List Module command. Sample 5-8 provides the syntax and usage. You can set the /app.name parameter to the name of the application path to examine. If you use the default application path for a site, you can list the modules enabled for the site. If you do not set this parameter, AppCmd returns the server-level configuration details.

Sample 5-8   List Module Syntax and Usage

Syntax
```
appcmd list module [[/module.name:]"ModuleName"]
[/app.name:"AppPath"]
```
Usage for Listing All Modules on a Server
```
appcmd list module
```
Usage for Listing All Modules for Applications or Sites
```
appcmd list modules /app.name:"Default Web Site/SalesApp"
```
Usage for Listing Specific Modules for Applications or Sites
```
appcmd list module "FormsAuthentication" /app.name:"Default Web Site/"

appcmd list modules /app.name:"Default Web Site/"
/type:System.Web.Security.FormsAuthenticationModule

appcmd list modules /app.name:"Default Web Site/" /
preCondition:managedHandler
```

Installing Native Modules

You manage the installation of native modules at the server level. The best way to install a module for the first time is to add the related role service as discussed in Chapter 2 in the section "Viewing and Modifying Role Services on Servers." Using the appropriate role service to install a module ensures that Setup inserts all necessary and related settings into the configuration files. If you subsequently uninstall a module by editing the configuration files or using IIS Manager, you can reinstall and enable a module at the server level by following these steps:

1. In IIS Manager, select the name of the server you want to work with in the left pane.

2. Access the Modules page by double-clicking the Modules feature. In the Actions pane, click Configure Native Modules.

3. In the Configure Native Modules dialog box, click Register. In the Register Native Module dialog box, shown in Figure 5-2, register the module you want to install by typing the module name and module executable path as per the appendix, "Comprehensive IIS 7.0 Module and Schema Reference."

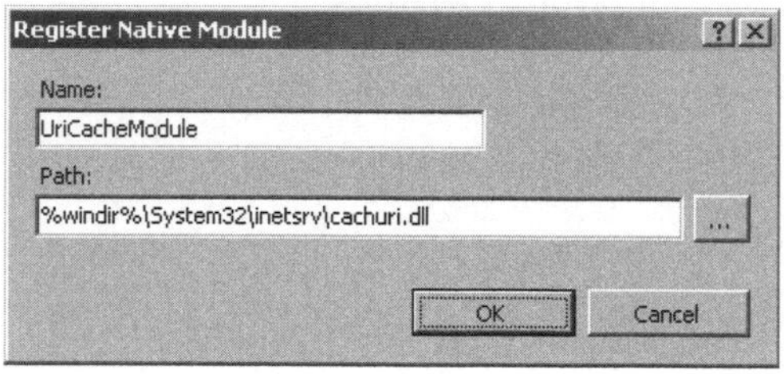

Figure 5-2   Register the module you want to install.

4. By default, modules you register are enabled automatically for use at the server level and below. If you don't want the module to be enabled in this way, you can disable the module as discussed in the section "Disabling Native and Managed Modules" later in this chapter. Click OK to complete the registration.

Using the IIS Command-line Administration Tool, you can install a native module by running the Install Module command. Sample 5-9 provides the syntax and usage. By default, modules are also added to the enabled list. If you don't want to enable the module you are installing, set the /add parameter to false.

Sample 5-9   Install Module Syntax and Usage

Syntax
```
appcmd install module /name:"ModuleName" /image:PathToDLL
[/add:true|false]
```
Usage
```
appcmd install module /name:"FastCGI"
/image:%windir%\System32\inetsrv\iisfcgi.dll
```

Enabling Native Modules

When you install a native module, the module is registered and enabled automatically for use. The registration entry is created in the <globalModules> section of the applicationHost.config file, and the enablement entry is created in the <modules>

section of the applicationHost.config file. If you disable a native module at the server level or another level of the configuration hierarchy, you can enable it as necessary by completing the following steps:

1. In IIS Manager, navigate to the level of the configuration hierarchy you want to manage.

2. Access the Modules page by double-clicking the Modules feature. In the Actions pane, click Configure Native Modules.

3. In the Configure Native Modules dialog box, shown in Figure 5-3, you'll see a list of modules that are registered (installed) but disabled. Select one or more registered modules to install, and then click OK.

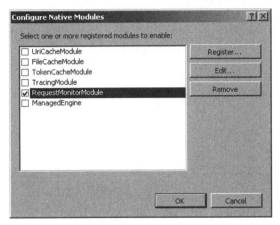

Figure 5-3   Select the native module or modules to enable.

In the IIS Command-line Administration Tool, you can enable a native module by using the Add Module command. Sample 5-10 provides the syntax and usage. You can use the /app.name parameter to set the level at which the module should be enabled. If you do not set this parameter, AppCmd enables the module for use at the server level.

Sample 5-10   Add Module Syntax and Usage for Native Modules

Syntax
```
appcmd add module /name:"ModuleName" [/app.name:"AppPath"]
[/parameter1:value1 ...]
```
Usage
```
appcmd add module /name:"WindowsAuthenticationModule"


appcmd add module /name:"WindowsAuthenticationModule"
/app.name:"Default Web Site/"
```

Enabling Managed Modules

Although managed modules are installed automatically as part of the .NET Framework, they are not enabled for use automatically. This means that you must enable any managed modules that you want to make available. Further, you must install and activate the ManagedEngine module to provide the necessary integration functionality between IIS and the .NET Framework.

You can enable managed modules by completing the following steps:

1. In IIS Manager, navigate to the level of the configuration hierarchy you want to manage.

2. Access the Modules page by double-clicking the Modules feature. In the Actions pane, click Add Managed Module.

3. In the Add Managed Module dialog box, shown in Figure 5-4, specify the managed module you want to enable by typing the module name and selecting the module's .NET library type as per the appendix.

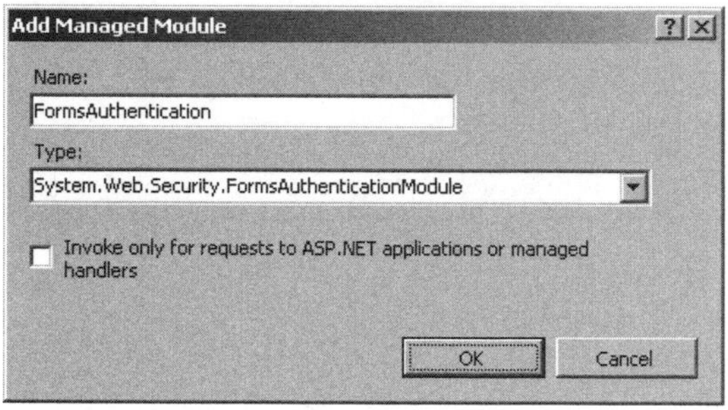

Figure 5-4   Specify the module name and type.

4. Select the Invoke Only For Requests To... check box if you want the managed module to process only requests made to ASP.NET applications or managed handlers. If you do not select this check box, IIS Manager will run the module for all requests in your applications.

> **Note**   Selecting the Invoke Only For Requests To check box ensures that the module is added to the <modules> section and has the managedHandler precondition. See the section "Controlling Managed Modules through the Configuration Files" earlier in this chapter for more information.

In the IIS Command-line Administration Tool, you can enable a managed module by using the Add Module command. Sample 5-11 provides the syntax and usage. You can use the /app.name parameter to set the level at which the module should be enabled. If you do not set this parameter, AppCmd enables the module for use at the server level.

Sample 5-11   Add Module Syntax and Usage for Managed Modules

Syntax
```
appcmd add module /name:"ModuleName" /type:ManagedModuleType
[/app.name:"AppPath"] [/precondition:managedHandler]
```
Usage
```
appcmd add module /name:"CustModule" /
type:CustNamespace.CustModuleClass /app.name:"Default Web Site/"
/precondition:managedHandler
```

Editing Native and Managed Module Configurations

The properties you can configure for a module depend on its type. With native modules, you can configure the module name and image (executable path). With managed modules, you can configure the module name and .NET library type. With either type of module, you can also set preconditions, such as the need to use a managedHandler.

You can edit a module's configuration by completing the following steps:

1. In IIS Manager, navigate to the level of the configuration hierarchy you want to manage. Keep in mind that you can manage native module configurations only at the server level.

2. Access the Modules page by double-clicking the Modules feature and then double-clicking the module you want to modify.

3. With native modules, you'll see the Edit Native Module Registration dialog box, which allows you to set the module name and path (image). With managed modules, you'll see the Edit Managed Module dialog box, which allows you to set the module's name, type, and managed handler requirements. After you make the necessary changes, click OK to save your new settings.

Tip   Managed modules can have different configurations at different levels of the configuration hierarchy. You can use this feature to remove managed handler requirements for a specific Web site or application. If you modify the configuration of a managed module at a lower level of the configuration hierarchy, you can click the module and then click Revert To Parent to restore the original configuration settings from the parent configuration level.

With the IIS Command-line Administration Tool, you can modify a module's configuration by using the Set Module command. Sample 5-12 provides the syntax and usage.

Sample 5-12   Set Module Syntax and Usage

Syntax
```
appcmd set module [[/module.name:]"ModuleName"]
[/app.name:"AppPath"] [/parameter1:value1 ...]
```

Usage

```
appcmd set module "ManagedEngine"
/image: "%windir%\Microsoft.NET\Framework\v2.0.50727\webengine.dll"
/preCondition:"preCondition="integratedMode,runtimeVersionv2.0,
bitness32"

appcmd set module "FormsAuthentication" /app.name:"Default Web Site/"
/type: "System.Web.Security.FormsAuthenticationModule"
/preCondition:managedHandler
```

Disabling Native and Managed Modules

You can disable a native or managed module at the server level or another level of the configuration hierarchy. When you disable a module at the server level, IIS removes the corresponding module entry from the <modules> section of the application-Host.config file. When you disable a module at another level, IIS inserts a remove entry into the <modules> section of the related Web.config. In the following example, an administrator has removed HttpCacheModule from a site or application:

```
<modules>
 <remove name="HttpCacheModule">
</modules>
```

Because disabling a module does not uninstall the module, a module disabled at one level is still available to be used at other levels of the configuration hierarchy. With this in mind, you can disable a module by completing the following steps:

1. In IIS Manager, navigate to the level of the configuration hierarchy you want to manage.

2. Access the Modules page by double-clicking the Modules feature.

3. Select the module you want to remove by clicking it, and then in the Actions pane, click Remove.

4. When prompted to confirm the action, click Yes.

With the IIS Command-line Administration Tool, you can disable a module by running the Delete Module command. Sample 5-13 provides the syntax and usage.

Sample 5-13   Delete Module Syntax and Usage

Syntax

```
appcmd delete module [[/module.name:]"ModuleName"]
[/app.name:"AppPath"]
```

Usage

```
appcmd delete module "CustModule"

appcmd delete module "CustModule" /app.name:"Default Web Site/SalesApp"
```

Uninstalling Native Modules

You manage the installation of native modules at the server level. When you uninstall a native module, the module is deregistered and disabled. As a result, IIS removes the registration entry from the <globalModules> section of the applicationHost.config file. This prevents the module from being used at other levels of the configuration hierarchy.

Before you can use IIS Manager to uninstall a native module, you must first disable the module at the server level. You can then uninstall the native module by completing the following steps:

1.   In IIS Manager, in the left pane, select the name of the server you want to work with.

2.   Access the Modules page by double-clicking the Modules feature. In the Actions pane, click Configure Native Modules.

3.   In the Configure Native Modules dialog box, select the module you want to uninstall, and then click Remove.

4.   When prompted to confirm the action, click Yes.

By using the IIS Command-line Administration Tool, you can uninstall a module by running the Uninstall Module command. Sample 5-14 provides the syntax and usage. By default, the /remove parameter is set to true so that the module is also removed from the enabled list.

Sample 5-14   Uninstall Module Syntax and Usage

Syntax
```
appcmd uninstall module [/module.name:]"ModuleName"
[/remove:true|false]
```
Usage
```
appcmd uninstall module /
name:"CertificateMappingAuthenticationModule" /remove:true
```

Sharing Global Configuration

A Web server farm is a group of IIS servers working together to provide common services. In large IIS installations like Web server farms, you'll often want all servers that provide the same services to share a common configuration. Don't worry—IIS 7.0 makes it easy for Web servers to share a common configuration. All you need to do is point the servers to a shared configuration location and then copy the desired configuration to this location.

Working with Shared Configurations

To facilitate a discussion on global configuration sharing, I'll refer to Web servers that share a global configuration as *shared servers*. The key to success with shared servers lies in careful management of the global configuration. Once sharing is set up, any configuration change you make to any one of the shared servers is applied to every other shared server. To avoid problems and the potential for multiple administrators to inadvertently change settings on different servers simultaneously, I recommend the following:

- Designating one administrator as the configuration administrator

- Using a nondedicated/dedicated configuration server

The configuration administrator is the central coordinator for changes to the shared server configuration. He or she is the only person who can authorize configuration changes. The fact that a prior request from this person is required to make configuration changes ensures that only one person at a time is making changes to the shared configuration.

With a nondedicated/dedicated configuration server, you make all configuration changes on a specific server. If this server is a part of the Web farm, it is a nondedicated configuration server, and any changes you make to the server are immediately applied to all servers in the Web farm. If this server is not a part of the Web farm and not used for other purposes, it is a dedicated configuration server and any changes you make to the server must be pushed out to the Web farm using the configuration export process. Because you can test changes prior to implementing them, there are definite advantages to using a dedicated configuration server.

Exporting and Sharing Global Configuration

Once you've configured a Web server with the settings you want to use, you can export its configuration to a central configuration location, such as a NTFS shared folder. Providing that all your Web servers can access this location, you can then enable your servers to access this location to obtain their global configuration settings. To protect the configuration files from unauthorized viewing, you create encryption keys as part of the configuration process.

On the fully configured server for which you want to share global configuration, you can export the configuration by completing the following steps:

1. In IIS Manager, in the left pane, select the name of the server you want to work with. Access the Shared Configuration page by double-clicking the Shared Configuration feature. In the Actions pane, click Export Configuration.

2. In the Export Configuration dialog box, type the folder path to the save location for the configuration files. For shared NTFS folders, this should be in the form of a Universal Naming Convention (UNC) path name, such as

\\FileServer23\WebConfig. If you want to select the path location rather than type it, click the options button and then use the Network node in the Browse For Folder dialog box to help you find the save location.

3. If you want to use alternate credentials or need additional permissions to access the save location, click Connect As. Type the user name and password and confirm the password of an account with appropriate permissions. Click OK.

> **Tip** For the export to be successful, the account you use must have Change permissions on the NTFS share and Modify permissions for NTFS.

4. In the Export Configuration dialog box, type and then confirm a strong password for the encryption keys that will be used to secure the configuration files. A strong password is at least eight characters long and contains at least three of these four elements: numbers, symbols, uppercase letters, and lowercase letters.

5. Click OK to export the configuration. If the export is successful, you'll see a prompt stating this. Click OK. Otherwise, if the export fails, note the error provided and correct any problems, such as insufficient permissions, and then repeat this procedure.

On servers that you want to use the shared configuration, you can apply the shared configuration by completing the following steps:

1. In IIS Manager, in the left pane, select the name of the server you want to work with. Access the Shared Configuration page by double-clicking the Shared Configuration feature. In the main pane, select the Enable Shared Configuration check box.

2. In the Physical Path text box, type the folder path to the shared configuration location. For shared NTFS folders, this should be in the form of a UNC path name, such as \\FileServer23\WebConfig. If you want to select the path location rather than type it, click the options button and then use the Network node in the Browse For Folder dialog box to help you find the save location.

3. Type the user name and password and confirm the password of an account with appropriate permissions to access the shared configuration location. The user name must be entered in DOMAIN\username format, such as CPANDL\wrstanek.

4. In the Actions pane, click Apply. When prompted, enter the encryption password and then click OK.

5. The computer's current IIS encryption keys are backed up and saved in the current configuration directory on the server. To restore these keys later, turn off shared configuration. When prompted about this, click OK again.

6. IIS Manager applies the shared global configuration. When prompted, confirm that the changes were successful before clicking OK. If IIS Manager was unable to apply the changes, ensure the NTFS and Share permissions on the shared

location are set appropriately for the account you specified previously and that you entered the correct encryption password.

7. Exit and then restart all instances of IIS Manager. If remote administration is allowed, you must restart the Web Management Service as well. In IIS Manager's left pane, select the server you just configured. Access the Management Service page by double-clicking the Management Service feature. In the Actions pane, click Restart.

If you no longer want a server to use a shared configuration, follow these steps to disable shared configuration:

1. In IIS Manager, in the left pane, select the name of the server you want to work with. Access the Shared Configuration page by double-clicking the Shared Configuration feature.

2. In the main pane, clear the Enable Shared Configuration check box. In the Actions pane, click Apply. When prompted, do one of the following:

   ❑ To restore the Web server's original configuration (that is, the configuration it was using prior to applying the shared configuration), click No. The server's original configuration is restored, along with its original encryption keys.

   ❑ To continue to use the current configuration, as specified in the shared configuration location, and copy this configuration over the original configuration, click Yes. The shared configuration is copied to the server, along with the shared encryption keys. Because sharing is disabled, any updates made to the shared configuration are not applied to the server.

3. When prompted, confirm that the changes were successful before clicking OK. If there are errors, they are likely due to NTFS and Share permissions on the shared location. Ensure permissions are set appropriately for the account you specified previously.

Chapter 6
Configuring Web Sites and Directories

Tasks for creating and managing Web sites and directories are broken down into several categories. You'll find sections in this chapter on Web site naming and identification, creating Web sites, creating virtual directories, and other topics.

Web Site Naming and Identification

Each Web site deployed in the organization has unique characteristics. Different types of Web sites can have different characteristics. Intranet Web sites typically use computer names that resolve locally and have private Internet Protocol (IP) addresses. Internet Web sites typically use fully qualified domain names (FQDNs) and public IP addresses. Intranet and Internet Web sites can also use host header names, allowing single IP address and port assignments to serve multiple Web sites.

Understanding IP Addresses and Name Resolution

Whether you're configuring an intranet or Internet site, your Web server must be assigned a unique IP address that identifies the computer on the network. An IP address is a numeric identifier for the computer. IP addressing schemes vary depending on how your network is configured, but they're normally assigned from a range of addresses for a particular network segment (also known as a *subnet*). For example, if you're working with a computer on the network segment 192.168.10.0, the address range you have available for computers is usually from 192.168.10.1 to 192.168.10.254.

Although numeric addresses are easy for machines to remember, they aren't easy for human beings to remember. Because of this, computers are assigned text names that are easy for users to remember. Text names have two basic forms:

- Standard computer names, which are used on private networks
- Internet names, which are used on public networks

Private networks are networks that are either indirectly connected to the Internet or completely disconnected from the Internet. Private networks use IP addresses that are reserved for private use and aren't accessible to the public Internet. Private network addresses fall into the following ranges:

- 10.0.0.0–10.255.255.255
- 172.16.0.0–172.31.255.255
- 192.168.0.0–192.168.255.255

Private networks that use Internet technologies are called *intranets*. Information is delivered on intranets by mapping a computer's IP address to its text name, which is the NetBIOS name assigned to the computer. Although Microsoft Windows components use the NetBIOS naming convention for name resolution, Transmission Control Protocol/Internet Protocol (TCP/IP) components use the Domain Name System (DNS). Under Windows, the DNS host name defaults to the same name as the NetBIOS computer name. For example, if you install a server with a computer name of CorpServer, this name is assigned as the NetBIOS computer name and the default DNS host name.

In contrast, public networks are networks that are connected directly to the Internet. Public networks use IP addresses that are purchased or leased for public use. Typically, you'll obtain IP address assignments for your public servers from the provider of your organization's Internet services. Internet service providers (ISPs) obtain blocks of IP addresses from the American Registry for Internet Numbers (ARIN). Other types of organizations also can purchase blocks of IP addresses.

On the Internet, DNS is used to resolve text names to IP addresses. With the DNS name *www.microsoft.com*, *www* identifies a server name and *microsoft.com* identifies a domain name. As with public IP addresses, domain names must be leased or purchased. You purchase domain names from name registrars, such as Internet Network Information Center (InterNIC). When a client computer requests a connection to a site by using a domain name, the request is transmitted to a DNS server. The DNS server returns the IP address that corresponds to the requested host name, and then the client request is routed to the appropriate site.

Don't confuse the public DNS naming system used on the Internet with the private naming system used on intranets. DNS names are configured on DNS servers and resolved to IP addresses before contacting a server. This fact makes it possible for a server to have multiple IP addresses, each with a different DNS name. For example, a server with an internal computer name of WebServer22 could be configured with IP addresses of 207.46.230.210, 207.46.230.211, and 207.46.230.212. If these IP addresses are configured as *www.microsoft.com*, *services.microsoft.com*, and *products.microsoft.com*, respectively, in the DNS server, the server can respond to requests for each of these domain names.

Understanding Web Site Identifiers

Each Web site deployed in your organization has a unique identity it uses to receive and to respond to requests. The identity includes the following:

- A computer or DNS name
- An IP address
- A port number
- An optional host header name

The way these identifiers are combined to identify a Web site depends on whether the host server is on a private or public network. On a private network, a computer called CorpIntranet could have an IP address of 10.0.0.52. If so, the Web site on the server could be accessed in the following ways:

- Using the Universal Naming Convention (UNC) path name: \\CorpIntranet or \\10.0.0.52

- Using a Uniform Resource Locator (URL): *http://CorpIntranet/* or *http://10.0.0.52/*

- Using a URL and port number: *http://CorpIntranet:80/* or *http://10.0.0.52:80/*

On a public network, a computer called Dingo could be registered to use the DNS name *www.microsoft.com* and the IP address of 207.46.230.210. If so, the Web site on the server could be accessed in either of the following ways:

- Using a URL: *http://www.microsoft.com/* or *http://207.46.230.210/*

- Using a URL and port number: *http:// www.microsoft.com:80/* or *http://207.46.230.210:80/*

Hosting Multiple Sites on a Single Server

Using different combinations of IP addresses, port numbers, and host header names, one can host multiple sites on a single computer. Hosting multiple sites on a single server has definite advantages. For example, rather than installing three different Web servers, one could host *www.microsoft.com*, *support.microsoft.com*, and *service.microsoft.com* on the same Web server.

One way to host multiple sites on the same server is to assign multiple IP addresses to the server. Figure 6-1 shows an example of this configuration.

To use this technique, you must follow these steps:

1. Configure the TCP/IP settings on the server so that there is one IP address for each site that you want to host.

2. Configure DNS so that the host names and corresponding IP addresses can be resolved.

3. Configure each Web site so that it uses a specific IP address.

With this technique, users can access the sites individually by typing the unique domain name or IP address in a browser. Following the example shown in Figure 6-1, you can access the Sales intranet by typing **http://SalesIntranet/** or **http://10.0.0.102/**.

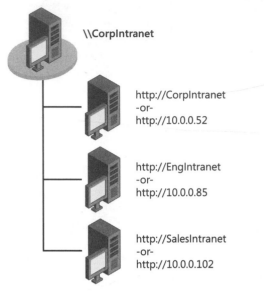

\\CorpIntranet

http://CorpIntranet
-or-
http://10.0.0.52

http://EngIntranet
-or-
http://10.0.0.85

http://SalesIntranet
-or-
http://10.0.0.102

Figure 6-1   You can use multiple IP addresses to host multiple Web sites on a single server.

Another technique you can use to host multiple sites on a single server is to assign each site a unique port number while keeping the same IP address, as shown in Figure 6-2. Users will then be able to do the following:

- Access the main site by typing the DNS server name or IP address in a browser, such as **http://Intranet/** or **http://10.0.0.52/**.

- Access other Web sites by typing the domain name and port assignment or IP address and port assignment, such as **http://Intranet:88/** or **http:// 10.0.0.52:88/**.

The final method you can use to host multiple sites on a single server is to use host header names. Host headers allow you to host multiple sites on the same IP address and port number. The key to host headers is a DNS name assignment that's configured in DNS and assigned to the site in its configuration.

An example of host header assignment is shown in Figure 6-3. Here, a single server hosts the sites CorpIntranet, EngIntranet, and SalesIntranet. The three sites use the same IP address and port number assignment but have different DNS names.

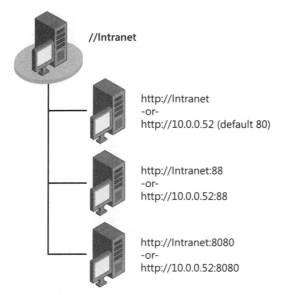

//Intranet

http://Intranet
-or-
http://10.0.0.52 (default 80)

http://Intranet:88
-or-
http://10.0.0.52:88

http://Intranet:8080
-or-
http://10.0.0.52:8080

Figure 6-2   Another technique is to use multiple port numbers to host multiple Web sites on a single server.

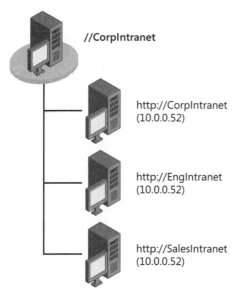

//CorpIntranet

http://CorpIntranet
(10.0.0.52)

http://EngIntranet
(10.0.0.52)

http://SalesIntranet
(10.0.0.52)

Figure 6-3   You can use host headers to support multiple Web sites on a single server with a single IP address.

To use host headers, you must do the following:

1. Configure DNS so that the host header names and corresponding IP addresses can be resolved.

2. Configure the primary Web site so that it responds to requests on the IP address and port number you've assigned.

3. Configure additional Web sites so that they use the same IP address and port number and also assign a host header name.

Using different IP addresses or different port numbers for each site ensures the widest compatibility because any Web browser can access the related sites without problems. However, as public IP addresses are valuable (and sometimes costly) resources, and non-standard ports require users to type the nonstandard port number, host headers are the most commonly used technique.

Host headers have specific drawbacks. Earlier versions of browsers that don't support Hypertext Transfer Protocol (HTTP) 1.1 are unable to pass host header names back to Internet Information Services (IIS). Although Microsoft Internet Explorer 3, Netscape Navigator 2, and later versions of these browsers support the use of host header names, earlier versions of these browsers don't, and visitors using earlier browsers will reach the default Web site for the IP address. After you configure host headers, you must also register the host header names you've used with DNS to ensure that the names are properly resolved.

Checking the Computer Name and IP Address of Servers

Before you configure Web sites, you should check the server's computer name and IP address. You can view the computer name by completing the following steps:

1. Click Start, and then click Control Panel. In the Control Panel's Classic View, double-click System. In the System console, under Computer Name, Domain, And Workgroup Settings, click Change Settings. Alternatively, you can click Advanced System Settings in the left pane.

2. On the Computer Name tab, you'll see the FQDN of the server and the domain or workgroup membership. The FQDN is the DNS name of the computer.

3. The DNS name is the name that you normally use to access the IIS resources on the server. For example, if the DNS name of the computer is www.microsoft.com and you've configured a Web site on port 80, the URL you use to access the computer from the Internet is *http://www.microsoft.com/*.

You can view the IP address and other TCP/IP settings for the computer by completing the following steps:

1. Click Start, and then click Control Panel. In Control Panel's Classic View, double-click Network And Sharing Center.

2. In the Network And Sharing Center, you'll see a list of tasks in the left pane. Click Manage Network Connections. This opens the Network Connections window.

3. Right-click Local Area Connection, and then select Properties. This opens the Local Area Connection Properties dialog box.

4. Open the Internet Protocol Version 4 (TCP/IPv4) Properties dialog box by double-clicking Internet Protocol Version 4 (TCP/IPv4).

5. The IPv4 Address and other TCP/IP settings for the computer are displayed, as shown in Figure 6-4.

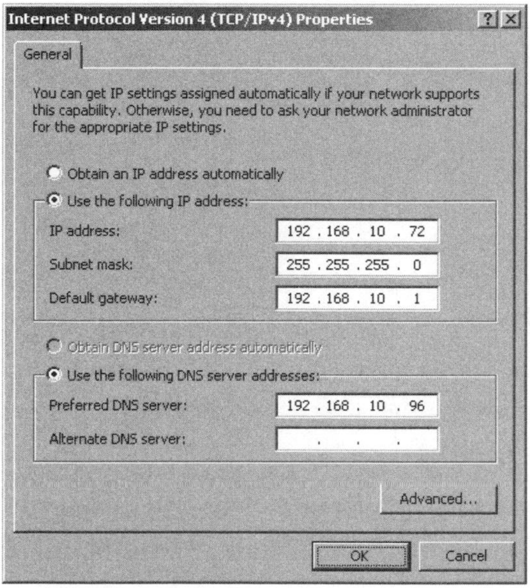

Figure 6-4 Use the Internet Protocol (TCP/IP) Properties dialog box to view and configure TCP/IP settings.

IIS servers should use static IP addresses. If the computer is obtaining an IP address automatically, you'll need to reconfigure the TCP/IP settings.

Examining Site Configuration

In IIS Manager, you can view a list of the Web sites installed on a server by clicking the node for the computer you want to work with in the left pane and then clicking the Sites node. Sites are listed by name, ID number, Web site status, binding, and path.

By using the IIS Command-line Administration Tool, you can list the existing sites on a server by running the List Site command. Type **appcmd list site** at a command prompt to list all the sites on a server. You can list details about a specific site or the settings of a specific site as shown in these examples:

```
appcmd list site "Default Web Site"
```

```
appcmd list site http://localhost/
```

```
appcmd list site /serverAutoStart:false
```

You'll then see a summary related to the site configuration, such as:

```
SITE "Shopping Site" (id:6,bindings:https:/*:443:,state:Stopped)
```

These details provided the following information:

- **"Shopping Site"** is the name of the site.

- **id:6** is the identification number of the site.

- **bindings:https:/*:443:** tells you the site uses HTTPS on port 443 and IIS listens for requests on all IP addresses.

- **state:Stopped** tells you that the Web site is stopped and is not active.

You can view the full configuration details for a site by using the /config parameter, such as:

```
appcmd list site "Default Web Site" /config
```

You'll then see a full listing of the configuration details for the site, such as:

```
<site name="Shopping" id="6" state="Starting">
  <bindings>
    <binding protocol="https" bindingInformation="*:443:" />
  </bindings>
  <limits />
  <logFile />
  <traceFailedRequestsLogging />
  <applicationDefaults />
  <virtualDirectoryDefaults />
  <application path="/" applicationPool="Shopping">
    <virtualDirectoryDefaults />
    <virtualDirectory path="/" physicalPath="C:\inetpub\shopping"
    userName="DevTeam" password="RubberChickens" />
  </application>
</site>
```

> **Note** When you are working with sites, applications, and virtual directories, you may need to provide logon credentials for authentication. Any credentials you provide are stored by default as encrypted text in the site, application, or virtual directory configuration. If you view the file with a text editor, you'll see the encrypted text. However, if you view the configuration details at the command prompt by running the List Site command with the /config parameter, you'll see the plaintext password as shown in this listing.

The full details do not include any inherited settings. To view the full configuration details, including inherited values, for a site, you must use the following syntax:

```
appcmd list site "SiteName" /config:*
```

Here is an example:

```
appcmd list site "Shopping Site" /config:*
```

You'll then see a full listing of the configuration details that includes inherited values, such as:

```
<site name="Shopping" id="6" serverAutoStart="true" state="Starting">
  <bindings>
    <binding protocol="https" bindingInformation="*:443:" />
  </bindings>
  <limits maxBandwidth="4294967295" maxConnections="4294967295"
  connectionTimeout="00:02:00" />
  <logFile logExtFileFlags="Date, Time, ClientIP, UserName, ServerIP,
Method,
  UriStem, UriQuery, HttpStatus, Win32Status, ServerPort, UserAgent,
  HttpSubStatus" customLogPluginClsid="" logFormat="W3C"
  directory="F:\inetpub\logs\LogFiles" period="Daily"
  truncateSize="20971520" localTimeRollover="false" enabled="true" />
  <traceFailedRequestsLogging enabled="false"
  directory="F:\inetpub\logs\FailedReqLogFiles" maxLogFiles="50"
  maxLogFileSizeKB="512" customActionsEnabled="false" />
  <applicationDefaults path="" applicationPool="" enabledProtocols="http" />
  <virtualDirectoryDefaults path="" physicalPath="" userName="" password=""
  logonMethod="ClearText" allowSubDirConfig="true" />
  <application path="/" applicationPool="Shopping"
enabledProtocols="http">
    <virtualDirectoryDefaults path="" physicalPath="" userName="" password=""
    logonMethod="ClearText" allowSubDirConfig="true" />
    <virtualDirectory path="/" physicalPath="C:\inetpub\shopping"
    userName="DevTeam" password="RubberChickens" logonMethod="ClearText"
    allowSubDirConfig="true" />
  </application>
</site>
```

Creating Web Sites

With IIS 7.0, you can create both unsecured and secured Web sites. Previous versions of IIS require you to configure a Certificate Authority (CA) to issue a site certificate prior to setting up Secure Sockets Layer (SSL) on a secured Web site, but IIS 7.0 does not require this. IIS 7.0 includes the necessary management features to create and manage SSL certificates. In fact, in most configuration scenarios, a self-signed certificate is created for a server during setup of IIS 7.0. For more information on SSL, see Chapter 11, "Managing Active Directory Certificate Services and SSL."

Creating a Web Site: The Essentials

When you install IIS, the setup process creates a default Web site. In most cases, you aren't required to change any network options to allow users access to the default Web site. You simply tell users the URL path that they need to type into their browser's Address field. For example, if the DNS name for the computer is *www.microsoft.com* and the site is configured for access on port 80, a user can access the Web site by typing **http://www.microsoft.com/** in the browser's Address field.

For name resolution, you must ensure that DNS is updated to include the appropriate records. Specifically, you'll need to ensure that either an A (address) or a CNAME (canonical name) record is created on the appropriate DNS server. An *A* record maps a host name to an IP address. A *CNAME* records sets an alias for a host name. For example, using this record, zeta.microsoft.com can have an alias as www.microsoft.com. If zeta.microsoft.com also hosts service.microsoft.com and sales.microsoft.com, you'd need CNAME records for these also.

On IIS 7.0, all Web Sites run within an application pool context. The settings of the application pool determine the pipeline mode used for requests and the Microsoft .NET Framework version. By default, IIS Manager creates a new application pool for any new site you create. This application pool uses the current .NET Framework version and the default, integrated pipeline mode. When you create a site, you can either accept the new application pool or select an existing application pool to associate with the site. Generally, you'll want to associate a site with a new application pool only when you want a non-standard configuration. For example, if you want a site to run in classic pipeline mode and use an earlier version of the .NET Framework, you could create the required application pool and then create a new Web site that uses this application pool.

The directories and files for the default Web site are created under *%Windir%* \Inetpub\Wwwroot. To help organize additional Web sites into a common directory structure, you might want to create your new site under *%windir%*\Inetpub also. Before you do this, however, you should consider carefully whether the underlying disk structure can support the increased file I/O of the new site. With high-traffic, extremely busy sites, you may need to put each site on a physically separate disk.

By default, IIS uses pass-through authentication for accessing the underlying physical directories used by Web sites and applications. This means that for anonymous access, the Internet user account (IUSR_*ServerName*) is used to access the site's physical directory and that for authenticated access, the actual account name of the authenticated user is used to access the site's physical directory. Thus, permissions for the physical directory must be set accordingly. If you want to map a Web site to a shared folder by using a UNC path, such as \\CentralStorage83\Inetpub\Sales_site, you can do this also. Because the shared folder is on a different server, you might need to set specific user credentials to access the shared folder. IIS Manager allows you to do this.

Creating an Unsecured Web Site

Users access unsecured Web sites by using HTTP. You can create a Web site that uses HTTP by completing the following steps:

1. If you're creating the Web site on a new server, ensure that the World Wide Web Publishing Service has been installed and started on the server.

2. If you want the Web site to use a new IP address, you must configure the IP address on the server before installing the site.

3. In IIS Manager, double-click the icon for the computer you want to work with, and then right-click Sites. On the shortcut menu, choose Add Web Site. This displays the Add Web Site dialog box, shown in Figure 6-5.

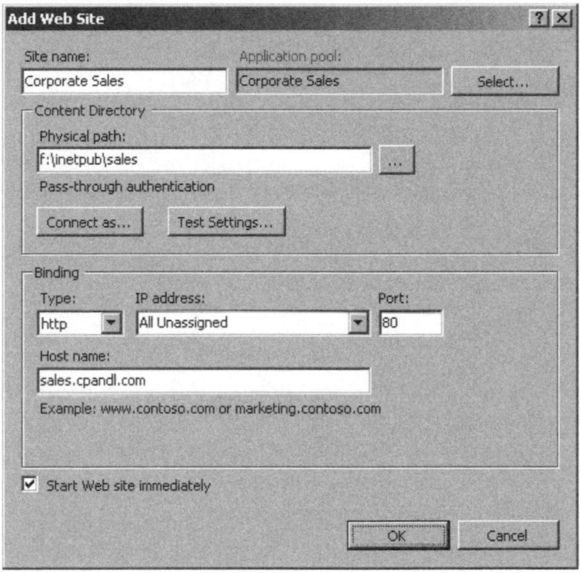

Figure 6-5   Create an unsecured Web site.

4. In the Web Site Name text box, type a descriptive name for the Web site, such as **Corporate Sales**. IIS Manager uses the name you provide to set the name of the new application pool to associate with the site. If you want to use an existing application pool instead of a new application pool, click Select. In the Select Application Pool dialog box, in the Application Pool drop-down list, select the application pool to associate with the site, and then click OK. Note that the .NET Framework version and pipeline mode of a selected application pool are listed on the Properties panel.

5. The Physical Path text box specifies the physical directory that contains the site's content. You can configure the physical path by using a local directory path or a shared folder. Keep the following in mind:

❑ To specify a local directory path for the site, click the selection button (...) to the right of the Physical Path text box. In the Browse For Folder dialog box, use the choices provided to select a directory for the Web site. This folder must be created before you can select it. If necessary, click Make New Folder to create the directory.

❑ To specify a shared folder for the site, type the desired UNC path in the appropriate text box, such as \\CentralStorage83\inetpub\sales_site. If you need to use alternate credentials to connect to the remote server specified in the UNC path, click Connect As. In the Connect As dialog box, choose Specific User, and then click Set. In the Set Credentials dialog box, type the name of the user account to use for authentication, type and confirm the account password, and then click OK.

Note   If you don't specify a user name and password, the user's Windows credentials are authenticated before allowing access. For an anonymous access site, IIS authenticates the credentials for the IUSR_*ServerName* account, so this account should have access to the shared folder. Otherwise, the network connection to the folder will fail. See the "Working with File and Folder Permissions" section in Chapter 10, "Managing Web Server Security," for more details on access permissions.

6. The Binding settings identify the Web site. To create an unsecured Web site, select HTTP as the type and then use the use the IP Address drop-down list to select an available IP address. Choose (All Unassigned) to allow HTTP to respond on all unassigned IP addresses that are configured on the server. Multiple Web sites can use the same IP address so long as the sites are configured to use different port numbers or host headers.

7. The TCP port for an unsecured Web site is assigned automatically as port 80. If necessary, type a new port number in the Port field. Multiple sites can use the same port as long as the sites are configured to use different IP addresses or host headers.

8. If you plan to use host headers for the site, type the host header name in the field provided. On a private network, the host header can be a computer name, such as EngIntranet. On a public network, the host header must be a DNS name, such as services.microsoft.com. The host header name must be unique within IIS.

9. By default, IIS starts the Web site immediately so long as the bindings you've supplied are unique. If you don't want to start the site immediately, clear the Start Web Site Immediately check box. In most cases, you'll want to finish setting the site's properties before you start the site and make it accessible to users.

By using the IIS Command-line Administration Tool, you can run the Add Site command to add an HTTP site to a server. Sample 6-1 provides the syntax and usage. Technically, bindings and physicalPath are optional, but a site won't work until these parameters are provided. Adding the physical path is what allows IIS to create the root virtual directory and root application for the site.

Sample 6-1   Adding an HTTP Site Syntax and Usage

Syntax
```
appcmd add site /name:Name /id:ID /bindings:http://UrlAndPort
/physicalPath:Path
```
Usage
```
appcmd add site /name:'Sales Site' /id:5 /bindings:
http://sales.adatum.com:80

appcmd add site /name:'Sales Site' /id:5 /bindings:http://*:8080

appcmd add site /name:'Sales Site' /id:5 /bindings:http/*:8080
/physicalPath:'c:\inetpub\mynewsite'
```

Creating a Secured Web Site

Users access secured Web sites by using SSL and HTTPS. Prior to creating a secured Web site, you must ensure that the certificate you want to use is available. You can create certificates as discussed in Chapter 11. You can create a Web site that uses HTTPS by completing the following steps:

1. Follow Steps 1–5 in the section "Creating an Unsecured Web Site," earlier in this chapter.

2. As shown in Figure 6-6, the Binding settings identify the Web site. To create a secured Web site, select HTTPS as the type, and then in the IP Address drop-down list, select an available IP address. Choose (All Unassigned) to allow HTTPS to respond on all unassigned IP addresses that are configured on the server. Multiple Web sites can use the same IP address as long as the sites are configured to use different port numbers or host headers.

3. The TCP port for a secured Web site is assigned automatically as port 443. If necessary, type a new port number in the Port field. Multiple sites can use the same port as long as the sites are configured to use different IP addresses or host headers.

4. Use the SSL Certificate drop-down list to select an available certificate to use for secure communications. After you select a certificate, click View to view details about the certificate.

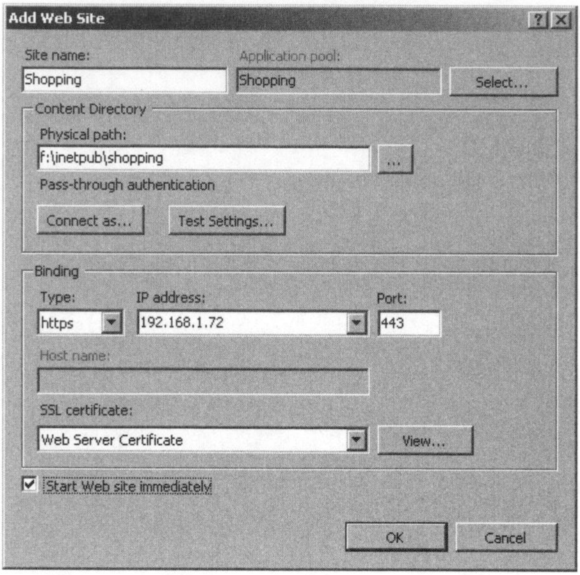

Figure 6-6   Create a secured Web site.

5. By default, IIS starts the Web site immediately as long as the bindings you've supplied are unique. If you don't want to start the site immediately, clear the Start Web Site Immediately check box. In most cases, you'll want to finish setting the site's properties before you start the site and make it accessible to users.

By using the IIS Command-line Administration Tool, you can run the Add Site command to add an HTTPS site to a server. Sample 6-2 provides the syntax and usage. As with unsecured sites, the bindings and physicalPath are optional, but a site won't work until these parameters are provided. Adding the physical path is what allows IIS to create the root virtual directory and root application for the site.

Sample 6-2   Adding an HTTPS Site Syntax and Usage

Syntax
```
appcmd add site /name:Name /id:ID /bindings:https://UrlAndPort
/physicalPath:Path
```
Usage
```
appcmd add site /name:'WWW Shopping Site' /id:6
/bindings:https://store.adatum.com:443

appcmd add site /name:'WWW Shopping Site' /id:6
/bindings:https://*:443

appcmd add site /name:'WWW Shopping Site' /id:6
/bindings:https://*:443 /physicalPath:'c:\inetpub\wwwstore'
```

Managing Web Sites and Their Properties

The sections that follow examine key tasks for managing Web sites and their properties. You configure Web site properties by using IIS Manager and the IIS Command-line Administration tool.

Working with Sites in IIS Manager

When you navigate to the Sites node in IIS Manager and select a site, the Actions pane displays a list of unique actions related to sites as shown in Figure 6-7. You can use the options in the Actions pane as follows:

- **Explore**   Opens the site's root directory in Windows Explorer. You can use this option to access the site's Web.config file or to manage the site's physical directories and content files.

- **Edit Permissions**   Opens the Properties dialog box for the site's root directory. By using the Properties dialog box, you can configure general settings, sharing, and security.

- **Edit Site**   Provides Bindings and Basic Settings options. The Bindings option allows you to view and manage the site's bindings. Basic Settings allows you to view and manage the site's application pool and physical path.

- **Manage Web Site**   Provides Start, Stop, and Restart options. These options allow you to manage the site's run state. A stopped site cannot be accessed by users.

- **Browse Web Site**   Provides Browse and View options for the site. The Browse options allow you to test the configuration of a specific binding. When you click a Browse link, IIS Manager starts the default browser and connects to the site using the related binding. View Applications displays a page that allows you to view and manage the site's applications. View Virtual Directories displays a page that allows you to view and manage the site's virtual directories.

- **Configure**   Provides Failed Request Tracing and Limits options. You can use Failed Request Tracing to trace failed requests through the IIS core. You can use Limits to control incoming connections to the Web site.

- **Help**   Displays the IIS Manager help documentation. Because the Help window is displayed on top of the IIS Manager window, you must minimize or close the Help window before you can return to IIS Manager.

Figure 6-7 Working with sites.

Right-clicking a site's node in the left pane displays a shortcut menu with similar, though slightly different, options. The Add Application option allows you to add an application to the site. The Add Virtual Directory option allows you to add a virtual directory to the site. Two additional options that are important are Switch To Content View and Switch To Features View. You can use these options to switch between the following views:

- **Content view** Shows the file contents of the physical directory related to a selected site, application, or virtual directory

- **Features view** Shows the managed features related to a selected site, application, or virtual directory

You can switch between the Content and Features view by right-clicking the site node and then selecting Switch To Content View or Switch To Feature View as appropriate.

You can use the shortcut menu to rename a Web site by right-clicking the site node and then selecting Rename. Next, edit the name of the site as necessary, and then press Enter.

When you right-click the site node and then point to Manage Web Site, you'll see an additional shortcut menu with these options:

- **Restart** Stops and then starts the site. If you suspect that IIS is not processing requests for a site appropriately, restarting the site can in some cases resolve this.

- **Start**   Starts a site if it is not running. A site can accept incoming requests only when it is started.

- **Stop**   Stops a site if it is running. A site cannot accept or process requests when it is stopped.

- **Browse**   Starts the default browser and connects to the site by using the default binding.

- **Advanced Settings**   Displays all the settings for a site in a single dialog box, allowing you to manage all settings except the site name and its bindings.

By using the IIS Command-line Administration Tool, you can start or stop a site by running the Start Site and Stop Site commands respectively. Samples 6-3 and 6-4 provide the syntax and usage.

Sample 6-3   Start Site Syntax and Usage

Syntax
```
appcmd start site [/site.name:]SiteNameOrURL
```
Usage
```
appcmd start site "Default Web Site"
```

Sample 6-4   Stop Site Syntax and Usage

Syntax
```
appcmd stop site [/site.name:]SiteNameOrURL
```
Usage
```
appcmd stop site "Default Web Site"
```

Configuring a Site's Application Pool and Home Directory

Each Web site on a server has an application pool and home directory. The application pool determines the request mode and .NET Framework version that IIS loads into the site's worker process. The home directory is the base directory for all documents that the site publishes. It contains a home page that links to other pages in your site. The home directory is mapped to your site's domain name or to the server name. For example, if the site's DNS name is *www.microsoft.com* and the home directory is C:\Inetpub\Wwwroot, browsers use the URL *http://www.microsoft.com/* to access files in the home directory. On an intranet, the server name can be used to access documents in the home directory. For example, if the server name is CorpIntranet, browsers use the URL *http://CorpIntranet/* to access files in the home directory.

You can view or change a site's home directory by completing the following steps:

1. In IIS Manager, navigate to the Sites node by double-clicking icon for the computer you want to work with and then double-clicking Sites.

2.   In the left pane, select the node for the site you want to work with.

3.   In the Actions pane, click Basic Settings. This displays the Edit Web Site dialog box, as shown in Figure 6-8.

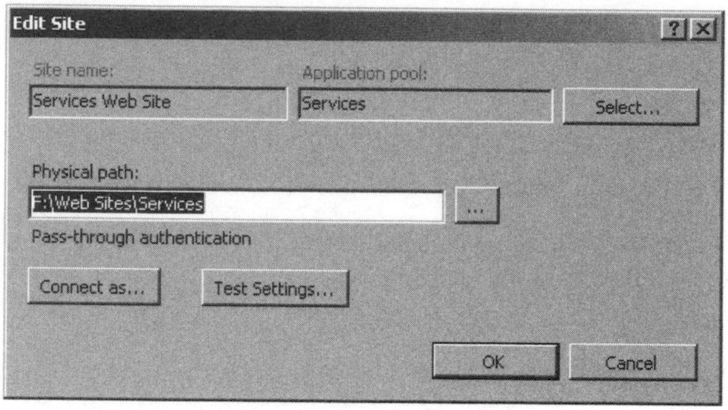

Figure 6-8   You can change a site's home directory at any time.

4.   The Application Pool text box lists the application pool currently associated with the site. To choose a different application pool, click Select. In the Select Application Pool dialog box, in the Application Pool drop-down list, select the application pool to associate with the site, and then click OK.

5.   If the directory you want to use is on the local computer, type the directory path, such as **C:\Inetpub\Wwwroot**, in the Physical Path text box. To browse for the folder, click the selection button to the right of the Physical Path text box. In the Browse For Folder dialog box, use the settings to select a directory for the Web site. This folder must be created before you can select it. If necessary, click Make New Folder in the Browse For Folder dialog box to create the directory.

6.   If the directory you want to use is on another computer and is accessible as a shared folder, type the desired UNC path, such as **\\WebServer22\CorpWWW**, in the Physical Path text box. If you need to use alternate credentials to connect to the remote server specified in the UNC path, click Connect As. In the Connect As dialog box, choose Specific User, and then click Set. In the Set Credentials dialog box, type the name of the user account to use for authentication, type and confirm the account password, and then click OK.

> **Caution**   Be careful when setting alternate pass-through credentials. The account you use should not have any additional privileges beyond those required to access content via the Web site. If necessary, you may want to create a new restricted account for this purpose.

7.   Click OK to close the Edit Web Site dialog box.

You cannot use the IIS Command-line Administration Tool to configure a site's application pool and home directory in the same way. Whereas IIS Manager maps these changes to the application pool and base virtual directory associated with the site, the IIS Command-line Administration tool does not, and you must edit the application pool and virtual directory settings to make the necessary changes.

Configuring Ports, IP Addresses, and Host Names Used by Web Sites

Throughout this chapter, I've discussed techniques you can use to configure multiple Web sites on a single server. The focus of the discussion has been on configuring unique identities for each site. In some instances, you might want a single Web site to have multiple domain names associated with it. A Web site with multiple domain names publishes the same content for different sets of users. For example, your company might have registered *example.com*, *example.org*, and *example.net* with a domain registrar to protect your company or domain name. Rather than publishing the same content to each of these sites separately, you can publish the content to a single site that accepts requests for each of these identities.

The rules regarding unique combinations of ports, IP addresses, and host names still apply to sites with multiple identities. This means that each identity for a site must be unique. You accomplish this by assigning each identity unique IP address, port, or host header name combinations.

> **Note**   When you've installed additional Windows Process Activation Service support components, you may find that IIS allows you to create non-HTTP binding types, including net.tcp, net.pipe, net.msmq, and msmq.formatname. These additional binding types are used to support process activation over Transmission Control Protocol (TCP), named pipes, and Microsoft Message Queuing (MSMQ). These binding types accept a single parameter: the binding information that includes the network address to listen for requests on. See the "Role Services for Application Servers" section of Chapter 2, "Deploying IIS 7.0 in the Enterprise," for more information on non-HTTP process activation.

To change the binding of a Web site, complete the following steps:

1. If you want the Web site to respond to a specific IP address, you must configure the IP address before updating the site.

2. In IIS Manager, navigate to the Sites node by double-clicking the icon for the computer you want to work with and then double-clicking Sites.

3. In the left pane, select the node for the site you want to work with.

4. In the Actions pane, click Bindings. This displays the Site Bindings dialog box, as shown in Figure 6-9.

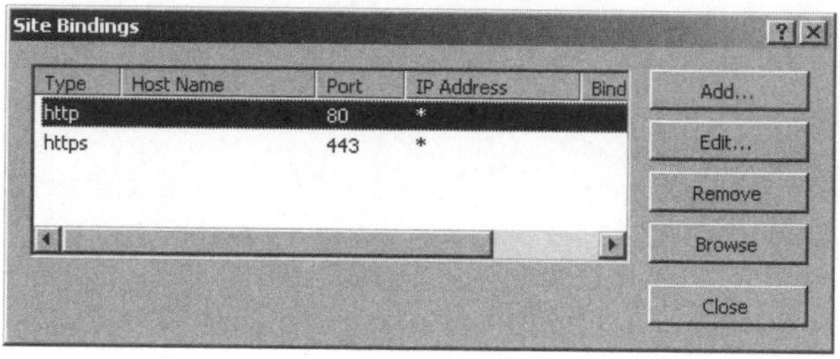

Figure 6-9   You modify a site's identity through the Site Bindings dialog box.

5. Use the Site Bindings dialog box to manage the site's binding by using the following settings:

   ❑ **Add**   Adds a new identity. To add a new identity, click Add. In the Add Site Binding dialog box, select the binding type, IP address, and TCP port to use. Optionally, type a host header name or select an SSL certificate as appropriate for the binding type. Click OK when you're finished.

   ❑ **Edit**   Allows you to edit the currently selected identity. To edit an identity, click the identity, and then click Edit. In the Edit Site Binding dialog box, select an IP address and TCP port to use. Optionally, type a host header name or select an SSL certificate as appropriate for the binding type. Click OK when you're finished.

   ❑ **Remove**   Allows you to remove the currently selected identity. To remove an identity, click the identity, and then click Remove. When prompted to confirm, click Yes.

   ❑ **Browse**   Allows you to test an identity. To test an identity, click the identity, and then click Browse. IIS Manager will then open a browser window and connect to the selected binding.

6. When you are finished working with bindings, click Close to close the Site Bindings dialog box.

By using the IIS Command-line Administration Tool, you can add, change or remove bindings by running the Set Site command. Samples 6-5 to 6-7 provide the syntax and usage. When working with the Set Site command, note that you must use the exact syntax shown. Unlike other commands in which you can omit quotes or use double-quotes, you must use single quotes where indicated. Additionally, because you are referencing into the bindings collection, the brackets ([]) in the syntax and usage examples are literal values rather than indicators of optional values. You must use the brackets to indicate that you are referencing into the bindings collection.

Caution   Failure to use the exact syntax expected with the bindings collections can result in the Web site becoming unstable. For example, improper use of quotes could cause AppCmd to create the site binding with quotes as part of the binding name. If this happens, the best way to correct the problem is to remove the binding and then add it again. Because you cannot remove the last binding associated with a site, you may need to create another binding and then remove the improperly formatted binding.

Sample 6-5   Adding Site Bindings Syntax and Usage

Syntax
```
appcmd set site /site.name:'Name'
/+bindings.[protocol='ProtocolType',
bindingInformation='IPAddress:Port:HostHeader']
```
Usage
```
appcmd set site /site.name:'WWW Shopping Site'
/+bindings.[protocol='https', bindingInformation='*:443:']
```

Sample 6-6   Changing Site Bindings Syntax and Usage

Syntax
```
appcmd set site /site.name:Name /bindings.[protocol='ProtocolType',
bindingInformation='OldBindingInfo'].bindingInformation:NewBindingInfo
```
Usage
```
appcmd set site /site.name: 'WWW Shopping Site'
/bindings.[protocol='https',
bindingInformation='*:443:'].bindingInformation:*:443:
shopping.cpandl.com
```

Sample 6-7   Removing Site Bindings Syntax and Usage

Syntax
```
appcmd set site /site.name:Name /-bindings.[protocol='ProtocolType',
bindingInformation='BindingInfo']
```
Usage
```
appcmd set site /site.name:'WWW Shopping Site'
/-bindings.[protocol='https', bindingInformation='*:443:']
```

Restricting Incoming Connections and Setting Time-Out Values

You can control incoming connections to a Web site in several ways. You can:

- Set a limit on the amount of traffic allowed to a Web site based on bandwidth usage.

- Set a limit on the number of simultaneous connections.

- Set a connection time-out value to ensure that inactive connections are disconnected.

Normally, Web sites have no bandwidth or connection limits, and this is an optimal setting in most environments. However, high bandwidth usage or a large number of connections can cause the Web site to slow down—sometimes so severely that nobody can access the site. To avoid this situation, you might want to limit the total bandwidth usage, the number of simultaneous connections, or both. When using limits, keep the following in mind:

- Once a bandwidth limit is reached, no additional bandwidth will be available to service new or existing requests. This means that the server would not be able to process new requests for both existing clients and new clients. One reason to set a bandwidth limit is when you have multiple sites sharing the same limited bandwidth connection and these sites are equally important. Keep in mind that most network connections are measured in *bits*, but you set the bandwidth limit in *bytes*.

- Once a connection limit is reached, no other clients are permitted to access the server. New clients must wait until the connection load on the server decreases; however, currently connected users are allowed to continue browsing the site. One reason to set a connection limit is to prevent a single Web site from overloading the resources of an entire server.

The connection time-out value determines when idle user sessions are disconnected. With the default Web site, sessions time out after they've been idle for 120 seconds (2 minutes). This prevents connections from remaining open indefinitely if browsers don't close them correctly.

You can modify a site's limits and time-outs by completing the following steps:

1. In IIS Manager, navigate to the Sites node by double-clicking the icon for the computer you want to work with and then double-clicking Sites.

2. In the left pane, select the node for the site you want to work with.

3. In the Actions pane, click Limits. You'll find Limits under Configure in the lower portion of the Actions pane. Clicking Limits displays the Edit Web Site Limits dialog box, as shown in Figure 6-10.

4. The Limit Bandwidth Usage check box controls bandwidth limits. To remove a bandwidth limit, clear this check box. To set a bandwidth limit, select this check box, and then type a limit in bytes.

5. The Connection Timeout field controls the connection time-out. Type a new value to change the current time-out setting.

6. The Limit Number Of Connections check box controls connection limits. To remove connection limits, clear this check box. To set a connection limit, select this check box, type a limit, and then click OK.

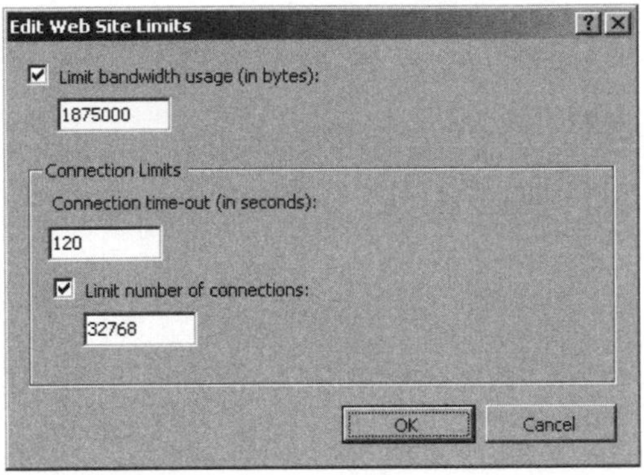

Figure 6-10   You modify a site's limits through the Edit Web Site Limits dialog box.

By using the IIS Command-line Administration Tool, you can run the Set Site command to set and remove limits for a site. Samples 6-8 and 6-9 provide the syntax and usage. Note that time-out values are set in the hh:mm:ss format in which the h position is for hours, the m position is for minutes, and the s position is for seconds. If you remove limits, the default values, such as 120 seconds for connection time-outs, are restored.

Sample 6-8   Setting Site Limits Syntax and Usage

Syntax

```
appcmd set site /site.name:Name [/limits.maxBandwidth:Bandwidth]
[/limits.maxConnections:MaxConnections]
[/limits.connectionTimeout:TimeOut]
```

Usage

```
appcmd set site /site.name:'WWW Shopping Site'
/limits.maxConnections:32768

appcmd set site /site.name:'WWW Shopping Site'
/limits.connectionTimeout:'00:01:30'
```

Sample 6-9   Removing Site Limits Syntax and Usage

Syntax

```
appcmd set site /site.name:Name [/-limits.maxBandwidth]
[/-limits.maxConnections] [/-limits.connectionTimeout]
```

Usage

```
appcmd set site /site.name:'WWW Shopping Site'
/-limits.maxConnections
```

Configuring HTTP Keep-Alives

The original design of HTTP opened a new connection for every file retrieved from a Web server. Because a connection isn't maintained, no system resources are used after the transaction is completed. The drawback to this design is that when the same client requests additional data, the connection must be reestablished, and this means additional traffic and delays.

Consider a standard Web page that contains a main HTML document and 10 images. With standard HTTP, a Web client requests each file through a separate connection. The client connects to the server, requests the document file, gets a response, and then disconnects. The client repeats this process for each image file in the document.

Web servers compliant with HTTP 1.1 support a feature called *HTTP Keep-Alives*. With this feature enabled as per the default configuration in IIS 7.0, clients maintain an open connection with the Web server rather than reopening a connection with each request. HTTP keep-alives are enabled by default when you create a new Web site. In most situations clients will see greatly improved performance with HTTP keep-alives enabled. Keep in mind, however, that maintaining connections requires system resources. The more open connections there are, the more system resources are used. To prevent a busy server from getting bogged down by a large number of open connections, you might want to limit the number of connections, reduce the connection time-out for client sessions, or both. For more information on managing connections, see the "Restricting Incoming Connections and Setting Time-Out Values" section earlier in this chapter.

To enable or disable HTTP keep-alives, follow these steps:

1. In IIS Manager, navigate to the level of the configuration hierarchy you want to manage. You can manage HTTP keep-alives for an entire server at the server level. You can manage HTTP keep-alives for a specific site at the site level.

2. When you group by area, the HTTP Response feature is listed under IIS. Double-click the HTTP Response feature.

3. In the Actions Pane, click Set Common Headers. This displays the Set Common HTTP Response Headers dialog box as shown in Figure 6-11.

4. Select Enable HTTP Keep-Alives to enable HTTP keep-alives. Clear this check box to disable HTTP keep-alives. Then click OK.

By using the IIS Command-line Administration Tool, you can run the Set Config command to enable or disable HTTP keep-alives. Sample 6-10 provides the syntax and usage. If you don't specify a site name, you will enable or disable HTTP keep-alives for the entire server.

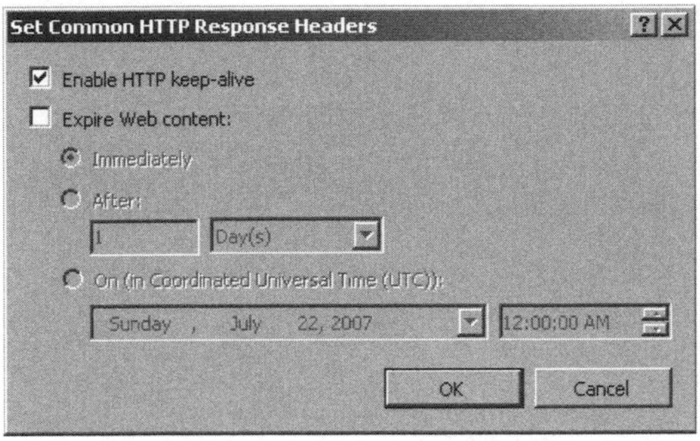

Set Common HTTP Response Headers

☑ Enable HTTP keep-alive
☐ Expire Web content:
   ⦿ Immediately
   ○ After:
       1 Day(s)
   ○ On (in Coordinated Universal Time (UTC)):
       Sunday , July 22, 2007   12:00:00 AM

OK   Cancel

Figure 6-11   Enable or disable HTTP keep-alives.

Sample 6-10   Enabling and Disabling HTTP Keep-Alives Syntax and Usage

Syntax
```
appcmd set config [SiteName] /section:httpProtocol
/allowKeepAlive:[true|false]
```
Usage
```
appcmd set config 'WWW Shopping Site' /section:httpProtocol
/allowKeepAlive:true

appcmd add site /name:'WWW Shopping Site' /id:6 /bindings:
https://*:443

appcmd add site /name:'WWW Shopping Site' /id:6 /bindings:
https://*:443 /physicalPath:'c:\inetpub\wwwstore'
```

Configuring Access Permissions in IIS Manager

In earlier releases of IIS, you configured access permissions for sites and virtual directories. In IIS 7.0, general access permissions are set through the access policy you've configured for the server's managed handlers as discussed in the "Controlling Managed Handlers through the Configuration Files" section of Chapter 5, "Managing Global IIS Configuration." From a perspective of content access, the standard types of access grant the following permissions:

- **Read**   Allows users to read documents, such as Hypertext Markup Language (HTML) files

- **Script**   Allows users to run scripts, such as ASP files or Perl scripts

- **Execute**   Allows users to execute programs, such as ISAPI applications or CGI executable files

You can configure access permissions by completing the following steps:

1. In IIS Manager, navigate to the level of the configuration hierarchy you want to manage. You can manage access permissions for an entire server at the server level. You can manage access permissions for a specific site at the site level.

2. When you group by area, the Handler Mappings feature is listed under IIS. Double-click the Handler Mappings feature.

3. In the Actions Pane, click Edit Feature Permissions.

4. In the Edit Feature Permissions dialog box, shown in Figure 6-12, select or clear permissions as appropriate, and then click OK to apply the settings.

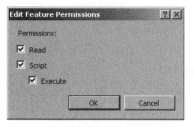

Figure 6-12   Set handler permissions for Web content.

Managing a Site's Numeric Identifier and AutoStart State

Every Web site has an associated numeric identifier and AutoStart state. IIS uses the numeric identifier for internally tracking the site, and you'll find it referenced in log files and trace files. IIS assigns the ID automatically when sites are created. Typically, the default Web site has an ID of 1, the second site created on a server has an ID of 2, and so on.

IIS uses the AutoStart state to determine whether to start the site automatically when the World Wide Web service is started. If the AutoStart state is set to True, IIS starts the site when the World Wide Web service is started. If the AutoStart state is set to False, IIS does not start the site when the World Wide Web service is started, so you must manually start the site.

You can configure a site's ID and AutoStart state by completing the following steps:

1. In IIS Manager, navigate to the Sites node by double-clicking the icon for the computer you want to work with and then double-clicking Sites.

2. In the left pane, select the node for the site you want to work with.

3. In the Actions pane, click Advanced Settings. You'll find Advanced Settings under Browse Web Site in the middle of the Actions pane. Clicking Advanced Settings displays the Advanced Settings dialog box, as shown in Figure 6-13.

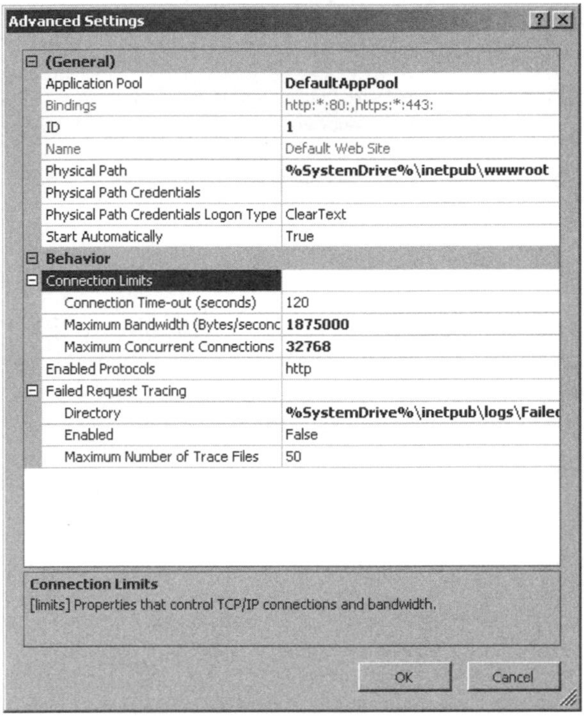

Figure 6-13   You modify a site's ID number and AutoStart state through the Advanced Settings dialog box.

4. ID lists the site's current ID number. To change the ID number, click in the column to the right and then type the desired ID number. The ID number you type cannot be in use already.

5. The Start Automatically item lists the site's current AutoStart state. To change the AutoStart state, click in the column to the right, and then in the selection list that appears, choose either True or False.

6. Click OK to save your settings. Changing the AutoStart state does not change the current run state of the site.

By using the IIS Command-line Administration Tool, you can change a site's ID number and AutoStart state by running the Set Site command. Sample 6-11 provides the syntax and usage. AppCmd will generate an error if you type an ID number that is already in use. In this case, you will need to choose a different ID number.

Sample 6-11   Set Site Syntax and Usage

Syntax
```
appcmd set site [/site.name:]SiteNameOrURL
[/serverAutoStart:true|false] [/id:Number]
```
Usage
```
appcmd set site "Default Web Site" /serverAutoStart:false /id:5
```

Deleting Sites

If you no longer need a site, you can delete the site by using IIS Manager or the IIS Command-line Administration tool. Deleting a site permanently removes the site configuration information from the IIS configuration files. This means that the site's configuration details, including any applications and virtual directories, are removed permanently. Deleting a site does not, however, delete the site's physical directories or content files. If you want to delete the physical directories or content files, you'll need to do this manually by using Windows Explorer.

> **Tip**   Rather than permanently deleting a site that you may need in the future, you may want to stop the site and then configure the site's AutoStart state to False as discussed in the "Managing a Site's Numeric Identifier and AutoStart State" section earlier in this chapter. This allows you to use the site in the future if necessary.

You can remove a site permanently by completing the following steps:

1. In IIS Manager, navigate to the Sites node by double-clicking the icon for the computer you want to work with and then double-clicking Sites.

2. In the left pane, right-click the node for the site you want to delete, and then select Remove.

3. When prompted to confirm the action, click Yes.

By using the IIS Command-line Administration Tool, you can remove a site by running the Delete Site command. Sample 6-12 provides the syntax and usage.

Sample 6-12   Delete Site Syntax and Usage

Syntax
```
appcmd delete [/site.name:]site SiteNameOrURL
```
Usage
```
appcmd delete site "Default Web Site"
```

Creating Directories

The directory structure of IIS is based primarily on the Windows Server file system, but it also provides additional functionality and flexibility. Understanding these complexities is critical to successfully managing IIS Web sites.

Understanding Physical and Virtual Directory Structures

Earlier in this chapter, I discussed home directories and how they were used. Beyond home directories, Microsoft Web sites also use the following:

- Physical directories
- Virtual directories

The difference between physical and virtual directories is important. A *physical* directory is part of the file system, and to be available through IIS, it must exist as a subdirectory within the home directory. A *virtual* directory is a directory that isn't necessarily contained in the home directory but is available to clients through an alias. Physical directories and virtual directories are configured and managed through the IIS Manager, but they're displayed differently. Physical directories are indicated with a standard folder icon. Virtual directories are indicated by a folder icon with a globe in the corner.

Both physical and virtual directories have permissions and properties that you can set at the operating system level and the IIS level. You set operating system permissions and properties in Windows Explorer–related dialog boxes. You set IIS permissions and properties in IIS Manager.

You create physical directories by creating subdirectories within the home directory by using Windows Explorer. You access these subdirectories by appending the directory name to the DNS name for the Web site. For example, you create a Web site with the DNS name *products.microsoft.com*. Users are able to access the Web site by using the URL *http://www.microsoft.com/*. You then create a subdirectory within the home directory called "search." Users are able to access the subdirectory by using the URL path *http://www.microsoft.com/search/*.

Even though locating your content files and directories within the home directory makes it easier to manage a Web site, you can also use virtual directories. Virtual directories act as pointers to directories that aren't located in the home directory. You access virtual directories by appending the directory alias to the DNS name for the site. If, for example, your home directory is D:\Inetpub\Wwwroot, and you store Microsoft Office Word documents in E:\Worddocs, you would need to create a virtual directory that points to the actual directory location. If the alias is *docs* for the E:\Worddocs directory, visitors to the *www.microsoft.com* Web site could access the directory by using the URL path *http://www.microsoft.com/docs/*.

Examining Virtual Directory Configuration

All virtual directories are associated with either a site's root application or a specific application. In IIS Manager, you can view a list of the virtual directories associated with a site's root application by selecting the site in the left pane and then under Actions, clicking View Virtual Directories. In IIS Manager, you can view a list of the virtual directories associated with a specific application by selecting the application in the left pane and then under Actions, clicking View Virtual Directories.

By using the IIS Command-line Administration Tool, you can list the existing virtual directories for an application by running the List Vdir command. Type **appcmd list vdir** at a command prompt to list all the virtual directories configured for any and all applications on a server. This listing will include the root virtual directories of all sites and applications configured on the server because these are created as virtual directories. The names of root virtual directories for sites and applications end in a slash. The names of virtual directories that are not mapped to sites and applications do not end in a slash.

You can list details about virtual directories according to the applications with which they are associated, as shown in these examples:

```
appcmd list vdir "Default Web Site/"
```

```
appcmd list vdir http://localhost/Sales
```

```
appcmd list vdir /app.name:"Default Web Site/Sales"
```

You'll then see a summary entry related to the virtual directory configuration, such as:

```
VDIR "Default Web Site/" (physicalPath:%SystemDrive%\inetpub\wwwroot)
```

You can also list details about virtual directories according to their virtual paths, as shown in this example:

```
appcmd list vdir /path:/Store
```

You'll then see a summary entry related to the virtual directory configuration, such as:

```
VDIR "Default Web Site/Store" (physicalPath:C:\store)
```

These details include the name of the virtual directory and the physical path of the virtual directory.

You can view the full configuration details for a virtual directory by using the /config parameter, such as:

```
appcmd list vdir "Default Web Site/" /config
```

You'll then see a full listing of the configuration details for the virtual directory, such as:

```
<virtualDirectory path="/" physicalPath="C:\inetpub\shopping"
userName="DevTeam" password="RubberChickens" />
```

The full details do not include any inherited settings. To view the full configuration details for a site, including inherited values, you must use the following syntax:

```
appcmd list vdir "VdirName" /config:*
```

Here is an example:

```
appcmd list vdir "Default Web Site/" /config:*
```

You'll then see a full listing of the configuration details that includes inherited values, such as:

```
<virtualDirectory path="/" physicalPath="C:\inetpub\shopping"
userName="DevTeam" password="RubberChickens" logonMethod="ClearText"
allowSubDirConfig="true" />
```

Creating Physical Directories

Within the home directory, you can create subdirectories to help organize your site's documents. You can create subdirectories within the home directory by completing the following steps:

1. In Windows Explorer, navigate to the home directory for the Web site.

2. In the Contents pane, right-click a blank area and then, on the shortcut menu, select New and then select Folder. A new folder is added to the Contents pane. The default name, New Folder, appears in the folder name area and is selected for editing.

3. Edit the name of the folder, and then press Enter. The best directory names are short but descriptive, such as Images, WordDocs, or Downloads.

> **Tip**   If possible, avoid using spaces as part of IIS directory names. Officially, spaces are illegal characters in URLs and must be replaced with an escape code. The escape code for a space is %20. Although most current browsers will replace spaces with %20 for you, earlier versions of browsers might not, so those versions won't be able to access the page.

4. The new folder inherits the default file permissions of the home directory and the default IIS permissions of the Web site. For details on viewing or changing permissions, see Chapter 10.

> **Tip**   IIS Manager doesn't display new folders automatically. You might need to click the Refresh button on the toolbar (or press F5) to display the folder.

Creating Virtual Directories

As stated previously, a virtual directory is a directory available to Internet users through an alias for an actual physical directory. In previous versions of IIS, you had to create the physical directory prior to assigning the virtual directory alias. In IIS 7.0, you can create the physical directory if one is needed when you create the virtual directory.

To create a virtual directory, follow these steps:

1. In IIS Manager, navigate to the level of the configuration hierarchy where you want to create the virtual directory. You can add a virtual directory to the site's root application by selecting the site's node. You can add a virtual directory to another application by selecting the application's node.

2. In the Actions pane, click View Virtual Directories. In the main pane, you'll see a list of the site's existing virtual directories (if any).

3. In the Actions pane, click Add Virtual Directory. This displays the Add Virtual Directory dialog box, shown in Figure 6-14.

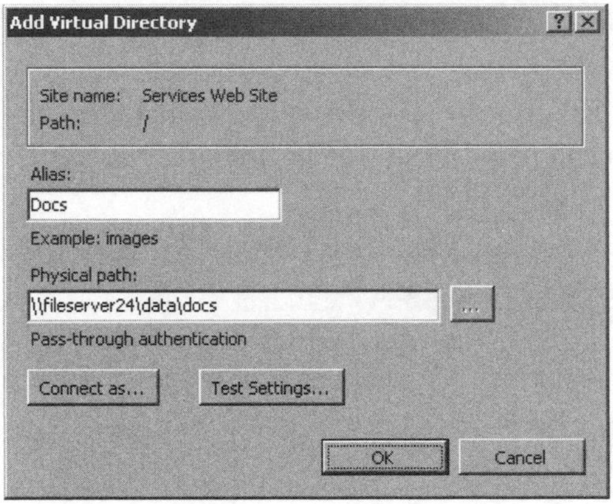

Figure 6-14   Create a virtual directory.

4. In the Alias text box, type the name you want to use to access the virtual directory. As with directory names, the best alias names are short but descriptive.

5. In the Physical Path text box, type the path to the physical directory where your content is stored, or click the selection button to the right of the Physical Path text box to search for a directory. The directory must be created before you can select it. If necessary, click Make New Folder in the Browse For Folder dialog box to create the directory before you select it. However, don't forget about checking and setting permissions at the operating system level as discussed in Chapter 10.

6. If you need to use alternate credentials to connect to the remote server specified in a UNC path, click Connect As. In the Connect As dialog box, choose Specific User, and then click Set. In the Set Credentials dialog box, type the name of the user account to use for authentication, type and confirm the account password, and then click OK.

7. Click OK to create the virtual directory.

Tip   When you set logon credentials for a virtual directory, the account name you provide must exist. By default, IIS Manager sets the logon type to ClearText. This means that IIS will use clear text when acquiring the user token necessary to access the physical path. Because IIS passes the logon user call over the back end on an internal network, using a clear-text call typically is sufficient. By editing a virtual directory's properties, you also have the option to set the logon type to Interactive, Batch, or Network. See the "Changing Virtual Directory Paths, Logon Methods, and More" section later in this chapter for more information.

By using the IIS Command-line Administration Tool, you can create virtual directories by running the Add Vdir command. Sample 6-13 provides the syntax and usage. Remember that the physical directory you point to must already exist.

Sample 6-13   Add Vdir Syntax and Usage

Syntax
```
appcmd add vdir /app.name:"ParentAppName" /path: "VirtualPath"
[/physicalPath: "Path"] [/logonMethod:Method] [/userName:User]
[/password:Password]
```
Usage
```
appcmd add vdir /app.name:"Default Web Site/" /path:"/Support" /
physicalPath:"c:\support"

appcmd add vdir /app.name:"Sales Site/" /path:"/Invoices"
/physicalPath:"c:\salesroot\invoices" /logonMethod:ClearText
/userName:SupportUser /password:RainyDayz
```

Managing Directories and Their Properties

When you navigate to a site node in IIS Manager and select a directory, the Actions pane displays a list of unique actions related to directories. With physical directories, denoted by a folder icon, the options allow you to explore the directory in Windows Explorer and edit permissions through the directory's Properties dialog box. You can also browse the folder in the default browser to test the configuration of a specific binding with regard to the selected physical directory. With virtual directories, denoted by a shortcut folder icon, you have additional options for editing a directory's basic and advanced settings. Basic settings allow you to view and manage a directory's physical path and connection credentials. Advanced settings allow you to view and manage a directory's physical path, connection credentials, and logon type.

Enabling or Disabling Directory Browsing

Unlike IIS 6, IIS 7.0 does not have a specific Browse policy that allows users to view a list of files if they enter the name of a valid directory that doesn't have a default file. Instead, you control whether directory browsing is allowed by using the Directory Browsing module. If you want users to be able to browse site directories, you must install, enable, and then configure the Directory Browsing module. Because you typically don't want users to be able to browse every directory on every site hosted on a server, you must be careful when using the Directory Browsing module. Specifically, you'll want to ensure that you enable this module only where necessary and appropriate. For example, if you want users to be able to browse a specific virtual directory, you can enable the module for this virtual directory but disable it elsewhere.

Note Keep in mind that these access permissions act as a layer on top of the server's file access permissions. You set file access permissions at the operating system level as discussed in the "Working with File and Folder Permissions" section of Chapter 10.

Once you've installed the Directory Browsing module, you can enable and configure directory browsing by completing these steps:

1. In IIS Manager, navigate to the level of the configuration hierarchy you want to manage. You can manage directory browsing for an entire server at the server level. You can manage directory browsing for a specific site at the site level.

2. When you group by area, the Directory Browsing feature is listed under IIS. Double-click the Directory Browsing feature.

3. If directory browsing is disabled, you can enable this feature by clicking Enable in the Actions pane.

4. Once directory browsing is enabled, you can use the check boxes to specify the information that IIS displays in a directory listing. The available check boxes are:

   ❑ **Time**. Lists the last modified time for each file

   ❑ **Size**. Lists the size of each file

   ❑ **Extension**. Lists the file extension along with the file name

   ❑ **Date**. Lists the last modified date for each file

   ❑ **Long Date**. Lists the last modified date for each file in extended format

5. Click Apply to save and apply your changes.

You can disable directory browsing by completing these steps:

1. In IIS Manager, navigate to the level of the configuration hierarchy you want to manage. You can manage directory browsing for an entire server at the server level. You can manage directory browsing for a specific site at the site level.

2. When you group by area, the Directory Browsing feature is listed under IIS. Double-click the Directory Browsing feature.

3. If directory browsing is enabled, you can disable this feature by clicking Disable in the Actions pane.

By using the IIS Command-line Administration Tool, you can run the Set Config command to enable or disable directory browsing. Sample 6-14 provides the syntax and usage. If you don't specify a virtual directory name, you will enable or disable directory browsing for the entire server. By including the /showFlags parameter, you can enter the flags in the form of a comma-separated list. The acceptable values are: Date, LongDate, Time, Size, and Extension.

Sample 6-14   Enabling and Disabling Directory Browsing Syntax and Usage

Syntax
```
appcmd set config [VdirName] /section:directoryBrowse
[/enabled:[true|false]] [/showFlags=Flags]
```
Usage
```
appcmd set config "WWW Shopping Site/Sales/" /section:directoryBrowse
/enabled:false /showFlags="Time, Size, Date, LongDate"
```

Modifying Directory Properties

You can modify the settings for a physical or virtual directory at any time. In Windows Explorer, you can set directory permissions and general directory properties by right-clicking the directory name and selecting Properties. In IIS Manager, you can display the same properties dialog box by selecting the physical or virtual directory in the left pane and then clicking Edit Permissions in the Actions pane.

You can configure IIS permissions by completing the following steps:

1. In IIS Manager, in the left pane, select the physical or virtual directory.

2. Double-click the Handler Mappings feature.

3. In the Actions Pane, click Edit Feature Permissions.

4. In the Edit Feature Permissions dialog box, select or clear permissions as appropriate, and then click OK to apply the settings.

Renaming Directories

You can rename physical and virtual directories in IIS Manager. When you rename a physical directory, the actual folder name of the directory is changed. When you rename a virtual directory, the alias to the directory is changed. The name of the related physical directory isn't changed.

To rename a physical directory, follow these steps:

1. In IIS Manager, in the left pane, select the physical directory you want to rename. The directory icon should show a folder. If the directory icon appears as a folder shortcut or a globe with pages in front of it, you've incorrectly selected a virtual directory or application. Do not use this technique with virtual directories or applications.

2. In the Actions pane, click Edit Permissions. This displays the Properties dialog box for the directory.

3. On the General tab, type the new name for the directory in the text box, and then click OK.

Caution   Browsers store file and directory paths in bookmarks. When you change a directory name, you invalidate any URL that references the directory in its path string. Because of this, renaming a directory might cause a return visitor to experience the 404 File Or Directory Not Found error. To resolve this problem, you might want to redirect browser requests to the new location by using the technique discussed in the "Redirecting Browser Requests" section of Chapter 7, "Customizing Web Server Content."

In IIS 7.0, you cannot rename virtual directories or applications through IIS Manager. The reason for this is that renaming a virtual directory or application would require several instance changes in the running IIS configuration. To rename a virtual directory, you could delete the existing virtual directory and then create a new one with the desired name. This won't preserve the original directory settings, however.

Changing Virtual Directory Paths, Logon Methods, and More

When you use virtual directories to access shared folders on remote servers, you can set the UNC path to use, logon credentials, and logon type. The logon credentials identify the user that should be impersonated when accessing the physical path for the virtual directory. The logon type specifies the type of logon operation to perform when acquiring the user token necessary to access the physical path. The logon types you can use are as follows:

- **ClearText**   IIS uses a clear-text logon to acquire the user token. Because IIS passes the logon user call over the back end on an internal network, using a clear-text call is typically sufficient. This is the default logon type.

- **Interactive**   IIS uses an interactive logon to acquire the user token. This gives the related account the Interactive identity for the logon session and makes it appear that the user is logged on locally.

- **Batch**   IIS uses a batch logon to acquire the user token. This gives the related account the Batch identity for the logon session and makes it appear that the user is accessing the remote server as a batch job.

- **Network**   IIS uses a network logon to acquire the user token. This gives the related account the Network identity for the logon session and makes it appear that the user is accessing the remote server over the network.

In IIS Manager, you can change a virtual directory's physical path, logon credentials, and logon type by completing the following steps:

When you navigate to a site node in IIS Manager and select a directory, the Actions pane displays a list of unique actions related to directories.

1. In IIS Manager, in the left pane, select the virtual directory, and then, in the Actions pane, click Advanced Settings. This displays the Advanced Settings dialog box.

2. Physical Path lists the current physical path for the virtual directory. To change the physical path, click in the column to the right, and then type the desired path. Alternately, click in the column to the right, and then click the selection button to display the Browse For Folder dialog box. Then use this dialog box to select the folder to use.

3. Physical Path Credentials lists the current logon credentials for the virtual directory. In most cases, only UNC paths require logon credentials. To change the logon credentials, click in the column to the right, and then click the selection button to display the Connect As dialog box. In the Connect As dialog box, choose Specific User, and then click Set. In the Set Credentials dialog box, type the name of the user account to use for authentication, type and confirm the account password, and then click OK.

4. Physical Path Credentials Logon Type lists the current logon type for the virtual directory. You need to set the logon type only when you've also set logon credentials. To change the logon type, click in the column to the right, and then in the drop-down list, select the desired logon type. Click OK to save your settings.

By using the IIS Command-line Administration Tool, you can configure a virtual directories path and logon details by running the Set Vdir command. Sample 6-15 provides the syntax and usage.

Sample 6-15   Set Vdir Syntax and Usage

Syntax
```
appcmd set vdir [[/vdir.name:]"VdirNameOrUrl"]
[/physicalPath:Path] [/logonMethod:Method] [/userName:User]
[/password:Password]
```
Usage
```
appcmd set vdir "Default Web Site/Invoices" /logonMethod:Network

appcmd set vdir /vdir.name:"Sales Site/Invoices"
/physicalPath:"c:\salesroot\invoices" /logonMethod:ClearText
/userName:SupportUser /password:RainyDayz
```

Deleting Directories

You can delete physical directories by using Windows Explorer. When you delete a physical directory, the directory and its contents are removed. When you delete local directories and files, Windows moves them to the Recycle Bin by default, but you can bypass the Recycle Bin by holding down the Shift key when deleting. You also can configure servers to bypass the Recycle Bin automatically when deleting (though this is not a recommended best practice).

You can delete virtual directories by using IIS Manager. When you delete a virtual directory, only the alias to the directory is removed. The actual contents of the related physical directory aren't changed.

To delete a virtual directory by using IIS Manager, follow these steps:

1. In the IIS Manager, right-click the virtual directory you want to delete, and on the shortcut menu, select Remove.

2. When asked to confirm the action, click Yes.

By using the IIS Command-line Administration Tool, you can delete a virtual directory by running the Delete Vdir command. Sample 6-16 provides the syntax and usage.

Sample 6-16   Delete Vdir Syntax and Usage

Syntax
```
appcmd delete vdir [[/vdir.name:]"VdirNameOrUrl"]
```
Usage
```
appcmd delete vdir "Default Web Site/Support"
```

Chapter 7
Customizing Web Server Content

Most Web administrators don't need to create Web server content. Typically, content creation is the job of Web designers, and content management is the job of Web administrators. Designers and administrators often work closely together to ensure that corporate sites, intranets, and extranets have the exact look and feel that management wants. A large part of this is customizing the way the Web server uses content. You might need to configure the server to redirect browser requests to other directories or Web sites. You might need to enable compression to improve performance or assign specific types of default documents to be used.

You can customize the content in many other ways, too. Rather than use generic error messages, you might want to create custom error messages that are specific to your company's Web pages. Custom error messages can contain menus, graphics, links, and text that help lost users find their way. If your organization uses unique types of content, you might need to configure servers to use additional content types. To help track advertising, you might want to create jump pages. To better manage outages, you might want to create an update site. These techniques and more are discussed in this chapter.

Don't worry. You don't have to master every technique in this chapter, but the more you know about customizing content and the options available, the better you'll be as an administrator. As discussed in Chapter 2, "Deploying IIS 7.0 in the Enterprise," and Chapter 3, "Core IIS 7.0 Administration," before Internet Information Services (IIS) 7.0 can serve static content, dynamic content, or both, you must enable the appropriate Common HTTP and Application Development role services.

Managing Web Content

Every Web site on a server has a home directory. The home directory is the base directory for all documents that the site publishes. Copying files into the home directory, a virtual directory, or any subdirectory of these directories is, in fact, how you publish documents on a Web site.

Documents inherit the default properties of the site and the default permissions of the Microsoft Windows folder in which they're placed. You can change these properties and permissions for each individual document or for all documents within a directory.

> **Caution** Browsers can cache file and directory paths in bookmarks. To prevent errors when renaming or deleting files, you might want to redirect browser requests to the new location using the technique discussed in the "Redirecting Browser Requests" section later in this chapter.

Opening and Browsing Files

You can open Web content files by using either Windows Explorer or IIS Manager. You can open files in a browser by using Windows Explorer. To do this, right-click the file, and then on the shortcut menu, select Open. This opens the file by using a directory path, such as D:\Inetpub\Wwwroot\Default.htm.

You can display most types of files in the default browser by opening them in this way. However, if the file is an .asp document or other type of dynamic content and the Web site is running, the file won't be displayed correctly. You must be browsing the file through IIS to view it correctly in Microsoft Internet Explorer.

By using the Content View in IIS Manager, you can browse files through IIS. To do this, navigate to the Web site node, and then in the main pane, click Content View. Next, right-click the file you want to browse, and then on the shortcut menu, select Browse. This opens the file using a localhost path, such as http://Localhost/Default.htm, rather than a directory path, and ensures that any type of file—static or dynamic—will appear correctly.

Modifying the IIS Properties of Files

You can modify the settings for a Web file at any time. You set file permissions and general file properties in the file's Properties dialog box. In Windows Explorer, right-click the file, and then select Properties to display the Properties dialog box. In IIS Manager, navigate to the Web site node, and then in the main pane, click Content View. Next, right-click the file you want to work with, and then on the shortcut menu, select Edit Permissions.

Renaming Files

To rename Web files in IIS Manager, follow these steps:

1. In IIS Manager, navigate to the Web site node, and then in the main pane, click Content View.

2. Right-click the file you want to work with, and then on the shortcut menu, select Edit Permissions. The file's Properties dialog box appears.

3. On the General tab, in the text box, type the new name for the file, and then click OK.

   Note The name change isn't reflected immediately in IIS Manager. To update the file listings, click Refresh Page. This button is located in the upper right corner of the IIS Manager window.

Deleting Files

Web content files are stored under the root directory path for the Web site and in the root directory path of any virtual directories associated with the Web site. You can use Windows Explorer to easily delete any files that are no longer needed. When you delete a file, Windows Explorer moves the file to the Recycle Bin by default, and it is deleted permanently when you empty the Recycle Bin.

Redirecting Browser Requests

Browser redirection is a useful technique to prevent errors when you rename or delete content within a Web site. When you redirect requests, you tell a browser to take the following actions:

- Look for files in another directory

- Look for files on a different Web site

- Look for a specific file instead of a set of files

- Run an application instead of accessing the requested files

Each of these redirection techniques is examined in the sections that follow. Tips for creating customized redirection routines are examined in the "Customizing Browser Redirection" section later in this chapter. As discussed in Chapter 2, the HTTP Redirection role service controls the availability of this feature.

Redirecting Requests to Other Directories or Web Sites

If you rename or delete a directory, you can redirect requests for files in the old directory to the new directory, another directory, or even another Web site. When a browser requests the file at the original location, the Web server instructs the browser to request the page using the new location. You redirect requests to other directories or Web sites as follows:

1. In IIS Manager, navigate to the level of the configuration hierarchy you want to manage. You can manage redirection for an entire site at the site level. You can manage directory browsing for a specific directory at the directory level.

2. When you group by area, the HTTP Redirect feature is listed under IIS in the main pane. Select the HTTP Redirect feature, and then in the Actions pane, click Open Feature.

3. On the HTTP Redirect page, select Redirect Requests To This Destination, as shown in Figure 7-1.

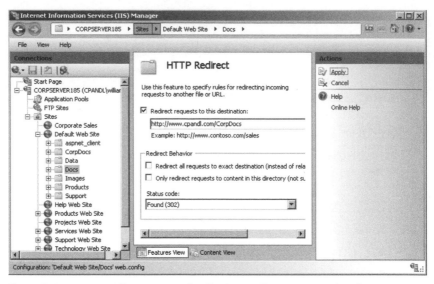

Figure 7-1 You can redirect requests for files in one directory to another directory.

4. In the Redirect Requests To This Destination field, type the Uniform Resource Locator (URL) of the destination Web site and directory. For example, to redirect all requests for http://www.cpandl.com/Docs to http://www.cpandl.com/CorpDocs, type **http://www.cpandl.com/CorpDocs**. To redirect all requests for files located at http://www.cpandl.com/Docs *to* techsupport.cpandl.com/CorpDocs, type **http://techsupport.cpandl.com/ CorpDocs**.

5. Click Apply. Now all requests for files in the old directory are mapped to files in the new directory. For example, if the browser requested http://www.cpandl.com/Docs/adminguide.htm, and you redirected requests to http://techsupport.cpandl.com/CorpDocs/, the browser would request http://techsupport.cpandl.com/CorpDocs/adminguide.htm.

Redirecting All Requests to Another Web Site

If you stop publishing a Web site but don't want users to reach a dead end if they visit, you should redirect requests for the old Web site to a specific page at the new site. You redirect requests to a specific page at another site by completing the following steps:

1. In IIS Manager, navigate to the site you want to manage. In the main pane, the HTTP Redirect feature is listed under IIS when you group by area. Double-click HTTP Redirect to open this feature.

2. On the HTTP Redirect page, select Redirect Requests To This Destination.

3. In the Redirect Requests To This Destination field, type the complete URL path to the page at the new site, such as **http://support.cpandl.com/oldsite.html**.

4. Under Redirect Behavior, select Redirect Requests To Exact Destination, and then click Apply. Now all requests for files at the old site are mapped to a specific page at the new site.

Redirecting Requests to Applications

If your organization's development team has created a custom application for the Web site, you can redirect all requests for files in a particular directory (or for the entire site, for that matter) to an application. Parameters passed in the URL can also be passed to the application; the technique you use to do this is as follows:

1. In IIS Manager, navigate to the level of the configuration hierarchy you want to manage. You can manage redirection for an entire site at the site level. You can manage directory browsing for a specific directory at the directory level.

2. In the main pane, the HTTP Redirect feature is listed under IIS when you group by area. Double-click HTTP Redirect to open this feature.

3. On the HTTP Redirect page, select Redirect Requests To This Destination.

4. In the appropriate field, type the application's URL including any variables needed to pass parameters to the program, such as http://Sales.cpandl.com /CorpApps/Login.exe?URL =$V+PARAMS=$P, where $V and $P are redirect variables. A complete list of redirect variables is provided in Table 7-1.

5. Under Redirect Behavior, select Redirect Requests To Exact Destination, and then click Apply. Now all requests for files in the directory or site are mapped to the application.

Customizing Browser Redirection

The previous sections looked at basic redirection techniques. Now it's time to break out the power tools and customize the redirection process. You can customize redirection anytime you select Redirect Requests To This Destination, and choose to redirect a URL.

In all of the previous discussions, when you selected Redirect Requests To This Destination, additional settings appeared in Redirect Behavior section. Without selecting additional check boxes, all requests for files in the old location were mapped automatically to files in the new location. You can change this behavior by changing any of the following settings in the Redirect Behavior section:

- **Redirect All Requests To Exact Destination**   Redirects requests to the destination URL without adding any other portions of the original URL. You can use this setting to redirect an entire site or directory to one file. For example, to redirect all requests for the http://www.cpandl.com/Downloads directory to the http://www.cpandl.com/Download.htm file, select this check box for the Downloads directory, and then in the Redirect Requests To This Destination field, type **http://www.cpandl.com/Download.htm**.

■ **Only Redirect Requests To Content In This Directory (Not Subdirectories)** Redirects files in a directory but does not affect files in subdirectories. For example, to redirect files in http://www.cpandl.com/products but not in http://www.cpandl.com/products/current or http://www.cpandl.com/products/upcoming, select this check box, and then in the Redirect Requests To This Destination field, type **http://www.cpandl.com/products**.

■ **Status Code** Sets the HTTP status code for the redirection. Use Found (302) to indicate a standard redirection (HTTP status code 302). Use Temporary (307) to indicate a temporary redirection (HTTP status code 307). Use Permanent (301) to indicate a permanent redirection (HTTP status code 301). Without configuring this setting, redirections are considered non-permanent, and the client browser receives the Standard (302) redirect message. Some browsers can use the Permanent (301) redirect message as the signal to permanently change a URL stored in cache or in a bookmark.

You can also customize redirection by using redirect variables. As Table 7-1 shows, you can use redirect variables to pass portions of the original URL to a destination path or to prevent redirection of a specific file or subdirectory.

Table 7-1   Redirect Variables for IIS

Variable	Description	Example
$S	Passes the matched suffix of the requested URL. The server automatically performs this suffix substitution; you use the $S variable only in combination with other variables.	If /Corpapps is redirected to /Apps, and the original request is for /Corpapps/Login.exe, / Login.exe is the suffix.
$P	Passes the parameters in the original URL, omitting the question mark used to specify the beginning of a query string.	If the original URL is /Scripts / Count.asp?valA=1&valB=2, the string "valA=1&valB=2" is mapped into the destination URL.
$Q	Passes the full query string to the destination.	If the original URL is /Scripts / Count.asp?valA=1&valB=2, the string "?valA=1&valB=2" is mapped into the destination URL.
$V	Passes the requested path without the server name.	If the original URL is //WebServer21 / Apps/Count.asp, the string "/Apps/ Count.asp" is mapped into the destination URL.
$0 through $9	Passes the portion of the requested URL that matches the indicated wildcard character.	If the original URL is //WebServer21/ Apps/Data.htm, $0 would be WebServer21, $1 would be Apps, and $2 would be Data.htm.
!	Use this variable to prevent redirecting a subdirectory or an individual file.	

By using the IIS Command-line Administration Tool, you can manage redirection by running the Set Config command and the httpRedirection section of the configuration file. Sample 7-1 provides the syntax and usage. See Table A-18 in the appendix, "Comprehensive IIS 7.0 Module and Schema Reference," for details on the related parameters. The default values for exactDestination and childOnly are *false*. The default value for httpResponseStatus is *Standard*.

Sample 7-1   Configuring Redirection Syntax and Usage

Syntax

```
appcmd set config ["ConfigPath"] /section:httpRedirect
[/enabled: true|false] [/destination: "DestPath"]
[/exactDestination: true|false] [/childOnly: true|false]
[/httpResponseStatus="Permanent" | "Standard" | "Temporary"]
```

Usage to Enable a Redirection Rule

```
appcmd set config "Default Web Site/Sales/" /section:httpRedirect
/enabled:true /destination: "http://sales.cpandl.com/"
```

Usage to Disable a Redirection Rule

```
appcmd set config "Default Web Site/Sales/" /section:httpRedirect
/enabled:false
```

Customizing Web Site Content and HTTP Headers

IIS sets default values for documents and Hypertext Transfer Protocol (HTTP) headers. You can modify these default values at the site, directory, and file level.

Configuring Default Documents

Default document settings determine how IIS handles requests that don't specify a document name. If a user makes a request using a directory path that ends in a directory name or forward slash (/) rather than a file name, IIS uses the default document settings to determine how to handle the request. As discussed in Chapter 2, the Default Document role service controls the availability of this feature.

When default document handling is enabled, IIS searches for default documents in the order in which their names appear in the default document list and returns the first document it finds. If a match isn't found, IIS checks to see if directory browsing is enabled, and if so returns a directory listing. Otherwise, IIS returns a 404–File Not Found error.

You can configure default document settings at the server, site, or directory level. This means that individual sites and directories can have default document settings that are different from the server as a whole. Standard default document names include

Default.htm, Default.asp, Index.htm, and Index.html. For optimal performance, you should:

- Limit the number of default documents to the essential few

- Order the default documents from the most frequently used to the least frequently used

If you do not follow these basic guidelines, you could seriously degrade the performance of IIS 7.0.

You can view current default document settings or make changes by following these steps:

1. In IIS Manager, navigate to the server, site, or directory you want to manage. In the main pane, the Default Document feature is listed under IIS when you group by area. Double-click Default Document to open this feature.

2. The settings on the Actions pane determine whether default documents are used. If default document handling is turned off and you want to turn it on, click Enable. If default document handling is turned on and you want to turn it off, click Disable.

3. As shown in Figure 7-2, the current default documents are listed in order of priority. You can use the following techniques to manage default documents:

   ❑ To change the priority order of a default document, select it and then click Move Up or Move Down in the Actions pane.

   ❑ To add a new default document, click Add in the Actions pane, type the name of the default document, such as **Index.html**, and then click OK.

   ❑ To remove a default document, click the default document that you want to remove and then click Remove in the Actions pane. When prompted to confirm, click Yes.

By using the IIS Command-line Administration Tool, you can manage default documents by running the Set Config command and the defaultDocument section of the configuration file. Sample 7-2 provides the syntax and usage for adding, changing, and removing HTTP headers. If any values you are setting include double quotation marks, you must escape the quotation character by enclosing it in double quotation marks. Additionally, because you are referencing into the files collection, the brackets ([]) in the syntax and usage examples are literal values rather than indicators of optional values. You must use the brackets to indicate that you are referencing into the files collection.

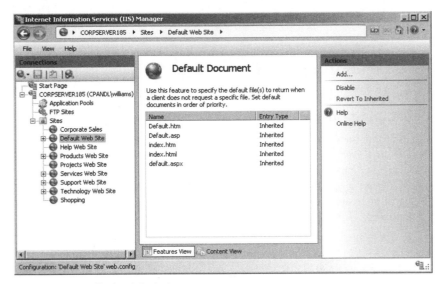

Figure 7-2 Specify the default documents to use.

Sample 7-2 Configuring Default Documents Syntax and Usage

Syntax
```
appcmd set config ["ConfigPath"] /section:defaultDocument
[/enable:true|false] [/files.[value='Value']
```
Usage for Enabling Default Documents
```
appcmd set config "Default Web Site" /section:defaultDocument
/enabled:true
```
Usage for Disabling Default Documents
```
appcmd set config "Default Web Site" /section:defaultDocument
/enabled:false
```
Usage for Adding Default Documents
```
appcmd set config /section:defaultDocument
/+files.[value="start.htm"]

appcmd set config /section:defaultDocument
/+files.[@start,value='start.htm']

appcmd set config /section:defaultDocument
/+files.[@end,value='start.htm']

appcmd set config /section:defaultDocument
/+files.[@2,value='start.htm']
```

Usage for Removing Default Documents
```
appcmd set config /section:defaultDocument
/-files.[value='start.htm']
```

```
appcmd set config /section:defaultDocument /-files.[@2]
```

Configuring Document Footers

You can configure IIS to automatically insert an HTML-formatted footer document on the bottom of every document it sends. The footer can contain copyright information, logos, or other important information. Although you can enable or disable at the site level, you must specify the default footer to use at the server level. This means that each IIS server can have a default footer that you can elect to use with individual sites hosted on the server.

To configure automatic footers, you need to create an HTML-formatted document and save it to a folder on a Web server's local hard disk drive. The footer document shouldn't be a complete HTML page. Instead, it should include only the HTML tags necessary for content that's to be displayed in the footer. Next, you need to use the IIS Command-line Administration Tool to specify the default document footer for the server. Afterward, you need to enable automatic footers for individual Web sites. Sample 7-3 provides examples for working with document footers.

Sample 7-3   Configuring Document Footers Syntax and Usage

Syntax
```
appcmd set config ["ConfigPath"] /section:staticContent
[/enableDocFooter:true|false] [/defaultDocFooter:'Value']
```
Usage for Setting a Document Footer
```
appcmd set config /section:staticContent
/defaultDocFooter:'footer.htm'
```
Usage for Enabling Document Footers
```
appcmd set config "Default Web Site" /section:staticContent
/enableDocFooter:true
```
Usage for Disabling Document Footers
```
appcmd set config "Default Web Site" /section:staticContent
/enableDocFooter:false
```

Configuring Included Files

You can use Server-Side Includes (SSI) directives to insert just about any type of document into a Web content file. SSI is a feature that becomes available when you install the Server-Side Includes role service.

When you install and enable the Server-Side Includes role service, you can use included content with .asp, .aspx, .shtm, and .shtml files. IIS uses the #*include* directive to insert the contents of a file into a Web page. The #*include* directive is the only SSI directive that can be used with both .asp and .shtm files. Although you could update the handler mappings for SSI to include .htm and .html files, this could seriously degrade your server's performance. Why? If you enable SSI for .htm and .html files, IIS would need to parse all .htm and .html files to see if they have included content. This additional parsing operation can slow down the overall request handling process on the server.

Included files can have any file name extension that IIS can process. However, a recommended best practice is to use the .inc file extension. IIS processes included files through the interpreter of the original calling page. Thus, if you want to include a .shtm or .shtml page that includes other types of SSI directives, you must call it from a .shtm or .shtml page. If you want to include an .asp or .aspx page that includes dynamic content, you must call it from an .asp or .aspx page.

When you are editing the content for a Web file, the syntax for including files is as follows:

```
<!-- #include file ="FileToInclude" -->
```

where FileToInclude is the name of the file to include and optionally its relative path from the current directory. By default, you can include files in the same directory or in subdirectories only. In the following example, the included file is in the same directory as the calling file:

```
<!-- #include file ="footer.inc" -->
```

To reference a subdirectory of the current directory, you include the subdirectory name as shown in this example:

```
<!-- #include file ="data\footer.inc" -->
```

If you turn on the Enable Parent Paths parameter for the ASP feature, you can include files in parent directories as shown in this example:

```
<!-- #include file ="..\footer.inc" -->
```

Following this, you could insert a custom footer into a set of documents by completing these steps:

1. Create the custom footer document.

2. Open a document in which you want to include the footer in Notepad or any other text editor.

3. Insert the appropriate include directive into the file.

4. Save the file, and then repeat this procedure for other documents that should include the footer.

Using Content Expiration and Preventing Browser Caching

Most browsers store documents that users have viewed in cache so that the documents can be displayed later without having to retrieve the entire page from a Web server. You can control browser caching by using content expiration. When content expiration is enabled, IIS includes document expiration information when sending HTTP results to a user. This enables the browser to determine if future requests for the same document need to be retrieved from the server or whether a locally cached copy is still valid.

You can configure content expiration at the server, site, directory, or file level. Server level settings affect all sites on a server. Site level settings affect all pages in the site. Directory-level settings affect all files in the directory and subdirectories of the directory. File-level settings affect the currently selected file only. Three content expiration settings are available:

- **Expire Immediately**   Forces cached pages to expire immediately, preventing the browser from displaying the file from cache. Use this setting when you need to ensure that the browser displays the most recent version of a dynamically generated page.

- **Expire After**   Sets a specific number of minutes, hours, or days during which the file can be displayed from cache. Use this setting when you want to ensure that the browser will retrieve a file after a certain period.

- **Expire On**   Sets a specific expiration date and time. The file can be displayed from cache until the expiration date. Use this setting for time-sensitive material that's no longer valid after a specific date, such as a special offer or event announcement.

Tip   In ASP pages, you can control content expiration by putting a Response.Expires entry in the HTTP header. Use the value *Response.Expires = 0* to force immediate expiration. Keep in mind that HTTP headers must be sent to the browser before any page content is sent.

Enabling Content Expiration

You set content expiration at site, directory, and file levels. Keep in mind that individual file and directory settings override site settings. So if you don't get the behavior you expect, check for file or directory settings that might be causing a conflict.

You can configure content expiration for a server, site, directory, or file by completing the following steps:

1. In IIS Manager, navigate to the server, site, directory, or file you want to manage. In the main pane, double-click HTTP Response Headers.

2. In the Actions pane, click Set Common Headers. This opens the Set Common HTTP Response Headers dialog box.

3. Select the Expire Web Content check box. Do one of the following and then click OK:

    ❑ To force cached pages to expire immediately, select Immediately.

    ❑ To set a specific number of minutes, hours, or days before expiration, select After, and then configure the expiration information in the appropriate fields.

    ❑ To set specific expiration date and time, select On, and then configure the expiration information in the appropriate fields.

By using the IIS Command-line Administration Tool, you can enable content expiration by running the Set Config command and the staticContent section of the configuration file. Sample 7-4 provides the syntax and usage for configuring the various content expiration modes. When you are setting maximum age, you set the age in terms of the maximum number of days, hours, minutes, and seconds for which content is valid. When you are setting content expiration, you set the expiration date in terms of the day, date, and time at which content expires.

Sample 7-4   Configuring Content Expiration Syntax and Usage

Syntax
```
appcmd set config ["ConfigPath"] /section:staticContent
[/clientCache.cacheControlMode:"NoControl" | "DisableCache"
 | "UseMaxAge" | "UseExpires"]
[/clientCache.cacheControlMaxAge:"DD.HH:MM:SS"]
[/clientCache.httpExpires:"Day, Date HH:MM:SS"]
```
Usage for Configuring Immediate Expiration
```
appcmd set config "Default Web Site" /section:staticContent
/clientCache.cacheControlMode:"DisableCache"
```
Usage for Setting Content Expiration
```
appcmd set config "Default Web Site" /section:staticContent
/clientCache.cacheControlMode:"UseExpires"
/clientCache.httpExpires:"Mon, 2 Mar 2009 00:00:00"
```
Usage for Setting Maximum Age
```
appcmd set config "Default Web Site" /section:staticContent
/clientCache.cacheControlMode:"UseMaxAge"
/clientCache.cacheControlMaxAge:"14.00:00:00"
```

Disabling Content Expiration

You set content expiration at site, directory, and file levels. Keep in mind that individual file and directory settings override site settings. So if you don't get the behavior you expect, check for file or directory settings that might be causing a conflict.

You can disable content expiration for a server, site, directory, or file by completing the following steps:

1. In IIS Manager, navigate to the server, site, directory, or file you want to manage. In the main pane, double-click HTTP Response Headers.

2. In the Actions pane, click Set Common Headers. This opens the Set Common HTTP Response Headers dialog box.

3. Clear the Expire Web Content check box, and then click OK.

By using the IIS Command-line Administration Tool, you can disable content expiration by running the Set Config command and the staticContent section of the configuration file. Sample 7-5 provides the syntax and usage for disabling content expiration.

Sample 7-5   Configuring Content Expiration Syntax and Usage

Syntax
```
appcmd set config ["ConfigPath"] /section:staticContent
/clientCache.cacheControlMode:"NoControl"
```
Usage
```
appcmd set config "Default Web Site" /section:staticContent
/clientCache.cacheControlMode:"NoControl"
```

Using Custom HTTP Headers

When a browser requests a document on a Web site handled by IIS, IIS normally passes the document with a response header prepended. Sometimes you might want to modify the standard header or create your own header for special situations. For example, you could take advantage of HTTP headers that are provided for by the HTTP standards but for which IIS provides no interface. Other times you might want to provide information to the client that you couldn't pass using standard HTML elements. To do this, you can use custom HTTP headers.

Custom HTTP headers contain information that you want to include in a document's response header. Entries in a custom header are entered as name value pairs. The Name portion of the entry identifies the value you're referencing. The Value portion of the entry identifies the actual content you're sending.

Custom HTTP headers typically provide instructions for handling the document or supplemental information. For example, the Cache-Control HTTP header field is used to control how proxy servers cache pages. A field value of *Public* tells the proxy server that caching is allowed. A field value of *Private* tells the proxy server that caching isn't allowed.

To view or manage custom HTTP headers for a server, site, directory, or file, follow these steps:

1. In IIS Manager, navigate to the server, site, directory, or file you want to manage. In the main pane, double-click HTTP Response Headers. The HTTP Response Headers pane shows currently configured headers in *name: value* format.

2. Use the following settings to manage existing headers or create new headers:

   ❑ **Add**   Adds a custom HTTP header. To add a header, click Add. Type a header name and a header value. Complete the process by clicking OK.

   ❑ **Edit**   Edits a custom HTTP header. To edit a header, select it, and then click Edit. In the Properties dialog box that appears, change the header information, and then click OK.

   ❑ **Remove**   Removes a custom HTTP header. To remove a header, select it, and then click Remove. When prompted to confirm the action, click Yes.

Note   When you are working with existing HTTP response headers, be sure to note whether the entry type is listed as local or inherited. Local entries are configured at the level you are working with. Inherited entries are configured at a higher level of the configuration hierarchy. If you edit an inherited entry, you will make a local (not global) change to the entry.

By using the IIS Command-line Administration Tool, you can manage HTTP headers by running the Set Config command. Samples 7-6 and 7-7 provide the syntax and usage for adding, changing, and removing HTTP headers. If any values you are setting include double quotation marks, you must escape the quotation character by enclosing it in double quotation marks. Additionally, because you are referencing into the customHeaders collection, the brackets ([]) in the syntax and usage examples are literal values rather than indicators of optional values.

Sample 7-6   Adding an HTTP Header Syntax and Usage

Syntax
```
appcmd set config ["ConfigPath"] /section:httpProtocol
/+customHeaders.[name='Name',value='Value']
```

Usage
```
appcmd set config "Default Web Site" /section:httpProtocol
/+customHeaders.[name='P3P',value='policyRef="""
http://www.cpandl.com/p3p.xml""""']
```

Sample 7-7   Removing an HTTP Header Syntax and Usage

Syntax
```
appcmd set config ["ConfigPath"] /section:httpProtocol
/-customHeaders.[name='Name',value='Value']
```
Usage
```
appcmd set config "Default Web Site" /section:httpProtocol
/-customHeaders.[name='P3P',
value='policyRef="""http://www.cpandl.com/p3p.xml"""']
```

Using Content Ratings and Privacy Policies

IIS 6 has a built-in content rating system that allows you to rate content according to levels of violence, sex, nudity, and offensive language. Because this feature was often misused, site ratings agencies no longer allow self-ratings. Because of this, IIS 7.0 no longer includes this feature, and ratings agencies now provide ratings directly to administrators for inclusion in Web sites when your organization joins or actively participates in a particular rating service.

In addition to content ratings, Web sites also can have privacy policies. Browsers such as Windows Internet Explorer rely on a Web site's compact privacy policy to determine how the site uses cookies. The World Wide Web Consortium (W3C) has published an official specification regarding Web privacy called the Platform for Privacy Preferences Project (P3P). P3P enables Web sites to report their privacy practices in a standard format that can be retrieved automatically and interpreted by user agents such as Web browsers. User agents rely on what is reported in the compact privacy policy and generally cannot determine whether cookies are used as reported. Because misuse of a privacy policy can get your organization into hot water, you should ensure that you answer the policy questions appropriately when you generate the policy reference file.

Real World   Several times a year, you should review the way your organization uses cookies and update your privacy policy as appropriate. Helping your organization's Web designers understand privacy policy and the reporting requirements can go a long way to ensuring that your site remains in compliance with privacy policy statements. If you educate the Web design team about privacy policy, they can tell you when they've made changes to cookies that affect privacy policy. You then can be proactive rather than reactive in maintaining privacy policies on your organization's Web sites.

You can learn more about P3P online at *http://www.w3.org/P3P/*. You can obtain details on privacy policy generators online at *http://www.w3.org/P3P/implementations*. Once you've created a P3P reference file for a site, you can copy the file to a directory on the site and reference it in the site's HTTP Response headers by following these steps:

1. Using Windows Explorer, copy the P3P reference file to the site's root directory or an appropriate subdirectory.

2. In IIS Manager, navigate to the site you want to manage. In the main pane, double-click HTTP Response Headers. The HTTP Response Headers pane shows currently configured headers in *name: value* format.

3. To add a header to reference the privacy policy, click Add. This opens the Add Custom HTTP Response Header dialog box.

4. In the Name field, type **P3P**.

5. In the Value field, type **policyref="*policyURL*"** where *policyURL* is the actual URL to the P3P reference file as shown in the example in Figure 7-3. Then click OK.

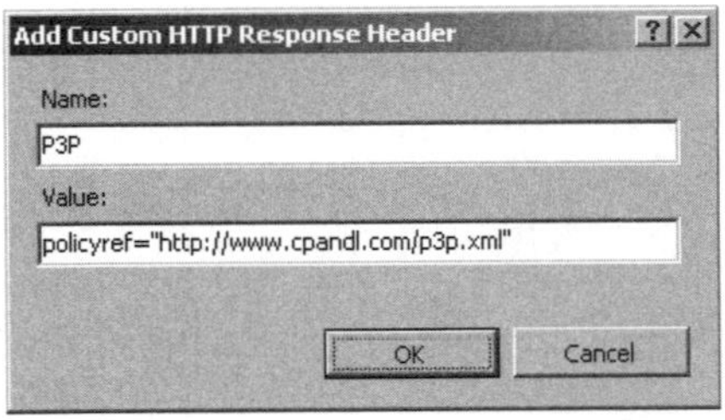

Figure 7-3 Reference your site's privacy policy file.

Improving Performance with Compression

IIS fully supports the HTTP 1.1 protocol and the compression enhancements it defines. By using HTTP compression, you can compress both static and dynamic results of HTTP queries for transmission to HTTP 1.1–compliant clients. Unlike early IIS releases, in which compression was implemented using an Internet Server Application Programming Interface (ISAPI) filter and could be enabled only for an entire server, IIS 7.0 builds in compression as a feature that you can control precisely to the file level.

By using IIS 7.0, you can enable and configure compression for both static and dynamic content. The Static Content Compression role service controls the availability of static content compression. The Dynamic Content Compression role service controls the availability of dynamic content compression.

IIS servers can get a big performance boost using static content compression. However, this isn't necessarily the case with dynamic content compression. Before you enable dynamic content compression, you need to look carefully at:

■ The size of the dynamic files

- The number of different dynamic files

- The way the dynamic files are being used

Once you have a firm understanding of how dynamic content is used on a site, you can optimize dynamic content caching to reduce the resource impact of dynamic content compression while reducing files sizes for faster transmission to client browsers. You optimize dynamic content caching by using ASP caching properties and output caching rules as discussed in Chapter 8, "Running IIS Applications."

Configuring Content Compression for an Entire Server

You can configure content compression for an entire server and all of the related sites by following these steps:

1. In IIS Manager, select the server you want to manage. In the main pane, double-click Compression. The main pane shows the current state of compression for the server as shown in Figure 7-4.

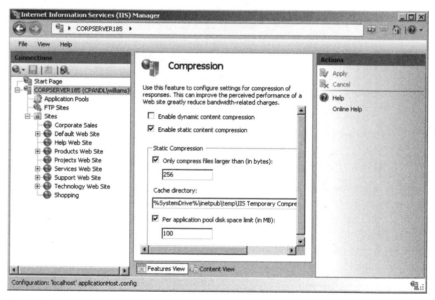

Figure 7-4   Manage compression for an entire server and all related sites.

2. To enable or disable static content compression, select or clear the Enable Static Content Compression check box as appropriate.

3. To enable or disable dynamic content compression, select or clear the Enable Dynamic Content Compression check box as appropriate.

4. If you've enabled static content compression, use the following check boxes to optimize compression:

❏ **Only Compress Files Larger Than (In Bytes)** Use the Only Compress Files Larger Than settings to set the minimum file size in bytes that you want to compress. By default, IIS compresses only files larger than 256 bytes. If you want to compress all files regardless of size, clear the related check box. Otherwise, select the related check box and specify the minimum file size to compress. On a busy server with many dozens or hundreds of small files, you might want to reduce the number of small files that IIS caches and must retrieve from the cache directory. This will reduce the resource drain from having to compress and retrieve small compressed files while allowing the server to focus on compressing larger files from which the biggest user-perceived performance improvement can be achieved. For example, in this scenario, you might want to compress files only when they are larger than 1023 bytes.

❏ **Cache Directory** Use the Cache Directory text box to specify the location where IIS stores static files after they are compressed. IIS stores static files until they expire or the content changes. The directory you use must be on an NTFS-formatted partition. The directory should not be compressed or encrypted.

❏ **Per Application Pool Disk Space Limit (In MB)** Use the Per Application Pool Disk Space Limit options to set the maximum amount of disk space in megabytes that you want IIS to use when compressing static content. By default, IIS stores up to 100 MB of compressed files for each application pool configured on the server. When the limit is reached, IIS automatically cleans up the temporary directory

5. Click Apply to save your settings.

By using the IIS Command-line Administration Tool, you can enable or disable content compression by running the Set Config command and the urlCompression section of the configuration file. Sample 7-8 provides the syntax and usage for enabling and disabling compression. The dynamicCompressionBeforeCache parameter controls whether IIS performs per-URL compression before caching the file. The default is *false*, which means that IIS caches a file (as appropriate per the current configuration) and then performs compression.

Sample 7-8 Enabling or Disabling Content Compression Syntax and Usage

Syntax
```
appcmd set config ["ConfigPath"] /section:urlCompression
[/doStaticCompression:true|false] [/doDynamicCompression:true|false]
[/dynamicCompressionBeforeCache:true|false]
```

Usage
```
appcmd set config "Default Web Site" /section:urlCompression
/doStaticCompression:true
```

By using the IIS Command-line Administration Tool, you can configure content compression by running the Set Config command and the httpCompression section of the configuration file. Sample 7-9 provides the syntax and usage for configuring compression. See Table A-11 in the appendix for a detailed description of each parameter.

Sample 7-9   Configuring Content Compression Syntax and Usage

Syntax
```
appcmd set config ["ConfigPath"] /section:httpCompression
[/cacheControlHeader:CacheTimeInSeconds]
[/doDiskSpaceLimiting:true|false]
[/dynamicCompressionDisableCpuUsage:true|false]
[/dynamicCompressionEnableCpuUsage:true|false]
[/dynamicCompressionLevel:Level]
[/maxDiskSpaceUsage:MaxSizeInMB]
[/minFileSizeForComp:MinSizeInBytes]
[/noCompressionForHttp10:true|false]
[/noCompressionForProxies:true|false]
[/noCompressionForRange:true|false]
[/sendCacheHeaders:true|false]
[/staticCompressionDisableCpuUsage:true|false]
[/staticCompressionEnableCpuUsage:true|false]
[/staticCompressionLevel:Level]
```
Usage
```
appcmd set config "Default Web Site" /section:httpCompression
/doDiskSpaceLimiting:true
```

Enabling or Disabling Content Compression for Sites and Directories

You can enable or disable static content compression for sites and directories by following these steps:

1. In IIS Manager, navigate to the site or directory you want to manage. In the main pane, double-click Compression. The main pane shows the current state of compression for the selected level.

2. To enable or disable static content compression, select or clear the Enable Static Content Compression check box as appropriate.

3. To enable or disable dynamic content compression, select or clear the Enable Dynamic Content Compression check box as appropriate.

4. Click Apply to save your settings.

Customizing Web Server Error Messages

IIS generates HTTP error messages when Web server errors occur. These errors typically pertain to bad client requests, authentication problems, or internal server errors. As the administrator, you have complete control over how error messages are sent back to clients. When you add the HTTP Custom Errors role service to a server, you can configure IIS to send generic HTTP errors or default custom error files, or you can create your own custom error files.

Understanding Status Codes and Error Messages

Status codes and error messages go hand in hand. Every time a user requests a file on a server, the server generates a status code. The status code indicates the status of the user's request. If the request succeeds, the status code indicates this, and the requested file is returned to the browser. If the request fails, the status code indicates why, and the server generates an appropriate error message based on this error code. This error message is returned to the browser in place of the requested file.

A status code is a three-digit number that might include a numeric suffix. The first digit of the status code indicates the code's class. The next two digits indicate the error category, and the suffix (if used) indicates the specific error that occurred. For example, the status code 403 indicates a forbidden-access problem, and within this access category a number of specific errors can occur: 403.1 indicates that execute access is denied, 403.2 indicates that read access is denied, and 403.3 indicates that write access is denied.

If you examine the Web server logs or receive an error code while trying to troubleshoot a problem, you'll see status codes. Table 7-2 shows the general classes for status codes. As you can see from the table, the first digit of the status code provides the key indicator as to what has actually happened. Status codes beginning with 1, 2, or 3 are common and generally don't indicate a problem. Status codes beginning with 4 or 5 indicate an error and a potential problem that you need to resolve.

Table 7-2   General Classes of Status Codes

Code Class	Description
1XX	Continue/protocol change
2XX	Success
3XX	Redirection
4XX	Client error/failure
5XX	Server error

Knowing the general problem is helpful when you're searching through log files or compiling statistics. When you're troubleshooting or debugging, you need to know the exact error that occurred. For this reason, IIS provides detailed error information that includes the HTTP status code and substatus code.

Tip Because of security concerns about providing complete details on errors, the HTTP substatus code is no longer passed to clients (in most instances). Instead, clients should see a general status code, such as 401 or 402. If you're trying to troubleshoot a problem, you might want to configure access logging so that the substatus codes are recorded in the server logs temporarily. That way you can view the logs to get detailed information on any errors.

Note In some cases, Internet Explorer might replace custom errors with its own HTTP error message. Typically, this is done when the error message is considered too small to be useful to the user. Internet Explorer attempts to determine message usefulness based on message size. When 403, 405, or 410 error messages are smaller than 256 bytes, or when 400, 404, 406, 500, 500.12, 500.13, 500.15, or 501 error messages are smaller than 512 bytes, the custom error message sent by IIS is replaced by a message generated by Internet Explorer.

Managing Custom Error Settings

When you add the HTTP Custom Errors role service to an IIS server, you can configure the way IIS handles error messages globally for the entire server and for individual sites and directories. By default, IIS displays detailed errors for local clients and terse errors for remote clients. IIS considers a local client to be any client with an IP address originating on the same network as the IIS server and a remote client to be a client with an IP address on any other network.

As Figure 7-5 shows, detailed errors includes the HTTP status code of the error in addition to the following information:

- **Description** A plain-language description of the error that occurred.

- **Error Code** An internal error code for IIS.

- **Module** The module in which the error occurred while processing the request. If the error occurred in the IIS server core, the module is listed as IIS Web Core.

- **Notification** The component that notified IIS about the error, such as the map request handler.

- **Requested URL** The URL requested including any related port used automatically, such as port 80 with HTTP requests and port 443 with HTTPS requests.

- **Physical Path** The local file path to which the request was mapped. If a user requests a file that does not exist, the file path will not be valid.

- **Logon User** The user account used to access the IIS server. With anonymous access to a server, the user is listed as Anonymous.

- **Logon Method**   The authentication method used to log on to the IIS server. With anonymous access to a server, the logon method is listed as Anonymous.

- **Handler**   The content handler that was processing the request when the error occurred, such as the StaticFile handler, which is used with standard HTML pages.

- **Most Likely Causes**   A list of the most likely causes of the error.

- **Things You Can Try**   A list of possible resolutions for the error.

- **Links And More Information**   Provides additional information about the error in addition to a link to more information on the Microsoft Web site.

Figure 7-5   IIS can return detailed errors to help users better understand problems that occur.

Terse errors, on the other hand, include only the HTTP status code of the error, the error description, and the server version information. The reason remote clients receive terse errors by default is to protect the integrity of your server and your network by ensuring that information that could be used maliciously is not passed to remote users.

Other security enhancements for IIS 7.0 ensure that IIS generates HTTP error responses only for a specific, limited subset of the HTTP status codes. By default, the error responses configured are: 401, 403, 404, 405, 406, 412, 500, 501, and 502. If IIS generated any related error codes or sub-error codes, IIS would provide an error response. These error responses are handled by files located in the *%SystemRoot%\Inetpub\Custerr\<LANGUAGE-TAG>* directory, where *LANGUAGE-TAG* is a placeholder for the default language of the client browser, such as en-us. If additional language packs are installed, this setting allows IIS to direct users to pages with the default language of their client browser. However, if no additional language packs are installed, IIS directs client browsers to pages with the default language of the server.

In the *%SystemRoot%\Inetpub\Custerr\<LANGUAGE-TAG>* directory, you'll find additional custom error files that you can configure for use in HTTP error responses. Because these files contain static content that is inserted into the error response, you can edit the files and optimize them for your environment. Further, because subcode errors are not configured by default, IIS returns general error responses, such as a 404 error rather than a 404.7 or 404.8 error. If you want IIS to be more specific about the exact error that occurred, you can add the appropriate custom error pages. However, don't do this without first considering the possible security implications of doing so. Always ask yourself if the additional information could be used maliciously, and err on the side of caution.

When you configure error responses, it doesn't have to be a choice between custom error pages and detailed errors. Instead of using either type of error response, you can configure a global default error page for an entire server, site, or directory. This error page can be a file with static content to insert into the error response, a URL to execute for dynamic content, or a redirection to a new URL.

You can tailor individual error responses in a similar way. This means that individual error responses can either be a file with static content to insert into the error response, a URL to execute for dynamic content, or a redirection to a new URL.

> **Real World**   When you use an .asp or .aspx file to handle custom errors, the error code and the original URL are passed to the dynamic page as query parameters. You must configure the dynamic page to read the parameters from the URL and set the status code appropriately. For example, if Notfound.asp is designed to handle 404 errors and the user accesses a page using the URL *http://www.cpandl.com/data.htm*, the dynamic page is invoked using the URL *http://www.cpandl.com/Not-Found.asp?404; http://www.cpandl.com/data.htm*, and your dynamic page must extract the 404 and *http://www.cpandl.com/data.htm* parameters from the URL.

Viewing and Configuring Custom Error Settings

You can view and configure custom error settings by performing these steps:

1. In IIS Manager, navigate to the server, site, or directory you want to manage. In the main pane, the Error Pages feature is listed under IIS when you group by area. Double-click Error Pages to open this feature.

2. You should now see a list of the configured HTTP error responses and how they're handled. Entries are organized by the following categories:

- ❑ **Status Code**   The HTTP status code for the error, which might include a suffix

- ❑ **Path**   The file path or URL path associated with the error response

- ❑ **Type**   The method used to handle the error (file, URL, or redirection)

- ❑ **Entry Type**   The type of entry as either local or inherited

3. When the server encounters an error, IIS can return customer error pages, detailed error pages, or a combination of the two depending on where the client is located. To view and configure how error responses are configured, click Edit Feature Settings.

4. In the Edit Feature Settings dialog box, shown in Figure 7-6, the options on the Error Responses panel control how the server handles error responses. By default, local clients see detailed error responses, and remote clients see custom error pages without additional details. To enhance security you might want all clients to see custom error pages without additional details; in this case, select Custom Error Pages. You'll rarely want to select Detailed Errors, because this setting provides detailed error responses to both local and remote clients.

5. Instead of providing clients with custom error responses, you can specify a default error page that IIS will display for all error responses. To set a default error page and override all other error response settings configured at this level, type the path to the default error page to use and specify the type of path as a file with static content to insert into the error response, a URL to execute for dynamic content, or a redirection to a new URL.

6. Click OK to save your settings.

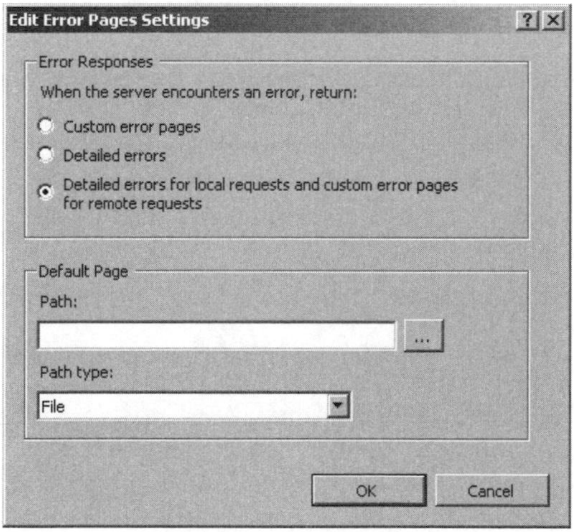

Figure 7-6   Configure error responses for local and remote clients.

By using the IIS Command-line Administration Tool, you can configure the error mode and default error page by running the Set Config command and the httpErrors section of the configuration file. Sample 7-10 provides the syntax and usage for configuring the error mode. Sample 7-11 provides the syntax and usage for configuring the default error page. See Table A-7 in the appendix for more information on the related attributes and their usage.

Sample 7-10   Configuring the Error Mode Syntax and Usage

Syntax
```
appcmd set config ["ConfigPath"] /section:httpErrors
[/errorMode: "DetailedLocalOnly"|"Custom"|"Detailed"]
```
Usage
```
appcmd set config "Default Web Site" /section:httpErrors
/errorMode: "DetailedLocalOnly"
```

Sample 7-11   Configuring a Default Error Page Syntax and Usage

Syntax
```
appcmd set config ["ConfigPath"] /section:httpErrors
[/defaultResponseMode:"File"|"ExecuteURL"|"Redirect"]
[/defaultPath:"Path"]
```
Usage
```
appcmd set config "Default Web Site" /section:httpErrors
/defaultResponseMode:"ExecuteURL"
/defaultPath:"C:\inetpub\errors\error.aspx"
```

Adding, Changing, and Removing Custom Error Responses

When you've configured IIS to return individual error responses rather than a default error page, you can manage the way IIS handles each error response. By default, IIS uses the settings you've configured for top-level status codes for any substatus codes you haven't configured. As with the default error page, you can configure error responses to be a file with static content to insert into the error response, a URL to execute for dynamic content, or a redirection to a new URL. When working with static content, you also can configure IIS to try to direct users to error responses for the default language for their client browser.

Adding Localized Custom Error Responses   You can add a localized custom error response by completing the following steps:

1. In IIS Manager, navigate to the server, site, or directory you want to manage. In the main pane, the Error Pages feature is listed under IIS when you group by area. Double-click Error Pages to open this feature.

2. You should now see a list of the configured error responses. Error responses listed as Local under Entry Type are configured at the current configuration level. To add a custom error response, in the Actions pane, click Add.

3. In the Add Custom Error Page dialog box, shown in Figure 7-7, type the status code you are configuring, such as 404.4 or 500.100.

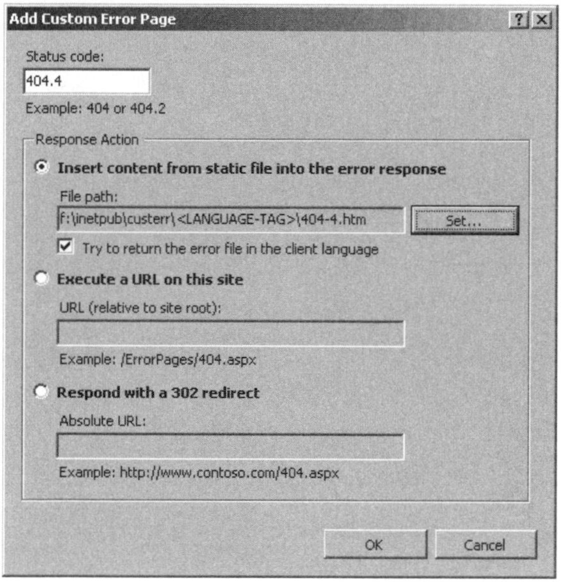

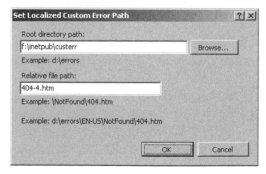

Figure 7-7   Use the Add Custom Error Page dialog box to configure a custom error response.

4. Because you want IIS to try to direct users to the default language for their client browser, select the Try To Return The Error File In The Client Language check box, and then click Set. This displays the Set Localized Custom Error Path dialog box as shown in Figure 7-8.

Figure 7-8   Set the custom error path.

5. Using the Root Directory Path settings, type or select the root directory path for the custom error page. The default root directory path is *%SystemRoot%*\Inetpub\Custerr.

6. In the Relative File Path text box, type the name of the error file. When working with the standard custom error pages, the file name is the name of the status code with a dash instead of a dot separating any applicable substatus and .htm as the file extension, such as 404-4.htm. The only exception in the standard custom error pages is for 500.100 error responses, which are handled by the 500-100.asp page.

7. Click OK twice to add the custom error page.

Tip When you click OK to close the Set Localized Custom Error Path dialog box, IIS Manager sets the full URL path to the custom error response for you. This includes the *<LANGUAGE-TAG>* placeholder variable. This placeholder is replaced at run time with the client's default language if available and with the server's default language otherwise.

Adding Non-localized Custom Error Responses You can add a non-localized custom error response by completing the following steps:

1. In IIS Manager, navigate to the server, site, or directory you want to manage. In the main pane, the Error Pages feature is listed under IIS when you group by area. Double-click Error Pages to open this feature.

2. In the Actions pane, click Add. In the Add Custom Error Page dialog box, type the status code you are configuring, such as 404.4 or 500.100.

3. Since you do not want IIS to try to direct users to the default language for their client browser, you have the following other options:

   ❑ **Insert Content From Static File Into The Error Response** Select this option to insert a static file into the error response, and then type the file path for the custom error page. Alternately, click Browse to use the Open dialog box to select the file to use.

   ❑ **Execute A URL On This Site** Select this option to execute a URL on this site, and then type a URL relative to the site root into the text box provided. The site root is located with the relative URL of /. Any subdirectories of the site root are below /. Following this, you could reference the 404-4.htm file in the ErrorPages subdirectory of a site by typing /**ErrorPages/404-4.htm**.

   ❑ **Respond With A 302 Redirect** Select this option to return the exact URL specified to the client along with a redirection status code. Type an absolute URL path, such as **http://www.cpandl.com/help/**.

4. Click OK.

Changing or Removing Custom Error Responses To change or remove a custom error response in IIS Manager, navigate to the server, site, or directory you want to manage. When you double-click Error Pages in the main pane, you should see a list of the configured error responses. Error responses listed as Local under Entry Type are configured at the current configuration level. You can now perform one of the following actions:

■ **Change a response action** To change the response action for a custom error response, click the related entry in the main pane, and then click Edit. In the Edit Custom Error Page, select a new response action, configure related settings as necessary, and then click OK.

■ **Change a status code** To change the status code for a custom error response, click the related entry in the main pane, and then click Change Status Code. Type the new status code, and then press Enter.

■ **Remove a custom error response** To remove a custom error response, click the related entry in the main pane, and then click Remove. When prompted to confirm, click Yes.

Using MIME and Configuring Custom File Types

Every static file that's transferred between IIS and a client browser has a data type designator, which is expressed as a Multipurpose Internet Mail Extensions (MIME) type. In the IIS configuration files, MIME type mappings allow you to configure extensions and associated content types that are served as static files.

Note Dynamic file types do not have MIME type mappings in the IIS configuration files. Instead, dynamic file types have handler mappings. Handler mappings, which also apply to certain types of static content, specify how a file should be processed. For more information on handlers and how they are used with IIS modules, see the "Extending IIS with Modules" section in Chapter 5, "Managing Global IIS Configuration."

Understanding MIME

To understand MIME, you need to know how servers use HTTP to transfer files. HTTP is a multipurpose protocol that you can use to transfer many types of files, including full-motion video sequences, stereo sound tracks, high-resolution images, and other types of media. The transfer of media files wouldn't be possible without the MIME standard. Web servers use MIME to identify the type of object being transferred. Object types are identified in an HTTP header field that comes before the actual data, and this allows a Web client to handle the object file appropriately.

Web servers set the MIME type by using the *Content_Type* directive, which is part of the HTTP header sent to client browsers. MIME types are broken down into categories, with each category having a primary subtype associated with it. Basic MIME types are summarized in Table 7-3.

Table 7-3   Basic MIME Types

Type	Description
Application	Binary data that can be executed or used with another application
Audio	A sound file that requires an output device to be broadcast
Image	A picture that requires an output device to view
Message	An encapsulated mail message
Multipart	Data consisting of multiple parts and possibly many data types
Text	Textual data that can be represented in any character set or formatting language
Video	A video file that requires an output device to preview
X-world	Experimental data type for 3-D world files

MIME subtypes are defined in three categories:

- **Primary**   Primary type of data adopted for use as a MIME content type

- **Additional**   Additional subtypes that have been officially adopted as MIME content types

- **Extended**   Experimental subtypes that haven't been officially adopted as MIME content types

You can easily identify extended subtypes because they begin with the letter x followed by a hyphen. Table 7-4 lists common MIME types and their descriptions.

Table 7-4   Common MIME Types

Type/Subtype	Description
Application/ mac-binhex40	Macintosh binary-formatted data
Application/msword	Microsoft Office Word document
Application/octet-stream	Binary data that can be executed or used with another application
Application/pdf	Adobe Acrobat Portable Document Format (PDF) document
Application/postscript	Postscript-formatted data
Application/rtf	Rich Text Format (RTF) document
Application/x-compress	Data that has been compressed using UNIX compress
Application/x- gzip	Data that has been compressed using UNIX gzip
Application/x-tar	Data that has been archived using UNIX tar
Application/x-zip-compressed	Data that has been compressed using PKZip or WinZip (or equivalent)

Table 7-4   Common MIME Types

Type/Subtype	Description
Audio/basic	Audio in a nondescript format
Audio/x-aiff	Audio in Apple Audio Interchange File Format (AIFF)
Audio/x-wav	Audio in Microsoft WAV format
Image/gif	Image in Graphics Interchange Format (GIF)
Image/jpeg	Image in Joint Photographic Experts Group (JPEG) format
Image/tiff	Image in Tagged Image File Format (TIFF)
Text/html	HTML-formatted text
Text/plain	Plain text with no HTML formatting
Video/mpeg	Video in the Moving Picture Experts Group (MPEG) format
Video/quicktime	Video in the Apple QuickTime format
Video/x-msvideo	Video in the Microsoft Audio Video Interleaved (AVI) format
X-world/x-vrml	Virtual Reality Modeling Language (VRML) world file

Hundreds of MIME types are configured using file-extension-to-file-type mappings. These mappings allow IIS to support just about any type of file that applications or utilities on the destination computer might expect. If a file doesn't end with a known extension, the file is sent as the default MIME type, which indicates that the file contains application data. In most cases use of the default MIME type means that the client is unable to handle the file or to trigger other utilities that handle the file. If you expect the client to handle a new file type appropriately, you must create a file-extension-to-file-type mapping.

MIME type mappings set at the server configuration level apply to all Web sites on the server. At the server configuration level, you can edit existing MIME types, configure additional MIME types, or delete unwanted MIME types. You can also create and manage additional MIME type mappings for individual sites and directories. When you do this, the MIME type mappings are available only in the site or directory in which they're configured.

Viewing and Configuring MIME Types

You can view and configure MIME types by completing the following steps:

1. In IIS Manager, navigate to the server, site, or directory you want to manage. You can view the MIME types for all Web sites on a server by selecting the server node. You can view the MIME types for sites and directories by selecting the appropriate nodes.

2. In the main pane, the MIME Types feature is listed under IIS when you group by area. Double-click MIME Types to open this feature. As shown in Figure 7-9, you should now see a list of configured MIME types by file extension and associated MIME type.

3. In IIS Manager, double-click the computer node for the IIS server you want to work with, and then select Properties.

4. Double-click MIME Types. As shown in Figure 7-9, you should see a list of the MIME types. Computer MIME types are active for all Web sites on the server.

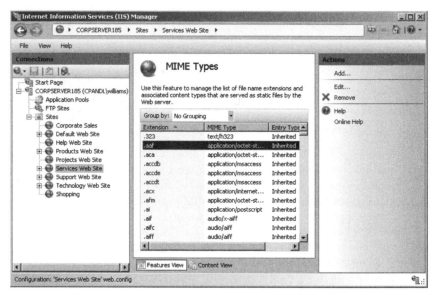

Figure 7-9   Use the MIME Types feature to view and configure computer MIME types.

5. Use the following settings to configure MIME types:

   ❑ **Add**   Adds a new MIME type. To add a MIME type, click Add. In the File Name Extension field, type a file extension such as .html, and then in the MIME Type field, type a MIME type such as text/html. Complete the process by clicking OK.

   ❑ **Edit**   Edits a MIME type mapping. To edit a MIME type, select it, and then click Edit. In the Edit MIME Type dialog box that appears, change the file extension and the content MIME type.

❑ **Remove**   Removes a MIME type mapping. To remove a MIME type, select it and then click Remove.

By using the IIS Command-line Administration Tool, you can manage MIME types by using the Set Config command and the staticContent section of the configuration file. Sample 7-12 provides the syntax and usage for adding and removing MIME types. Because you are referencing into the *fileExtension* collection, the brackets ([]) in the syntax and usage examples are literal values rather than indicators of optional values. You must use the brackets to indicate that you are referencing into the *fileExtension* collection.

Sample 7-12   Configuring MIME Types Syntax and Usage

Syntax
```
appcmd set config ["ConfigPath"] /section:staticContent
[ /+"[fileExtension='Extension',mimeType='MIMEType']" |
/-"[fileExtension='Extension',mimeType='MIMEType']" ]
```
Usage for Adding MIME Types
```
appcmd set config ["ConfigPath"] /section:staticContent
/+"[fileExtension='.htm',mimeType='text/html']"
```
Usage for Removing MIME Types
```
appcmd set config ["ConfigPath"] /section:staticContent
/-"[fileExtension='.htm',mimeType='text/html']"
```

Additional Customization Tips

Update sites, jump pages, and error forwarding are three additional techniques you can use to customize your IIS Web sites. Each of these techniques is discussed in the sections that follow.

Using Update Sites to Manage Outages

An update site allows you to handle outages in a way that's customer-friendly. Use the update sites function to display aclternate content when your primary sites are offline. So rather than seeing an error message where the user expects to find content, the user sees a message that provides information regarding the outage plus additional helpful information.

Each Web site you publish should have an update site. You create update sites by completing the following steps:

1. Create or arrange for someone else to create a Web page that can be displayed during outages. The page should explain that you're performing maintenance on the Web site and that the site will be back online shortly. The page can also

provide links to other sites that your organization publishes so that the user has somewhere else to visit during the maintenance.

2. Use Windows Explorer to create a directory for the update site. The best location for this directory is on the Web server's local drive. Afterward, copy the content files created by the Web development team into this directory.

> **Tip** I recommend that you create a top-level directory for storing the home directories and then create subdirectories for each update site. For example, you can create a top-level directory called D:\UpdateSites and then use sub-directories called WWWUpdate, ServicesUpdate, and ProductsUpdate to store the files for www.cpandl.com, services.cpandl.com, and products.cpandl.com, respectively.

3. In IIS Manager, select the main node for the computer you want to work with. If the computer isn't shown, connect to it.

4. Click the Sites node. You should now see a list of Web sites already configured on the server. You should write down the host header, IP address, and port configuration of the primary site you want to mimic during outages. To view this information, right-click the desired Web site, and then choose Bindings.

5. Create a new site using the configuration settings you just noted. Name the site so that it clearly identifies the site as an update site. For example, if you are creating an update site for the corporate Web Site, name the update sites "Update Site for the Corporate Web." Ensure that the new site doesn't start by clearing the Start Web Site Immediately check box before you click OK to add the Web site.

6. Perform the following tasks:

   ❑ Enable default content pages.

   ❑ Remove the existing default documents.

   ❑ Add a default document and set the document name to the name of the outage page just created.

7. By using the site's Custom Errors feature, edit the properties for 401, 403, 404, 405, 406, 412, 500, 501, and 502 errors. These errors should have the Message Type set to File and have a File path that points to your new outage page.

8. Update other site features as necessary.

Once you create the update site, you can activate it as follows:

1. Use IIS Manager to stop the primary site prior to performing maintenance, and then start the related update site.

2. Confirm that the update site is running by visiting the Web site in your browser. If the site is properly configured, you should be able to append any file name to the URL and be directed to the outage page.

3. Perform the necessary maintenance on the primary site. When you're finished, stop the update site and then start the primary site.

4. Confirm that the primary site is running by visiting the Web site in your browser.

Using Jump Pages for Advertising

A *jump page* is an intermediate page that redirects a user to another location. You can use jump pages to track click-throughs on banner advertisements or inbound requests from advertising done by the company.

With banner ads, jump pages ensure that users visit a page within your site before moving off to a page at an advertiser's site. This allows you to track the success of advertising on your site. Here's how it works:

1. A page in your site has a banner ad that is linked to a jump page on your site.

2. A user clicks on the ad and is directed to the jump page. The Web server tracks the page access and records it in the log file.

3. The jump page is configured to redirect the user to a page on the advertiser's Web site.

With corporate advertising, jump pages ensure that you can track the source of a visit to advertising done by the company. This allows you to track the success of your company's advertising efforts. Here's how it works:

1. The marketing department develops a piece of advertising collateral—for instance, a product brochure. Somewhere in the brochure, there's a reference to a URL on your site. This is the URL for the jump page you've configured.

2. A user types in the URL to the jump page as it was listed in the ad. The Web server tracks the page access and records it in the log file.

3. The jump page is configured to redirect the user to a page on your Web site where the advertised product or service is covered.

Each jump page you create should be unique, or you should create a dynamic page that reads an embedded code within the URL and then redirects the user. For example, you can create a page called Jump.asp that reads the first parameter passed to the script as the advertising code. Then you can create a link in the banner ad that specifies the URL and the code, such as Jump.asp?4408.

Handling 404 Errors and Preventing Dead Ends

Users hate dead ends, and that's just what a 404 error represents. Rather than having the browser display an apparently meaningless 404–File Or Directory Not Found error, you should throw the user a lifeline by doing one of two things:

- Replacing the default error file with a file that provides helpful information and links

- Redirecting all 404 errors to your site's home page

Either technique makes your Web site a better place to visit. This feature could be the one thing that separates your Web site from the pack.

Chapter 8
Running IIS Applications

Not long ago, when Web sites were primarily static Hypertext Markup Language (HTML) pages, the most serious problems facing Web administrators were configuring multiple sites on the same server and keeping the server running without failure. With the growing importance of Web servers not just on the Internet but also everywhere within the organization, different issues have emerged. Web servers must do more—and not just with respect to handling and responding to requests. Web servers must provide services, host applications, and serve dynamic content, all of which IIS can do using Internet Server Application Programming Interface (ISAPI) applications, Common Gateway Interface (CGI) programs, Active Server Pages (ASP) applications, and Microsoft ASP.NET applications.

Managing ISAPI and CGI Application Settings

As discussed in Chapter 3, "Core IIS 7.0 Administration," ISAPI and CGI are two basic types of IIS applications. ISAPI provides the core functionality for IIS 7.0 when applications use classic pipeline mode. ISAPI acts as a layer over IIS that can be extended using ISAPI applications, Active Server Pages (ASP), ASP.NET, and third-party extensions. CGI programs pass information to servers through environment variables that capture user input in forms in addition to details about the user, the user's browser, and the user's operating system.

Understanding ISAPI Applications

Although ISAPI applications are being replaced by the new IIS 7.0 modules API, IIS 7.0 maintains support for ISAPI applications. ISAPI applications fall into two categories:

- ISAPI filters
- ISAPI extensions

You can use both filters and extensions to modify the behavior of IIS. ISAPI filters are dynamic-link libraries (DLLs) or executables that are loaded into memory when the World Wide Web Publishing Service is started and remain in memory until the IIS server is shut down. ISAPI filters are triggered when a Web server event occurs on the IIS server. For example, an ISAPI filter can control which files are mapped to a URL, modify the response sent by the server, and perform other actions to modify the behavior of the server.

You can apply ISAPI filters globally or locally. Global filters affect all IIS Web sites running on a server and are loaded into memory when the World Wide Web Publishing Service is started. Local filters are called site filters. Site filters affect a single IIS Web site and can be dynamically loaded into memory when a request that uses such a filter is made to the site.

ISAPI filters aren't ideal choices when you need to perform long-running operations, such as database queries, or when you want to process the entire body of requests. In these instances, ISAPI extensions work better.

Like ISAPI filters, ISAPI extensions are defined as DLLs or executables. Unlike global filters, which are loaded with the World Wide Web Publishing Service, extensions are loaded on demand and are executed in response to client requests. Normally, ISAPI extensions are used to process the data received in requests for specific types of files. For example, when a client makes a request for a file that has an .asp extension, IIS uses the Asp.dll ISAPI extension to process the contents of ASP and return the results to the client for display. IIS provides classic ASP.NET functionality through an ISAPI filter (aspnet_filter.dll), which in turn calls an ISAPI extension (aspnet_isapi.dll).

When you install ASP and ASP.NET, default ISAPI extensions are configured for use on the Web server. ISAPI extensions are configured to respond to specific types of Hypertext Transfer Protocol (HTTP) requests or all HTTP requests for files with a specific file extension. Table 8-1 summarizes the key types of HTTP requests.

Table 8-1   HTTP Request Types Used with ISAPI Extensions

Request Type	Description
DELETE	A request to delete a resource. This request normally isn't allowed unless the user has specific privileges on the Web site.
GET	A request to retrieve a resource. This is the standard request for retrieving files.
HEAD	A request for an HTTP header. The return request doesn't contain a message body.
OPTIONS	A request for information about communications options.
POST	A request to submit data as a new subordinate of a resource. It is typically used for posting data from filled-out forms.
PUT	A request to store the enclosed data with the resource identifier specified. It is typically used when uploading files through HTTP.
TRACE	A request to trace the client's submission for testing or debugging.

Configuring ISAPI and CGI Restrictions

ISAPI and CGI restrictions control the ISAPI and CGI extensions that are allowed to run on a Web server. You configure restrictions only at the server configuration level. In IIS Manager, to view currently configured restrictions as either a CGI (.exe) or an ISAPI (.dll) file extension, select the server node, and then double-click the ISAPI And CGI Restrictions feature. On the ISAPI And CGI Restrictions page, shown in Figure 8-1, extensions are listed by:

- **Description** A brief description or friendly name for the related ISAPI or CGI application.

- **Restriction** The restriction status. If an extension is permitted to run, its restriction status is listed as Allowed. Otherwise, its restriction status is listed as Not Allowed.

- **Path** The execution path for the related ISAPI or CGI application.

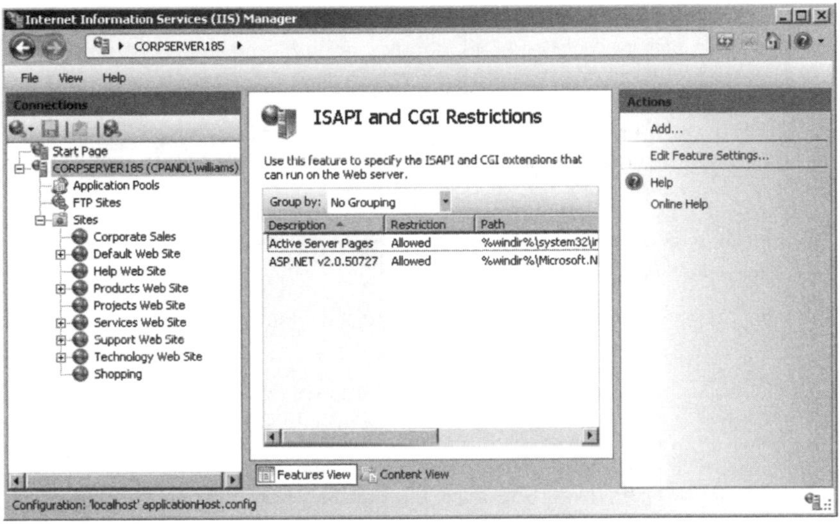

Figure 8-1 Determine which ISAPI and CGI extensions are allowed to run.

Some of the commonly allowed extensions you'll see include:

- **ASP.DLL** This ISAPI extension implements ASP functionality.

- **ASPNET_ISAPI.DLL** This ISAPI extension provides the processing functions for ASP.NET in classic pipeline mode.

- **OCSPISAPI.DLL** This ISAPI extension implements the certification status protocol for Certificate Services.

- **MSW3PRT.DLL** This ISAPI extension provides the processing functions for Internet printing.

Note Because the ASPNET_ISAPI.DLL extension is version-specific, you may see multiple versions of the extension registered. Specifically, there'll be one extension for each version of the Microsoft .NET Framework configured. Remove older versions of this extension only when you are sure they are no longer in use.

By default, only extensions listed as Allowed can run on the server. You can modify this configuration to allow unspecified CGI modules, unspecified ISAPI modules, or both to run without restriction. To modify this behavior, as may be necessary during development or temporarily for troubleshooting, you can allow unspecified extensions to run by completing the following steps:

1. In IIS Manager, select the server node, and then double-click ISAPI And CGI Restrictions.

2. In the Actions pane, click Edit Feature Settings. The Edit ISAPI And CGI Restrictions Settings dialog box appears.

3. You can now allow unspecified CGI modules, unspecified ISAPI modules, or both to run by selecting the related check boxes. To prevent unspecified CGI modules, unspecified ISAPI modules, or both from running, clear the related check boxes. When you are finished, click OK to save your settings.

Caution   Allowing unspecified modules to run on a Web server is a serious security risk. To prevent possible malicious use of the extension functionality, you should rarely allow unspecified modules to run on a Web server.

You can configure an Allowed or Not Allowed restriction for an extension by completing the following steps:

1. In IIS Manager, select the server node, and then double-click ISAPI And CGI Restrictions.

2. In the Actions pane, click Add. The Add ISAPI Or CGI Restriction dialog box appears.

3. Click the selection button to the right of the ISAPI Or CGI Path text box, and then in the Open dialog box, select the executable to configure as either a CGI (.exe) or an ISAPI (.dll) file extension.

4. If you wish, type a description of the extension.

5. To allow the extension to run, select the Allow Extension Path To Execute check box. To prevent the extension from running, do not select this check box. Click OK to add the restriction.

You can work with restrictions in a variety of other ways, as follows:

■ To change a currently set restriction from Allowed to Not Allowed, click the extension, and then in the Actions pane, click Deny.

■ To change a currently set restriction from Not Allowed to Allowed, click the extension, and then in the Actions pane, click Allow.

■ To modify an extension's execution path, description, and restriction status, click the extension, and then in the Actions pane, click Edit. In the Edit ISAPI Or

CGI Restriction dialog box, make the necessary changes to the restriction configuration, and then click OK.

- To remove an extension from the restriction list, click the extension, and then in the Actions pane, click Remove. When prompted to confirm the action, click Yes.

By using the IIS command-line administration tool, you can configure ISAPI and CGI restrictions by using the Set Config command and the IsapiCgiRestriction section of the configuration file. Sample 8-1 provides the syntax and usage.

Sample 8-1   Configuring ISAPI and CGI Restrictions Syntax and Usage

Syntax
```
appcmd set config ["ConfigPath"] /section:IsapiCgiRestriction
[/notListedIsapisAllowed:true|false]
[/notListedCgisAllowed:true|false]
```
Usage
```
appcmd set config "Default Web Site" /section:IsapiCgiRestriction
/notListedIsapisAllowed:true /notListedCgisAllowed:true
```

Configuring ISAPI Filters

ISAPI filters are DLLs that enhance the functionality provided by IIS. In IIS Manager, you can view currently configured filters by selecting a server or site node and then double-clicking the ISAPI Filters feature. On the ISAPI Filters page, you'll see a list of defined filters listed by name, executable, and entry type. Local entries are configured at the level you are working with. Inherited entries are configured at a higher level of the configuration hierarchy.

When you've configured a server to use ASP.NET, the standard filter you'll see is aspnet_filter.dll, which enables classic pipeline mode. Because this filter is version-specific, you may see multiple versions of the extension registered. Specifically, there'll be one extension for each version of the .NET Framework configured. Remove older versions of this extension only when you are sure they are no longer in use. Typically, no other standard filters are configured.

You can configure an ISAPI filter for use by completing the following steps:

1. In IIS Manager, select the server node, and then double-click ISAPI Filters.

2. In the Actions pane, click Add. This displays the Add ISAPI Filter dialog box.

3. In the Filter Name text box, type a descriptive name for the filter.

4. Click the selection button to the right of the Executable text box, in the Open dialog box, select the filter's DLL, and then click OK to add the filter.

You can edit, rename, or remove ISAPI filters by using the following techniques:

- To modify an ISAPI filter's executable path, click the filter entry you want to modify, and then click Edit. In the Edit ISAPI Filter dialog box, click the selection button to the right of the Executable text box, in the Open dialog box, select the filter's DLL, and then click OK to save your changes.

- To rename a filter, click the filter entry to select it, and then click Rename. Type the new name for the filter, and then press Enter.

- To remove a filter that is no longer needed, click the filter entry you want to remove, and then click Remove. When prompted to confirm the action, click Yes.

Configuring CGI Settings

You can control the way CGI applications are executed by using the settings on the CGI configuration page. You can set a time-out value for CGI applications, isolate CGI applications in their own console window, or configure CGI applications to run at the system or user level.

To view the currently configured CGI settings, in IIS Manager, navigate to the level of the configuration hierarchy you want to manage, and then access the CGI page by double-clicking the CGI feature. On the CGI page, you can configure the way CGI applications are used by using the following techniques:

- You can modify the time-out for CGI applications by typing the desired time-out in the Time-Out text box. Use the hh:mm:ss format where hh is for hours, mm is for minutes, and ss is for seconds. The default value is 00:15:00 (15 minutes). In most cases, you'll want a relatively short time-out value. The reason for this is that when CGI applications time out, IIS removes the related process and frees up the resources it used. Increase the time-out period only when users are experiencing problems with long-running requests that are processed through CGI applications.

- You can specify whether each CGI application runs in a separate console window by setting the Use New Console For Each Invocation option. The default value is False. If the value is set to True, each CGI application creates a new console window when started, which isolates each application and prevents problems with one CGI application from affecting another CGI application (in most cases). However, because creating a new console window for each CGI application uses additional resources on the server, there is a trade-off to be made between application isolation and resource usage.

- You can specify whether a CGI application process is created in the system context or in the context of the requesting user by using the Impersonate User feature. The default value is True. When True, IIS creates CGI application processes in the context of the requesting user. When False, IIS creates CGI application processes in the system context. Run CGI applications in a system context only when there is a specific need to do so, such as when an application requires the additional permissions available to the system user. Otherwise, run CGI applications in the user context to enhance security and reduce the possibility of malicious use of elevated privileges.

By using the IIS command-line administration tool, you can configure CGI settings by using the Set Config command and the Cgi section of the configuration file. Sample 8-2 provides the syntax and usage.

Sample 8-2   Configuring CGI Settings Syntax and Usage

Syntax
```
appcmd set config ["ConfigPath"] /section:Cgi
[/createCGIWithNewConsole:true|false]
[/createProcessAsUser:true|false]
[/timeout: "hh:mm:ss"
```
Usage
```
appcmd set config "Default Web Site" /section:Cgi
/createCGIWithNewConsole:true /createProcessAsUser:true
/timeout: "00:10:00"
```

Managing ASP Settings

ASP is a server-side scripting environment used to create dynamic Web applications. An ASP application is a collection of resource files and components that are grouped logically. Logically grouping files and components as an application allows IIS to share data within the application and to run the application as a shared, pooled, or isolated process. You can have multiple applications per Web site, and you can configure each application differently.

IIS resource files include ASP pages, HTML pages, GIF images, JPEG images, and other types of Web documents. An ASP page is a file that ends with the .asp extension that includes HTML, a combination of HTML and scripting, or only scripting. Scripts within ASP pages can be intended for processing by a client browser or the server itself. Scripts designed to be processed on the server are called server-side scripts and can be written using Microsoft Visual Basic Scripting Edition (VBScript), Microsoft JScript, or any other scripting language available on the server.

ASP provides an object-based scripting environment. Server-side scripts use the built-in objects to perform common tasks, such as tracking session state, managing errors, and reading HTTP requests sent by clients. ASP scripts can also use Component Object Model (COM) components. Prebuilt components are available in the standard IIS 7.0 installation and are included in the *%SystemRoot%*\System32\Inetsrv directory on the IIS server.

Controlling ASP Behavior

To view the currently configured ASP behavior settings, in IIS Manager, navigate to the level of the confiuration hierarchy you want to manage, and then access the ASP page, by double-clicking the ASP feature. On the ASP page, shown in Figure 8-2, you'll find a variety of settings under the Behavior node.

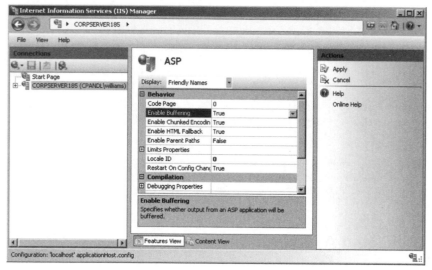

Figure 8-2 Review the ASP behavior settings.

For ASP, buffering is a key option that affects server performance and resource usage. When buffering is enabled, as per the default setting, IIS completely processes ASP pages before sending content to the client browser. When buffering is disabled, IIS returns output to the client browser as the page is processed. The advantage to buffering is that it allows IIS to respond dynamically to events that occur while processing the page. IIS can take one of the following actions:

- Abort sending a page or transfer the user to a different page

- Clear the buffer and send different content to the user

- Change HTTP header information from anywhere in your ASP script

A disadvantage of buffering is that users have to wait for the entire script to be processed before content is delivered to their browser. If a script is long or complex, the user might have to wait for a long time before seeing the page. To counter potential delays associated with buffering, developers often insert Flush commands at key positions within the script. If your development team does this, they should be aware that this causes additional connection requests between the client and server, which might also cause performance problems.

Other options that control the behavior of ASP include Code Page, Enable Chunked Encoding, Enable HTML Fallback, Enable Parent Paths, Locale ID, Restart On Config Change, and Script Language. Code Page sets the default code page that IIS should use when working with non-Unicode character data. The default setting is zero (0), which indicates that IIS should use the code page used by the server for storing and displaying non-Unicode character data.

Enable Chunked Encoding determines whether HTTP 1.1 chunked transfer encoding is enabled. The default is True. All HTTP 1.1–compliant applications, such as Web browsers, support chunked encoding. With chunked encoding, IIS transfers the body of responses as a series of message chunks, each with its own size indicator, following by an optional trailer containing entity-header fields. This allows dynamically generated content to be transferred along with the information necessary for the recipient to verify that it has received the full message. If chunked encoding is disabled, IIS transfers responses to requests using standard encoding, and client browsers have no way to verify that the full response has been received. If chunked encoding is enabled, IIS transfers responses to requests by using chunked encoding, and client browsers can verify that the full response has been received.

Enable HTML Fallback determines whether HTML is used as a fallback when the ASP request queue is full. The default is True. When set to True and the request queue is full, ASP will substitute an HTML file that has _asp added to the file name and return the file if found. For example, if the name of the requested .asp file is inventory.asp, the name of the .htm file that is returned will be inventory_asp.htm. If the file does not exist or you've disabled fallback and the request queue is full, IIS returns a 500.13 (Web Server is too busy) HTTP error to the client.

Enable Parent Paths determines whether ASP pages allows paths relative to parent directories in addition to the current directory. The default is False. When enabled, ASP pages can use relative paths to access parent directories of the current directory. For example, a script could reference ../Build.htm, where ".." is a reference to the current directory's parent directory. When disabled, ASP pages cannot use parent paths.

Locale ID sets the default locale identifier (LCID) for an application. Locale identifiers control the formatting of numbers, currencies, dates, and times. The default setting is zero (0), which indicates that IIS should use the locale identifier used by the server.

Restart On Config Change determines whether IIS automatically restarts ASP applications when you change critical configuration properties that affect how applications are used. The default is True. To restart an application, IIS stops and then starts the application. This means that all resources used by the application are freed. This also means, however, that any requests currently being processed will fail and that new requests for the application aren't processed until the application is started.

Script Language sets the default scripting language for ASP pages. Two scripting engines are installed with a standard IIS installation. These scripting engines are for

VBScript and JScript. You can reference these scripting engines by using the values VBScript and JScript, respectively. The default scripting language in a standard IIS installation is VBScript. In ASP pages, you can override the default language by using the <%@LANGUAGE%> directive.

You manage ASP behavior settings by completing the following steps:

1. In IIS Manager, navigate to the level of the configuration hierarchy you want to manage, and then access the ASP page by double-clicking the ASP feature.

2. On the ASP page, under Behavior, set the following options to configure ASP behavior: Code Page, Enable Buffering, Enable Chunked Encoding, Enable HTML Fallback, and Enable Parent Paths.

3. On the ASP page, under Compilation, use the Script Language option to set the default scripting language.

In the Actions pane, click Apply.

By using the IIS command-line administration tool, you can configure ASP behavior settings by using the Set Config command and the ASP section of the configuration file. Sample 8-3 provides the syntax and usage.

Sample 8-3   Configuring ASP Behavior Settings Syntax and Usage

Syntax
```
appcmd set config ["ConfigPath"] /section:Asp
[/codepage: "CodePage"]
[/bufferingOn: true|false]
[/enableChunkedEncoding: true|false]
[/enableAspHtmlFallback: true|false]
[/enableParentPaths: true|false]
[/lcid: "LocaleID"]
[/enableApplicationRestart: true|false]
[/scriptLanguage: "ScriptLanguage"]
```
Usage
```
appcmd set config "Default Web Site" /section:Asp
/bufferingOn: true /enableChunkedEncoding: true
```

Customizing Request Handling for ASP

Many different options control the way ASP handles and responds to requests. To view the related ASP settings, in IIS Manager, navigate to the level of the configuration hierarchy you want to manage, and then access the ASP page by double-clicking the ASP feature. On the ASP page, under Behavior, expand the Limits Properties node to see the related properties.

Client Connection Test Interval sets the period of time a request should be queued. If the request is queued longer than the specified time, ASP checks to determine whether the client is still connected before running a request. If the client is no longer connected, the request is not processed and is deleted from the queue. The default is 00:00:03 (3 seconds).

Maximum Requesting Entity Body Limit determines the maximum number of bytes allowed in the entity-body of an ASP request. The default is 200,000 bytes (195 KB). If the maximum value is exceeded, IIS truncates the request or generates an error.

Queue Length determines the maximum number of concurrent ASP requests that are permitted in the ASP request queue. The default is 3000. IIS does not allow any new requests when the queue has reached the maximum value. If you've disabled HTML fallback and the request queue is full, IIS returns a 500.13 (Web Server is too busy) HTTP error to the client.

Request Queue Timeout sets the period of time that an ASP request is allowed to wait in the queue. The default is 00:00:00 (infinite), allowing a request to be queued indefinitely. If you set a specific time-out, IIS removes requests older than the time-out period automatically and does not attempt to process them. All requests that wait in the queue are also subject to the Client Connection Test Interval.

Response Buffering Limit sets the maximum size of the ASP response buffer. If response buffering is enabled, this property controls the maximum number of bytes that an ASP page can write to the response buffer before a flush occurs. The default is 4,194,304 bytes (4096 KB).

Script Timeout determines the default length of time that IIS allows an ASP script to run before attempting to stop the script and writing an event to the Windows event log. The default is 00:01:30 (90 seconds).

Threads Per Processor Limit determines the maximum number of worker threads per processor that IIS can create to handle ASP requests. The default is 25. Once the per-processor thread limit is reached, IIS will not generate new threads to handle ASP requests. This doesn't necessarily mean that request processing will fail. Worker processes associated with application pools are responsible ultimately for handling requests. Worker processes can use additional threads to improve responsiveness and handling of requests. If no new threads are available, worker processes must handle requests by using currently allocated threads.

You can customize request handling for ASP by completing the following steps:

1. In IIS Manager, navigate to the level of the configuration hierarchy you want to manage and then access the ASP page by double-clicking the ASP feature.

2. On the ASP page, under Behavior, expand the Limits Properties node by double-clicking it.

3. Use the Limit Properties to configure request handling for ASP.

4. In the Actions pane, click Apply.

By using the IIS command-line administration tool, you can configure request-handling settings by using the Set Config command and the Asp\limits section of the configuration file. Sample 8-4 provides the syntax and usage.

Sample 8-4   Configuring Request Handling Settings Syntax and Usage

Syntax
```
appcmd set config ["ConfigPath"] /section:Asp
[/limits.queueConnectionTestTime: "hh:mm:ss"]
[/limits.maxRequestEntityAllowed: "RequestLimit"]
[/limits.requestQueueMax: "QueueLength"]
[/limits.queueTimeout: "hh:mm:ss"]
[/limits.bufferingLimit: "BufferingLimit"]
[/limits.scriptTimeout: "hh:mm:ss"]
[/limits.processorThreadMax: "ThreadLimit"]
```
Usage
```
appcmd set config "Default Web Site" /section:Asp
/limits.queueConnectionTestTime: "00:00:05"
/limits.requestQueueMax: "5000"
```

Optimizing Caching for ASP

IIS compiles ASP pages at run time when they're first requested, and then the compiled code is stored in the file cache where it can be reused without recompiling. The way IIS caches ASP pages depends on these caching properties:

- **Cache Directory Path**   Sets the name of the directory that ASP uses to store compiled ASP templates to disk after overflow of the in-memory cache. The default is *%SystemDrive%* \Inetpub\Temp\ASP Compiled Templates.

- **Enable Type Library Caching**   Determines whether Type Library caching is enabled. The default value, True, enables Type Library caching.

- **Maximum Disk Cached Files**   Sets the maximum number of compiled ASP templates that can be stored on disk. The default value is 2000. The valid range is from 0 to 2147483647 files.

- **Maximum Memory Cached Files**   Sets the maximum number of precompiled script files to cache in memory. The default value is 500 files. The valid range is from 0 to 2147483647 files.

- **Maximum Script Engines Cached**   Sets the maximum number of scripting engines that IIS will keep cached in memory. The default value is 250 cached scripting engines. The valid range is from 0 to 2147483647 script engines.

You can optimize caching for ASP by completing the following steps:

1. In IIS Manager, navigate to the level of the configuration hierarchy you want to manage and then access the ASP page by double-clicking the ASP feature.

2. On the ASP page, expand the Caching Properties node by double-clicking it.

3. In Caching Properties, configure caching settings for ASP.

4. In the Actions pane, click Apply.

By using the IIS command-line administration tool, you can configure caching settings by using the Set Config command and the Asp\session section of the configuration file. Sample 8-5 provides the syntax and usage.

Sample 8-5   Configuring Caching Settings Syntax and Usage

Syntax
```
appcmd set config ["ConfigPath"] /section:Asp
[/session.diskTemplateCacheDirectory: "DirectoryPath"]
[/session.enableTypelibCache: true|false]
[/session.maxDiskTemplateCacheFiles: "NumFiles"]
[/session.scriptFileCacheSize: "CacheSize"]
[/session.scriptEngineCacheMax: "NumEngines"]
```
Usage
```
appcmd set config "Default Web Site" /section:Asp
/session.enableTypelibCache: true
/session.maxDiskTemplateCacheFiles: "2500"
```

Customizing COM+ Execution for ASP

ASP can use different types of Component Object Model components. The way those components are used depends on these Com Plus Properties for ASP:

- **Enable Side By Side Component**   Determines whether COM+ side-by-side assemblies are enabled. When True, ASP applications can use COM+ side-by-side assemblies to specify which version of a system DLL or COM component to use. The default is False.

- **Enable Tracker**   Determines whether the COM+ tracker is enabled. When True, you can debug applications by using the COM+ tracker. The default is False.

- **Execute In MTA**   Determines whether ASP can run scripts in a multithreaded execution mode. The default is False. When True, ASP can use multiple threads to execute scripts (but scripts must be designed for and compliant with multithreading).

- **Honor Component Threading Model** Determines whether IIS examines the threading model of any components that your application creates. The default is False. If True, IIS checks the threading model of any components that your application creates to ensure that it is appropriate. Otherwise, IIS does not check the threading model.

- **Partition ID** When COM+ partitioning is used, Partition ID sets the GUID of the COM+ partition. This value is not used when COM+ partitioning is disabled.

- **Side By Side Component** When side-by-side execution is enabled, sets the name of the COM+ application. This value is not used when side-by-side execution is disabled.

- **Use Partition** Determines whether COM+ partitioning is used to isolate applications into their own COM+ partitions. When this property is set to True, you must specify a value for the Partition ID element.

You can customize the way ASP uses COM+ components by completing the following steps:

1. In IIS Manager, navigate to the level of the configuration hierarchy you want to manage, and then access the ASP page by double-clicking the ASP feature.

2. On the ASP page, under Services, expand the Com Plus Properties node by double-clicking it.

3. Use Com Plus Properties to configure COM+ component handling for ASP.

4. In the Actions pane, click Apply.

By using the IIS command-line administration tool, you can configure COM+ settings by using the Set Config command and the Asp\comPlus section of the configuration file. Sample 8-6 provides the syntax and usage.

Sample 8-6 Configuring COM+ Handling Settings Syntax and Usage

Syntax
```
appcmd set config ["ConfigPath"] /section:Asp
[/comPlus.appServiceFlags: true|false]
[/comPlus.appServiceFlags: true|false]
[/comPlus.executeInMta: true|false]
[/comPlus.trackThreadingModel: true|false]
[/comPlus.partitionID: "PartitionGUID"]
[/comPlus.sxsName: "AppName"]
[/comPlus.usePartition: true|false]
```
Usage
```
appcmd set config "Default Web Site" /section:Asp
/comPlus.appServiceFlags: true
/comPlus.executeInMta: true
```

Configuring Session State for ASP

Session state plays a significant role in IIS performance and resource usage. When session state is enabled, IIS creates a session for each user who accesses an ASP or ASP.NET application. Session information is used to track the user within the application and to pass user information from one page to another. For example, your company might want to track individual user preferences within an application, and you can use sessions to do this.

By default, IIS uses in-process session state management. The way sessions work in this mode is fairly straightforward. The first time a user requests an ASP or ASP.NET page with a specified application, IIS generates one of the following:

- A *Session* object containing all values set for the user session, including an identifier for the code page used to display the dynamic content, a location identifier, a session ID, and a time-out value

- A *Session.Contents* collection, which contains all the items that the application has set in the session

- A *Session.StaticObjects* collection, which contains the static objects defined for the application

The *Session* object and its associated properties are stored in memory on the server. The user's session ID is passed to the user's browser as a cookie. As long as the browser accepts cookies, the session ID is passed back to the server on subsequent requests. This is true even if the user requests a page in a different application. The same ID is used in order to reduce the number of cookies sent to the browser. If the browser doesn't accept cookies, the session ID can't be maintained, and IIS can't track the user session by using this technique. In this case, you could track the session state on the server.

Session state is enabled by default for all IIS applications. By default, sessions time out in 20 minutes. This means that if a user doesn't request or refresh a page within 20 minutes, the session ends and IIS removes the related *Session* object from memory. Worker process recycling can affect session management. If a worker process is recycled or otherwise cleared out of memory, the session state could be lost. If this happens, you won't be able to recover the session data.

As you might imagine, tracking sessions can use valuable system resources. You can reduce resource usage by reducing the time-out interval or disabling session tracking altogether. Reducing the time-out interval allows sessions to expire more quickly than usual. Disabling session tracking tells IIS that sessions shouldn't be automatically created. You can still start sessions manually within the application. Simply place the <%@ENABLESESSIONSTATE = True%> directive in individual ASP pages.

For ASP pages, you control session state management by using the ASP feature. In IIS Manager, navigate to the level of the configuration hierarchy you want to manage, and then display the ASP page by double-clicking the ASP feature. On the ASP page, expand the Session Properties node by double-clicking it. You can then use the following Session properties to manage caching for ASP:

■ **Enable Session State**   Determines whether session state persistence is enabled for applications. The default is True.

■ **Maximum Sessions**   Sets the maximum number of concurrent sessions that IIS will allow. The default is 4294967295.

■ **New ID On Secure Connection**   Determines whether IIS generates a new cookie when a transition from a non-secure to a secure connection is made. The default is True, and in most cases, you'll want to keep this value.

■ **Timeout**   Sets the period of time that IIS maintains a session object after the last request associated with the object is made. The default is 00:20:00. For a high-usage application in which you expect users to move quickly from page to page, you might want to set a fairly low time-out value, such as 5 or 10 minutes. On the other hand, if it's critical that the user's session is maintained to complete a transaction, you might want to set a long time-out value, such as 60 minutes.

By using the IIS command-line administration tool, you can configure session state settings by using the Set Config command and the Asp\session section of the configuration file. Sample 8-7 provides the syntax and usage.

Sample 8-7   Configuring Session State Settings for ASP Syntax and Usage

Syntax
```
appcmd set config ["ConfigPath"] /section:Asp
[/session.allowSessionState: true|false]
[/session.max: "MaxSessions"
[/session.keepSessionIdSecure: true|false]
[/session.timeout: "hh:mm:ss"
```
Usage
```
appcmd set config "Default Web Site" /section:Asp
/session.allowSessionState: true
/session.timeout: "00:15:00"
```

Configuring Debugging and Error Handling for ASP

One of the best ways to troubleshoot an IIS application is to enable debugging. Debugging is handled through server-side and client-side configuration settings. Server-side debugging allows IIS to throw errors while processing ASP pages and to display a prompt that allows you to start the Microsoft Script Debugger. You can then use the debugger to examine your ASP pages. Client-side debugging involves sending debugging information to the client browser. You can then use this information to help determine what's wrong with IIS and the related ASP page.

You can use the following debugging options to help you detect and diagnose problems. Calculate Line Numbers determines whether ASP should calculate and store the line number of each executed line of code. The default is True. If set to True, ASP can report the line number on which an error occurred during execution. Otherwise, ASP does not report the line number in error reports.

Catch COM Component Exceptions determines whether ASP pages trap exceptions thrown by COM components. The default is True. If set to True, ASP attempts to catch exceptions, which prevents the exception from being handled elsewhere, such as the scripting engine or the IIS worker process. If set to False, ASP does not attempt to catch exceptions, which could lead to the exception being handled elsewhere and could also cause termination of the worker process.

Other debugging options are:

- **Enable Client-Side Debugging**   Determines whether debugging is enabled for ASP on the client. The default is False. If set to True, client-side debugging is enabled, which may be necessary for troubleshooting and diagnostics.

- **Enable Log Error Requests**   Determines whether IIS writes ASP errors to the IIS log files. The default is True. If set to True, IIS writes ASP errors to the IIS log files.

- **Enable Server-Side Debugging**   Determines whether debugging is enabled for ASP on the server. The default is False. If set to True, server-side debugging is enabled, which may be necessary for troubleshooting and diagnostics.

- **Log Errors To NT Log**   Determines whether IIS writes ASP errors to the Windows event logs. The default is False. If set to True, IIS writes ASP errors to the Windows event logs, which may be necessary for troubleshooting and diagnostics.

- **Run On End Functions Anonymously**   Determines whether the *SessionOnEnd* and *ApplicationOnEnd* global ASP functions should be run as the anonymous user. The default is True. If set to True, the functions are run as the anonymous user. If set to False, the functions are not run at all.

- **Script Error Message**   Sets the error message to send to the browser if specific debugging errors are not sent to the client. The default message sent is "An error occurred on the server when processing the URL. Please contact the system administrator."

- **Send Errors To Browser**   Determines whether IIS writes ASP errors to client browsers. The default is False. If set to True, IIS writes ASP errors to client browsers, such as may be necessary for troubleshooting and diagnostics.

You manage debugging and error handling settings by completing the following steps:

1. In IIS Manager, navigate to the level of the configuration hierarchy you want to manage, and then access the ASP page by double-clicking the ASP feature.

2. On the ASP page, under Compilation, expand the Debugging Properties node by double-clicking it.

3. On the ASP page, under Compilation, set the Debugging Properties options to configure the way ASP should debug and handle errors.

4. In the Actions pane, click Apply.

Caution   Server-side debugging of ASP applications is designed for development and staging servers and not necessarily for production servers. If you enable server-side debugging on a production server, you might notice a severe decrease in performance for the affected application.

By using the IIS command-line administration tool, you can configure debugging settings by using the Set Config command and the ASP section of the configuration file. Sample 8-8 provides the syntax and usage.

Sample 8-8   Configuring Debugging for ASP Syntax and Usage

Syntax
```
appcmd set config ["ConfigPath"] /section:Asp
[/calcLineNumber: true|false]
[/exceptionCatchEnable: true|false]
[/appAllowClientDebug: true|false]
[/logErrorRequests: true|false]
[/appAllowDebugging: true|false]
[/errorsToNTLog: true|false]
[/runOnEndAnonymously: true|false]
[/scriptErrorMessage: true|false]
[/scriptErrorSentToBrowser: true|false]
```
Usage
```
appcmd set config "Default Web Site" /section:Asp
/exceptionCatchEnable: true
/errorsToNTLog: true
```

Managing ASP.NET Settings

ASP.NET moves away from the reliance on ISAPI and ASP to provide a reliable framework for Web applications that takes advantage of the Microsoft .NET Framework. ASP.NET is, in fact, a set of .NET technologies for creating Web applications. With ASP.NET, developers can write the executable parts of their pages using any .NET-compliant language, including Microsoft Visual C#, Microsoft Visual Basic, and Microsoft JScript.

Unlike ASP, ASP.NET has components that are precompiled prior to run time. These precompiled components are called *assemblies*. Compiled assemblies not only load and run faster than ASP pages, but they also are more secure. As you might recall from the discussion in Chapter 3, whereas ASP.NET can process requests in either classic pipeline mode or integrated pipeline mode, only the integrated mode allows IIS to process requests directly.

Note Server-level configuration changes for ASP.NET features are made in the Web.config file in the *%SystemRoot%*\Microsoft.NET\Framework*Framework Version*\Config folder, where *FrameworkVersion* is the version of the .NET Framework you are using, such as V2.0.50727. Site-level and application-level configuration changes for ASP.NET features are made in the Web.config file stored in the site or application folder.

Configuring Session State Settings for ASP.NET

In the default configuration, IIS manages session state for ASP.NET in much the same way as it manages session state for ASP. Beyond the basic settings, however, you have many more options. For ASP.NET pages, you use the Enable Session State setting of the Pages And Controls feature as the master control to turn on or off session state management or to configure IIS to use a read-only session state. You use the Session State feature to fine tune how session state management is used.

By default, IIS maintains session state in process as does ASP. Each ASP.NET application configured on your server can have its own session state settings. When you've activated the ASP.NET State Service and configured it to start automatically, you can use out-of-process session state management for ASP.NET. Out-of-process state management ensures that session state information is preserved when an application's worker process is recycled. You can configure out-of-process state management to use a State Server or a Microsoft SQL Server database. Before you configure a SQL Server for session state, you must run the InstallSqlState.sql script on the server. By default, this script is stored in *%SystemRoot%*\Microsoft.NET\Framework*FrameworkVersion*, where *FrameworkVersion* is the version of the .NET Framework you are using, such as V2.0.50727.

You turn on or off session state management or use a read-only session state by following these steps:

1. In IIS Manager, navigate to the level of the configuration hierarchy you want to manage, and then display the Pages And Controls page by double-clicking the Pages And Controls feature.

2. On the Pages And Controls page, shown in Figure 8-3, the Enable Session State text box shows the current session state. As necessary, change this setting to False to disable session state maintenance, True to enable session state maintenance, or ReadOnly to use a read-only session state.

3. In the Actions pane, click Apply to save your settings.

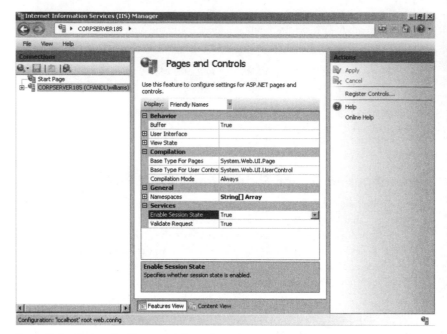

Figure 8-3   Review the Pages and Controls settings.

Once you've enabled a ReadWrite or ReadOnly session state, you can use the settings of the Session State feature to optimize the session state configuration. Follow these steps:

1. In IIS Manager, navigate to the level of the configuration hierarchy you want to manage, and then display the Session State page by double-clicking the Session State feature.

2. On the Session State Mode Settings frame in the main pane, shown in Figure 8-4, use the following options to set the session state mode:

    ❑ **Not Enabled**   Select this option to disable session state.

    ❑ **In Process**   Select this option to store session state data for a managed-code application in the worker process where the application runs. This is the default setting.

    ❑ **Custom**   Select this option to configure IIS to use a custom provider to handle session state for ASP.NET applications.

    ❑ **State Server**   Select this option to enable the ASP.NET State Service and store session state data outside the worker process where the application runs. The ASP.NET State Service stores the session state in an internal database by default or in a database of your choosing. You must start the service and configure it for automatic startup.

❑ **SQL Server** Select this option to configure IIS to use a SQL Server database to store session state data instead of storing it in the worker process where the application runs. The ASP.NET State Service stores the session state in the SQL Server database you designate. You must start the service and configure it for automatic startup.

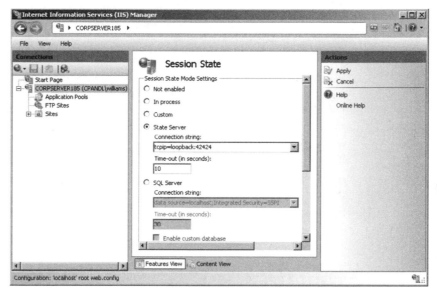

Figure 8-4 Configure the session state mode for ASP.NET.

3. With the State Server or SQL Server option, the Connection String text box sets the connection string that is used to connect to the state server or SQL Server. If you click the related selection drop-down list, you can choose a previously created connection string to use. If you click the related Create button, you create the required connection string by using the Create Connection String dialog box.

4. With the State Server or SQL Server option enabled, the related Time-Out text box sets the time, in seconds, that the connection will be maintained. The default for a state server is 10 seconds. The default for a server running SQL Server is 30 seconds.

5. With the SQL Server option enabled, you can select the Enable Custom Database check box to enable a custom SQL Server database for storing session state data.

6. On the Cookie Settings pane, in the Mode drop-down list, select the desired item to specify how cookies are used to store session state data. The items are:

- ❑ **Auto Detect** IIS uses cookies if the browser supports cookies and cookie support is enabled. Otherwise, IIS doesn't use cookies.

- ❑ **Use Cookies** Allows IIS to track the session state by using cookies. IIS passes the session state in cookies for all requests between a client browser and the Web server. Because cookies do not require redirection, cookies allow you to track session state more efficiently than any of the methods that do not use cookies. Using cookies also has several other advantages. Cookies allow users to bookmark Web pages, and they ensure that state is retained if a user leaves one site to visit another and then returns to the original site.

- ❑ **Use Device Profile** IIS uses cookies if the device profile supports cookies regardless of whether cookie support is enabled or disabled. The only time that IIS doesn't use cookies is when the device profile indicates that the browser doesn't support cookies.

- ❑ **Use URI** IIS inserts the session ID as a query string in the Uniform Resource Identifier (URI) request, and then the URI is redirected to the originally requested URL. Because the changed URI request is used for the duration of the session, no cookie is necessary.

7. Keep the following in mind when you are specifying how cookies are used to store session state data:

- ❑ When you use the Auto-Detect cookie, Use Device Profile, or Use URI modes, the Regenerate Expired Session ID check box is selected automatically. This ensures that IIS rejects and reissues session IDs that do not have active sessions. You should require that expired session IDs be regenerated because this ensures that IIS expires and regenerates tokens, which gives a potential attacker less time to capture a cookie and gain access to server content. If you want to disable session ID regeneration, as may be necessary when initially testing a new deployment in a development environment, clear this check box. Be sure to re-enable this feature later to enhance server security.

- ❑ When you use the Auto-Detect cookie, Use Cookies, or Use Device Profile modes, the entry in the Time-Out (In Minutes) text box sets the period of time that IIS maintains a session object after the last request associated with the object is made. The default time-out is 20 minutes. For a high-usage application in which you expect users to move quickly from page to page, you might want to set a fairly low time-out value, such as 5 or 10 minutes. On the other hand, if it's critical that the user's session is maintained to complete a transaction, you might want to set a long time-out value, such as 60 minutes.

❑ When you use the Auto-Detect cookie, Use Cookies, or Use Device Profile modes, the Name text box sets a name for the cookie. The default is ASP.NET_SessionId. To enhance security, you may want to change this value to a name that isn't as readily identifiable as the session ID.

❑ The Use Hosting Identity For Impersonation option enables Windows authentication for remote connections using the host process identity. Typically, this is the setting you want to use to ensure that IIS can read and write session state data.

8. In the Actions pane, click Apply to save your settings.

Configuring SMTP E-Mail Settings

E-mail services are an important part of most Internet, intranet, and extranet server operations. Often, you'll find that applications installed on a server generate e-mail messages that need to be delivered. For this purpose, IIS includes the Simple Mail Transfer Protocol (SMTP) feature so that IIS can deliver e-mail messages for Web applications that use the System.Net.Mail API. The configuration restricts the sending of messages that are generated by remote users, which include the Internet Guest account and any other named user on the Web server. The configuration also restricts relaying of e-mail through SMTP.

SMTP is just one of several components that make up a typical e-mail system. Windows Server 2008 includes the optional SMTP Server feature to provide a more robust solution. However, if you want to receive e-mail and store it on the server so that users and applications can retrieve it, you need to install a full-featured messaging server in the enterprise, such as Microsoft Exchange Server 2007.

You can use the SMTP E-mail feature in two key ways. You can use this feature to deliver e-mail messages generated by applications to a specific SMTP server running on the local system or a remote server. Or you can use this feature to drop e-mail directly into the pickup directory for later processing by an application or for direct processing by an SMTP server running on the local system. Because SMTP servers monitor their pickup directories continuously for new messages, any message placed in this directory is picked up and transferred to a queue directory for further processing and delivery.

E-mail messages have To, Cc, Bcc, and From fields to determine how the message should be handled. To, Cc, and Bcc fields are used to determine where the message should be delivered. The From field indicates the origin of the message. E-mail addresses, such as *williams@tech.microsoft.com*, have three components:

■ An e-mail account, such as *williams*

■ An at symbol (@), which separates the account name from the domain name

■ An e-mail domain, such as *tech.microsoft.com*

The key component that determines how the server handles messages is the e-mail or service domain. Service domains can be either local or remote. A *local service domain* is a Domain Name System (DNS) domain that's serviced locally by the server. A *remote service domain* is a DNS domain that's serviced by another server or mail gateway.

You can deliver e-mail to a locally hosted or remote SMTP server by completing the following steps:

1. In IIS Manager, navigate to the level of the configuration hierarchy you want to manage, and then display the SMTP E-Mail page by double-clicking the SMTP E-Mail feature.

2. On the SMTP E-Mail page, shown in Figure 8-5, in the E-Mail Address text box, type the address you want to use as the default address from which e-mail messages are sent.

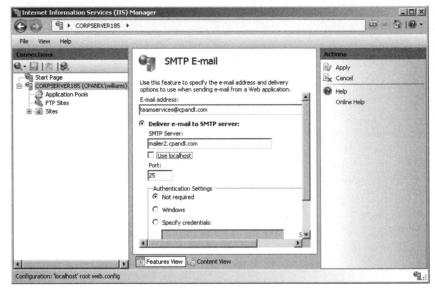

Figure 8-5   Configure SMTP E-mail settings.

3. Select the Deliver E-Mail To SMTP Server option.

4. In the SMTP Server text box, type the fully qualified domain name of the SMTP server, such as mailer5.adatum.com. Or select the Use Localhost check box to set the name of the SMTP server to localhost, allowing System.Net.Mail to send e-mail directly to the SMTP server on the local computer.

5. In the Port text box, type the TCP port number to use to connect to the SMTP server. The standard TCP port for SMTP is 25, so this is the default and recommended setting.

6. The Authentication Settings options allow you to specify the authentication mode and credentials. If your SMTP server does not require authentication, choose Not Required. Otherwise, choose one of the following options:

   ❏ **Windows**   Choose this to use the application identity for connecting to the SMTP server.

   ❏ **Specify Credentials**   Choose this to specify a user name and password for connecting to the SMTP server. Credentials are sent as clear text across the network. To specify credentials, click Set. Type the user name, type and then confirm the user password, and then click OK.

7. In the Actions pane, click Apply to save your settings.

You can deliver e-mail to a pickup directory by completing the following steps:

1. In IIS Manager, navigate to the level of the configuration hierarchy you want to manage, and then display the SMTP E-Mail page by double-clicking the SMTP E-Mail feature.

2. On the SMTP E-Mail page, in the E-Mail Address text box, type the address you want to use as the default address from which e-mail messages are sent.

3. Select the Store E-Mail In Pickup Directory option, and then click Browse.

4. Use the Browse For Folder dialog box to specify the location of the pickup directory, and then click OK.

5. In the Actions pane, click Apply to save your settings.

Configuring Key/Value Pairs for ASP.NET Applications

When you are working with managed code applications, you may need to store information used by an application as key/value pairs in the application's Web.config file. Storing application settings in this way ensures that the stored values can be accessed from anywhere within the application. If you store application settings at the server or site level, multiple applications could access and use the same settings. With this in mind, you can view and work with key/value pairs for applications by completing the following steps:

1. In IIS Manager, navigate to the level of the configuration hierarchy you want to manage.

2. Access the Application Settings page by double-clicking the Application Settings feature.

3. In the main pane, you'll see a list of the currently defined key/value pairs. Be sure to note whether the entry type is listed as local or inherited. Local entries are configured at the level you are working with. Inherited entries are configured at a higher level of the configuration hierarchy.

4. Use the following techniques to work with application settings:

❑ **Add a setting** Click Add. In the Add Application Setting dialog box, type the name and value for the application setting, and then click OK.

❑ **Edit a setting** Click the setting you want to modify, and then click Edit. In the Edit Application Setting dialog box, type the desired name and value for the application setting, and then click OK.

❑ **Remove a setting** Click the setting you want to remove, and then click Remove. When prompted to confirm the action, click Yes.

Configuring Settings for ASP.NET Pages and Controls

Web applications that use ASP.NET include Web pages to provide the user interface and controls to provide drop-in functionality. As with ASP, you can optimize the way ASP.NET is used through a variety of configuration settings. You can also make additional functionality available by registering custom controls that applications can use.

Registering Custom Controls

Managed code applications can use any custom controls that are registered for use with IIS. As an administrator, you probably won't need to install controls, but you may need to validate control configurations. To view currently registered controls, in IIS Manager, navigate to the level of the configuration hierarchy you want to manage, double-click the Pages And Controls feature, and then in the Actions pane, click Register Controls. In the main pane, you should then see a list of the currently registered controls. Controls are listed by tag prefix, associated source or assembly, and entry type. Local entries are configured at the level you are working with. Inherited entries are configured at a higher level of the configuration hierarchy.

You can add a custom control by following these steps:

1. In IIS Manager, navigate to the level of the configuration hierarchy you want to manage, double-click the Pages And Controls feature, and then, in the Actions pane, click Register Controls.

2. In IIS Manager, on the Controls Page, click Add Custom Control. The Add Custom Control dialog box appears as shown in Figure 8-6.

3. In the Tag Prefix text box, type the tag prefix assigned to the control, such as **aspx**.

4. In the Namespace text box, type the ASP.NET namespace in which the custom control type is defined, such as **System.Web.UI.WebControls.WebParts**.

5. In the Assembly text box, type the assembly details associated with the custom control. This includes the control's top-level namespace, version, culture, and any additional information required to register the assembly properly, such as its public key token. Then click OK.

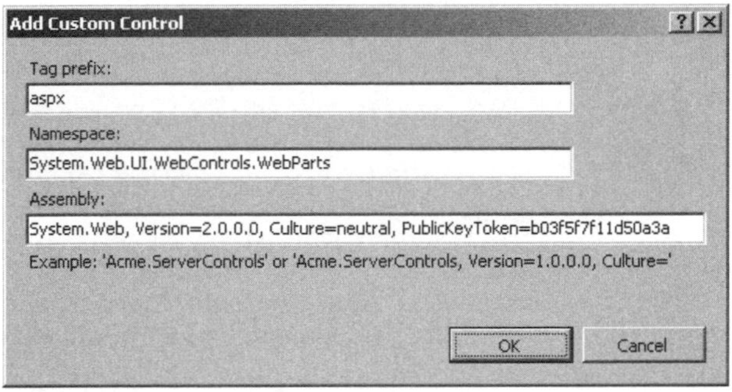

Figure 8-6   Register a custom control.

You can edit registered control entries by clicking the control entry you want to modify and then clicking Edit. In the Edit Custom Control dialog box, modify the settings as necessary, and then click OK to save your changes. To remove a registration entry for a custom control that is no longer needed, click the control entry you want to remove, and then click Remove. When prompted to confirm the action, click Yes.

Configuring ASP.NET Settings for Pages and Controls

You can modify the way ASP.NET is used by Web applications by using the configuration settings on the Pages And Controls page in IIS Manager. To access this page, navigate to the level of the configuration hierarchy you want to manage, and then double-click the Pages And Controls feature.

Table 8-2 summarizes the available ASP.NET settings for pages and controls. In the related server, site, or application Web.config file, you manage these settings by using the sessionState configuration section.

Table 8-2   Settings for Pages and Controls

Setting	Description
Base Type for Pages (pageBaseType)	Sets the base type that .aspx pages inherit by default. The default value in most cases is System.Web.UI.Page. This value can be overridden by the *Inherits* attribute.
Base Type for User Controls (userControlBaseType)	Sets the base type that user controls inherit by default. The default value in most cases is System.Web.UI.UserControl.
Buffer (buffer)	Determines whether .aspx pages and .ascx controls use response buffering. The default setting is True. When True, IIS uses response buffering in much the same way as it uses response buffering for ASP.

Table 8-2   Settings for Pages and Controls

Setting	Description
Compilation Mode (compilationMode)	Determines whether an ASP.NET page or control should be compiled at run time. The default is Always, which ensures that pages and controls are always compiled at run time. A value of Never specifies that pages and controls are not compiled and should be interpreted instead. A value of Auto allows IIS to compile pages and controls as necessary and otherwise set them to be interpreted.
Enable Authenticated View State (enableViewStateMAC)	Determines whether ASP.NET should run a message authentication code (MAC) on the page's view state when the page is posted back from the client. The default setting is True.
Enable Session State (enableSessionState)	Specifies whether and how IIS maintains session state information for ASP.NET applications. The default setting is True. When True, IIS maintains session state information for ASP.NET. Alternately, you can use a value of ReadOnly to have IIS maintain non-editable, read-only session state data. If you don't want IIS to maintain session state information for ASP.NET, configure this setting to False.
Enable View State (enableViewState)	Determines whether the page maintains the view state and the view state of any server controls it contains when the current page request ends. The default setting is True.
Master Page File (masterPageFile)	Sets an optional master page path relative to the local configuration file. This allows applications to reference locations in the master page path by name rather than full file path.
Maximum Page State Field Length (maxPageStateFieldLength)	Sets the maximum number of characters for individual view state fields. When the value is greater than zero (0), IIS breaks the view state field into chunks that are less than the specified length. Clients receive this chunked view state as a series of view state fields rather than a single, possibly very long view state field. When the value is set to -1, IIS does not chunk the view state field and instead sends the entire value to the client in a single view state field.
Namespaces (namespaces)	Specifies the namespaces included for all pages. IIS imports these namespaces during assembly pre-compilation. If you expand the Namespaces node, you'll see a list of namespaces that will be imported.

Table 8-2   Settings for Pages and Controls

Setting	Description
Style Sheet Theme (styleSheetTheme)	Sets the optional name of the theme folder that IIS will use to apply a theme before control declarations. You can specify a theme to apply after control declaration by using the theme attribute.
Theme (theme)	Sets the optional name for the theme that is used for pages that are in the scope of the configuration file. The specified theme must exist as either an application or a global theme. If the theme does not exist, IIS generates an HttpException exception.
Validate Request (validateRequest)	Determines whether ASP.NET validates requests to screen for potentially dangerous or malicious input. The default setting is True, which causes ASP.NET to validate input from client browsers. Although you should rarely disable validation, you can do so by using a value of False.

You can configure the list of namespaces that IIS imports during assembly pre-compilation by completing the following steps:

1. To view currently configured Pages And Controls settings, in IIS Manager, navigate to the level of the configuration hierarchy you want to manage, and then double-click the Pages And Controls feature.

2. On the Pages And Controls page, expand the Namespaces node to display a list of namespaces that will be included during assembly pre-compilation.

3. If you click the Namespaces entry, IIS Manager displays a selection button on the far right side of the second column. Clicking this button displays the String Collection Editor dialog box, which you can use to edit the imported namespace values. Edit the namespace entries as necessary. Add additional namespaces by typing each additional namespace on a separate line.

4. When you are finished editing namespace values, click OK. In the Actions pane, apply the changes to the configuration by clicking Apply.

Connecting to Data Sources

IIS can store connection strings used by managed code applications to connect to local and remote data sources, which can include SQL Server databases and other types of databases. To view currently configured connection strings, in IIS Manager, navigate to the level of the configuration hierarchy you want to manage, and then access the Connection Strings page by double-clicking the Connection Strings feature. In the main pane, you'll see a list of the currently defined connection strings. Local entries are configured at the level you are working with. Inherited entries are configured at a higher level of the configuration hierarchy.

You can create a connection string for SQL Server by completing the following steps:

1. In IIS Manager, navigate to the level of the configuration hierarchy you want to manage, and then access the Connection Strings page by double-clicking the Connection Strings feature.

2. On the Connection Strings page, in the Actions pane, click Add. This displays the Add Connection String dialog box, shown in Figure 8-7.

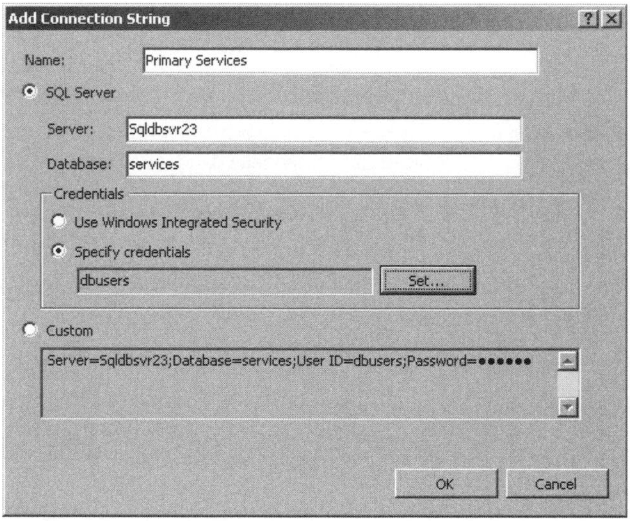

Figure 8-7 Add a connection to a SQL Server database.

3. In the Name text box, type the name of the connection string, such as **SqlServerCustDb**. This name must be the same name that you reference in your application code to retrieve data that uses this connection string. You cannot change the name later without re-creating the connection string.

4. In the Server text box, type the name of the SQL server that hosts the database.

5. In the Database text box, type the name of the SQL server database.

6. Select one of the following Credentials options to specify the security credentials that are used to connect to the database:

   ❑ **Use Windows Integrated Security** Configures the connection string so that the application uses the current Windows identity established on the operating system thread to access the SQL Server database. Use this option to pass through authenticated Windows domain credentials to the database.

Note   You can use integrated security only when SQL Server runs on the same computer as IIS or when you've configured delegation between computers. Additionally, all application users must be in the same domain so that their credentials are available to IIS.

❏ **Specify Credentials**   Configures the connection string to use a specific SQL Server user name and password. Use this option when you do not want to pass through user credentials to the database for authentication. After you select Specify Credentials, click Set. In the Set Credentials dialog box, type the SQL Server user name to use for the connection. After you type and then confirm the password for this user, click OK.

7. Click OK to close the Add Connection String dialog box.

You can create a custom connection string for other types of database servers by completing the following steps:

1. In IIS Manager, navigate to the level of the configuration hierarchy you want to manage, and then access the Connection Strings page by double-clicking the Connection Strings feature.

2. On the Connection Strings page, in the Actions pane, click Add. This displays the Add Connection String dialog box, with the Custom option enabled, as shown in Figure 8-8.

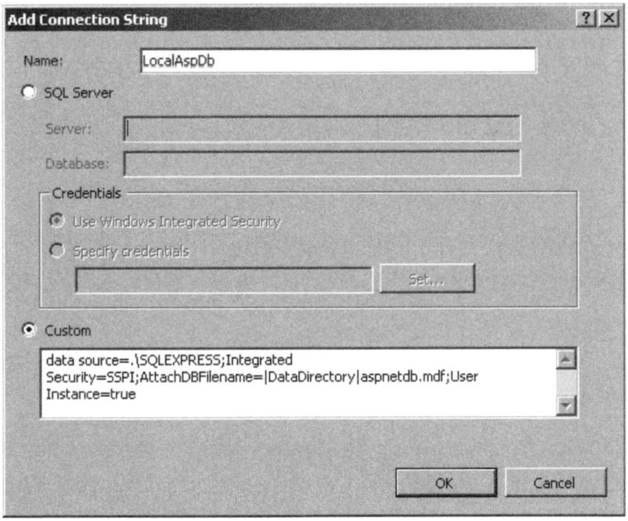

Figure 8-8   Add a connection to a data source.

3. In the Name text box, type the name of the connection string, such as **LocalSqlServer**. This name must be the same name that you reference in your application code to retrieve data that uses this connection string. You cannot change the name later without re-creating the connection string.

4. Select the Custom option, and then type the connection string. The connection string should by formatted as appropriate for the type of database to which you are connecting. Your organization's application developer or database administrator should be able to provide the required connection string. The following example connects to a local SQL Express database, which is stored in the aspnetdb.mdf file:

```
Data source=.\SQLEXPRESS;Integrated Security=SSPI;
AttachDBFilename=|DataDirectory|aspnetdb.mdf;User Instance=true
```

5. Click OK to close the Add Connection String dialog box.

To edit an existing connection string, select the string that you want to modify, and then click Edit. In the Edit Connection String dialog box, modify the settings as necessary, and then click OK to save your changes. To remove a connection string that is no longer needed, select the connection string you want to remove, and then click Remove. When prompted to confirm the action, click Yes.

Managing .NET Framework Settings

In ASP.NET applications, you can use the functions and features provided by the .NET Framework to establish connections to databases, control access to applications, and much more. Key configuration areas for connecting to databases include Connection Strings and .NET Providers. Key configuration areas for controlling applications include: .NET Profiles, .NET Users, and .NET Roles. You can also configure settings for .NET Trust Levels, .NET Compilation, and .NET Globalization.

Configuring .NET Providers

When you have managed code applications that use provider-based services to store data in a database or other data store, you'll need to configure .NET providers to manage .NET roles, .NET users, and .NET profiles. .NET providers have helper functions that allow managed code applications to connect to databases by using previously defined connection strings and perform the necessary management tasks for working with .NET roles, .NET users, and .NET profiles.

Because .NET roles, .NET users, and .NET profiles all have different purposes, different .NET providers are required for working with each of these features:

- .NET Roles providers supply an interface between the ASP.NET role management service and role data sources.

- .NET Users providers supply an interface between the ASP.NET membership service and membership data sources.

- .NET Profile providers supply an interface between the ASP.NET profile service and profile data sources.

To view the default .NET providers and any additional providers that you've created, in IIS Manager, navigate to the level of the configuration hierarchy you want to manage, and then double-click the Providers feature. On the Providers page, in the Feature drop-down list, choose the type of .NET provider you want to view and manage. Associated providers are listed by:

- **Name**   Show the descriptive name that is assigned to the provider for easy identification.

- **Type**   Shows the .NET type for the provider. All providers are implemented in managed code.

- **Entry Type**   Shows the scope of the provider as either Local or Inherited.

Table 8-3 provides an overview of the default .NET providers that are available when you've enabled ASP.NET for application development.

Table 8-3   Default .NET Providers

Provider	Associated .NET Type	Description
AspNetSqlRoleProvider	System.Web.Security. SqlRoleProvider	For working with .NET roles stored in the Windows Internal Database associated with the IIS installation.
AspNetWindowsToken- RoleProvider	System.Web.Security. WindowsTokenRole- Provider	For working with Windows security tokens associated with .NET roles.
AspNetMembershipProvider	System.Web.Security. SqlMembershipProvider	For managing .NET user memberships stored in the Windows Internal Database associated with the IIS installation.
AspNetSqlProfileProvider	System.Web.Profile. SqlProfileProvider	For managing .NET profiles stored in the Windows Internal Database associated with the IIS installation.

You can configure additional .NET providers for managing .NET roles, .NET users, and .NET profiles stored in a database or other data store by following these steps:

1. Each .NET provider requires a connection string to the data source you want to use. If you haven't already created the required connection string as discussed in the "Connecting To Data Sources" section earlier in this chapter, do so now.

2. On the Providers page in IIS Manager, in the Feature drop-down list, select the feature you want to manage with the provider. Choose .NET Roles if you want to use the provider to create or manage .NET Roles in the related data source. Choose .NET Users if you want to use the provider to create or manage .NET Users in the related data source. Choose .NET Profile if you want to use the provider to create or manage .NET Profiles in the related data source.

3. In the Actions pane, click Add. As shown in Figure 8-9, this displays the Add Provider dialog box.

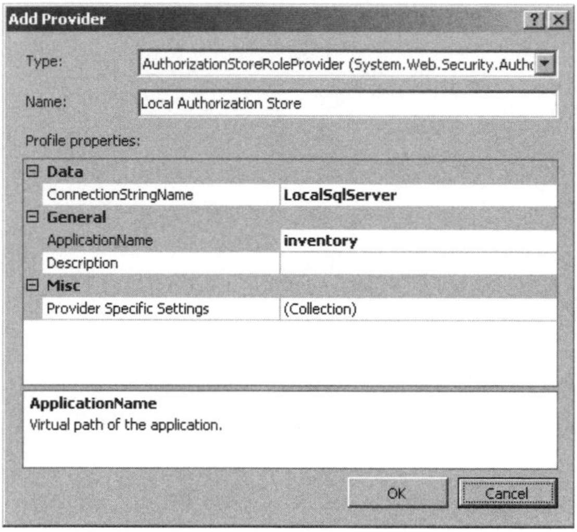

Figure 8-9   Add a provider for ASP.NET applications.

4. In the Type selection drop-down list, choose the .NET type to associate with the .NET provider, such as AuthorizationStoreRoleProvider.

5. In the Name text box, type a unique name for the .NET provider, such as **AspNet AuthorizationStoreRoleProvider**.

6. If you are creating a .NET provider for .NET users, use the Behavior options to specify these profile properties:

   ❑   EnablePasswordReset for enabling the password reset functionality

   ❑   EnablePasswordRetrieval for enabling password retrieval from a data store

   ❑   RequiresQuestionAndAnswer for requiring a security question and correct answer to reset a user password

   ❑   RequiresUniqueEmail for requiring a unique e-mail address for each user

   ❑   StorePasswordInSecureFormat for storing the user password in a secure (encrypted) format

7. Click in the ConnectionStringName text box to activate the related selection list. In the drop-down list, choose the previously created connection string that the .NET provider should use.

8. The entry in the ApplicationName text box sets the virtual path of a specific application that uses the provider. If you do not specify a value, the value is set at run time to that of the current application making the connection request, per HttpContext.Current.Request.ApplicationPath.

9. In the Description text box, type an optional description of the provider, and then click OK.

Although you cannot edit or remove default .NET providers, you can edit, rename, or remove any .NET providers you've created:

■ To edit user-created .NET providers, click the provider entry you want to modify, and then click Edit. In the Edit Provider dialog box, modify the settings as necessary, and then click OK to save your changes.

■ To rename a user-created provider, click the provider entry to select it, and then click Rename. Type the new name for the provider, and then press Enter.

■ To remove an entry for a user-created provider that is no longer needed, click the provider entry you want to remove, and then click Remove. When prompted to confirm the action, click Yes.

Configuring .NET Trust Levels

The active .NET Trust Level sets the level of trust that is applied to managed modules, handlers, and applications. The trust levels you can use for servers, sites, and applications follow:

■ **Full (internal)**   Indicates that ASP.NET applications are fully trusted. This grants application permissions to access any resource that is subject to operating system security and allows all privileged operations.

■ **High (web_hightrust.config)**   Indicates that ASP.NET applications are highly trusted. This restricts application permissions so that an application cannot perform any of the following actions: call unmanaged code, call serviced components, write to the event log, access Microsoft Message Queuing (MSMQ) service queues, or access data sources.

■ **Medium (web_mediumtrust.config)**   Indicates that ASP.NET applications are moderately trusted. This restricts application permissions so that in addition to not being able to perform any of the actions restricted by the High trust level, an application cannot perform any of the following tasks by default: access files outside the application directory, access the registry, or make network or Web service calls.

- **Low (web_lowtrust.config)**   Indicates that ASP.NET applications are somewhat trusted. This restricts application permissions so that in addition to not being able to perform any of the actions restricted by the High and Medium trust levels, an application cannot perform either of the following tasks by default: write to the file system or call the *Assert* method.

- **Minimal (web_minimaltrust.config)**   Indicates that ASP.NET applications are minimally trusted. This restricts application permissions so that it has only execute permissions. No other permissions are granted by default.

You can configure the .NET trust level for a server, site, or application by completing the following steps:

1. In IIS Manager, navigate to the level of the configuration hierarchy you want to manage, and then display the .NET Trust Levels page by double-clicking the .NET Trust Levels feature.

2. On the .NET Trust Levels page, in the Trust Level drop-down list, set the desired trust level. Click Apply to save your settings.

In the related server, site, or application Web.config file, you can configure the trust level by using the level attribute of the trust configuration section. The valid values are: Full, High, Medium, Low, and Minimal.

Configuring .NET Profiles

.NET profiles allow you to store any custom information that applications require. Generally speaking, you'll have two types of properties: global properties that you want to use for all applications, and application-specific properties that apply only to a specific application. You can make it easier to work with properties by grouping similar properties. You can do this according to the application they are used with or according to how the property is used.

In IIS Manager, you can view currently configured properties for .NET profiles by double-clicking the .NET Profile feature. This feature is available only at or below a site level. On the .NET Profile page, you'll see a list of the currently defined properties. Local entries are configured at the level you are working with. Inherited entries are configured at a higher level of the configuration hierarchy.

You can work with .NET profiles in a variety of ways:

- To disable or enable the .NET Profile feature, in the Actions pane, click Disable or Enable.

- To set the default provider for .NET profiles, in the Actions pane, click Set Default Provider, select a default provider, and then click OK. By default, ASP.NET uses a SqlProfileProvider instance named AspNetSqlProfileProvider to connect to a SQL Server database on the local computer. A Windows Internal Database is provided for this purpose.

- To create a group container for properties, in the Actions pane, click Add Group, type a group name, and then click OK.

- When you select a group, you can add a new property to the group by clicking Add Property To Group, providing the property details, and then clicking OK.

- To add a property without placing it in a group, click Add Property, provide the property details, and then click OK.

- When you select a property, you can edit, rename, or remove it by configuring the related settings in the Actions pane.

You can set the following details for profile properties:

- **Name** Sets the name of the profile property.

- **Data Type** Sets the data type of the property. This can be either a common data type such as String, or a custom data type.

- **Default Value** Sets the default value of the property.

- **Serialization Option** Sets the serialization formatting for the property as string, binary, XML, or provider-specific.

Properties can also be read-only and accessible to anonymous users.

Configuring .NET Roles

.NET Roles allow you to group a set of users and perform security-related operations, such as authorization, on a whole set of users. In IIS Manager, to view currently configured .NET Roles, double-click the .NET Roles feature. This feature is available at or below a site level only. On the .NET Roles page, enable roles that are currently disabled by clicking Enable in the Actions pane. You'll see a list of the currently defined roles. Roles are listed by name and by the number of users assigned to a role.

You can work with .NET Roles in a variety of ways:

- To set the default provider for .NET profiles, in the Actions pane, click Set Default Provider, select a default provider, and then click OK. By default, the ASP.NET Role Manager uses a SqlRoleProvider instance named AspNetSqlRoleProvider, which stores role information in a SQL Server database. A Windows Internal Database is provided for this purpose.

- To define a role, in the Actions pane, click Add, provide the necessary role details, and then click OK. The role uses the default provider automatically.

- To change the default provider for a role, click the role you want to edit, and then click Edit. In the Edit .NET Role dialog box, select the default provider to use, and then click OK.

Note   The ASP.NET Role Manager is designed to support custom role and user assignment and cannot be used to manage Windows users and groups. This is why the default provider is set as SqlRoleProvider and not as WindowsTokenRoleProvider. SqlRoleProvider supports custom user and role assignment through SQL Server and is ideally suited to medium and large deployments. The WindowsTokenRoleProvider uses role information based on Windows domain accounts and is useful only if your application runs on a network in which all users have domain accounts. The WindowsTokenRoleProvider relies on Windows authentication to determine the groups in which a user is allowed to be a member.

Configuring .NET Users

You can use .NET Users to help you manage user identities that are defined for applications. .NET Users can be used to perform authentication, authorization, and other security-related operations.

To view currently configured .NET Users, in IIS Manager, double-click the .NET Users feature. This feature is available at or below a site level only. On the .NET Users page, you'll see a list of the currently defined users. Users are listed by name, e-mail address, date created, and last login.

You can work with .NET Users in a variety of ways:

- To set the default provider for .NET users, in the Actions pane , click Set Default Provider, select a default provider, and then click OK. By default, the ASP.NET Users Manager uses a SqlMembershipProvider instance named AspNetSql-MembershipProvider, which stores user information in a SQL Server database. A Windows Internal Database is provided for this purpose.

- To create a user, in the Actions pane, click Add., and then follow the wizard prompts. You'll need to supply the user name and default e-mail address. Type and then confirm the password for the user. You can also select or type a security question and provide an answer for this question. If the RequiresQuestion-AndAnswer property is set for the .NET Users provider, this question and answer can be used to reset the user password.

- To specify the roles to associate with a .NET user, select a user, and then in the Actions pane, click Add . Then use the options provided to specify the roles associated with the user.

- To change the default provider for a user, click the user you want to edit, and then click Edit. In the Edit .NET Users Settings dialog box, select the default provider to use, and then click OK.

Configuring .NET Compilation

.NET Compilation properties allow you to manage the way IIS performs batch compilations of ASP.NET application code. In IIS Manager, to view currently configured .NET compilation settings, navigate to the level of the configuration hierarchy you want to manage, and then double-click the .NET Compilation feature. On the .NET Compilation page, you'll see a list of the currently defined settings. These settings are used as described in Table 8-4. In the related server, site, or application Web.config file, you can use the compilation configuration section to configure these settings.

Table 8-4   .NET Compilation Settings

Setting	Description
Assemblies (assemblies)	Specifies the assemblies to include during compilation. If you expand the Assemblies node, you'll see a list of assemblies that will be included. Click Select to edit the assemblies list.
Batch Compilations (batch)	Determines whether batch processing is supported. The default is True, enabling batch compilation. To disable batch compilation, use a value of False.
Code Sub Directories	Specifies the subdirectories that contain code. If you expand the Code Sub Directories node, you'll see a list of subdirectories that will be included. Click Select to edit the subdirectories list.
Debug (debug)	Determines whether the debugger is enabled or disabled. The default is False, disabling debugging. To enable debugging, use a value of True.
Default Language (defaultLanguage)	Sets the default programming language to use in dynamic compilation files. The default is Visual Basic ("vb"). You can also select C#.
Explicit Compile Option (explicit)	Determines whether to set the Visual Basic explicit compile option. The default is True. If True, all variables must be declared explicitly by using a Dim, Private, Public, or ReDim statement. To remove the requirement for explicit declarations, use a value of False.
Maximum File Size (maxBatchGeneratedFileSize)	Sets the maximum size, in kilobytes, of the generated source files per batched compilation. The default is 1000 KB. If a source file exceeds the maximum size, the compiler reverts to single compilation mode for the source file.
Maximum Size of Batch (maxBatchSize)	Sets the maximum number of pages per batched compilation. The default is 1000. When ASP.NET reaches the maximum number of files, it closes the current batch session and starts a new one as necessary.

Table 8-4   .NET Compilation Settings

Setting	Description
Number of Recompiles (numRecompilesBeforeAppRestart)	Specifies the number of dynamic recompiles of resources that can occur before IIS restarts the application. The default is 15. If this value is reached, IIS restarts the application.
Strict Compile Option (strict)	Determines whether to set the Visual Basic strict compile option. The default is False, meaning that the strict compile option is not set.
Timeout (batchTimeout)	Sets the time-out period for batch compilation. If compilation cannot be completed in the time-out period, the compiler reverts to single compilation mode for the current page. The default is 00:15:00 (15 minutes).
Temporary Directory (tempDirectory)	Sets the directory to use for temporary file storage during compilation. The default value is an empty string, which allows ASP.NET to use its default working directory.
Url Line Pragmas (urlLinePragmas)	Determines whether the line pragmas (used to introduce machine-dependent code in a controlled fashion) generated by ASP.NET should use URLs instead of physical paths. The default is False, meaning that ASP.NET will use physical paths. To use URLs instead, use a value of True.

You can configure the list of assemblies to use during .NET Compilation by completing the following steps:

1. To view currently configured .NET compilation settings, in IIS Manager, navigate to the level of the configuration hierarchy you want to manage, and then double-click the .NET Compilation feature.

2. On the .NET Compilation page, expand the Assemblies node to display a list of assemblies that will be included for compilation.

3. If you click the Assemblies entry, IIS Manager displays a selection button on the far right side of the second column. Clicking this button displays the String Collection Editor dialog box, which you can use to edit the included assemblies. Edit the assembly entries as necessary. Add additional assemblies by entering each additional assembly on a separate line. Enter * as the last entry to include all other assemblies.

4. When you are finished editing assembly values, click OK. In the Actions pane, click Apply to apply the changes to the configuration.

Configuring .NET Globalization

IIS is capable of supporting multiple language environments. *Globalization* is the process of internationalizing application code, then localizing the application to other languages and cultures. With applications that have been globalized, IIS can present application content in the appropriate encoding and format for the client locale.

You can configure globalization options to support globalized applications on the .NET Globalization page. To access this page, in IIS Manager, navigate to the level of the configuration hierarchy you want to manage, and then double-click the .NET Globalization feature. On the .NET Globalization page, you'll see a list of the currently defined settings. These settings are used as described in Table 8-5. In the related server, site, or application Web.config file, you can configure these settings by using the globalization configuration section.

Table 8-5   .NET Globalization Settings

Setting	Description
Culture (culture)	Sets the default culture for processing incoming Web requests.
Enable Client Based Culture (enableClientBasedCulture)	Determines whether the client culture settings are evaluated. The default is False, meaning that the client culture settings are not evaluated. If True, ASP.NET sets the Culture and UICulture properties based on the AcceptLanguage header field value that is sent by the client browser.
File (fileEncoding)	Sets default the file encoding for .aspx, .asmx, and .asax file parsing. Unicode and UTF-8 files that are saved with the byte-order mark prefix are automatically recognized, regardless of the value for this attribute. The default file encoding in the U.S. is Windows-1252.
Requests (requestEncoding)	Sets the assumed encoding for incoming requests, including posted data and query strings. If a request includes a request header that contains an *Accept-Charset* attribute, the value of this attribute overrides this setting. The default encoding is UTF-8. In most case, requests, response headers, and responses encoding should be set in the same way.
Response Headers (responseHeaderEncoding)	Sets the content encoding of response headers. The default encoding is UTF-8.
Responses (responseEncoding)	Sets the content encoding of responses. The default encoding is UTF-8.
UI Culture (uiCulture)	Sets the default UI culture for use in processing incoming Web requests.

Chapter 9
Managing Applications, Application Pools, and Worker Processes

Chapter 8, "Running IIS Applications," discussed the essentials for customizing the application environment. That chapter's focus was broad and discussed issues related to all types of applications that you can host on IIS. In this chapter, I focus on advanced application configuration issues that are specific to running dynamic applications, such as:

- Managing .NET configurations

- Creating applications and application pools

- Configuring multiple worker processes for applications

- Recycling worker processes manually and automatically

- Optimizing application performance

As you might expect, the discussion in this chapter applies primarily when you are working with Active Server Pages (ASP) and Microsoft ASP.NET, and you must be logged on as an administrator or run commands as an administrator to perform the tasks this chapter discusses.

Defining Custom Applications

You use IIS Manager to configure custom applications. As part of the standard installation, Web sites have a prespecified application that allows you to run custom programs without making changes to the environment. You could, for example, copy your ASP files to a site's base directory and run them without creating a separate application. Here, the ASP application runs as a default application within the context of the site's application pool.

Each application has a starting point. The starting point sets the logical namespace for the application. That is, the starting point determines the files and folders that are included in the application. Every file and folder in the starting point is considered part of the application.

You can set application starting points for the following:

- An entire site

- A directory

- A virtual directory

When you specify a site-wide application, all files in all the Web site's subdirectories are considered to be a part of the application. When you specify an application for a standard or virtual directory within a site, all files in all subdirectories in this directory are considered part of the application and are no longer considered to be a part of the site application.

To get better control over sites and related applications, you should configure separate contexts for key applications. Application contexts are specified using basic and advanced application settings. Basic application settings include the following:

- **Alias** Sets the relative URL path for the application.

- **Physical Path** Sets the base directory for the application. All files in all subdirectories of the base directory are considered to be part of the application.

- **Application Pool** Determines which application pool is used with the application. You can configure multiple application pools, and each can have a different worker process configuration.

Advanced application settings include Physical Path Credentials and Physical Path Credentials Logon Type. Physical Path Credentials sets the credentials for the user identity that should be impersonated when IIS accesses application files on a remote share. If you need to use alternate credentials to connect to the remote server specified in a Universal Naming Convention (UNC) path, you can specify user credentials or use the default pass-through authentication mode. With pass-through authentication, IIS uses the credentials of the requesting user. For authenticated requests, IIS uses the logged on credentials of the authenticated user. For non-authenticated requests, IIS uses the Internet Guest account (IUSR_*hostname*).

Physical Path Credentials Logon Type specifies the type of logon operation to perform when acquiring the user token necessary to access the physical path. The logon types you can use are as follows:

- **ClearText** IIS uses a clear-text logon to acquire the user token. As IIS passes the logon user call over the back end on an internal network, using a clear-text call typically is sufficient. This is the default logon type.

- **Interactive** IIS uses an interactive logon to acquire the user token. This gives the related account the Interactive identity for the logon session and makes it appear that the user is logged on locally.

- **Batch** IIS uses a batch logon to acquire the user token. This gives the related account the Batch identity for the logon session and makes it appear that the user is accessing the remote server as a batch job.

- **Network** IIS uses a network logon to acquire the user token. This gives the related account the Network identity for the logon session and makes it appear that the user is accessing the remote server over the network.

These basic and advanced settings create an application context within which an application runs. Application contexts are specified at the directory level. All files in all subdirectories of an application's base directory are considered to be part of the application. Because of this, one way to create applications is to follow these steps:

1. In Microsoft Windows Explorer, create a directory that will act as the application's starting point, and then set appropriate Windows access permissions on the directory.

2. Use IIS Manager to create an application that maps to the physical directory.

3. Configure application settings for the directory as described in the "Creating Applications" section later in this chapter.

Because IIS Manager now allows you to create a required physical directory and set Windows permissions, you can also create applications by using the following technique:

1. Use IIS Manager to create an application that maps to a new directory.

2. Configure application settings for the directory as described in the "Creating Applications" section later in this chapter.

3. In IIS Manager, use the application's Edit Permissions setting to set appropriate Windows access permissions on the directory.

Managing Custom IIS Applications

As part of the standard installation, all Web sites created in IIS have a default application that's set as a site-wide application, meaning that its starting point is the base directory for the Web site. The default application allows you to run custom applications that use the preconfigured application settings. You don't need to make any changes to the environment. You can, however, achieve better control by specifying applications with smaller scope, and the sections that follow tell you how to do this.

Viewing Applications

To view all applications associated with a site, in IIS Manager, select the site node, and then in the Actions pane, click View Applications. As Figure 9-1 shows, you'll then see the applications created within the site listed by:

- **Virtual Path**   Lists the virtual path to the application within the site context

- **Physical Path**   Lists the physical path to the base directory for the application

- **Site**   Lists the site to which the application belongs

- **Application Pool**   Lists the application pool in which the application runs

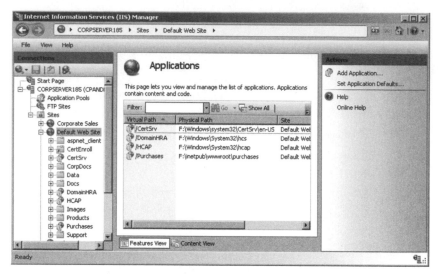

Figure 9-1   Review the applications associated with a site.

With the IIS command-line administration tool, you can list applications by using the List App command. Sample 9-1 provides the syntax and usage.

Sample 9-1   List App Syntax and Usage

Syntax
```
appcmd list app [[/app.name:]AppNameOrURL] [/site.name:"SiteName"]
[/apppool.name:"AppPoolName"][/path: "VirtualPath"]
[/parameter1:value1 ...]
```
Usage
```
appcmd list app "Default Web Site/Sales"

appcmd list apps /site.name:"Default Web Site"

appcmd list apps /apppool.name:"DefaultAppPool"

appcmd list apps /path:/Sales
```

Configuring Default Settings for New Applications

In a standard configuration, new applications are configured to use the default application pool, pass-through authentication, and clear text for the logon type. If you use the same settings for most applications, you may want to modify the default settings. To do this, follow these steps:

1. In IIS Manager, select the site node you want to work with, and then in the Actions pane, click View Applications.

2. On the Applications page, in the Actions pane, click Set Application Defaults.

3. The Application Pool text box lists the current default application pool. To change the default value, click the selection button. In the Select Application Pool dialog box, select the application pool to use in the Application Pool drop-down list, and then click OK.

4. The Physical Path Credentials text box is blank by default to indicate that IIS uses pass-through authentication. If you need to use alternate credentials to connect to the remote server specified in a UNC path, click the selection button. In the Connect As dialog box, choose Specific User, and then click Set. In the Set Credentials dialog box, type the name of the user account to use for authentication, type and confirm the account password, and then click OK.

5. The Physical Path Credentials Logon Type text box lists the default type of logon operation to perform when acquiring the user token necessary to access the physical path. The logon types you can use are ClearText, Interactive, Batch, and Network. Click OK to save your settings.

With the IIS command-line administration tool, you can configure the default application pool by using the *applicationPool* attribute of the applicationDefaults configuration section. You can configure the Physical Path Credentials and Physical Path Credentials Logon Type by using the *username*, *password*, and *logonMethod* attributes of the virtualDirectoryDefaults configuration section. Samples 9-2 and 9-3 provide the syntax and usage.

Sample 9-2   Setting the Default Application Pool Syntax and Usage

Syntax
```
appcmd set config ["ConfigPath"] /section:applicationDefaults
[/applicationPool:"AppPoolName"]
```
Usage
```
appcmd set config "Default Web Site" /section:applicationDefaults
/applicationPool:"Standard App Pool"
```

Sample 9-3   Configuring Default Path Settings Syntax and Usage

Syntax
```
appcmd set config ["ConfigPath"] /section:virtualDirecdtoryDefaults
[/userName:"UserName"] [/password:"Password"]
[/logonMethod:"LogonType"]
```
Usage
```
appcmd set config "Default Web Site"
/section:virtualDirecdtoryDefaults /logonMethod:"ClearText"
```

Creating Applications

IIS applications are collections of resource files and components that are grouped together to take advantage of key IIS features. You can create an application by completing the following steps:

1. In IIS Manager, right-click the site, directory, or virtual directory under which you want to create the application, and then select Add Application. This displays the dialog box shown in Figure 9-2.

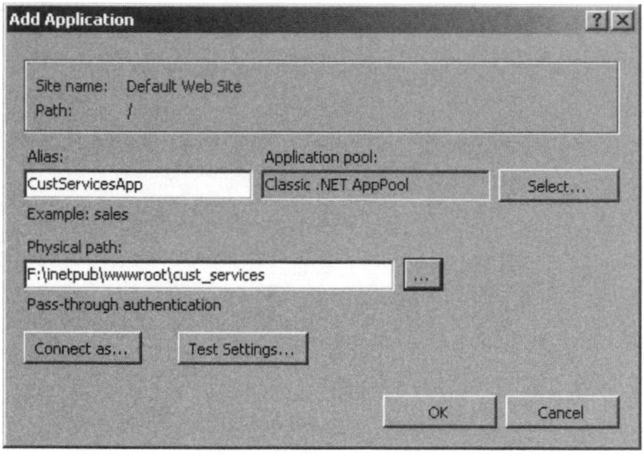

Add Application

Site name: Default Web Site
Path: /

Alias: Application pool:
CustServicesApp   Classic .NET AppPool   Select...
Example: sales

Physical path:
F:\inetpub\wwwroot\cust_services   ...

Pass-through authentication

Connect as...   Test Settings...

                                    OK   Cancel

Figure 9-2   Use the Add Application dialog box to configure custom applications.

2. In the Alias text box, type the relative URL of the application. For example, if you are creating the application under the default Web site at *http://www.cpandl.com* and set the alias as Inventory, the application can be accessed using the URL *http://www.cpandl.com/Inventory*.

   Caution   Make sure you use an appropriate alias. You cannot change an application's alias.

3. The default application pool is listed in the Application Pool text box. Although you can use the default application pool, it's better to create pools for specific types of applications. To do so, click the Select button. In the Select Application Pool dialog box, select the application pool to use in the Application Pool drop-down list, and then click OK.

   Note   When you select an application pool in the Select Application Pool dialog box, the Microsoft .NET Framework version and pipeline mode are listed as properties. Be sure to select an application pool using the appropriate .NET Framework version and pipeline mode.

4. In the Physical Path text box, type the path to the physical directory where the application content is stored, or click the selection button to the right of the Physical Path text box to search for a directory. The directory must be created before you can select it. If necessary, in the Browse For Folder dialog box, click Make New Folder to create the directory before you select it. However, don't forget about checking and setting permissions at the operating system level as discussed in Chapter 10, "Managing Web Server Security."

5. If you need to use alternate credentials to connect to the remote server specified in a UNC path, click Connect As. In the Connect As dialog box, choose Specific User, and then click Set. In the Set Credentials dialog box, type the name of the user account to use for authentication, type and confirm the account password, and then click OK twice.

Tip   When you set logon credentials for an application, the account name you provide must exist. By default, IIS Manager sets the logon type to ClearText. This means that IIS will use clear text when acquiring the user token necessary to access the physical path. Because IIS passes the logon user call over the back end on an internal network, using a clear-text call typically is sufficient. By editing an application's properties, you also have the option to set the logon type to Interactive, Batch, or Network. See the "Changing Application Settings" section later in this chapter for more information.

With the IIS command-line administration tool, you can create applications by using the Add App command. Sample 9-4 provides the syntax and usage.

Sample 9-4   Add App Syntax and Usage

Syntax
```
appcmd add app /site.name: "ParentSiteName" /path: "VirtualPath"
/physicalPath: "Path"
```
Usage
```
appcmd add app /site.name:"Default Web Site" /path: "/Sales"
/physicalPath: "c:\inetpub\wwwroot\Sales"
```

When you create an application, a related virtual directory is created automatically. You can use this virtual directory to set the logon type and credentials for an application. The related command is Add Vdir. Sample 9-5 provides the syntax and usage.

Sample 9-5   Setting the Logon Type and Credentials Syntax and Usage

Syntax
```
appcmd add vdir /app.name:"ParentAppName" /path: "VirtualPath"
[/physicalPath: "Path"] [/logonMethod:Method] [/userName:User]
[/password:Password]
```

Usage

```
appcmd add vdir /app.name:"Default Web Site/Sales" /path:"/Support"
/physicalPath:"c:\support"

appcmd add vdir /app.name:"Sales Site/" /path:"/Invoices"
/physicalPath:"c:\salesroot\invoices" /logonMethod:ClearText
/userName:SupportUser /password:RainyDayz
```

Converting Existing Directories to Applications

Existing physical and virtual directories can be easily converted to applications, giving them separate contexts. To convert a directory to an application, follow these steps:

1. In IIS Manager, right-click the directory or virtual directory that you want to convert to an application, and then select Convert To Application. This displays the Add Application dialog box shown previously in Figure 9-2. The application alias and physical path are set automatically based on the directory you selected and cannot be changed.

2. The default application pool is listed in the Application Pool text box. To use a different application pool, click the Select button. In the Select Application Pool dialog box, select the application pool to use in the Application Pool drop-down list, and then click OK.

3. If you need to use alternate credentials to connect to the remote server specified in a UNC path, click Connect As. In the Connect As dialog box, choose Specific User, and then click Set. In the Set Credentials dialog box, type the name of the user account to use for authentication, type and confirm the account password, and then click OK twice.

With the IIS command-line administration tool, you can convert a directory to an application in the same way as you create an application. See Samples 9-4 and 9-5 for examples.

Changing Application Settings

An application's alias (virtual path) cannot be changed. You can change any other application's settings by following these steps:

1. In IIS Manager, select the site node you want to work with, and then in the Actions pane, click View Applications.

2. On the Applications page, click the application you want to work with, and then do one or both of the following:

   ❑ To edit the application's basic settings (which includes all settings except the logon type), select the application, and then, in the Actions pane, click Basic Settings. This displays the Edit Application dialog box, which you can use to change the application settings in much the same way as you set them in the first place by using the Add Application dialog box.

❑   To edit the application's advanced settings, in the Actions pane, click Advanced Settings. This displays the Advanced Settings dialog box, which you can use to change the application settings.

3.   Applications can have associated virtual directories. To view and manage the virtual directories associated with an application, select the application you want to work with, and then click View Virtual Directories. You can now work with the virtual directories associated with the previously selected application.

With the IIS command-line administration tool, you can change application settings via the virtual directory associated with the application. See Sample 9-6 for the related syntax and usage. Several application settings are configurable only from a command prompt. These settings control the bindings and protocols that are enabled for an application.

Sample 9-6   Set Application Protocols Syntax and Usage

Syntax
```
appcmd set app [/app.name:]AppNameOrURL
[/bindings:value1 ...]
[/enabledProtocols:value1 ...]
```
Usage
```
appcmd set app "Default Web Site/Sales" /bindings:
http://www.cpand1.com:8080

appcmd set app "Default Web Site/Sales" /enabledProtocols:http
```

Configuring Output Caching for Applications

Output caching improves performance by returning a processed copy of a served content from cache, resulting in reduced overhead on the server and faster response times. IIS 7.0 supports output caching in both user mode and kernel mode. Kernel-mode caching is enabled by default to ensure that cached responses are served from the kernel rather than from IIS user mode, giving IIS an extra boost in performance and increasing the number of requests IIS can process. Whether an individual application uses user-mode caching or kernel-mode caching depends on the application configuration as well as the caching rules that you define.

With the attributes of the Caching configuration section, you can control the way caching is used. Sample 9-7 provides the syntax and usage. The *enabled* attribute turns user-mode output caching on or off. If set to True, user mode is enabled for output caching. Otherwise, user-mode output caching is disabled. The *enableKernelModeCache* attribute controls whether kernel-mode output caching is enabled. If set to True, kernel mode is enabled for output caching. Otherwise, kernel-mode caching is disabled. The *maxCacheSize* attribute sets the maximum size, in megabytes, of the in-memory cache used for both the user-mode and kernel-mode caches. If this attribute is set to zero (0), IIS uses half the available physical or virtual memory (whichever is less) for caching. *maxResponseSize* sets the maximum size, in bytes, of responses that can be stored in the output cache for both the user-mode and kernel-mode caches. The default value is 262144 bytes (256 KB). If the response size is large than this value, the response is not stored in the output cache.

Note   At the server level, you set the master caching configuration and all the configuration options are available. At other configuration levels, you can control only whether output caching, kernel caching, or both are enabled.

Sample 9-7   Configuring Output Caching Syntax and Usage

Syntax
```
appcmd set config ["ConfigPath"] /section:caching
[/enabled:true|false] [/enableKernelModeCache:true|false]
[/maxCacheSize:"MaxStoredCacheInMB"]
[/maxResponseSize:"MaxSizeInBytes"]
```
Usage
```
appcmd set config "Default Web Site" /section:caching
/enableKernelModeCache:true
```

In IIS Manager, you can configure the maximum cached response size and cache size limit for output caching by completing the following steps:

1. Navigate to the level of the configuration hierarchy you want to manage, and then double-click the Output Caching feature.

2. On the Output Caching page, click Edit Feature Settings. This displays the Edit Output Cache Settings dialog box, shown in Figure 9-3.

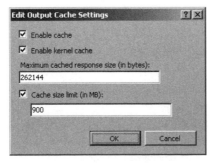

Figure 9-3   Configure output caching.

3. If you are working at the server configuration level, you can configure user-mode and kernel-mode caching:

    ❑   To enable user-mode caching, select Enable Cache. Clear this option to disable user-mode caching.

    ❑   To enable kernel-mode caching, select Enable Kernel Cache. Clear this option to disable kernel-mode caching.

4. In the Maximum Cached Response Size text box, type the maximum cached response size in bytes. The default value, 262144 bytes (256 KB), is appropriate in many instances. However, if your site has applications which can return large responses, such as database result sets, you'll want to increase this value accordingly.

5. To have IIS manage the cache size, clear the Cache Size Limit check box. To set a specific limit, select this check box, and then type a limit value in megabytes (MB). Click OK to save your settings.

Tip   On a dedicated Web server, you can set a specific cache limit to allow IIS to use more than half of the available physical or virtual memory. Before you do this, however, you should determine memory usage baselines for the server through monitoring. On a non-dedicated server, you can set a specific cache limit of less than half of the available physical or virtual memory to ensure that memory is available for other applications running on the server. In this configuration, you sacrifice IIS performance and responsiveness to ensure other applications can run on the server.

You can also create output-caching rules that control how IIS performs output caching for specific types of files. You can cache files until they change or until a specified time interval has elapsed. You also can have multiple cached versions of files based on query string variables or HTTP headers. For example, you may want to allow multiple cached versions of files based on locale. This would allow IIS to store different language versions of a file in cache.

The best way to configure output-caching rules is as follows:

■   At the server level, you set the caching rules that you want to apply to all sites and applications running on the server.

■   At the site and application level, you set the remote caching rules that you do not want to apply at that level.

■   At the site and application level, you add caching rules as necessary that use the default settings for cache monitoring.

In IIS Manager, you can create an output caching by completing the following steps:

1. Navigate to the level of the configuration hierarchy you want to manage, and then double-click the Output Caching feature. Keep in mind that you can customize the caching process only at the server level. At other levels, you can apply only the default settings.

2. On the Output Caching page, click Add. This displays the Add Cache Rule dialog box, shown in Figure 9-4.

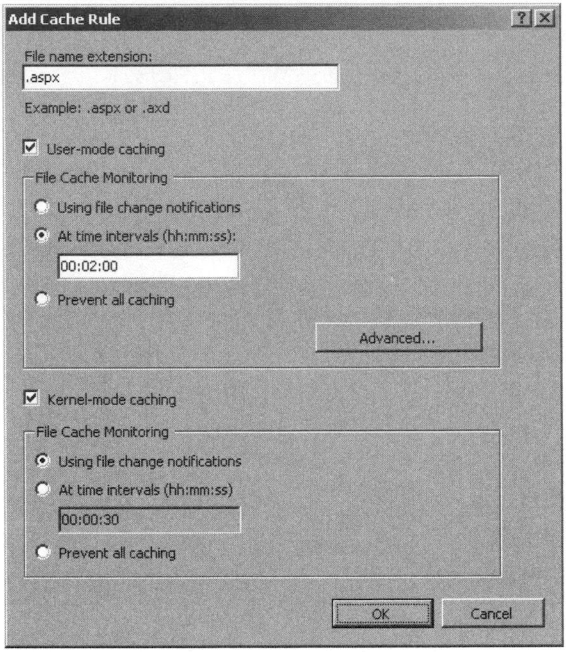

Figure 9-4   Create an output cache rule.

3. In the File Extension text box, type the file extension for which the rule will be applied, such as .aspx or .axd.

> **Note**   Be sure to use the correct file extension. You cannot change the file extension later. Because of this, you would need to delete and then re-create the rule using the correct file extension.

4. To prevent user-mode caching for this file extension, select the User-Mode Caching check box and then select Prevent All Caching. To enable and configure user-mode caching, select the User-Mode Caching check box and then perform one or more of the following actions as necessary:

❑ Once IIS caches a file, it monitors the file to determine whether the cache needs to be updated. To configure monitoring based on change notifications, select the Using File Change Notifications option. To configure monitoring for a specified time interval, select At Time Intervals, and then type an appropriate time interval, such as 00:01:00.

❑   IIS can cache multiple versions of files based on query string variables. To allow multiple versions of files to be cached based on the language, click Advanced. Select the Query String Variables check box, and then type Locale. To allow multiple versions of files to be cached based on regional settings, select the Query String Variables check box, and then type Culture. Separate multiple values with a comma and a space.

❑   IIS can cache multiple versions of files based on HTTP headers. To allow multiple versions of files to be cached based on a header value, click Advanced. Select the Headers check box, and then type the header keyword, such as Accept-Language or Accept-Charset. Separate multiple values with a comma and a space.

5. To prevent kernel-mode caching for this file extension, select the Kernel-Mode Caching check box and then select Prevent All Caching. To enable and configure user-mode caching, select the User-Mode Caching check box and then configure file cache monitoring. Once IIS caches a file, it monitors the file to determine whether the cache needs to be updated. To configure monitoring based on change notifications, select the Using File Change Notifications option. To configure monitoring for a specified time interval, select At Time Intervals, and then type an appropriate time interval, such as 00:01:00.

6. Click OK to create the cache rule.

You can work with cache rules in a variety of other ways:

■   To modify the rule definition, click the rule, and then click Edit. In the Edit Cache Rule dialog box, make the necessary changes to the rule, and then click OK.

■   To block an inherited rule so that IIS doesn't apply at the current configuration level, click the rule, and then click Remove.

■   To remove a rule permanently, click the rule, and then in the Actions pane, click Remove. When prompted to confirm the action, click Yes.

Deleting IIS Applications

If you find that you no longer need an application, you should remove it to free up the resources that it's using. Deleting an application removes the application context only; it does not remove the underlying directories or content.

To delete an application, follow these steps:

1. In IIS Manager, select the site node you want to work with, and then in the Actions pane, click View Applications.

2. On the Applications page, click the application you want to remove, and then in the Actions pane, click Remove.

3. When prompted to confirm that you want to remove the application, click Yes.

With the IIS command-line administration tool, you can delete an application by using the Delete App command. Sample 9-8 provides the syntax and usage.

Sample 9-8   Delete App Syntax and Usage

Syntax
```
appcmd delete app [/app.name:]AppNameOrURL
```
Usage
```
appcmd delete app "Default Web Site/Sales"
```

Managing ASP.NET and the .NET Framework

Every Web administrator should become intimately familiar with ASP.NET and the .NET Framework. You should know how to configure and manage the related components and applications. As you've seen in Chapter 8, ASP.NET and .NET Framework configurations are fairly complex. To ensure success, you'll need to work closely with your organization's engineers and developers during planning, staging, and deployment.

Installing ASP.NET and the .NET Framework

To use applications that incorporate the .NET Framework, you must install ASP.NET on your IIS servers. ASP.NET is the central Windows component that allows an IIS server to run ASP.NET applications. Like the .NET Framework, ASP.NET technology is advancing rapidly. Several implementations of ASP.NET are already available, and many more will be developed in the coming months and years.

Unlike many application implementations, in which you have to remove previous application or component versions before installing new applications or components, you don't have to remove previous versions of ASP.NET. The reason is that the .NET Framework supports side-by-side execution of applications and components running different versions of ASP.NET. Side-by-side execution is made possible because applications and the components they use run within isolated process boundaries. Each worker process runs its own instance of the ASP.NET components that it needs and is isolated from other processes.

You can install multiple versions of ASP.NET on an IIS server. You enable the default version of ASP.NET and .NET by installing and enabling the ASP.NET and .NET Extensibility role services. You can install additional versions of ASP.NET on an IIS server. Typically, you do this by running the .NET Framework setup program (Dotnetfx.exe) for the version you want to install. Installing a newer version of the .NET Framework could reconfigure ASP.NET applications installed on the IIS server to use the version you're installing. Specifically, this happens when the version you're installing is a new version that represents a minor revision (as determined by the version number). For example, if ASP.NET applications are currently configured to use ASP.NET version 2.0.50727 and you're installing a newer version, ASP.NET applications would be configured to use components in the new version automatically. Here, 50727 represents the build number, and 2.0 are the major and minor version numbers, respectively.

After you install a new version of the .NET Framework, you'll need to ensure that IIS is configured properly so that the new version of ASP.NET it contains can be used in both the Classic and Integrated pipeline modes. You do this by ensuring that the related aspnet_filter.dll is added as an ISAPI filter and that the related aspnet_isapi.dll is allowed as an ISAPI and CGI restriction. Each version of the .NET Framework installed on a server has different components and tools. The base directory for the .NET Framework is *%SystemRoot%*\Microsoft.NET\Framework. Below the base directory, you'll find separate subdirectories for each version of the .NET Framework you've installed.

One of the tools in the version subdirectory is the ASP.NET IIS Registration tool. This tool controls the mapping of ASP.NET applications to a specific ASP.NET version. If you want to install an additional ASP.NET version so that it can be used on the server, you can use this tool to do it. Complete the following steps:

1. On the Start menu, choose Run.

2. In the Open field, type **cmd,** and then click OK.

3. At the command prompt, type **cd %SystemRoot%\Microsoft.NET\Framework,** and then press Enter.

4. Run the **dir** command to obtain a directory listing. Note the available version subdirectories, and then change to the directory containing the ASP.NET version you want to use.

5. List the installed versions of ASP.NET and view how those versions are configured by running **aspnet_regiis -lv** and then **aspnet_regiis -lk**. Then do one of the following:

   ❑ If you want all application pools to use this ASP.NET version (as long as it's a newer version and represents a compatible build as determined by the version and build number), run **aspnet_regiis -i.**

   ❑ If you want to register this ASP.NET version on the server but don't want to reconfigure application pools to use it, run **aspnet_regiis -ir.**

Tip It's important to note that each version of ASP.NET installed on a server has a separate set of performance counter objects. Because of this, if you want to monitor a particular ASP.NET application's performance, you'll need to configure monitoring of the performance counter objects specific to the version of ASP.NET used by the application.

Deploying ASP.NET Applications

Now that you've configured the application directory structure, you're ready to deploy your ASP.NET applications. To deploy applications, copy the necessary ASP.NET files, such as .asmx or .aspx files, to the application directory. Application binaries and assemblies (DLLs) are copied to the Bin subdirectory for the application.

Any time you need to update or change the files in the deployment directory, simply copy the new versions of the ASP.NET files and binaries to the appropriate directory. When you do this, ASP.NET automatically detects that files have been updated. In response, ASP.NET compiles a new version of the application and loads it into memory as necessary to handle new requests. Any current requests are handled without interruption by the previously created application instance. When that application instance is no longer needed, it's removed from memory.

ASP.NET handles changes to the Web.config file in the same way. If you modify the Web.config file or application pool properties while IIS is running, ASP.NET compiles a new version of the application and loads it into memory as necessary to handle new requests. Any current requests are handled without interruption by the previously created application instance. When that application instance is no longer needed, it's removed from memory.

Uninstalling .NET Versions

Sometimes you no longer want an older version of ASP.NET to run on a server. In this case you can uninstall the unneeded ASP.NET version. When you uninstall an older version of ASP.NET, ASP.NET applications that used the version are reconfigured so that they use the highest remaining version of ASP.NET that's compatible with the version you're uninstalling.

Remember, the version number determines compatibility. If no other compatible versions are installed, applications that used the version of ASP.NET you're uninstalling are left in an unconfigured state, which might cause the entire contents of ASP.NET pages to be served directly to clients, thereby exposing the code those pages contain.

If you want to uninstall an additional version of ASP.NET, follow these steps:

1. On the Start menu, choose Run.

2. In the Open field, type **cmd**, and then click OK.

3. At the command prompt, type cd **%SystemRoot%\Microsoft.NET\Framework**, and then press Enter.

4. Run the **dir** command to obtain a directory listing. Note the available version subdirectories and then change to the directory containing the ASP.NET version you want to remove.

5. List the installed versions of ASP.NET and view how those versions are configured by running **aspnet_regiis -lv** and then running **aspnet_regiis -lk**.

6. To uninstall the ASP.NET version whose components are in the current subdirectory, run **aspnet_regiis -u**. This uninstalls the ASP.NET version and the performance counter objects used by the ASP.NET version.

Note   If you want to uninstall all ASP.NET versions installed on a server, run **aspnet_regiis -ua**.

Working with Application Pools

Application pools set boundaries for applications and specify the configuration settings that applications they contain use. Every application pool has a set of one or more worker processes assigned to it. These worker processes specify the memory space that applications use. By assigning an application to a particular application pool, you're specifying that the application:

- **Can run in the same context as other applications in the application pool**   All applications in a particular application pool use the same worker process or processes, and these worker processes define the isolation boundaries. These applications must use the same version of ASP.NET. If applications in the same application pool use different versions of ASP.NET, errors will occur and the worker processes might not run.

- **Should use the application pool configuration settings**   Configuration settings are applied to all applications assigned to a particular application pool. These settings control recycling of worker processes, failure detection and recovery, CPU monitoring, and much more. Application pool settings should be optimized to work with all applications they contain.

The sections that follow provide techniques for creating, configuring, and optimizing application pools.

Viewing Application Pools

You manage application pools on a per-server basis. In IIS Manager, you can view all the application pools configured on a server by expanding the server node and then clicking the Application Pools node. As Figure 9-5 shows, you'll then see a list of applications created within the site listed by:

- **Name**   Lists the name of the application pool

- **Status**   Lists the status of an application pool as Started or Stopped

- **.NET Framework Version**   Lists the .NET Framework version that the application pool uses

- **Managed Pipeline Mode** Lists the request processing mode used by the application as Integrated or Classic

- **Identity** Lists the account under which the application pool runs, such as NetworkService

- **Applications** Lists the number of applications that are configured to run in the application pool

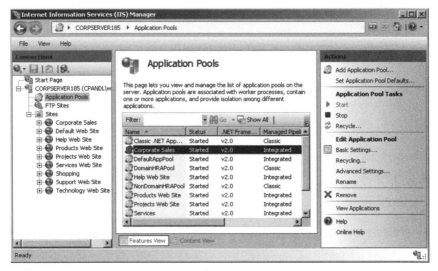

Figure 9-5 Review the application pools configured on the server.

With the IIS command-line administration tool, you can list a server's application pools by running the List AppPool command. Sample 9-9 provides the syntax and usage.

Sample 9-9 List AppPool Syntax and Usage

Syntax
```
appcmd list apppool [[/apppool.name:]"AppPoolName"]
[/managedRuntimeVersion:"Version"]
[/managedPipelineMode: Integrated|Classic]
[/queueLength:"queueLength"]
[/autoStart:true|false]
```

Usage
```
Appcmd list apppool

appcmd list apppool "DefaultAppPool"

appcmd list apppool /autoStart:false
```

Several utility commands are provided to help you work with application pools and track their worker processes. With the List Wp command, you can list the worker processes currently running on a server. Sample 9-10 provides the syntax and usage.

Sample 9-10   List Wp Syntax and Usage

Syntax
```
appcmd list wp [[/process.name:]"ProcessID"] [/wp.name:"ProcessID"]
[/apppool.name:"AppPoolName"]
```
Usage
```
appcmd list wp


appcmd list wp "4291"


appcmd list wp /apppool.name:"DefaultAppPool"
```

With the List Request command, you can list the requests currently executing on a server and optionally find requests that have been executing for longer than a specified time in milliseconds. Sample 9-11 provides the syntax and usage.

Sample 9-11   List Request Syntax and Usage

Syntax
```
appcmd list request [[/process.name:]"ProcessID"]
[/request.name: "ProcessID"] [/site.name:"SiteName"]
[/wp.name:"WpName"] [/apppool.name:"AppPoolName"]
[/elapsed:Milliseconds]
```
Usage
```
appcmd list request


appcmd list request /wp.name:4125


appcmd list request /apppool.name:DefaultAppPool


appcmd list request /site.name:"Default Web Site"
```

Configuring Default Settings for New Application Pools

In a standard configuration, new application pools are configured to use a number of settings that determine exactly how an application pool works. If you use the same settings for most application pools, you may want to modify the default settings. To do this, follow these steps:

1. In IIS Manager, expand the node for the server you want to work with, and then click the Application Pools node.

2. On the Application Pools page, in the Actions pane, click Set Application Pool Defaults.

3. In the Application Pool Defaults dialog box, configure the default settings for application pools, and then click OK.

Table 9-1 provides a summary of the default settings for application pools. Each setting is listed alphabetically according to its related configuration area, such as CPU or Process Model. With the IIS command-line administration tool, you can configure these settings using the following syntax:

```
appcmd set config /section:applicationPools
/applicationPoolDefaults.SubAttribute:Value
```

where SubAttribute is a listed sub attribute and Value is the desired value, such as:

```
appcmd set config /section:applicationPools
/applicationPoolDefaults.enable32BitAppOnWin64:true
```

All time intervals are set hh:mm:ss format. These same sub attributes are used with application pools when you want to configure their settings from a command prompt. To configure settings for an individual application pool, use the following syntax:

```
appcmd set apppool "AppPoolName" /[Attribute.]SubAttribute:Value
```

where AppPoolName is the name of the application pool, Attribute is a listed attribute, SubAttribute is a listed sub attribute, and Value is the desired value, such as:

```
appcmd set apppool "CustServicesAppPool" /cpu.resetInterval:30
```

Note Hyphens are added in this table for readability. Sub attribute names do not have hyphens in actual usage.

Table 9-1 Settings for Configuring Application Pools

UI Name	Sub Attribute	Description
General		
	enable32BitApp-OnWin64	When True, enables 32-bit applications to run using 32-bits on a 64-bit system.
.NET Framework Version	managedRuntime-Version	Sets the .NET Framework version.
Managed Pipeline Mode	managedPipe-lineMode	Sets the managed pipeline mode
Name	name	Sets the application pool name.
Queue Length	queueLength	Sets the maximum number of queued requests.
Start Automatically	autoStart	When True, the application pool starts when it is created or when IIS starts.
CPU		

Table 9-1   Settings for Configuring Application Pools

UI Name	Sub Attribute	Description
Limit	cpu.limit	Sets the maximum CPU time in 1/1000th of a percent that the worker processes in an application pool can use over the limit interval.
Limit Action	cpu.action	Sets the action IIS takes if the CPU limit is reached as either NoAction for logging only or KillW3WP to stop the application pool for the duration of the limit interval.
Limit Interval	cpu.resetInterval	Sets the period of time in minutes for tracking the CPU limit or resetting an application pool if a limit is reached.
Processor Affinity Enabled	cpu.smpAffinitized	When True, forces worker processes for an application to run on specific CPUs.
Processor Affinity Mask	cpu.smpProcessor-AffinityMask	Sets a hexadecimal mask that controls which CPUs worker processes are associated with when processor affinity is enabled.
Process Model		
	passAnonymous-Token	When True, allows passing an anonymous user token.
	processModel.manu-alGroupMembership	When True, allows manual group membership assignment.
Identity	processModel.identityType	Sets the user account under which the worker processes run.
Idle Time-Out	processModel.idle-TImeout	Sets the amount of time a worker process can remain idle before it shuts down.
Load User Profile	processModel.load-UserProfile	When True, IIS loads the user profile for the application pool identity.
Maximum Worker Processes	processModel.max-Processes	Sets the maximum number of worker processes.
Password	processModel.pass-word	Sets the password for a "SpecificUser" identity. Available in UI when you are setting credentials.
Ping Enabled	processModel.ping-ingEnabled	When True, IIS periodically checks worker processes to ensure that they are active.
Ping Maximum Response Time	processModel.ping-ResponseTime	Sets the maximum time that a worker process is given to respond to a ping. If this time is exceeded, IIS terminates the process.
Ping Period	processModel.ping-Interval	Sets the interval between pings.

Table 9-1   Settings for Configuring Application Pools

UI Name	Sub Attribute	Description
Shutdown Time Limit	processModel.shutdownTimeLimit	Sets the maximum amount of time a worker process is given to finish processing requests and shutdown. If this time is exceeded, IIS terminates the process.
Startup Time Limit	processModel.startupTimeLimit	Sets the maximum amount of time a worker process is given to start and initialize. If this time is exceeded, IIS terminates the process.
UserName	processModel.userName	Sets user name for the "SpecificUser" identity. Available in UI when you are setting credentials.
Process Orphaning		
Enabled	failure.orphanWorkerProcess	When True, a nonresponsive worker process is abandoned instead of terminated. This allows debugging and should be used only during troubleshooting.
Executable	failure.orphanActionExe	Sets the executable to run when a worker process is abandoned, such as %SystemDrive%\Dbgtools\Ntsd.exe.
Executable Parameters	failure.orphanActionParams	Sets the parameters to pass to the executable that is run when a worker process is abandoned.
Recycling		
Disable Overlapping Recycle	recycling.disallowOverlappingRotation	If an application does not support multiple instances, set this value to True. When True, IIS waits for an existing process to exit before starting another process during recycling.
Disable Recycling for Configuration Changes	recycling.disallowRotationOnConfigChange	When True, IIS doesn't recycle the application pool when the configuration is changed (and as a result some changes aren't applied until a later restart).
Generate Recycle Event Log Entry	recycling.logEventOnRecycle	Determines the types of events that IIS logs when recycling application pools.
Private Memory Limit	recycling.periodicRestart.privateMemory	Sets the maximum amount of private memory in kilobytes that a worker process can use before IIS recycles it. Use a value of zero to set no limit.
Regular Time Interval	recycling.periodicRestart.time	Sets the period of time in minutes after which IIS routinely recycles an application pool. Use a value of zero to set a regular recycling interval.

Table 9-1   Settings for Configuring Application Pools

UI Name	Sub Attribute	Description
Request Limit	recycling.periodic-Restart.requests	Sets the maximum requests an application pool can process before IIS recycles it. Use a value of zero to set no limit.
Specific Times	recycling.periodic-Restart.schedule. [value='timespan'] .value	Sets specific times when the application pool is recycled.
Virtual Memory Limit	recycling.periodic-Restart.memory	Sets the maximum amount of virtual memory in kilobytes that a worker process can use before IIS recycles it. Use a value of zero to set no limit.
Rapid-Fail Protection		
"Service Unavailable" Response Type	failure.loadBalancer-Capabilities	When rapid-fail protection is enabled, determines how "Service Unavailable" errors are handled. With HttpdLevel, an HTTP 503 error is returned. With TcpLevel, IIS resets the connection.
Enabled	failure.rapidFail-Protection	When True, rapid-fail protection is enabled.
Failure Interval	failure.rapidFail-ProtectionInterval	When rapid-fail protection is enabled, sets the time interval during which the maximum number of failures must occur before the application pool is shut down.
Maximum Failures	failure.rapidFail-ProtectionMaxCrashes	When rapid-fail protection is enabled, sets the maximum number of failures permitted in the failure interval before the application pool is shut down.
Shutdown Executable	failure.auto-ShutdownExe	When rapid-fail protection is enabled, sets the executable to run when an application pool is shut down.
Shutdown Executable Parameters	failure.auto-ShutdownParams	When rapid-fail protection is enabled, sets the parameters to pass to the executable to run when an application pool is shut down.

Creating Application Pools

Application pools specify the isolation boundaries for Web applications. You can use application pools to optimize the performance, recovery, and monitoring of Web applications. An application's scope can range from an entire Web site to a single virtual directory. This means that you can specify default applications for Web sites that your IIS server hosts, and you can specify Web applications with very specific scopes.

To create an application pool, follow these steps:

1. In IIS Manager, expand the node for the server you want to work with, and then click the Application Pools node.

2. On the Application Pools page, in the Actions pane, click Add Application Pool. This displays the Add Application Pool dialog box shown in Figure 9-6.

Figure 9-6 Use the Add Application Pool dialog box to set the name, .NET Framework version, and pipeline mode for the application pool.

3. In the Name text box, type the name of the application pool. The name should be short but descriptive.

> **Tip** You might want to number the application pools to identify them uniquely. For example, you might create AppPool #1, AppPool #2, and so on. Or you might want to identify the purpose of the application pool in the name. For example, you might have CustRegPool, ProdCatPool, and TechNetPool.

4. You can now use the .NET Framework Version drop-down list to select the .NET Framework version that the application pool should use, such as .NET Framework Version 2.0.50727. If the application pool is not for ASP.NET applications and has no managed code components, you can select No Managed Code.

5. In the Managed Pipeline Mode drop-down list, you can choose either the Integrated or Classic pipeline mode. If an application pool uses Classic mode, IIS processes the requests in the application pool by using separate processing pipelines for IIS and ISAPI. If an application pool uses Integrated mode, IIS processes the requests in an application pool by using an integrated processing pipeline for IIS and ASP.NET. See the "Understanding and Using ASP.NET Applications" section in Chapter 3, "Core IIS Administration," for more information.

6. By default, the application pool is configured to start as soon as you click OK, and it is also configured to start automatically whenever you start IIS. If you'd rather start the application pool manually, clear the Start Application Pool Immediately check box.

7. Click OK to create the application pool.

With the IIS command-line administration tool, you can create an application pool by using the Add AppPool command. Sample 9-12 provides the syntax and usage. Attributes listed in Table 9-1 are valid also. The only mandatory attribute is the application pool name. If you don't set additional attributes, AppCmd uses the current default settings to determine the appropriate values.

Sample 9-12   Add AppPool Syntax and Usage

Syntax
```
appcmd add apppool /name:"AppPoolName"
[/managedRuntimeVersion:"Version"]
[/managedPipelineMode: Integrated|Classic]
[/queueLength:"queueLength"]
[/autoStart:true|false]
```
Usage
```
Appcmd add apppool /name:CustServicesAppPool
/managedPipelineMode: Integrated

Appcmd add apppool /name:CustServicesAppPool
/autoStart:false
```

Changing Application Pool Settings

In IIS Manager, you can change application pool settings on the Application Pools page. To rename an application pool, click the entry to select it, and then click Rename. Type the new name for the application pool, and then press Enter.

You can change any other application pool settings by following these steps:

1. In IIS Manager, expand the node for the server you want to work with, and then click the Application Pools node.

2. On the Application Pools page, click the application pool you want to work with, and then do one of the following:

   ❑ To edit the application pool's basic settings, in the Actions pane, click Basic Settings. This displays the Edit Application Pool dialog box, which you can use to change the application pool's .NET Framework, version, managed pipeline mode, and startup setting.

   ❑ To edit the application pool's advanced settings, in the Actions pane, click Advanced Settings. This displays the Advanced Settings dialog box, which you can use to change all application pool settings.

3. Application pools can have associated applications. To view and manage the applications associated with an application pool, click the application pool you want to work with, and then click View Applications. You can now work with the applications associated with the previously selected application pool.

With the IIS command-line administration tool, you can change basic application pool settings by using the Set AppPool command. See Sample 9-13 for the related syntax and usage. Attributes listed in Table 9-1 are valid as well.

Sample 9-13   Set AppPool Syntax and Usage

Syntax
```
appcmd set apppool [/apppool.name:]"AppPoolName"
[/managedRuntimeVersion:"Version"]
[/managedPipelineMode: Integrated|Classic]
[/queueLength:"queueLength"]
[/autoStart:true|false]
```

Usage
```
Appcmd set apppool /name:CustServicesAppPool
/managedRuntimeVersion:"v2.0"


Appcmd set apppool /name:CustServicesAppPool
/queueLength:"1100"
```

Assigning Applications to Application Pools

Applications assigned to the same pool share the same configuration settings. These settings control recycling of worker processes used by applications in the pool, failure detection and recovery, the identity under which the worker processes run, and more. You should assign applications to the same pool only when they have similar requirements. If an application has unique requirements, you might want to assign it to a separate application pool that's used only by that application.

To assign an application to an application pool, follow these steps:

1. In IIS Manager, select the node for the site you want to work with, and then in the Actions pane, click View Applications.

2. On the Web Applications page, click the application you want to work with, and then click Basic Settings. This displays the Edit Application dialog box.

3. The Application Pool text box lists the application pool currently associated with the application. To change this value, click the Select button. In the Select Application Pool dialog box, select the application pool to use in the Application Pool list. Then click OK twice to save your settings.

Applications assigned to the same application pool can't use different versions of ASP.NET. If you assign applications that use different ASP.NET versions to the same pool, the worker process might not run at all.

Configuring Application Pool Identities

The application pool identity determines the account under which the application pool's worker processes run. In most cases, this identity is the Network Service account, which has limited permissions and privileges. If a particular application needs additional permissions or privileges, it's a good idea to create a separate application pool for that application and then configure the application pool identity to use an account that has those permissions. In most cases you should use one of the other predefined accounts, such as Local Service or Local System, but you can also use the IWAM account or any other account that you configure.

To configure the application pool identity, follow these steps:

1. In IIS Manager, expand the node for the server you want to work with, and then click the Application Pools node.

2. On the Application Pools page, click the application pool you want to work with, and then click Advanced Settings.

3. Under Process Model, click the Identity entry, and then click the related selection button.

4. Do one of the following:

   ❑ If you want to use the built-in Network Service, Local Service, or Local System accounts, select Built-in Account, and then in the drop-down list, select the appropriate account. Click OK and skip the remaining steps.

   ❑ If you want to specify a user account, select Custom Account, and then click Set. In the Set Credentials dialog box, type the user name for the account. Type and then confirm the account password, and then click OK twice.

> **More Info**   For detailed information on working with the Network Service, Local Service, Local System, and accounts, see the section titled "IIS User and Group Essentials" in Chapter 10.

Starting, Stopping, and Recycling Worker Processes Manually

Sometimes you might want to restart or recycle the worker processes that an application pool is using. You might want to do this if you suspect that an application is leaking memory or is otherwise affecting server performance or if users are experiencing undetermined or intermittent problems.

Starting and Stopping Worker Processes Manually

When you stop worker processes for an application pool, the related IIS 7.0 processes (W3wp.exe) are terminated, and as a result, all resources used by the worker processes are freed. This also means, however, that any requests currently being processed will fail and that new requests for the applications aren't processed until you start the application pool again, at which time Http.sys looks for requests in the application pool queue and then starts new worker processes as necessary to handle any pending requests.

The World Wide Web service can also stop an application pool. Typically, this occurs when rapid-fail protection is triggered, meaning that there were a certain number of worker process failures in a specified time period. In the standard configuration, five worker process failures within a five-minute interval trigger rapid-fail protection. Application pools can also be stopped when they're configured to use a nonexistent identity or if different applications use different versions of ASP.NET.

To stop and then start an application pool, follow these steps:

1. In IIS Manager, expand the node for the server you want to work with, and then click the Application Pools node.

2. On the Application Pools page, click the application pool you want to stop, and then click Stop.

3. Worker processes used by applications in the application pool are terminated. To start request processing for applications in the pool, click the application pool, and then click Start.

Tip Clients trying to access an application in a stopped application pool might see an HTTP Error 503: Service Unavailable message. If users tell you they're seeing this message, and you haven't stopped the application pool, check to see if the application pool is started. If it isn't, start it, and then check the error logs to determine what happened while closely monitoring for additional failures.

With the IIS command-line administration tool, you can start and stop application pools by using the Start AppPool and Stop AppPool commands respectively. See Samples 9-14 and 9-15 for the related syntax and usage. The *Wait* attribute determines whether AppCmd waits for the application pool to start or stop before returning. When you wait for the application pool to start or stop, you can use the *timeout* attribute to specify the maximum amount of time in milliseconds to wait.

Sample 9-14   Start AppPool Syntax and Usage

Syntax
```
appcmd start apppool [[/apppool.name:]"AppPoolName"] [/wait]
[/timeout:WaitTimeMilliseconds]
```
Usage
```
appcmd start apppool "MyAppPool"
```

Sample 9-15   Stop AppPool Syntax and Usage

Syntax
```
appcmd start apppool [[/apppool.name:]"AppPoolName"] [/wait]
[/timeout:WaitTimeMilliseconds]
```
Usage
```
appcmd stop apppool "MyAppPool"
```

Recycling Worker Processes Manually

An alternative to abruptly terminating worker processes used by an application pool is to mark them for recycling. Worker processes that are actively processing requests continue to run while IIS starts new worker processes to replace them. Once the new worker processes are started, Http.sys directs incoming requests to the new worker processes, and the old worker processes are able to continue handling requests until they shut down. With this approach, you minimize any service interruptions while ensuring that any resources used by old worker processes are eventually freed.

With recycling, the startup and shutdown processes can be limited by the Startup Time Limit and Shutdown Time Limit values set for the application pool. If IIS can't start new worker processes within the set time limit, a service interruption would occur because IIS would be unable to direct requests to the new processes. If IIS stops old worker processes when the shutdown time limit is reached and those processes are still handling requests, a service interruption would occur because the requests wouldn't be processed further.

To recycle the worker processes used by an application pool, follow these steps:

1. In IIS Manager, expand the node for the server you want to work with, and then click the Application Pools node.

2. On the Application Pools page, click the application pool you want to recycle, and then click Recycle.

With the IIS command-line administration tool, you can recycle application pools by using the Recycle AppPool command. See Sample 9-16 for the related syntax and usage.

Sample 9-16   Recycle AppPool Syntax and Usage

Syntax
```
appcmd recycle apppool [[/apppool.name:]"AppPoolName"]
[/parameter1:value1 ...]
```
Usage
```
appcmd recycle apppool "MyAppPool"
```

Configuring Worker Process Startup and Shutdown Time Limits

Whenever IIS starts or shuts down worker processes, it attempts to do so within prescribed time limits. The goal is to ensure timely startup of worker processes so that Http.sys can direct incoming requests to new worker processes and shut down old worker processes after they complete the processing of existing requests.

Graceful startup and shutdown of worker processes, however, is dependent on the amount of time allowed for startup and shutdown. If these values are set too low, service might be interrupted—a new worker process might not get started in time to accept incoming requests, or an old worker process might be terminated before it can finish processing requests. If these values are set too high, system resources might be tied up waiting for a transition that isn't possible. An existing worker process might be nonresponsive, or the server might be unable to allocate additional resources to start new worker processes while the old processes are still running.

Real World   Listen carefully to user complaints about failed requests, time-outs, and other errors. Frequent complaints can be an indicator that you need to take a close look at the worker process recycling configuration as discussed in the "Configuring Worker Process Recycling" section later in this chapter. If you believe you've optimized worker process recycling but users are still experiencing problems, take a look at the startup and shutdown time limits.

Ideally, you'll select a balanced startup and shutdown time that reflects the server's load and the importance of the applications in the application pool. By default, the startup and shutdown time limits are both set to 90 seconds. Here are some rules of thumb for setting startup and shutdown time limits:

- For application pools with applications that have long-running processes, such as those that require extensive computations or extended database lookups, you might want to reduce the startup time limit and extend the shutdown time limit, particularly if the server consistently experiences a moderate or heavy load.

- For application pools in which it's more important to ensure that the service is responsive than to ensure that all requests go through, you might want to reduce both the startup and shutdown time limits, particularly if applications have known problems, such as memory leaks or frequent hangs.

To configure worker process startup and shutdown time limits, complete the following steps:

1. In IIS Manager, expand the node for the server you want to work with, and then click the Application Pools node.

2. On the Application Pools page, click the application pool you want to work with, and then click Advanced Settings.

3. Under Process Model, in the Startup Time Limit and Shutdown Time Limit fields, set the maximum time allowed for worker process startup and shutdown respectively (in seconds). Click OK.

Configuring Multiple Worker Processes for Application Pools

Multiple worker processes running in their own context can share responsibility for handling requests for an application pool. This configuration is also referred to as a *Web garden*. When you set up a Web garden, each new request is assigned to a worker process according to a round-robin scheme. Round-robin is a load balancing technique used to spread the workload among the worker processes that are available.

> **Note**   It's important to note that worker processes aren't started automatically and don't use resources until they're needed. Rather, they're started as necessary to meet the demand based on incoming requests. For example, if you configure a maximum of five worker processes for an application pool, there may be at any given time from zero to five worker processes running in support of applications placed in that application pool.

If a single application is placed in an application pool serviced by multiple worker processes, all available worker processes will handle requests queued for the application. This is a multiple worker process–single application configuration, and it's best used when you want to improve the application's request-handling performance and reduce any possible contention for resources with other applications. In this case the application might have heavy usage during peak periods and moderate-to-heavy usage during other times, or individuals using the application might have specific performance expectations that must be met if possible.

If multiple applications are placed in an application pool serviced by multiple worker processes, all available worker processes handle requests queued for any applicable application. This is a multiple worker process–multiple application configuration, and it's best used when you want to improve request-handling performance and reduce resource contention for multiple applications but don't want to dedicate resources to any single application. In this case the various applications in the application pool might have different peak usage periods or might have varying resource needs.

To configure multiple worker processes for an application pool, follow these steps:

1. In IIS Manager, expand the node for the server you want to work with, and then click the Application Pools node.

2. On the Application Pools page, click the application pool you want to work with, and then click Advanced Settings.

3. Under Process Model, in the Maximum Worker Processes text box, specify the number of worker processes that the application pool should use, and then click OK.

Real World   When you assign multiple worker processes to a busy application pool, keep in mind that each worker process uses server resources when it's started and might affect the performance of applications in other application pools. Adding worker processes won't resolve latency issues caused by network communications or bandwidth, and it can reduce the time it takes to process requests only if those requests were queued and waiting and not being actively processed. A poorly engineered application will still respond poorly, and at some point, you'd need to look at optimizing the application code for efficiency and speed.

Configuring Worker Process Recycling

Manual recycling of worker processes might work when you're troubleshooting, but on a day-to-day basis you probably don't have time to monitor resource usage and responsiveness for worker processes. For IIS to handle worker process recycling for you, you'll want to configure some type of automatic worker process recycling. Automatic worker process recycling can be configured to occur:

- **After a specific time period**   Recycles worker processes based on the amount of time they've been running. This is best used when applications have known problems running for extended periods of time.

- **When a certain number of requests are processed**   Recycles worker processes based on the number of requests processed. This is best used when applications fail based on usage.

- **At specific scheduled times during the day**   Recycles worker processes based on a defined schedule. This is best used when applications have known problems running for extended periods of time and you don't want processes to be recycled during a peak usage period. Here, you'd schedule recycling when you expect application usage to be at its lowest for the day.

- **When memory usage grows to a specific point**   Recycles worker processes when they use a certain amount of virtual (paged) or private (nonpaged) memory. This is best used when applications have known or suspected memory leaks.

The sections that follow discuss techniques for configuring automatic worker process recycling. When you configure recycling, keep in mind that unless you disable overlapped recycling, active worker processes continue to run while IIS starts new worker processes to replace them. Once the new worker processes are started, Http.sys directs incoming requests to the new worker processes, and the old worker processes are able to continue handling requests until they shut down. The startup and shutdown processes can be limited by the Startup Time Limit and Shutdown Time Limit values set for the application pool. If these values are set inappropriately, new worker processes might not start, and old worker processes might shut down before they've finished processing current requests.

Recycling Automatically by Time and Number of Requests

When applications have known problems running for extended periods of time and handling requests in peak loads, you probably want to configure automatic recycling by time, by number of requests, or both. To configure automatic recycling by time and number of requests, follow these steps:

1. In IIS Manager, expand the node for the server you want to work with, and then click the Application Pools node.

2. On the Application Pools page, click the application pool you want to work with, and then click Advanced Settings.

3. If any application running in the application pool does not support multiple instances, set Disable Overlapped Recycle to True. Otherwise, you'll want to allow overlapped recycling (in most cases) by setting this option to False.

4. To recycle worker processes after a specified period of time, select Regular Time Interval (In Minutes), and then type the number of minutes that you want to elapse before worker processes are recycled.

   Tip   In most cases it's prudent to schedule worker process recycling to take place at specific off-peak usage times rather than to set hard limits based on run time or number of requests handled. If you schedule recycling, you control when recycling occurs and can be reasonably sure that it won't occur when the application usage is high.

5. To recycle a worker process after processing a specified number of requests, select Request Limit, and then type the number of requests that you want to be processed before the worker process is recycled.

6. To recycle worker processes according to a specific schedule, select Specific Times, and then click the related selection button. You can use the TimeSpan Collection Editor to:

   - ❑ **Add a scheduled recycle time**   Click Add. In the right pane under TimeSpan, click in the Value text box. Set a recycle time on a 24-hour clock.

   - ❑ **Edit a scheduled recycle time**   Click the recycle time you want to change, and then in the right pane, under TimeSpan, in the Value text box, type the desired recycle time.

   - ❑ **Remove a scheduled recycle time**   Click the recycle time you want to delete, and then click Remove.

   - ❑ **Save the scheduled recycle times**   Click OK to close the TimeSpan Collection Editor and save your recycle times.

7. Click OK to apply the settings.

Recycling Automatically by Memory Usage

When applications have known or suspected memory leaks, you probably want to configure automatic recycling based on virtual or private memory usage. To configure automatic recycling of worker processes based on memory usage, follow these steps:

1. In IIS Manager, expand the node for the server you want to work with, and then click the Application Pools node.

2. On the Application Pools page, click the application pool you want to work with, and then click Advanced Settings.

3. Virtual memory usage refers to the amount of paged memory written to disk that the worker process uses. To limit virtual memory usage and automatically recycle a worker process when this limit is reached, select Virtual Memory Limit (KB), and then type the virtual memory limit in the corresponding field.

> **Tip** In most cases, you'll want to establish the baseline virtual and private memory usage for an application before configuring memory recycling. If you don't do this, you might find that worker processes are being recycled at the most inopportune times, such as when the server is experiencing peak usage loads. A good rule of thumb is to allow private memory usage of at least 1.5 times the baseline usage you see and to allow virtual memory usage of at least 2 times the private memory usage. For example, if your baseline memory usage monitoring shows that the application typically uses 128 MB of private memory and 96 MB of virtual memory, you might allow memory usage of up to at least 192 MB for private memory and 256 MB for virtual memory.

4. Private memory usage refers to the amount of physical RAM that the worker process uses. To limit private memory usage and automatically recycle a worker process when this limit is reached, select Private Memory Limit (KB), and then in the corresponding field, type the memory limit. Then click OK to apply the settings.

Maintaining Application Health and Performance

Maintaining the health and performance of Web applications is an important part of your job as a Web administrator. Fortunately, IIS has many built-in functions to make this task easier, including:

- CPU monitoring and automated shutdown of runaway worker processes

- Worker process failure detection and recovery

- Request queue limiting to prevent server flooding

- Idle worker process shutdown to recover resources

Each of these tasks is discussed in the sections that follow.

Configuring CPU Monitoring

Typically, when a process consistently uses a high percentage of CPU time, there's a problem with the process. The process might have failed or might be running rampant on the system. You can configure IIS to monitor CPU usage and perform either of the following CPU performance monitoring options:

- **Take No Action (NoAction)**   IIS logs the CPU maximum usage event in the System event log but takes no corrective action.

- **Shut Down the Worker Process (KillW3wp)**   IIS logs the event and requests that the application pool's worker processes be recycled, based on the Shutdown Time Limit, set in the Process Model section.

To enable and configure IIS to monitor the CPU usage of worker processes, follow these steps:

1. In IIS Manager, expand the node for the server you want to work with, and then click the Application Pools node.

2. On the Application Pools page, click the application pool you want to work with, and then click Advanced Settings.

3. Under CPU, in the Limit field, set the maximum percentage of CPU usage that triggers event logging, worker process recycling, or both, in 1/1000ths of a percent.

    Tip   Typically, you'll want to set a value to at least 90000 (90 percent). However, to ensure that worker processes are recycled only when they're blocking other processes, you should set the value to 100000 (100 percent).

4. Use the Limit Interval (In Minutes) to specify how often IIS checks the CPU usage.

    Caution   In most cases you won't want to check the CPU usage more frequently than every five minutes. If you monitor the CPU usage more frequently, you might waste resources that could be better used by other processes.

5. Next, choose one of the following:

    ❑   If you want to log the CPU usage event but not have IIS attempt to shut down worker processes, in the Limit Action list, select NoAction.

    ❑   If you want to log the CPU usage event and have IIS attempt to shut down the worker processes used by the application pool, in the Limit Action list, select KillW3wp.

6. Click OK.

If you want to disable CPU monitoring, follow these steps:

1. In IIS Manager, expand the node for the server you want to work with, and then click the Application Pools node.

2. On the Application Pools page, click the application pool you want to work with, and then click Advanced Settings.

3. Disable CPU monitoring by setting the Limit Interval to zero (0), and then click OK.

Configuring Failure Detection and Recovery

You can configure application pools to monitor the health of their worker processes. This monitoring includes processes that detect worker process failure and then take action to recover or prevent further problems on the server.

Process pinging is central to health monitoring. With *process pinging*, IIS periodically checks to see if worker processes are responsive. This means that IIS sends a ping request at a specified interval to each worker process. If a worker process fails to respond to the ping request, either because it doesn't have additional threads available for processing incoming requests or because it's hung up, IIS flags the worker process as unhealthy. If the worker process is in an idle but unresponsive state, IIS terminates it immediately, and a replacement worker process is created. Otherwise, the worker process is marked for recycling as discussed previously in this chapter.

To configure health monitoring, complete the following steps:

1. In IIS Manager, expand the node for the server you want to work with, and then click the Application Pools node.

2. On the Application Pools page, click the application pool you want to work with, and then click Advanced Settings.

3. To enable process pinging, set Ping Enable to True, and then use the Ping Period and Ping Maximum Response Time options to set the ping interval and the maximum time to wait for a ping response in seconds. Here are some guidelines:

    ❑   For low-priority applications or applications that are used infrequently, you might want to use intervals of several minutes. This ensures that the responsiveness of applications is checked only as often as necessary and that IIS waits an appropriate amount of time for a response.

    ❑   On a busy server or a server with many configured applications, you might want to set longer intervals than usual. This will reduce resource usage due to ping requests and give the application pool longer to respond.

    ❑   For high-priority applications in which it's critical that applications run and be responsive, you might want to set a ping interval of five minutes or less and a maximum response time of one minute (60 seconds) or less.

This ensures that the application pool is checked frequently and that the responsiveness of applications is checked frequently.

4. To improve responsiveness for important applications by preventing idle processes from being shut down after a specified period of time, set Idle Time-out to zero (0).

5. Click OK.

You can also configure application pools for rapid-fail protection. When rapid-fail protection is enabled, IIS stops an application pool if there are a certain number of worker process failures in a specified time period. In the standard configuration, five worker process failures within a five-minute interval trigger rapid-fail protection.

To configure rapid-fail protection, complete the following steps:

1. In IIS Manager, expand the node for the server you want to work with, and then click the Application Pools node.

2. On the Application Pools page, click the application pool you want to work with, and then click Advanced Settings.

3. To enable rapid-fail protection, under Rapid-Fail Protection, set Enabled to True.

4. To cause IIS to stop the application pool if there are a certain number of worker process failures in a specified time period, set the Failure Interval and Maximum Failures options respectively.

5. Set the Service Unavailable Response Type option to HttpLevel to have IIS return an HTTP 503 error when the application pool is stopped because of rapid-fail protection. Set this option to TcpLevel to have IIS reset the connection otherwise.

6. Click OK to save your settings.

Note Keep in mind that these monitoring and recovery techniques aren't perfect, but they're helpful. They won't detect all types of failures. For instance, they won't detect problems with the application code, such as conditions that cause the application to return an internal error, and they won't detect a nonblocking error state, such as when the worker process can allocate new threads but is unable to process current threads.

Shutting Down Idle Worker Processes

Although worker processes start on demand based on incoming requests, and thus resources are allocated only when necessary, worker processes don't free up the resources they use until they're shut down. In a standard configuration, worker processes are shut down after they've been idle for 20 minutes. This ensures that any physical or virtual memory used by the worker process is made available to other processes running on the server, which is especially important if the server is busy.

Tip Shutting down idle worker processes is a good idea in most instances, and if system resources are at a premium, you might even want idle processes shut down sooner than 20 minutes. For example, on a moderately busy server with many configured sites and applications and on which there are intermittent resource issues, reducing the idle time-out could resolve the problems with resource availability.

Caution Shutting down idle worker processes can have unintended consequences. For example, on a dedicated server with ample memory and resources, shutting down idle worker processes clears cached components out of memory. These components must be reloaded into memory when the worker process starts and requires them, which might make the application seem unresponsive or sluggish.

To configure the idle process shutdown time, follow these steps:

1. In IIS Manager, expand the node for the server you want to work with, and then click the Application Pools node.

2. On the Application Pools page, click the application pool you want to work with, and then click Advanced Settings.

3. Choose one of the following:

   ❑ To allow idle processes to be shut down after a specified period of time, set Idle Time-Out to the desired shutdown time in minutes.

   ❑ To prevent idle processes from being shut down after a specified period of time, set Idle Time-Out to zero (0).

4. Click OK.

Limiting Request Queues

When hundreds or thousands of new requests pour into an application pool's request queue, the IIS server can become overloaded and overwhelmed. To prevent this from occurring, you can limit the length of the request queue. Once a queue limit is set, IIS checks the queue size each time before adding a new request to the queue. If the queue limit has been reached, IIS rejects the request and sends the client an HTTP Error 503: Service Unavailable message.

Real World The standard limit for the default application pool is 1000 requests. On a moderately sized server with few applications configured, this might be a good choice. However, on a server with multiple CPUs and lots of RAM, this value might be too low. On a server with limited resources or many applications configured, this value might be too high. Here, you might want to use a formula of Memory Size in Megabytes × Number of CPUs × 10 / Number of Configured Applications to determine the size of the average request queue.

This is meant to be a guideline to give you a starting point for consideration and not an absolute rule. For example, on a server with two CPUs, 2048 MB of RAM, and 24 configured applications, the size of the average request queue limit would be around 1,700 requests. You might have some applications configured with request queue limits of 1,000 and others with request queue limits of 2,000. However, if the same server had only one configured application, you probably wouldn't want to configure a request queue limit of 10,000 or more.

To configure the request queue limit, follow these steps:

1. In IIS Manager, expand the node for the server you want to work with, and then click the Application Pools node.

2. On the Application Pools page, click the application pool you want to work with, and then click Advanced Settings.

3. Perform one of the following:

    ❑ To specify and enforce a request queue limit, set the Queue Length to the desired limit.

    ❑ To remove the request queue limit, set the Queue Length option to zero (0).

4. Click OK.

Note   Requests that are already queued remain queued even if you change the queue limit to a value that's less than the current queue length. The only consequence here would be that new requests wouldn't be added to the queue until the current queue length is less than the queue limit.

Deleting IIS Application Pools

If you find that you no longer need an application pool, you can remove it by following these steps:

1. In IIS Manager, expand the node for the server you want to work with, and then click the Application Pools node.

2. On the Application Pools page, click the application pool you want to remove, and then in the Actions pane, click Remove.

3. When prompted to confirm that you want to remove the application, click Yes.

With the IIS command-line administration tool, you can delete an application pool by using the Delete AppPool command. Sample 9-17 provides the syntax and usage.

Sample 9-17   Delete AppPool Syntax and Usage

Syntax
```
appcmd delete apppool [[/apppool.name:]"AppPoolName"]
```
Usage
```
appcmd delete apppool "CustServicesAppPool"
```

Chapter 10
Managing Web Server Security

As you've seen throughout this book, security features are integrated into many areas of Internet Information Services (IIS) 7.0. In this chapter, you'll learn how to manage areas of Web server security that we have not yet discussed. Web servers have different security considerations from those of standard Windows Server 2008 configurations. On a Web server, you have three levels of security:

- **Windows security**   At the operating system level, you create user and group accounts, configure access permissions for files and directories, and set policies.

- **IIS security**   At the level of Internet Information Services (IIS), you set content permissions, authentication controls, and delegated privileges.

- **.NET security**   At the application level, you can control access to managed code applications by using the security features built into the Microsoft .NET Framework.

Windows security, IIS security, and .NET security can be completely integrated. The integrated security model allows you to use authentication based on user and group membership in addition to standard Internet-based authentication. It also allows you to use a layered permission model to determine access rights and permissions for applications and content. Before users can access files and directories, you must ensure that the appropriate users and groups have access at the operating system level. Then you must set IIS security permissions that grant permissions for content that IIS controls. Finally, you can use .NET Profile, .NET Users, and .NET Roles to manage top-level access to managed code applications.

Managing Windows Security

Before setting IIS security permissions, you use operating system tools to perform the following security tasks:

- Create and manage accounts for users and groups
- Configure access permissions for files and folders
- Set group policies for users and groups

Each of these topics is discussed in the sections that follow.

Working with User and Group Accounts

Windows Server 2008 provides user accounts and group accounts. User accounts determine permissions and privileges for individuals. Group accounts determine permissions and privileges for multiple users.

IIS User and Group Essentials

You can set user and group accounts at the local computer level or at the domain level. Local accounts are specific to an individual computer and aren't valid on other machines or in a domain unless you specifically grant permissions. Domain accounts, on the other hand, are valid throughout a domain, which makes resources in the domain available to the account. Typically, you'll use specific accounts for specific purposes:

- Use local accounts when your IIS servers aren't part of a domain or you want to limit access to a specific computer.

- Use domain accounts when the servers are part of a Windows domain and you want users to be able to access resources throughout that domain.

User accounts that are important on IIS servers include:

- **Local System** By default, all standard IIS services log on using the local system account. This account is part of the Administrators group on the Web server and has all user rights on the Web server. If you configure application pools to use this account, the related worker processes have full access to the server system, which may present a serious security risk.

- **Local Service** A limited-privilege account that grants access to the local system only. The account is part of the Users group on the Web server and has the same rights as the Network Service account, except that it is limited to the local computer. Configure application pools to use this account when worker processes don't need to access other servers.

- **Network Service** By default, all applications log on using the network service account. When IIS is using out-of-process session state management, the ASP.NET State Service also uses this account by default. This account is part of the Users group on the Web server and provides fewer permissions and privileges than the Local System account (but more than the Local Service account). Specifically, processes running under this account can interact throughout a network by using the credentials of the computer account.

- **IUSR_*ComputerName*** Internet guest account used by anonymous users to access Internet sites. The account grants anonymous users limited user rights and is also known as the *anonymous user identity*.

When you install IIS 7.0, the IIS_IUSRS group is also created. If you use a specific user identity for an application pool, you must make this identity a member of the IIS_IUSRS group to ensure that the account has appropriate access to resources. See the section "Configuring Application Pool Identities" in Chapter 9, "Managing Applications, Application Pools, and Worker Processes," for details on configuring the application pool identity.

Table 10-1 details key user rights assigned to IIS user and group accounts by default. You can make changes to these accounts if necessary. For added security, you can configure IIS to use different accounts from the standard accounts provided. You can also create additional accounts.

Table 10-1   Important User Rights Assigned by Default to IIS User and Group Accounts

Default User Right	Local Service	Network Service	IUSR	IIS_IUSRS
Access This Computer From The Network	X	X	X	X
Adjust Memory Quotas For A Process	X	X		
Allow Log On Locally			X	
Bypass Traverse Checking	X	X	X	X
Change The System Time	X			
Change The Time Zone	X			
Create Global Objects	X	X		
Generate Security Audits	X	X		
Impersonate A Client After Authentication	X	X		X
Increase Process Working Set			X	
Log On As A Batch Job				X
Log On As A Service		X		
Replace A Process-Level Token	X	X		

Managing the IIS Service Logon Accounts

The standard IIS services use the local system account to log on to the server. Using the local system account allows the services to run system processes and perform system-level tasks. You really shouldn't change this configuration unless you have very specific needs or want to have strict control over the IIS logon account's privileges and rights. If you decide not to use this account, you can reconfigure the logon account for an IIS service by completing the following steps:

1. In the Computer Management console, in the left pane, connect to the IIS server whose services you want to manage.

2. Expand the Services And Applications node by clicking the plus sign (+) next to it, and then choose Services.

3. In the right pane, right-click the service you want to configure, and then choose Properties.

4. Click the Log On tab, as shown in Figure 10-1.

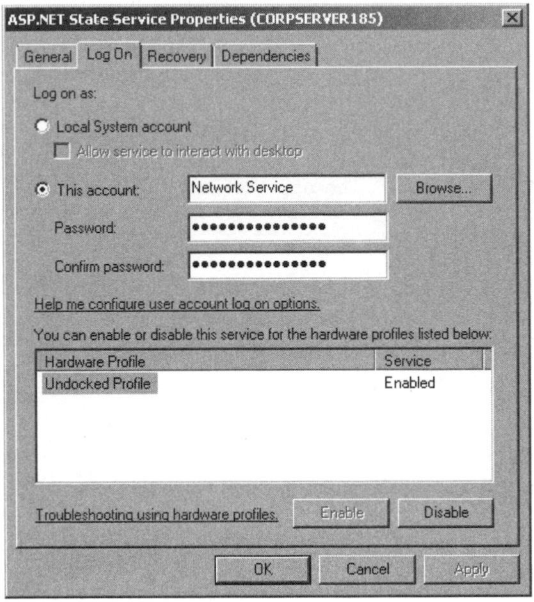

Figure 10-1 Use the Log On tab to configure the service logon account.

5. Choose one of the following:

   ❑ If the service should log on using the system account (the default for most services), select Local System Account.

   ❑ If the service should log on using a specific user account, select This Account. Be sure to type an account name and password in the appropriate fields. Click the Browse button to search for a user account if necessary.

6. Click OK.

> **More Info**   If you use a specific user identity for a service, you'll need to assign privileges and logon rights to the account you use. For more information on these and other account permissions, see the *Windows Server 2008 Administrator's Pocket Consultant* (Microsoft Press, 2008).

Managing the Internet Guest Account

You manage the Internet Guest account at the IIS security level and at the Windows security level. At the IIS security level, you specify the user account to use for anonymous access. Normally, you manage anonymous access at the server or site level, and all related files and directories inherit the settings you use. You can change this behavior for individual files and directories as necessary.

To change the configuration of the anonymous user account for an entire server or another configuration level, complete the following steps:

1. In IIS Manager, navigate to the level of the configuration hierarchy you want to manage, and then double-click Authentication.

2. On the Authentication page, in the main pane, click Anonymous Authentication, and then in the Actions pane, click Edit.

3. The IUSR_*ComputerName* account is the default Internet guest account. Choose one of the following based on the user account you want to specify:

   ❑ If you want to specify a different user account, select Specific User, and then click Set. In the Set Credentials dialog box, type the user name for the account. Type and then confirm the account password, and then click OK twice.

   ❑ If you want to use the application pool identity rather than a specific user account, select Application Pool Identity, and then click OK.

Note   When Anonymous Access is enabled, users don't have to log on using a user name and password. IIS automatically logs the user on using the anonymous account information provided for the resource. If Anonymous Authentication isn't listed as Enabled on the Authentication page, the resource is configured for named account access only. To enable anonymous access, click Anonymous Authentication, and then in the Actions pane, click Enable. However, you should do this only if you're sure that the resource doesn't need to be protected.

At the Windows security level, you perform all other account management tasks, including:

- Enabling or disabling accounts
- Unlocking the account after it has been locked out
- Changing group membership

Working with File and Folder Permissions

Every folder and file used by IIS can have different access permissions. You set these access permissions at the Windows security level. The sections that follow provide an overview of permissions. You'll learn the basics, including how to view and set permissions.

File and Folder Permission Essentials

The basic permissions you can assign to files and folders are summarized in Table 10-2. The basic permissions are created by combining special permissions, such as Traverse Folder and Execute File, into a single easily managed permission. If you want granular control over file or folder access, you can use advanced permissions to assign special permissions individually. For more information on special permissions, see the *Windows Server 2008 Administrator's Pocket Consultant*.

Table 10-2   File and Folder Permissions Used by Windows Server

Permission	Meaning for Folders	Meaning for Files
Read	Permits viewing and listing files and subfolders	Permits viewing or accessing the file's contents
Write	Permits adding files and subfolders	Permits writing to a file
Read And Execute	Permits viewing and listing files and subfolders and executing files; inherited by files and folders	Permits viewing and accessing the file's contents and executing the file
List Folder Contents	Permits viewing and listing files and subfolders and executing files; inherited by folders only	N/A
Modify	Permits reading and writing of files and subfolders; allows deletion of the folder	Permits reading and writing of the file; allows deletion of the file
Full Control	Permits reading, writing, changing, and deleting files and subfolders	Permits reading, writing, changing, and deleting the file

Whenever you work with file and folder permissions, you should keep the following in mind:

- Read is the only permission needed to run scripts. Execute permission applies only to executables.

- Read access is required to access a shortcut and its target.

- Giving a user permission to write to a file but not to delete it doesn't prevent the user from deleting the file's contents. A user can still delete the contents.

- If a user has full control over a folder, the user can delete files in the folder regardless of the permission of the files.

IIS uses the following users and groups to configure file and folder access:

- **Administrators**   Allows administrators to access IIS resources.

- **Creator Owner**   Allows the account that created a resource to access the resource.

- **System**   Allows the local system to access the resource.

- **Users**   Allows named accounts to access the resource (including the Local Service and Network Service accounts, which are user accounts).

- **IIS_IUSRS**   Allows you to set specific permission for special identities that are members of the IIS_IUSRS group. To prevent malicious users from gaining access to files and modifying them, you can deny this account Full Control, Modify, and Write permission on important directories.

When you grant Read permission to these users and groups, anyone who has access to your Internet or intranet Web site will be able to access the files and folders. If you want to restrict access to certain files and folders, you should set specific user and group permissions and then use authenticated access rather than anonymous access. With authenticated access, IIS authenticates the user before granting access and then uses the Windows permissions to determine what files and folders the user can access.

As you evaluate the permissions, you might want to apply to files and folders used by IIS, refer to Table 10-3. This table provides general guidelines for assigning permissions based on content type.

Table 10-3   General Guidelines for Permissions Based on Content Type

File Type	File Extension	Permission
CGI scripts and executables	.exe, .dll, .cmd	Users (Execute), Administrators (Full Control), System (Full Control)
Dynamic content	.asp, .aspx, .vbs, .js, .pl	Users (Read Only), Administrators (Full Control), System (Full Control)
Include files	.inc, .shtm, .shtml, .stm	Users (Read Only, Deny Write), Administrators (Full Control), System (Full Control)
Static content	.txt, .rtf, .gif, .jpg, .jpeg, .htm, .html, .doc, .ppt, .xls	Users (Read Only, Deny Write), Administrators (Full Control), System (Full Control)

Instead of setting permissions on individual files, you should organize content by type in subdirectories. For example, if your Web site used static, script, and dynamic content, you could create subdirectories called WebStatic, WebScripts, and WebDynamic. You would then store static, script, and dynamic content in these directories and assign permissions on a per-directory basis. Don't forget to consider whether it's prudent to specifically deny a permission, such as Full Control, Modify, or Write.

Viewing File and Folder Permissions

You view security permissions for files and folders in Windows Explorer or in IIS Manager by completing the following steps:

1. Open Windows Explorer or IIS Manager as appropriate. In Windows Explorer, right-click the file or folder you want to work with, and then select Properties. In IIS Manager, navigate to the site node or folder node you want to work with, and then in the Actions pane, click Edit Permissions.

2. You should now see the Properties dialog box for the file or folder you previously selected. On the General tab, be sure to note any NTFS attributes, such as Read only or Hidden, that are being applied, because you might need to change these.

3. Select the Security tab. In the Group Or User Names list box, select the user, computer, or group whose permissions you want to view. If check boxes in the Permissions For list are dimmed, it means that the permissions are inherited from a parent object.

Setting File and Folder Permissions

You can set permissions for files and folders by completing the following steps:

1. Open Windows Explorer or IIS Manager as appropriate. In Windows Explorer, right-click the file or folder you want to work with, and then select Properties. In IIS Manager, navigate to the site node or folder node you want to work with, and then in the Actions pane, click Edit Permissions.

2. In the Properties dialog box, select the Security tab, select a user, computer, or group, and then click Edit. This displays an editable version of the Security tab, as shown in Figure 10-2.

3. Users or groups that already have access to the file or folder are listed in the Group Or User Names list box. You can change permissions for these users and groups by doing the following:

   ❑ Select the user or group you want to change.

   ❑ Use the Permissions For list box to grant or deny access permissions.

   Note Inherited permissions are dimmed. If you want to override an inherited permission, select the opposite permission. For example, if, because of inheritance, a user is granted a permission you don't want that user to have, you could override the inheritance by explicitly denying the permission in the Permissions For list box.

4. Click Add to set access permissions for additional users, contacts, computers, or groups. This displays the Select Users, Computers, Or Groups dialog box. You can select computer accounts and configure their permissions only if you are a member of a domain.

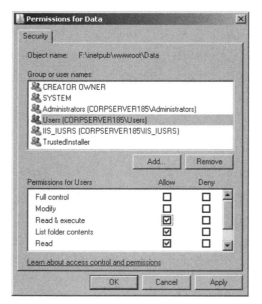

Figure 10-2   Use the Security tab to configure basic permissions for the file or folder.

5. In the Select Users, Computers, Or Groups dialog box, select the users, computers, or groups for which you want to set access permissions, and then click OK.

6. In the Group Or User Names list box, select the user, computer, or group you want to configure, and then use the fields in the Permissions For list box to allow or deny permissions. Repeat for other users, computers, or groups.

7. Click OK when you're finished.

Working with Group Policies

Group policies are another aspect of Windows security that you need to understand. You'll use group policies to automate key security administration tasks and to manage IIS resources more effectively. Group policies for sites, domains, and organizational units (OUs) can be configured only for computer, group, and user accounts that are part of a domain.

Group Policy Essentials

Group policies provide central control over privileges, permissions, and capabilities of users and computers. You can think of a policy as a set of rules that you can apply to multiple computers and to multiple users. Because computers can be a part of larger organizational groups, you can apply multiple policies. The order in which policies are applied is extremely important in determining which rules are enforced and which rules are not.

When multiple policies are in place, the policies are applied in the following order:

1. Local group policies that affect the local computer only

2. Site group policies that affect all computers that are part of the same site, which can include multiple domains

3. Domain polices that affect all computers in a specific domain

4. Organizational unit policies that affect all computers in an organizational unit

5. Child organizational unit policies that affect all computers in a subcomponent of an organizational unit

As successive policies are applied, the rules in those policies override the rules set in the previous policy. For example, domain policy settings have precedence over the local Group Policy settings. Exceptions allow you to block, override, and disable policy settings. A discussion of exceptions is outside the scope of this book.

Policy settings are divided into two broad categories: those that affect computers and those that affect users. Computer policies are applied during system startup. User policies are applied during logon.

Two graphical user interface (GUI) tools are provided for managing Active Directory Group Policy: Group Policy Object Editor and Group Policy Management Console. Although both are used to manage Active Directory Group Policy, you can think of Group Policy Object Editor as a basic editor and Group Policy Management Console as an advanced editor. By using Group Policy Object Editor, you can view and configure policy settings for a specific Group Policy Object (GPO). By using Group Policy Management Console, you can view, configure, and manage policy settings for Group Policy Objects in any forest and domain to which you can connect and have appropriate administrator permissions. Management features in Group Policy Management Console enable you to import, export, back up, and restore GPOs. You can also use Group Policy Management Console to plan Group Policy changes and to determine how group policies are being applied to particular computers and users.

To use the Group Policy Object Editor and related features to access and use site, domain, and OU policies, complete the following steps:

1. For sites, open the Active Directory Sites and Services console to create a GPO that is linked to the site. For domains and OUs, open the Active Directory Users and Computers console to create a GPO that is linked to the domain or OU.

2. In the left pane of the appropriate Active Directory window, right-click the site, domain, or OU for which you want to create or manage Group Policy. Then on the shortcut menu, select Properties. The Properties dialog box opens.

3. In the Properties dialog box, click the Group Policy tab. You can now:

   ❑ **Create a new policy** To create a new policy, click New. Type a name for the policy, and then press Enter. Then click Edit to configure the new policy.

❑ **Edit an existing policy** To edit an existing policy, select the policy, and then click Edit. You can then edit the policy settings.

❑ **Change the priority of a policy** To change the priority of a policy, click the Up or Down button to change its position in the Group Policy Object Links list.

The Group Policy Management Console is included with Windows 2000 Server and later releases of the Windows operating system. To use the Group Policy Management Console and related features to access and work with site, domain, and OU policies, complete the following steps:

1. When you add the Group Policy Management feature using the Add Feature Wizard, the Group Policy Management Console is available on the Administrative Tools menu. Click Start, point to Administrative Tools, and then select Group Policy Management.

2. In the MMC, you'll see two top-level nodes: Group Policy Management (the label for the console root) and Forest (a node representing the forest to which you are currently connected). When you expand the Forest node, you'll then see the following nodes:

   ❑ **Domains** Provides access to the policy settings for domains in the related forest. By default, you are connected to your logon domain and can add connections to other domains. If you expand a domain, you'll be able to access Default Domain Policy, the Domain Controllers OU (and the related Default Domain Controllers Policy), and Group Policy Objects defined in the domain.

   ❑ **Sites** Provides access to the policy settings for sites in the forest. Sites are hidden by default.

   ❑ **Group Policy Modeling** Provides access to the Group Policy Modeling Wizard, which you can use to help you plan policy deployment and simulate settings for testing purposes. The wizard also provides access to any saved policy models.

   ❑ **Group Policy Results** Provides access to the Group Policy Results Wizard. For each domain to which you are connected, you have all the related Group Policy Objects and OUs available to work with in one location.

3. You can now:

   ❑ **Create a new policy** Right-click the site, domain, or OU you want to work with, and then select Create And Link A GPO Here. In the New GPO dialog box, type a descriptive name for the new GPO, and then click OK. The GPO is now created and linked to the site, domain, or OU. Right-click the GPO, and then choose Edit. This opens the Group Policy Object Editor. You can then edit the policy settings.

❏ **Edit an existing policy** Expand the site, domain, or OU node in which the related policy is stored. Right-click the policy, and then choose Edit. This opens the Group Policy Object Editor.

You manage local group policies for an individual computer by completing the following steps:

1. Click Start, point to All Programs, and then point to Accessories.

2. Right-click Command Prompt, and then select Run As Administrator.

3. At the command prompt, type **mmc**. This opens an empty Microsoft Management Console (MMC).

4. On the File menu, select Add/Remove Snap-In.

5. In the Add Or Remove Snap-In dialog box, under Available Snap-Ins, select Local Group Policy Object Editor, and then click Add.

6. By default, the editor works with the local computer's Group Policy Object (GPO), so you need only click Finish to accept this as the default.

7. Click OK. You can now manage the local policy on the selected computer.

Tip There is another way to start the Group Policy Object Editor for the local computer: On the Start menu, click Run, in the Run box type **gpedit.msc**, and then press Enter.

Group policies for passwords, account lockout, and auditing are essential to your Web server's security. Guidelines for password policies are as follows:

■ Set a minimum password age for all accounts. I recommend 2–3 days.

■ Set a maximum password age for all accounts. I recommend 30 days.

■ Set a minimum password length. I suggest the minimum be set at eight characters to start.

■ Enable secure passwords by enforcing password complexity requirements.

■ Enforce password history. I recommend using a value of 5 or more.

Guidelines for account lockout polices include the following:

■ Set an account lockout threshold. In most cases accounts should be locked after five bad attempts.

- Set account lockout duration. In most cases you'll want to lock out accounts indefinitely.

- Reset the lockout threshold after 30–60 minutes.

Guidelines for auditing include the following:

- Audit system event success and failure

- Audit logon event success and failure

- Audit failed object access attempts

- Audit successful and failed policy changes

- Audit successful and failed account management

- Audit successful and failed account logon

Techniques for managing these policies are examined in the sections that follow. For more detailed information on policy management, see the *Windows Server 2008 Administrator's Pocket Consultant.*

Setting Account Policies for IIS Servers

You can set account policies by completing the following steps:

1. Access the group policy container you want to work with as described in the "Group Policy Essentials" section of this chapter. Expand the Computer Configuration node, then Windows Settings, then Security Settings, and finally, Account Policies.

2. You can now manage account policies. For domains, sites, and OUs, you'll have Password Policy, Account Lockout Policy, and Kerberos Policy nodes. For local computers, you'll have Password Policy and Account Lockout Policy nodes only.

3. To configure a policy, double-click its entry or right-click it and select Properties. This opens a Properties dialog box for the policy. Then do one of the following:

    ❑ For a local policy, the Properties dialog box will be different from that for a site, domain, or OU. Use the appropriate fields to configure the local policy. Skip the remaining steps; they apply to global group policies.

    ❑ For a site, domain, or OU, all policies are either defined or not defined—that is, they're either configured for use or not configured for use. A policy that isn't defined in the current container could be inherited from another container.

4. Select or clear the Define This Policy Setting check box to determine whether a policy is defined.

5. Policies can have additional fields for configuring the policy. Often, these fields have the following option buttons:

   ❏ **Enabled**   Turns on the policy restriction

   ❏ **Disabled**   Turns off the policy restriction

Setting Auditing Policies

Auditing is the best way to track what's happening on your IIS server. You can use auditing to collect information related to resource usage, such as file access, system logon, and system configuration changes. Whenever an action occurs that you've configured for auditing, the action is written to the system's security log, where it's stored for your review. You access the security log from Windows Event Viewer.

You can set auditing policies by completing the following steps:

1. Access the Group Policy container you want to work with as described in the "Group Policy Essentials" section in this chapter. Expand the Computer Configuration node, Windows Settings, Security Settings, and Local Policies. Then select Audit Policy.

2. You now have access to the following auditing options:

   ❏ **Audit Account Logon Events**   Tracks events related to user logon and logoff.

   ❏ **Audit Account Management**   Tracks account management. Events are generated anytime user, computer, or group accounts are created, modified, or deleted.

   ❏ **Audit Directory Service Access**   Tracks access to the Active Directory service. Events are generated whenever users or computers access the directory.

   ❏ **Audit Logon Events**   Tracks events related to user logon, logoff, and remote connections to network systems.

   ❏ **Audit Object Access**   Tracks system resource usage for files, directories, shares, printers, and Active Directory objects.

   ❏ **Audit Policy Change**   Tracks changes to user rights, auditing, and trust relationships.

   ❏ **Audit Privilege Use**   Tracks the use of user rights and privileges, such as the right to back up files and directories, but doesn't track system logon or logoff.

   ❏ **Audit Process Tracking**   Tracks system processes and the resources they use.

   ❏ **Audit System Events**   Tracks system startup, shutdown, and restart, in addition to actions that affect system security or the security log.

3. To configure an auditing policy, double-click its entry or right-click it and select Properties. This opens a Properties dialog box for the policy.

4. Select Define These Policy Settings, and then select the Success check box, the Failure check box, or both. Success logs successful events, such as successful logon attempts. Failure logs failed events, such as failed logon attempts.

5. Click OK when you're finished.

Managing IIS Security

After setting operating system security, use IIS security to set the Web server and execute permissions for content by:

■ Configuring handler mappings

■ Configuring authentication methods

■ Setting authorization rules for application access

■ Controlling access by IP address or Internet domain name

■ Managing feature delegation and remote administration

Each of these topics is discussed in the sections that follow. When working with this myriad of security features, keep in mind that all these related features collectively determine whether IIS grants access to a particular client and user. For example, if the client IP address or domain name is denied access, a user won't be able to log in to get authenticated.

Configuring Handler Mappings for Applications

Handler mappings are used to specify the ISAPI extensions, CGI programs, IIS modules, and managed types that are available to handle incoming requests. As discussed in Chapter 5, "Managing Global IIS Configuration," each type of content that IIS can work with has a specific handler mapping. A handler mapping identifies the module used to process requests for files with a specific file extension or a specific file name. IIS Setup creates handler mappings automatically when you install and enable related role services or modules.

To view the general handler mappings, in IIS, navigate to the level of the configuration hierarchy you want to manage, and then double-click the Handler Mappings feature. On the Handler Mappings page, shown in Figure 10-3, you'll see the configured handler mappings listed by:

■ **Name**   The name of the handler mapping.

■ **Path**   The file extension or file name for which the handler will process a response.

- **State**   The current state as either Enabled or Disabled. If a handler requires a type of access that is not enabled in the access policy at that level, the handler is disabled.

- **Path Type**   The type of path to which the handler is mapped:

  ☐ File, if the mapping applies to a file

  ☐ Directory, if the mapping applies to a directory

  ☐ Unspecified, if the mapping does not apply to a specific path type

- **Handler**   The module or managed type that responds to the request as specified in the mapping.

- **Entry Type**   The type of entry as either Local or Inherited.

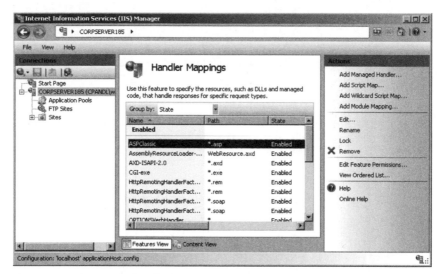

Figure 10-3   Review the handler mappings that are configured.

You can configure and manage three general types of handler mappings:

- **Mappings for IIS modules**   Allow IIS to process specific requests through IIS modules configured on the Web server. For example, the PageHandlerFactory-ISAPI-2.0 handler mapping specifies that the IsapiModule handler process requests for .aspx files when IIS is using Classic mode.

- **Mappings for managed handlers**   Allow IIS to process specific requests through handlers written in managed code. For example, the PageHandlerFactory-

Integrated handler mapping specifies that the System.Web.UI.PageHandlerFactory handler process requests for .aspx files when IIS is using Integrated mode.

■ **Mappings for scripts and executables** Allow IIS to process specific requests through ISAPI filters and extensions permitted to run on the Web server. For example, the ASPClassic handler mapping specifies that the IsapiModule handler process requests for .asp files.

Note Script maps provide backward compatibility with earlier versions of IIS. Executables must be written to the CGI specification, and dynamic link libraries must support the ISAPI extension interfaces. If you map a type of request to an .exe file, the CgiModule will load the associated executable when a request enters the server and it matches the handler mapping. If you map a type of request to a .dll file, IsapiModule will load the DLL when a request enters the server and it matches the handler mapping. For example, IIS 7.0 includes a handler mapping for Active Server Pages (ASP). All requests for .asp files are processed by asp.dll, which is loaded by IsapiModule because asp.dll is an ISAPI extension.

You can create handler mappings by completing the following steps:

1. IIS Manager, navigate to the level of the configuration hierarchy you want to manage, and then double-click the Handler Mappings feature.

2. On the Handler Mappings page, click Add Managed Handler, Add Script Map, or Add Module Mapping as appropriate for the type of handler mapping you are creating.

   Note By default, when you add a managed handler, the handler will run only in application pools configured to use Integrated mode. To allow the new managed handler to be used in Classic mode, you must add the handler to the <httphandlers> section in the Web.config file.

3. In the Request Path text box, type a file name extension or file name with an extension for which you want the handler to process requests. File extensions don't have to have file type associations at the operating system level and can have more than three characters. If you wanted the handler to process all requests made for files with the extension .zip, type ***.zip**. Alternatively, if you want the handler to run all requests made for a specific file, type the file name and its extension, such as **Custom.zip**.

   ❑ For a managed handler, in the Type drop-down list, select the class type of the managed handler, such as System.Web.DefaultHttpHandler.

   ❑ For a module map, in the Module drop-down list, select the module that will process related requests, such as FastCgiModule.

   ❑ For a script map and optionally for a module map, in the Executable text box, specify the script or executable that will process related requests.

Click the selection button to the right of the Executable text box to display the Open dialog box, which you can use to select the executable. The executable must be in a directory that's accessible to IIS, such as the *%SystemRoot%*\System32 or *%SystemRoot%*\System32\Inetsrv directory.

4. In the Name text box, type a descriptive name for the handler mapping.

5. Click the Request Restrictions button to open the Request Restrictions dialog box and specify additional, optional restrictions for the handler mapping. The Request Restrictions dialog box has two tabs:

   ❑ **Mapping** Use the settings on the Mapping tab to limit the ways the handler can be invoked. Select the Invoke Handler Only If Request Is Mapped To check box, and then choose File to limit the handler to file requests, Folder to limit the handler to folder requests, or File Or Folder to limit the handler to file or folder requests.

   ❑ **Verbs** Use the settings on the Verbs tab to limit the HTTP request types that can be used to invoke the handler. Either allow all HTTP verbs to be used, or specify a list of allowed HTTP verbs, such as GET, HEAD, POST, and DEBUG. For a detailed list of HTTP request types, refer to Table 8-1 in Chapter 8, "Running IIS Applications."

   ❑ **Access** Access policy, together with a handler's required access setting, determines whether a handler can run. The access policy for handlers can be set to grant read, write, script, and execute permissions. If a handler requires a permission that is not enabled in the access policy, the handler will be disabled, and unless there is another handler that can process the request, all requests that are processed by that handler will fail.

6. Click OK twice to close all open dialog boxes and create the handler mapping.

To configure access policy that specifies the type of access permissions allowed for handlers at the current configuration level, click Edit Feature Permissions, and then, in the Edit Feature Permissions dialog box, select the allowed permissions or clear the denied permissions in the Permissions list. When you select a permission check box in the Edit Feature Permissions dialog box, the State column on the Handler Mappings page displays Enabled for the handlers that are enabled by the selection. Similarly, when you clear a selection in the Edit Feature Permissions dialog box, the State column on the Handler Mappings page displays Disabled for the handlers that are disabled by the selection. You can preview the handlers that are enabled or disabled by viewing the Handler Mappings page. If you click OK, any changes you've made to permissions are saved. If you click Cancel instead of OK, any changes you've made are not saved.

You can edit, rename, or remove handler mappings by using the following techniques:

- To modify a handler mapping's settings, click the handler mapping you want to modify, and then click Edit. In the Edit dialog box, make the necessary changes, and then click OK.

- To rename a handler mapping, click the entry to select it, and then click Rename. Type the new name for the filter, and then press Enter.

- To remove a handler mapping that is no longer needed, click the entry you want to remove, and then click Remove. When prompted to confirm the action, click Yes.

Setting Authentication Modes

Authentication modes control access to IIS resources. You can use authentication to allow anonymous access to public resources, to create secure areas within a Web site, and to create controlled access to Web sites and applications. When authentication is enabled, IIS uses the account credentials supplied by a user to determine whether the user has access to a resource and to determine which permissions the user has been granted.

Understanding Authentication

The authentication modes available on a Web server depend on the authentication modules you've installed and enabled for use. A complete list of related modules is provided in Chapter 2, "Deploying IIS 7.0 in the Enterprise," but a basic list of authentication modes follows:

- **Anonymous authentication**   With anonymous authentication, IIS automatically logs users on with an anonymous or guest account. This allows users to access resources without being prompted for user name and password information. Because the first request all browsers send to a Web server is for anonymous access, you must disable anonymous authentication at the appropriate configuration level if you want to restrict access to content.

- **ASP.NET Impersonation**   With ASP.NET Impersonation, a managed code application can run as either the user authenticated by IIS or a designated account that you specify when configuring this mode.

- **Basic authentication**   With basic authentication, users are prompted for logon information. When it's entered, this information is transmitted unencrypted (as clear text) across the network. If you've configured secure communications on the server as described in the "Working with SSL" section of Chapter 11, "Managing Active Directory Certificate Services and SSL," you can require clients to use Secure Sockets Layer (SSL). When you use SSL with basic authentication, the logon information is encrypted before transmission.

- **Active Directory Client Certificate authentication**   With Client Certificate authentication, IIS can map Active Directory client certificates for authentication across multiple servers. This lets IIS automatically authenticate clients without using other authentication methods. If you enable this mode, you cannot use IIS certificate mapping for any other sites hosted on the server.

- **Digest authentication**   With digest authentication, user credentials are transmitted securely between clients and servers. Digest authentication is a feature of HTTP 1.1 and uses a technique that can't be easily intercepted and decrypted. This feature is available only when IIS is configured on a server that is part of an Active Directory domain. The client is required to use a domain account, and the request must be made by Microsoft Internet Explorer 5.0 or later.

- **IIS Client Certificate mapping authentication**   With IIS Client Certificate authentication, IIS can map client certificates for authentication across multiple servers. This lets IIS automatically authenticate clients without using other authentication methods. If you enable this mode, you cannot use Active Directory Client Certificate mapping for any other sites hosted on the server.

- **Integrated Windows authentication**   With integrated Windows authentication, IIS uses standard Windows security to validate the user's identity. Instead of prompting for a user name and password, clients relay the logon credentials that users supply when they log on to Windows. These credentials are fully encrypted without the need for SSL, and they include the user name and password needed to log on to the network. The only Web browsers that support Integrated Windows Authentication are versions of Internet Explorer.

- **ASP.NET Forms-based authentication**   With ASP.NET Forms-based authentication, you manage client registration and authentication at the application level instead of relying on the authentication mechanisms in IIS 7.0. As the mode name implies, users register and provide their credentials using a login form. By default, this information is passed as clear text. To avoid this, you should use SSL encryption for the login page and other internal application pages.

By default, only anonymous authentication is enabled for IIS resources. Anonymous authentication is enabled as part of the server core. You can apply authentication on a global or local basis. You configure global authentication modes via the server configuration level. You set local authentication modes at the site, application, directory, or file configuration level.

Before you start working with authentication modes, you should keep the following in mind:

- When you combine anonymous access with authenticated access, users have full access to resources that are accessible anonymously via the Internet guest account. If this account doesn't have access to a resource, IIS attempts to authenticate the user using the authentication techniques you've specified. If these authentication methods fail, the user is denied access to the resource.

- When you disable anonymous access, you're telling IIS that all user requests must be authenticated using the authentication modes you've specified. Once the user is authenticated, IIS uses the user's account credentials to determine access rights.

■ When you combine basic authentication with integrated or digest authentication, Internet Explorer attempts to use integrated Windows authentication or digest authentication before using basic authentication. This means that users who can be authenticated using their current account credentials won't be prompted for a user name and password.

In addition, before you can use digest authentication, you must enable reversible password encryption for each account that will connect to the server using this authentication technique. IIS and the user's Web browser use reversible encryption to manage secure transmission and unencryption of user information. To enable reversible encryption, follow these steps:

1. To start Active Directory Users And Computers, click Start, point to Administrative Tools, and then click Active Directory Users And Computers.

2. Double-click the user name that you want to use with digest authentication.

3. On the Account tab, under Account Options, select Store Password Using Reversible Encryption, and then click OK.

4. Repeat steps 1–3 for each account that you want to use with digest authentication.

Enabling and Disabling Authentication

You can enable or disable anonymous access to resources at the server, site, application, directory, or file level. If you enable anonymous access, users can access resources without having to authenticate themselves (as long as the Windows permissions on the resource allow this). If you disable anonymous access, users must authenticate themselves before accessing resources. Authentication can occur automatically or manually depending on the browser used and the account credentials the user previously entered.

You can enable or disable authentication at a particular configuration level by completing the following steps:

1. In IIS Manager, navigate to the level of the configuration hierarchy you want to manage, and then double-click the Authentication feature.

2. On the Authentication page, shown in Figure 10-4, you should now see the available authentication modes. If a mode you want to use is not available, you'll need to install and enable the related module.

3. To enable or disable anonymous access, select Anonymous Authentication, and then click Enable or Disable as appropriate.

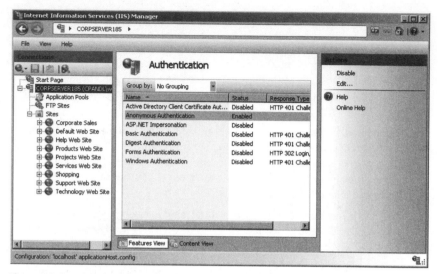

Figure 10-4 View the available authentication modes.

4. Select and then use the related Enable, Disable, and Edit links in the Actions pane to configure the authentication methods you want to use. Keep the following in mind:

❑ Disabling basic authentication might prevent some clients from accessing resources remotely. Clients can log on only when you enable an authentication method that they support.

❑ A default domain isn't set automatically. If you enable basic authentication, you can choose to set a default domain that should be used when no domain information is supplied during the logon process. Setting the default domain is useful when you want to ensure that clients authenticate properly.

❑ With basic and digest authentication, you can optionally specify the realm that can be accessed. Essentially, a *realm* is the DNS domain name or Web address that will use the credentials that have been authenticated against the default domain. If default domain and realm are set to the same value, the internal Windows domain name may be exposed to external users during the user name and password challenge/response.

❑   If you enable ASP.NET Impersonation, you can specify the identity to impersonate. By default, IIS uses pass-through authentication and the identity of the authenticated user is impersonated. You can also specify a specific user if necessary.

❑   If you enable forms authentication, you can set the login URL and cookies settings used for authentication. See the "FormsAuthenticationModule" section in the appendix, "Comprehensive IIS 7.0 Module and Schema Reference," for details on the related options.

❑   If you enable passport authentication, all other authentication settings are ignored. As a result, the server will use this technique to authenticate only for the specified resource.

Setting Authorization Rules for Application Access

You can use authorization rules to control access to Web content. An authorization rule specifies which users, roles, and groups are allowed to or restricted from accessing content at a specific configuration level. The two types of authorization rules are:

■   **Allow Authorization Rules**   Grants access to Web content at a specific configuration level

■   **Deny Authorization Rules**   Denies access to Web content at a specific configuration level

To view the current authorization rules at a particular configuration level, navigate to the level of the configuration hierarchy you want to manage, and then double-click the Authorization Rules feature. On the Authorization Rules page, shown in Figure 10-5, you'll then see a list of applicable authorization rules listed by:

■   **Mode**   Lists the type of rule as either Allow or Deny.

■   **Users**   Lists the user types, names, or groups to which the rule applies.

■   **Roles**   Lists the user roles to which the rule applies.

■   **Verbs**   Lists the HTTP verbs to which the rule applies. Applicable only when a rule is limited to specific HTTP verbs.

■   **Entry Type**   Lists the entry type as Local or Inherited.

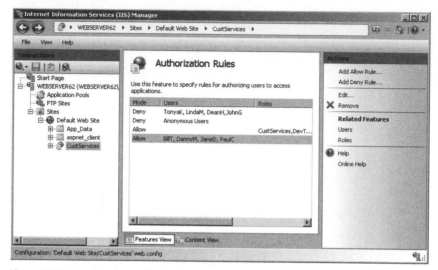

Figure 10-5   Review the authorization rules for the selected configuration level.

You can set an Allow or Deny authorization rule by completing the following steps:

1. In IIS Manager, navigate to the level of the configuration hierarchy you want to manage, and then double-click the Authentication Rules feature.

2. On the Authorization Rules page, you should now see the currently configured authorization rules.

3. You can now set an authorization rule. To add an allow rule, click Add Allow Rule. To add a deny rule, click Add Deny Rule. Figure 10-6 shows the Add Allow Authorization Rule dialog box.

4. Use the options in the dialog box to specify the users to which the rule applies. With regard to users, these rules can be applied to:

   ❑ All users, meaning that both anonymous and authenticated users are either granted or denied access

   ❑ Anonymous users, meaning that all anonymous unauthenticated users are either granted or denied access

   ❑ Specified roles or user groups, meaning that authenticated users who are members of specific Windows roles and user groups are either granted or denied access

   ❑ Specified users, meaning that specific authenticated users are either granted or denied access

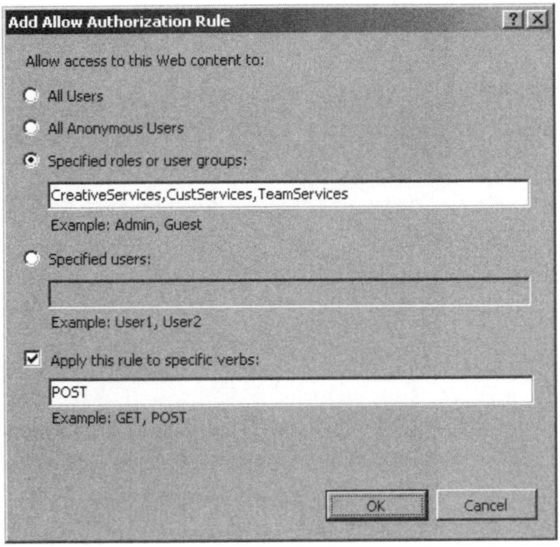

Figure 10-6   Set the authorization rule.

5. Authorization rules can be applied to all HTTP requests or to requests only with specific HTTP verbs, such as GET and POST. To apply the rule to specific HTTP verbs, select the Apply This Rule To Specific Verbs check box, and then type the verbs to use in a comma-separated list.

6. Click OK to set the rule.

You can edit or remove authorization rules by using the following techniques:

■ To modify a rule's settings, click the authorization rule you want to modify, and then click Edit. In the Edit dialog box, make the necessary changes, and then click OK.

■ To remove a rule that is no longer needed, click the entry you want to remove, and then click Remove. When prompted to confirm the action, click Yes.

Configuring IPv4 Address and Domain Name Restrictions

By default, IIS resources are accessible to all IPv4 addresses, computers, and domains, which present a security risk that might allow your server to be misused. To control use of resources, you might want to grant or deny access by IP Version 4 (IPv4) address, network ID, or domain. When you grant or deny access, keep the following in mind:

■ Granting access allows a computer to make requests for resources but doesn't necessarily allow users to work with resources. If you require authentication, users still need to authenticate themselves.

■ Denying access to resources prevents a computer from accessing those resources. Therefore, users of the computer can't access the resources—even if they could have authenticated themselves with a user name and password.

You can establish or remove restrictions globally at the server level and for individual sites, applications, and directories. The three types of restriction settings are:

- **General Restriction settings** Determine whether unspecified clients are allowed or denied access and whether domain name restrictions are enabled or disabled. An unspecified client is a computer for which there is no other restriction rule.

- **Allow Restriction rules** Grant access to a specific IP address, a range of IPv4 addresses, or a specific domain name.

- **Deny Authorization rules** Deny access to a specific IP address, a range of IPv4 addresses, or a specific domain name.

IPv4 address ranges are set based on the IPv4 address for the network ID and the related subnet mask. With standard classful networks, the network ID is the .0 address for the network, such as 192.168.1.0. By default, domain name restrictions are disabled. The reason for this is that when you grant or deny access by domain, IIS must perform a reverse Domain Name System (DNS) lookup on each connection to determine whether the connection comes from the domain. These reverse lookups can severely increase response times for the first query each user sends to your site.

To view the current restriction rules at a particular configuration level, navigate to the level of the configuration hierarchy you want to manage, and then double-click the IPv4 And Domain Restrictions feature. On the IPv4 And Domain Restrictions page, shown in Figure 10-7, you'll see a list of applicable restriction rules listed by:

- **Mode** Lists the type of rule as either Allow or Deny

- **Requestor** Lists the specific IPv4 address, IPv4 address range, or domain to which the rule applies

- **Entry Type** Lists the entry type as Local or Inherited

You can configure the general restriction settings by completing the following steps:

1. In IIS Manager, navigate to the level of the configuration hierarchy you want to manage, and then double-click the IPv4 And Domain Restrictions feature.

2. On the IPv4 And Domain Restrictions page, in the Actions pane, click Edit Feature Settings.

3. Set the restriction rule for unspecified clients, that is, clients that do not fall under any other restriction rule. To grant access to unspecified clients, set the Access For Unspecified Clients drop-down list to Allow. To deny access to unspecified clients, set the Access For Unspecified Clients drop-down list to Deny.

4. To allow domain name restrictions to be used in addition to IPv4 address restrictions, select the Enable Domain Name Restrictions check box.

5. Click OK to configure the restriction settings.

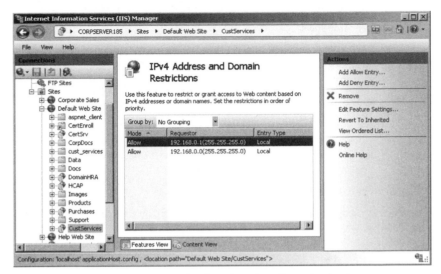

Figure 10-7   Review the restrictions for the selected configuration level.

You can set an allow or deny restriction by completing the following steps:

1. In IIS Manager, navigate to the level of the configuration hierarchy you want to manage, and then double-click the IPv4 And Domain Restrictions feature.

2. On the IPv4 And Domain Restrictions page, you should now see the currently configured IPv4 address and domain restrictions.

3. You can now specify a restriction. To add an allow restriction, click Add Allow Entry. To add a deny restriction, click Add Deny Entry. Figure 10-8 shows the Add Allow Restriction Rule dialog box.

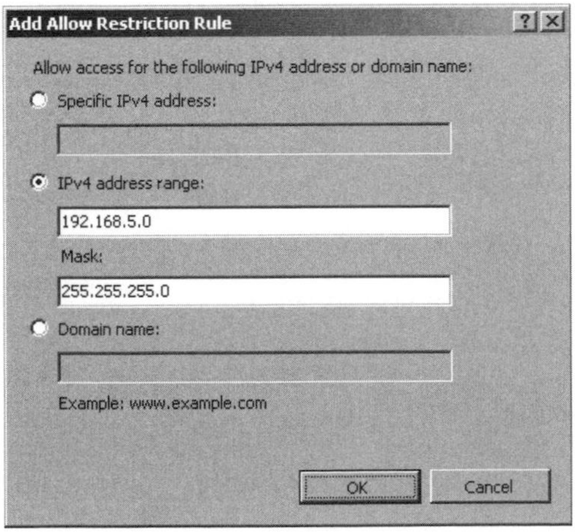

Figure 10-8   Create a restriction rule.

4. Create the Allow Access or Deny Access list. The settings you can specify for each option are as follows:

    ❑   For a single computer, select Specific IPv4 Address, and then type the IPv4 address for the computer, such as **192.168.5.50**.

    ❑   For groups of computers, select IPv4 Address Range, and then type the subnet address, such as **192.168.0.0**, and the subnet mask, such as **255.255.255.0**.

    ❑   For a domain name, select Domain Name, and then type the fully qualified domain name (FQDN), such as *eng.microsoft.com*. (Domain name restrictions must be enabled.)

5. Click OK to create the rule.

To remove a rule that is no longer needed, click the entry you want to remove, and then click Remove. When prompted to confirm the action, click Yes.

Managing Feature Delegation and Remote Administration

The Web Management Service (WMSVC) enables remote and delegated management of IIS using IIS Manager based on either Windows credentials only or Windows credentials and IIS Manager credentials. In addition to the Management Service feature, discussed in the "Enabling and Configuring Remote Administration" section of Chapter 3, "Core IIS Administration," you can use the following IIS features to control the way delegation and remote administration works:

- IIS Manager Users
- IIS Manager Permissions
- Feature Delegation

Each of these features is discussed in the sections that follow. When working with these features, keep in mind that they are used with IIS Manager for the purposes of delegation and remote administration. For local logon, any administrator user can use IIS Manager for administration of a local Web server. Furthermore, any user with direct access to content and configuration files can manipulate those files as appropriate for the file system permissions they've been granted.

Creating and Configuring IIS Manager User Accounts

The IIS Manager Users feature allows you to create accounts for individuals that act as Web site or Web application administrators when using IIS Manager for remote administration. When you specify an IIS manager, you set the permitted user name and password for the user, creating an IIS Manager account. You can then manage this account in IIS Manager. Options are available for enabling, disabling, and removing accounts as and for changing account passwords.

By default, IIS Manager permissions are based on Windows credentials. If you want to allow IIS Manager accounts to also be used, you must enable this option by completing the following steps:

1. In IIS Manager, select the server node, and then double-click Management Service.

2. On the Management Service page, the Identity Credentials options control whether IIS Manager accounts can be used. Do one of the following:

   ❏ If the Management Service is currently running and the Windows Credentials Or IIS Manager Credentials option is not selected, in the Actions pane, click Stop. Select the Windows Credentials Or IIS Manager Credentials option, click Apply, and then click Start.

   ❏ If the Management Service is not running and has not been configured, see the "Enabling and Configuring Remote Administration" section of Chapter 3.

You can configure IIS managers only at the server configuration level. To create and configure IIS managers, follow these steps:

1. In IIS Manager, select the server node, and then double-click the IIS Manager Users feature.

2. On the IIS Manager Users page, you should now see the currently configured IIS managers listed by user name and account status.

3. To create an IIS manager, in the Actions pane, click Add User. In the Add User dialog box, type the desired user name for the account. Type and confirm the account password, and then click OK.

4. You can work with IIS manager accounts by using the following techniques:

   ❏ To change an account password, click the user name you want to modify, and then click Change Password. In the Change Password dialog box, type and confirm the account password, and then click OK.

   ❏ To disable an account so that it cannot be used, click the user name, and then click Disable.

   ❏ To enable an account, click the user name, and then click Enable.

   ❏ To remove an account that is no longer needed, click the user name that you want to remove, and then click Remove. When prompted to confirm the action, click Yes.

Configuring IIS Manager Permissions

IIS Manager permissions control who can perform remote administration in IIS Manager. You configure IIS Manager permissions for individual sites, applications, or directories. Any permissions you apply at the site, application, or directory level also automatically apply to all lower configuration levels.

To grant a user permission to manage IIS remotely using IIS Manager, follow these steps:

1. In IIS Manager, select the configuration level below the server node for which you are configuring remote administration, and then double-click the IIS Manager Permissions feature.

2. On the IIS Manager Permissions page, you should now see a list of users who have been delegated remote administration privileges in IIS Manager. To see only users with permissions for a selected site, click Show Only Site Users.

3. In the Actions pane, click Allow User. In the Allow User dialog box, choose one of the following options:

   ❑ **Windows**   Choose Windows if you want to configure permissions based on a Windows account.

   ❑ **IIS Manager**   Choose IIS Manager if you want to configure permissions based on an IIS Manager account.

4. Click Select. Use the dialog box provided to choose the account to use, and then click OK.

To deny a user permission to manage IIS remotely using IIS Manager, follow these steps:

1. In IIS Manager, select the configuration level below the server node for which you are configuring remote administration, and then double-click the IIS Manager Permissions feature.

2. On the IIS Manager Permissions page, you should now see a list of users who have been delegated remote administration privileges in IIS Manager. To see only users with permissions for a selected site, click Show Only Site Users.

3. Click the user account that should no longer have administration permissions at or below the selected level, and then click Deny User.

Configuring Feature Delegation

Feature Delegation settings configure the delegation state at the server level or for individual sites for lower configuration levels in IIS Manager. These settings also determine the state of the related section in the applicationHost.config file. To configure Feature Delegation for all sites on a server, you configure feature delegation at the server level. To configure Feature Delegation for all application and directories within a site, you configure feature delegation at the site level.

As shown in Figure 10-9, each feature, with two noted exceptions, has one of the following delegation states:

■ **Read/Write**   Enables remote administrators to view and change the feature. It also unlocks the configuration section in the applicationHost.config file, allowing settings for this feature to be read from and written to web.config files.

- **Read Only** Enables remote administrators to view but not change the feature. It also locks the configuration section in the applicationHost.config file, preventing settings for this feature to be read from and written to web.config files.

- **Not Delegated** Prevents remote administrators from viewing or changing the feature. Also locks the configuration section in the applicationHost.config file, preventing settings for this feature to be read from and written to Web.config files.

With the .NET Roles and .NET Users features, you'll see the delegation state specified as either Configuration Read/Write or Configuration Read Only. These settings work the same as Read/Write and Read Only but are distinguished from other features because configuration information can come not only from configuration files, but also from a database.

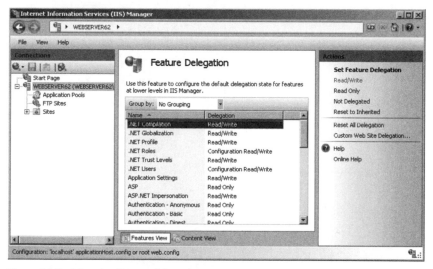

Figure 10-9   View the feature delegation state.

You can configure the delegation state by completing the following steps:

1. Open IIS Manager. To configure the delegation state at the server level for all lower configuration levels, select the server node, and then double-click Feature Delegation. To configure the delegation state of an individual site, select the server node, double-click Feature Delegation, and then in the Actions pane, click Custom Web Site Configuration. On the Feature Delegation or Custom Web Site Delegation page, you should now see the delegation state for each feature in IIS Manager.

2. You can now use the following techniques to manage delegation:

   ❑ To change the delegation state, select the feature you want to work with, and then configure the Actions pane options to set the delegation state as Read/Write, Read Only, Configuration Read/Write, Configuration Read Only, or Not Delegated.

   ❑ When you are working with the Custom Web Site Delegation page, you can reset a feature to its inherited value by selecting the feature and then clicking Reset To Inherited.

   ❑ To reset the delegation state for all IIS features to their original state (as per the default value in schema), click Reset All Delegation.

Chapter 11

Managing Active Directory Certificate Services and SSL

Active Directory Certificate Services and Secure Sockets Layer (SSL) provide an extra layer of security for your Web server. You use Certificate Services and SSL to protect sensitive information such as passwords, credit card numbers, or payment information. Certificate Services and SSL protect sensitive information by encrypting the data sent between client browsers and your server. *Encryption* is the process of encoding information by using a mathematical algorithm that makes it difficult for anyone other than the intended recipient to view the original information.

Internet Information Services (IIS) transfers encrypted data to a client browser by using the SSL protocol. With SSL, servers and clients can use certificates to provide proof of identity prior to establishing a secure connection. Once a connection is established, clients and servers use the secure SSL channel to transfer information. This information is encrypted using a technique that the clients and servers can interpret to extract the original information.

Understanding SSL

IIS supports SSL protocol version 3. SSL 3 enables encrypted data transfers between client browsers and Web servers. The sections that follow provide an overview on how SSL works and how it's used.

Using SSL Encryption

As stated previously, encryption is the process of encoding information by using a mathematical algorithm that makes it difficult for anyone other than the intended recipient to view the original information. The encryption algorithm uses a mathematical value, called a *key*, to scramble the data so that the key must be used to recover the data.

Many techniques are available for encrypting information so that it can be exchanged. Some encryption techniques use a combination of public and private keys—the public key can be shared and the private key can't. Some encryption techniques use shared secret keys that are transferred between authenticated systems. SSL uses a technique called *public key encryption*, which combines private, public, and shared secret (session) keys.

In public key encryption, there are three keys:

- A public key that's available to any application that requests it
- A private key that's known only to its owner
- A session key that's created using public and private key data

IIS uses the public key encryption component in SSL to establish sessions between clients and servers. You should use SSL whenever you want to provide additional protection for data that's transferred between clients and servers. Some specific instances in which you might want to use Certificate Services and SSL follow:

- When you remotely manage the Web server by using the Administration Web site or operator administration pages
- When your Web site has secure areas that contain sensitive company documents
- When your Web site has pages that collect sensitive personal or financial information from visitors
- When your Web site processes orders for goods or services and you collect credit or other personal information from customers

With SSL, users connect to Web pages by using a secure Uniform Resource Locator (URL) that begins with *https://*. The *https* designator tells the browser to try to establish a secure connection with IIS. SSL connections for Web pages are made on port 443 by default, but you can change the port designator as necessary. As you set out to work with SSL, keep in mind that you can't use host headers with SSL. With SSL, Hypertext Transfer Protocol (HTTP) requests are encrypted, and the host header name within the encrypted request can't be used to determine the correct site to which a request must be routed.

After the client browser contacts the server by using a secure URL, the server sends the browser its public key and server certificate. Next, the client and server negotiate the level of encryption to use for secure communications. The server always attempts to use the highest level of encryption it supports. Once the encryption level is established, the client browser creates a session key and uses the server's public key to encrypt this information for transmission. Anyone intercepting the message at this point wouldn't be able to read the session key—only the server's private key can decrypt the message.

The IIS server uses its private key to decrypt the message sent by the client. The SSL session between the client and the server is now established. The session key can be used to encrypt and decrypt data transmitted between the client and server.

To recap, secure SSL sessions are established using the following technique:

1. The user's Web browser contacts the server by using a secure URL.
2. The IIS server sends the browser its public key and server certificate.

3. The client and server negotiate the level of encryption to use for the secure communications.

4. The client browser encrypts a session key with the server's public key and sends the encrypted data back to the server.

5. The IIS server uses its private key to decrypt the message sent by the client, and the session is established.

6. Both the client and the server use the session key to encrypt and decrypt transmitted data.

Using SSL Certificates

Not reflected in the previous discussion is the way in which SSL uses certificates. You can think of a certificate as an identity card that contains information needed to establish the identity of an application or user over a network. Certificates enable Web servers and users to authenticate one another before establishing a connection. Certificates also contain keys needed to establish SSL sessions between clients and servers.

In most cases certificates used by IIS, Web browsers, and Certificate Services conform to the X.509 standard. For this reason, they're often referred to as X.509 certificates. Different versions of the X.509 standard have been issued (see RFC 3280 for more information on this standard), and these versions have been revised from time to time. Two types of X.509 certificates are used:

- Client certificates, which contain identifying information about a client

- Server certificates, which contain identifying information about a server

Certificate authorities issue both types of certificates. A *certificate authority (CA)* is a trusted agency responsible for confirming the identity of users, organizations, and their servers and then issuing certificates that confirm these identities. Before issuing a client certificate, CAs require that you provide information that identifies you, your organization, and the client application you're using. Before issuing a server certificate, CAs require that you provide information that identifies your organization and the server you're using.

When you're choosing CAs to create your server certificates, you have several options. If you use Certificate Services, your organization can act as its own CA. When you act as your own CA, you use the following process to enable SSL on your Web server:

1. Install Active Directory Certificate Services on a server in the domain, and then generate the root CA certificate.

2. Generate a certificate request file for each Web site on your server that has a unique name, and then use the certificate request files to create server certificates for your Web sites.

3. Install the certificates and then enable SSL on each applicable Web site.

4. Client browsers won't recognize and trust your root CA certificate. To get browsers to trust the root CA, the user must install the certificate in the browser's authorities store.

5. Initiate SSL connections by using URLs that begin with *https://*.

Instead of using your own CAs, you can use third-party CAs—and there's an advantage to doing so. The third-party authority can vouch for your identity, and dozens of vendors are already configured as trusted CAs in Web browsers. In Microsoft Internet Explorer version 5 or later, you can obtain a list of trusted authorities by completing the following steps:

1. On the Tools menu, select Internet Options. The Internet Options dialog box appears.

2. On the Content tab, click Certificates. The Certificates dialog box appears.

3. On the Trusted Root Certification Authorities tab. you should now see a list of trusted root CAs.

When you use a trusted third-party authority, you follow a different procedure on your Web server to enable SSL than when you act as your own root CA:

1. Create a certificate request file for each Web site on your server that has a unique name.

2. Submit the certificate request files to a trusted third-party authority such as Verisign. The CA will process the requests and send you certificates.

3. Complete the certificate request by installing the certificate, and then enable SSL on each applicable Web site.

4. Client browsers initiate SSL sessions by using a secure URL beginning with *https://*.

Regardless of whether you act as your own CA or use a trusted CA, you still must manage the server certificates, and you use Active Directory Certificate Services to do this. Server certificates can expire or be revoked, if necessary. For example, if your organization is an Internet service provider (ISP) that issues its own certificates, you might want your customers' server certificates to expire annually. This forces customers to update their certificate information at least once a year to ensure that it's current. You also might want to revoke a certificate when a customer cancels service.

Understanding SSL Encryption Strength

An SSL session's encryption strength is directly proportional to the number of bits in the session key. This means that session keys with a greater number of bits are considerably more difficult to crack and, thus, are more secure.

The most commonly used encryption levels for SSL sessions are 40-bit, 128-bit, and 256-bit. Encryption at the 40-bit level is adequate for most needs, including e-commerce. Encryption at the 128-bit level provides added protection for e-commerce. Encryption at the 256-bit level provides superior protection for sensitive personal and financial information. Most versions of Microsoft Windows Server shipped in the United States are configured with 256-bit encryption.

Don't confuse the encryption level for SSL sessions (the strength of the session key expressed as bits) with the encryption level for SSL certificates (the strength of the certificate's public and private keys expressed as bits). Most encryption keys (public and private) have a bit length of 512 or higher. When a user attempts to establish an SSL session with your Web server, the user's browser and the server use the bit length of their encryption keys to determine the strongest level of encryption possible. If the encryption keys use 512 bits, the level of encryption is set to 40 bits. If the encryption keys use 1024 bits, the level of encryption is set to 128 bits. If the encryption keys use 2048 bits, the level of encryption is set to 256 bits. Other key bit lengths and encryption levels are available.

Working with Active Directory Certificate Services

Active Directory Certificate Services allows you to issue and revoke digital certificates. You can use these certificates to enable SSL sessions and to authenticate the identity of your intranet, extranet, or Internet Web site.

Understanding Active Directory Certificate Services

Active Directory Certificate Services is a Windows service that runs on a designated certificate server. Certificate servers can be configured as one of four types of CAs:

- **Enterprise root CA**   The certificate server at the root of the hierarchy for a Windows domain. It's the most trusted CA in the enterprise and must be a member of the Active Directory service and have access to it.

- **Enterprise subordinate CA**   A certificate server that will be a member of an existing CA hierarchy. It can issue certificates but must obtain its own CA certificate from the enterprise root CA.

- **Stand-alone root CA**   The certificate server at the root of a non-enterprise hierarchy. It's the most trusted CA in its hierarchy and doesn't need access to Active Directory.

- **Stand-alone subordinate CA**   A certificate server that will be a member of an existing non-enterprise hierarchy. It can issue certificates but must obtain its own CA certificate from the stand-alone root CA in its hierarchy.

Certificate servers aren't required to be dedicated to Active Directory Certificate Services and can be the same servers you use for Web publishing. However, it's a good idea to designate specific servers in your domain that will act as certificate servers and to use these servers only for that purpose.

Real World To safeguard the root CA from malicious users, you should create multiple levels in the CA hierarchy. For example, in an enterprise, you'd set up an enterprise root CA and then set up one or more enterprise subordinate CAs. You'd then issue certificates to users and computers only through the subordinate CAs. This safeguard should help ensure that the root CA's private key can't be easily compromised.

Once you install Active Directory Certificate Services on a computer, you're limited in what you can and can't do with the computer. Specifically, you can't do the following:

- You can't rename a computer that has Certificate Services installed.

- You can't change the domain membership of a computer that has Certificate Services installed.

You manage Certificate Services by using a Microsoft Management Console (MMC) snap-in called the Certificate Authority snap-in and a Web-based Active Server Pages (ASP) application that can be accessed in a standard Web browser. In the snap-in, you have full control over Certificate Services. The Web-based application, on the other hand, is used primarily to retrieve Certificate Revocation Lists (CRLs), to request certificates, and to check on pending certificates. You can access the Web-based application from the following URL: *http://hostname/certsrv*.

Figure 11-1 shows the Certification Authority snap-in's main window. As you can see, five containers are under the root authority. These containers are used as follows:

- **Revoked Certificates** Contains all certificates that have been issued and then revoked.

- **Issued Certificates** Contains all certificates that have been approved and issued by the Certificate Services administrator.

- **Pending Requests** Contains all pending certificate requests for this CA. If you're an administrator on the certificate server, you can approve requests by right-clicking them and selecting Issue. The default configuration is to process requests automatically, which means that no administrator involvement is required.

- **Failed Requests** Contains any declined certificate requests for this CA. If you're an administrator on the certificate server, you can deny requests by right-clicking them and selecting Deny.

Note The label for the root node of the snap-in is set to the name of the CA. In the example, the CA name is Corporate Root CA.

- **Certificate Templates**   Contains a set of certificate templates that are configured for different intended purposes. These templates provide basic rules for the various types of certificates. To install additional certificate templates, right-click Certificate Templates, select New, and then click Certificate Template To Issue. (Certificate Templates are available only with enterprise root and subordinate CAs.)

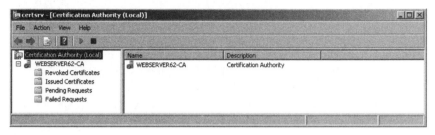

Figure 11-1   Use the Active Directory Certificate Services snap-in to manage Certificate Services.

Installing Active Directory Certificate Services

If the server isn't running IIS and you want to be able to retrieve CRLs to request certificates or to check on pending certificates through a browser, you must install IIS prior to installing Active Directory Certificate Services. To install Active Directory Certificate Services, complete the following steps:

1. Log on to the certificate server by using an account with Administrator privileges or, if you're creating an enterprise CA, Enterprise Administrator privileges.

2. Start Server Manager by clicking the Server Manager icon on the Quick Launch toolbar or by clicking Start, pointing to Administrative Tools, and then clicking Server Manager.

3. In Server Manager, in the left pane, select the Roles node, and then scroll down until you see the details section for the role you want to manage. In the details section for the role, click Add Role Services. This starts the Add Role Services Wizard. If the Before You Begin page appears, click Next.

4. On the Select Role Services page, select Active Directory Certificate Services, and then click Next. Read the introductory message, and then click Next.

5. The Certificate Authority role service is selected by default. Select these additional role services to install as necessary: Certificate Authority Web Enrollment and Online Certificate Status Protocol.

6. On the Specify Setup Type page, select the setup type as enterprise or stand-alone, and then click Next.

7. On the Specify CA Type page, specify the CA type as either root CA or subordinate CA.

8. All CAs must have a private key to generate and issue certificates. On the Setup Private Key page, select Create A New Private Key, and then click Next.

9. Use the settings on the Configure Cryptography For CA page to select a cryptographic provider, hash algorithm, and bit length for the CA's private key. Ensure that your selections are appropriate for the CA's intended use. If you are unsure, accept the default settings. Click Next when you are ready to continue.

10. On the Configure CA Name page, type the common name for the CA, such as **Corporate Root CA**. As necessary, set the distinguished name suffix for the CA name, and then click Next.

11. On the Set Validity Period page, set the CA certificate's expiration date. Most CA certificates are valid for at least five years. Click Next.

12. Specify the storage location for the configuration database and log. By default, the certificate database and log are stored in the *%SystemRoot%*\System32\CertLog folder. Click Next.

> **Tip**   If hundreds or thousands of users use your CA, you might want the database and log files to be stored on separate drives. By placing these files on separate drives, you can improve the CA's performance and responsiveness. In all cases the database and log files should be on NTFS volumes. This ensures that the security permissions can be set to restrict access to these files by user account.

13. Click Install to complete the process. When the installation completes, click Close. If you installed Certificate Services on a computer running IIS, you can configure these services for Web access (as described in the section "Accessing Certificate Services in a Browser," immediately following).

Accessing Certificate Services in a Browser

When you install Certificate Services on a computer running IIS, the default (or primary) Web site is updated so that you can perform key certificate tasks through a Web browser. These tasks include:

- Retrieving CRLs

- Requesting certificates

- Checking on pending certificates

The structures that make Web-based requests possible are files configured for use in the two following virtual directories:

- **CertSrv**   Contains files necessary for Web-based access to Certificate Services. It is located in *%SystemRoot%*\System32\CertSrv by default. This directory is set up as a pooled application called CertSrv.

- **CertEnroll**   Contains files necessary for controlling Certificate Services. It is located in *%SystemRoot%*\System32\CertSrv\CertEnroll by default.

Tip   If these directories aren't available for some reason, you can create virtual directories that map aliases to their physical locations. At a command prompt, type **certutil –vroot**. The command-line utility Certutil creates the necessary virtual directories for you and maps them to their default locations.

Once you've configured Web-based access to Certificate Services, you can access these services by typing **http://*hostname*/certsrv/**, where *hostname* is the Domain Name System (DNS) or NetBIOS name of the host server, such as *ca.microsoft.com* or CASrvr. Figure 11-2 shows the main page for Certificate Services.

Figure 11-2   Use the Web-based interface to retrieve CA certificates or revocation lists, to request certificates, or to check on pending certificates.

Starting and Stopping Certificate Services

Active Directory Certificate Services runs as a Windows service on the certificate server. You can stop and start this service on a local system by completing the following steps:

1. In Administrative Tools, click Certification Authority to open the Certification Authority snap-in.

2. Right-click the root node for the CA, and then select All Tasks.

3. Select Stop Service to stop Certificate Services.

4. Select Start Service to start Certificate Services.

You can stop and start services on a remote system by completing the following steps:

1. In Administrative Tools, click Certification Authority to open the Certification Authority snap-in.

2. Right-click the Certification Authority node, and then on the shortcut menu, select Retarget Certification Authority. The Certification Authority dialog box appears.

3. Select Another Computer, type the name of the computer to which you want to connect, and then click Finish. You can also type the server's Internet Protocol (IP) address or fully qualified domain name (FQDN), or you can click Browse to search for the computer.

4. In the Certification Authority snap-in, right-click the root node for the CA, and then select All Tasks.

5. Select Stop Service to stop Certificate Services.

6. Select Start Service to start Certificate Services.

Backing Up and Restoring the CA

If your organization publishes its own CA, you should back up the CA information routinely. Backing up the CA information ensures that you can recover critical CA data, including:

- CA private key and certificate

- CA configuration information

- CA log and pending request queue

You can perform two types of backups through the Certification Authority snap-in:

- **Standard**   Creates a full copy of certificate database, logs, and pending request queues.

- **Incremental**   Creates a partial copy of certificate database, logs, and pending request queues. This copy contains only the changes since the last standard backup.

In a very large CA implementation, you can perform incremental backups of the database, logs, and queues by selecting Perform Incremental Backups. To use incremental backups, you must do the following:

1. First perform a standard backup.

2. Perform successive incremental backups at later dates.

When you use incremental backups, you must also restore incrementally. To do this, complete the following steps:

1. Stop Certificate Services.

2. Restore the last standard backup.

3. Restore each incremental backup in order.

4. Start Certificate Services.

Creating CA Backups

To back up the CA information on your certificate server, complete the following steps:

1. Create a folder that Certificate Services can use to store the backup information. This directory must be empty, and you should create it on the local machine where Certificate Services is installed.

2. Start the Certification Authority snap-in, right-click the root node for the CA, choose All Tasks, and then select Back Up CA. This starts the Certification Authority Backup Wizard.

> **Note**   Certificate Services must be running when you back up the CA. If the service isn't running, you'll see a prompt asking you if you want to start the service. Click OK.

3. Click Next, and then select the items you want to back up, as shown in Figure 11-3. The options are:

   ❑   Private Key And CA Certificate

   ❑   Certificate Database And Certificate Database Log

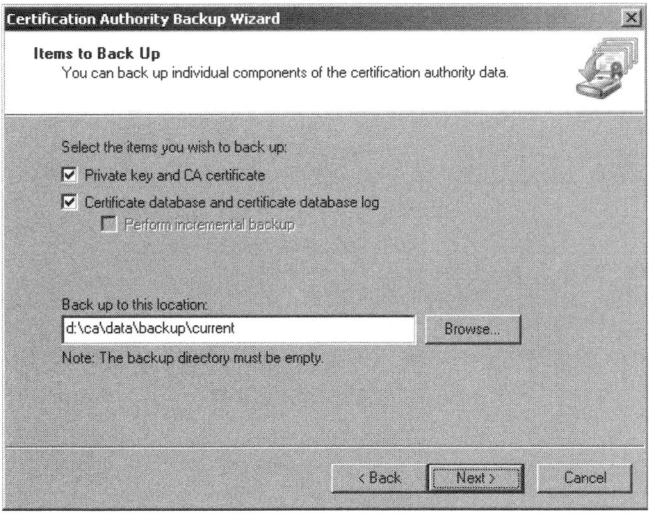

Figure 11-3   Specify the certification items that you want to back up.

4. If this is an incremental backup, select Perform Incremental Backup. Incremental backups can be performed only when backing up the certificate database and log.

5. In the Back Up To This Location field, type the file path to the backup folder, or click Browse to search for this folder. If you specify a folder that doesn't exist, you'll be given the option of creating it.

6. Click OK or Next. Type and then confirm a password that will be used to protect the private key and CA certificate files.

7. Click Next, and then click Finish. The wizard creates a backup of the selected data.

Recovering CA Information

If you ever need to recover the CA information, you can do this by completing the following steps:

1. The Certificate Services can't be running when you restore the CA. In the Certification Authority snap-in, right-click the root node for the CA, choose All Tasks, and then select Stop Service.

2. Right-click the root node a second time, choose All Tasks, and then select Restore CA. This starts the Certification Authority Restore Wizard.

3. Click Next, and then select the items you want to restore. The options are:

   ❑ Private Key And CA Certificate

   ❑ Certificate Database And Certificate Database Log

4. In the Restore From This Location field, type the file path to the backup folder, or click Browse to search for this folder. You should always restore the last complete backup before restoring any incremental backups.

5. Click Next. Type the password used to protect the CA files, and then click Next again.

6. Click Finish. The wizard restores the selected data and starts the Certificate Services service.

Configuring Certificate Request Processing

Unlike previous versions of Certificate Services, the version shipping with IIS 7.0 is configured for autoenrollment by default. This means that authorized users can request a certificate, and the CA automatically processes the certificate request so that the user can immediately install the certificate.

If you want to view or change the default request processing policy, follow these steps:

1. In Administrative Tools, click Certification Authority to open the Certification Authority snap-in.

2. Right-click the CA node, and then select Properties. The Properties dialog box appears.

3. On the Policy Module tab, click Properties.

4. If you want to process requests manually, select "Set The Certificate Request Status To Pending. The Administrator Must Explicitly Issue The Certificate."

5. If you want the CA to process requests automatically, select Follow The Settings In The Certificate Template, If Applicable. Otherwise, Automatically Issue The Certificate.

6. Click OK twice.

Approving and Declining Pending Certificate Requests

If you've configured the CA so that certificates must be manually processed, you'll find that pending certificate requests are displayed in the Certification Authority snap-in's Pending Requests container.

You can approve pending requests by completing the following steps:

1. In Administrative Tools, click Certification Authority to open the Certification Authority snap-in.

2. Select the Pending Requests container. You will see a list of pending requests if there are any.

3. Right-click the request that you want to approve, choose All Tasks, and then select Issue.

4. Certificate Services generates a certificate based on the request and places this certificate in the Issued Certificates container.

5. Certificates are valid for one year. After this period they must be renewed.

You can decline pending certificate requests by doing the following:

1. In Administrative Tools, click Certification Authority to open the Certification Authority snap-in.

2. Select the Pending Requests container. You should see a list of pending requests.

3. Right-click the request that you want to decline, choose All Tasks, and then select Deny.

4. When prompted to confirm the action, select Yes.

> **Caution**   Denied requests are moved to the Failed Requests container and can't be restored. The user must resubmit a new request.

Generating Certificates Manually in the Certification Authority Snap-In

Once you've issued a certificate, you can manually create the certificate file that you need to install. To do this, complete the following steps:

1. In Administrative Tools, click Certification Authority to open the Certification Authority snap-in.

2. Select the Issued Certificates container. You should see a list of certificates issued by this root CA, if any.

3. Right-click the certificate that you want to generate, and then select Open. The Certificate dialog box appears.

4. On the Details tab, select Copy To File. The Certificate Export Wizard opens. Click Next.

5. Select the Base-64 Encoded X.509 (.CER) export file format, and then click Next.

6. Specify the name of the file you want to export. Be sure to use .cer as the file extension. Click Browse if you want to use the Save As dialog box to set the file location and name.

7. Click Next, and then click Finish. After the Certificate Export Wizard confirms that the certificate was successfully exported, click OK. You can now install the certificate file as described in the "Processing Pending Requests and Installing Site Certificates" section of this chapter.

Revoking Certificates

Server certificates are valid for one year and can be revoked if necessary. Typically, you revoke a certificate when there's a change in the site's status or when the customer for whom you issued the certificate cancels the service subscription. To revoke a certificate, complete the following steps:

1. In Administrative Tools, click Certification Authority to open the Certification Authority snap-in.

2. Select the Issued Certificates container. You should see a list of issued certificates.

3. Right-click the certificate that you want to revoke, choose All Tasks, and then select Revoke Certificate. The Certificate Revocation dialog box appears.

4. In the Reason Code drop-down list, select a reason for the revocation, and then click Yes. The CA marks the certificate as revoked and moves it to the Revoked Certificates container.

By default, CAs publish CRLs weekly and CRL changes daily. You can change this setting through the Revoked Certificates Properties dialog box by performing the following steps:

1. In Administrative Tools, click Certification Authority to open the Certification Authority snap-in.

2. Right-click the Revoked Certificates container, select Properties, and then in the CRL Publication Interval fields, set a new interval for publishing the CRL and CRL changes. Then click OK.

Reviewing and Renewing the Root CA Certificate

The root CA certificate is valid for the period that was specified when the certificate was created. To view the expiration date or to review the certificate properties, complete the following steps:

1. In Administrative Tools, click Certification Authority to open the Certification Authority snap-in.

2. Right-click the root node for the CA, and then select Properties. This displays the Root CA Properties dialog box.

3. On the General tab, click View Certificate.

4. Use the Certificate dialog box to review the root CA certificate's properties, including the valid from and to dates.

The root CA certificate is usually valid for five years. If you're approaching the end of the five-year period, you should renew the certificate. You should also renew the root CA certificate if one of the following situations exists:

■ The signing key is compromised.

■ A program requires a new signing key to be used with a new certificate.

■ The current CRL is too big and you want to move some of the information to a new CRL.

When you renew the root CA certificate, you can generate new public and private keys. Do this if the key has been compromised or a new key is required.

To renew the root CA certificate, complete the following steps:

1. Log on locally to the CA server.

2. Right-click the root node for the CA again, choose All Tasks, and then select Renew CA Certificate.

3. If prompted to stop Certificate Services, click Yes. Certificate Services can't be running when you renew the CA. The Renew CA Certificate dialog box appears.

4. In the Renew CA Certificate dialog box, select Yes if you want to generate a new public and private key pair. Otherwise, select No.

5. Click OK. Certificate Services is restarted automatically and a new certificate is issued.

Creating and Installing Certificates

You have two options for creating and installing certificates. You can use your own Certificate Services to generate your certificates, or you can use a trusted third-party authority. When you use Certificate Services, you manage the certificate creation, expiration, and revocation process. When you create certificates through trusted third-party authorities, you let the trusted authority manage the certificate creation, expiration, and revocation process. Either way, the basic tasks you need to perform to create and install a certificate are as follows:

1. Create a certificate request.

2. Submit the request to the authority of your choice or to your own root authority.

3. When you receive the response from the authority, process the pending request and install the certificate.

4. Ensure that SSL is enabled and that secure communications are configured properly.

Creating Certificate Requests

Each Web site hosted on your Web server needs a separate certificate if you want SSL to work properly. The first step in the certificate creation process is to generate a certificate request.

You can generate a self-signed certificate request by following these steps:

1. In IIS Manager, select the server node, and then double-click the Server Certificates feature.

2. On the Server Certificates page, you'll see a list of certificates that the Web server can use. In the Actions pane, click Create Self-Signed Certificate.

3. In the Specify Friendly Name dialog box, type a friendly name for the certificate, such as Default Web Site, and then click OK to create the self-signed certificate.

You can generate a certificate request to submit to CAs by completing the following steps:

1. In IIS Manager, select the server node, and then double-click the Server Certificates feature.

2. On the Server Certificates page, you'll see a list of certificates that the Web server can use. In the Actions pane, click Create Certificate Request.

3. Set the following properties as shown in Figure 11-4:

   ❑ **Common Name**   Sets your Web site's common name. When the certificate is used on an intranet (or internal network), the common name may be one word, and it can also be the server's NetBIOS name, such as CorpIntranet. When the certificate will be used on the Internet, the common name must be a valid DNS name, such as *www.microsoft.com*.

   ❑ **Organization**   Sets your company's legal name, such as Microsoft Corporation.

   ❑ **Organizational Unit**   Sets the division in your company responsible for the certificate, such as Technology Department.

   > **Note**   Third-party authorities will use the organization name, the site's common name, and the geographical information you supply to validate your request for a certificate. If you don't type this information correctly, you won't be issued a certificate.

   ❑ **City/Locality**   Type the city or locality in which your company is located.

   ❑ **State/Province**   Type the full name of the state or province in which your company is located.

   ❑ **Country/Region**   Select the country or region for your company.

   > **Caution**   Don't use abbreviations when typing geographic data. Some authorities won't accept abbreviated geographic information, and you'll have to resubmit your request.

4. Click Next.

5. Use the options on the Cryptographic Service Provider Properties page to select a cryptographic provider, hash algorithm, and bit length for the certificate's private key. Ensure that your selections are appropriate for the certificate's intended use. If you are unsure, accept the default settings. Click Next when you are ready to continue.

6. You need to specify the file name and path for the certificate request file, such as C:\certreq.txt. Type a new path, or click the selection button to select a path and file name in the Specify Save As File Name dialog box.

7. Click Finish to complete the request generation process.

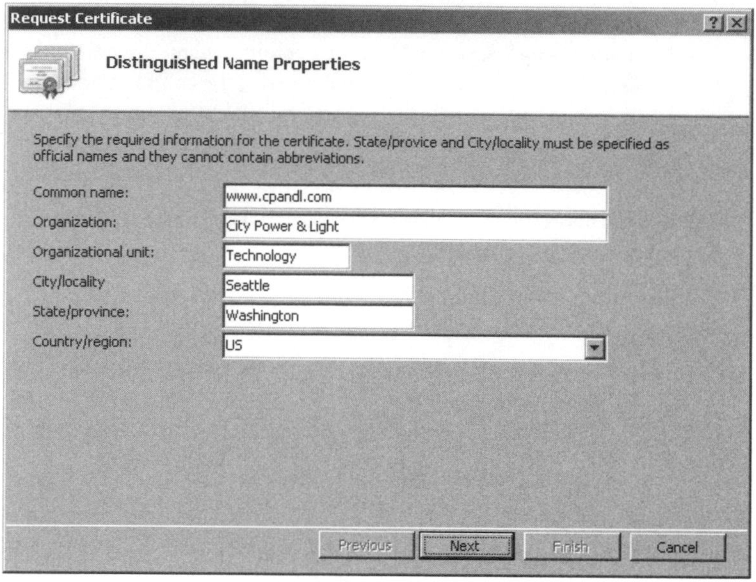

Figure 11-4 Specify the name properties for the certificate.

Real World The common name is typically composed of *Host + Domain Name*, such as *www.microsoft.com* or *products.microsoft.com*. Certificates are specific to the common name that they have been issued to at the Host level. The common name must be the same as the Web address you'll be accessing when connecting to a secure site. For example, a certificate for the domain *microsoft.com* will receive a warning if accessing a site named *www.microsoft.com* or *services.microsoft.com* because *www.microsoft.com* and *services.microsoft.com* are different from *microsoft.com*. You'd need to create a certificate for the correct common name.

Submitting Certificate Requests to Third-Party Authorities

After you create a CSR, you can submit it to a third-party authority such as Verisign. The CSR is stored as American Standard Code of Information Interchange (ASCII) text in the file you specified in Step 6 in the "Creating Certificate Requests" section. It contains your site's public key and your identification information. When you open this file, you'll find the encrypted contents of the request, such as:

```
--BEGIN NEW CERTIFICATE REQUEST--
MIXCCDCCAnECAQAwczERMA8GA1UEAxMIZW5nc3ZyMDExEzARBgNVBAsTClRlY2hu
b2xvZ3kxEzARBgNVBAoTCkRvbWFpbi5Db20xEjAQBgNVBAcTCVZhbmNvdXZlcjET
MBEGA3UECBMKV2FzaGluZ3RvbjELMAkGA1UEBhMCVVMwgZ8wDQYJKoZIhvcNAQEB
BQADgY0AMIGJAoGBALElbrvIZNRB+gvkdcf9b7tNns24hB2Jgp5BhKi4NXc/twR7
C+GuDnyTqRs+C2AnNHgb9oQkpivqQNKh2+N18bKU3PEZUzXHOpxxjhaiT8aMFJhi
3bFvD+gTCQrw5BWoV9/Ff5Ud3EF5TRQ2WJZ+JluQQewo/mXv5ZnbHsM+aLy3AgMB
```

```
AAGgggFTMBoGCisGAQQBgjcNAgMxDBYKNS4wLjIxOTUuMjA1BgorBgEEAYI3AgEO
MScwJTAOBgNVHQ8BAf8EBAMCBPAwEwYDVR01BAwwCgYIKwYWWQUHAwEwgfOGCisG
AQQBgjcNAgIxge4wgesCAQEeWgBNAGkAYwByAG8AcwBvAGYAdAAgAFIAUwBBACAA
UwBDAGgAYQBuAG4AZQBsACAAQwByAHkAcAB0AG8AZwByAGEACAB0AGkAYwAgAFAA
cgBvAHYAaQBkAGUAcgOBiQBfE24DPqBwFp1R15/xZDY8Cugoxbyymtwq/tAPZ6dz
Pr9Zy3MNnkKQbKcsbLR/4t9/tWJIMmrFhZonrx12qBfICoiKUXreSK89OILrLEto
1frm/dycoXHhStSsZdm25vszv827FKKk5bRW/vIIeBqfKnEPJHOnoiG6UScvgA8Q
fgAAAAVVAAAMAOGCSqGSIb3DQEBBQUAA4GBAFZc6K4S04BMUnR/8Ow3J/MS3TYi
HAvFuxnjGOCefTq8Sakzvq+uazUO3waBqHxZ1f32qGr7karoD+fq8dX27nmhOzpp
Rz1DXrxR35mMC/yP/fpLmLb51sxOt1379PdS4trvWUFkfY93/CkUi+nrQt/uZHY3
NOSThxf73VkfbsE3
--END NEW CERTIFICATE REQUEST--
```

Most CAs require you to submit the certificate request as part of a formal site registration process. In this registration process you'll be asked to submit the request file in an e-mail message or through an online form. When using e-mail, you simply attach the request file to the message and send it. When using an online form, you can copy the entire text of the request—including the BEGIN and END statements—to the clipboard and paste this into the online form. You can use Microsoft Notepad to do this. Or you might be able to browse for the file to insert and let the server paste the data into the form for you.

After the CA reviews your certificate request, the CA either approves or declines it. If the CA approves the request, you'll receive an e-mail message with the signed certificate attached or a notice to visit a location where you can retrieve the signed certificate. The certificate is an ASCII text file that you can view in Notepad, and it can be decrypted only with the private key you generated previously. As before, the contents of the file are encrypted and include BEGIN and END statements, as in this example:

```
--BEGIN CERTIFICATE--
MXXCWjCCAgQCED1pyIenknxBt43eUZ7JF9YwDQYJK  oZIhvcNAQEEBQAwgakxFjAU
BgNERAoTDVZ1cm1TaWduLCBJbmMxRzBFBgNVBAsTP  nd3dy52ZXJppc21nbi5jb20v
cmVwb3NpdG9yeS9UZXXN0Q1BTIE1uY29ycC4gQnkgU  mVmLiBMaWFiLiBMVEQuMUYw
RAYDVQQLEz1G45IgVmVyaVNpZ24gYXV0aG9yaXp1Z  CBOZXN0OaW5nIG9ubHkuIeev
IGFzc3VyYW5jZXMgKEM345MxOTk3MB4XDTAwMTEwN  zAwMDAwMFoXDTAwMTEyMTIz
NTk1OVowczELMAkGA1UEBhMCVVMxEzARBgNVBAgTC  1dhc2hpbmd0b24xEjAQBgNV
BAcUCVZhbmNvdXZlcjETMBEGA1UEChQKRG9tYW1uL  kNvbTETMBEGA1UECxQKVGVj
aG5vbG9neTERMA8GA1UEAxQIZW5nY3ZyQWEwgZ8wD  QYJKoZIhvcNAQEBBQADgYOA
MIGJAoGBALE1brvIZNRB+gvkdcf9b7tNns24hB2Jgp5BhKi4NXc/  twR7C+GuDnyT
qRs+C2AnNHgb9oQkpivqQNKh2+N18bKU3PEZUzXHO  prtyhaiT8aMFJhi3bFvD+gT
CQrw5BWoV9/Ff5Ud3EF5TRQ2WJZ+J1uQQewo/  mXnTZnbHsM+aLy3AgMBAAEwDQYJ
KoZIhvcNAQEBBQADQQCQIrhq5UmsPYzwzKVHIiLDD  nkYunbhUpSNaBfUSYdv1AU1
Ic/37OrdN/E1ZmOutOMbCWIXKrOJk5q8F6T1bqwe
--END CERTIFICATE-
```

Save the certificate file to a location that you can access when using IIS Manager. You should use .cer as the file extension. Then process and install the certificate as described in the "Processing Pending Requests and Installing Site Certificates" section of this chapter.

Submitting Certificate Requests to Certificate Services

After you create a CSR, you can submit it to Active Directory Certificate Services by using the Web-based interface. To do this, complete the following steps:

1. The CSR is stored as ASCII text in the file you specified in Step 6 in the "Creating Certificate Requests" section. Open this file in Notepad and copy the entire text of the request, including the BEGIN and END statements, to the clipboard (press Ctrl+A and then press Ctrl+C).

2. You're now ready to submit the request to Certificate Services. Start your Web browser, and then type in the Certificate Services URL, such as *http://ca.microsoft.com/certsrv/*. You should see the main page for Certificate Services. If you don't, you might not have configured Web access correctly.

3. Select Request A Certificate.

4. On the Request A Certificate page, select Advanced Certificate Request.

5. Select Submit A Certificate Request Using A Base-64-Encoded ... Request. This option tells Certificate Services that you're going to submit a request that's Base64-encoded.

6. Paste the request into the Saved Request field (press Ctrl+V).

7. Click Submit. If you've completed this process correctly, the final page shows you that your request has been received and is pending approval by the CA. If there's a problem with the request, you'll see an error page telling you to contact your administrator for further assistance. On the error page you can click Details to get more information on the error. You might need to re-create the certificate request or go back to ensure that you haven't accidentally inserted additional spacing or characters in the request submission.

8. If you're also the CA, you can use the Certification Authority snap-in to handle the request. See the "Approving and Declining Pending Certificate Requests" section of this chapter.

Once the request has been approved, use the Web-based interface to retrieve the signed certificate. To do this, complete the following steps:

1. Start your Web browser, and then type in the Certificate Services URL, such as *http://ca.microsoft.com/certsrv/*.

2. Click View The Status Of A Pending Certificate Request.

3. You should see a list of pending requests. Requests are listed with a description and a date/time stamp. Click the request for the site you want to work with.

> **Note** If you can't access the certificate file online, you can have the certificate administrator generate the certificate manually. See the "Generating Certificates Manually in the Certification Authority Snap-In" section of this chapter.

4. If a certificate has been issued for the request, you should see a page stating that the certificate you requested was issued to you. On this page, select Base 64 Encoded, and then click Download Certificate.

5. You should see a File Download dialog box. Click Save.

6. Use the Save As dialog box to select a save location for the certificate file, click Save, then Close. You should use .cer as the file extension. Then process and install the certificate as described in the section "Processing Pending Requests and Installing Site Certificates," immediately following.

Tip   The default save location is the Downloads subfolder in your user data folder. I recommend placing all certificate files and requests in a common folder on the Web server's local file system. You should safeguard this folder so that only administrators have access.

Processing Pending Requests and Installing Site Certificates

Once you receive the certificate back from the authority, you can install it by completing the following steps:

1. In IIS Manager, select the server node, and then double-click the Server Certificates feature.

2. On the Server Certificates page, you'll see a list of certificates that the Web server can use. In the Actions pane, click Complete Certificate Request.

3. Type the path and file name to the certificate file returned by the authority, or click the selection button to search for the file.

4. Type a friendly name for the certificate, such as Default Web Site.

5. Click OK. Check the SSL configuration, and manage the certificate as necessary.

Working with SSL

Installing a site certificate automatically enables SSL so that it can be used, but you might need to change the default settings. You'll need to configure and troubleshoot SSL as necessary.

Configuring SSL Ports

Once you install a certificate on a Web site, you can use a site's bindings to change the SSL port the site uses. To add a binding for SSL, follow these steps:

1. In IIS Manager, navigate to the Sites node by double-clicking the icon for the computer you want to work with, and then double-clicking Sites.

2. In the left pane, select the node for the site you want to work with.

3. In the Actions pane, click Bindings. In the Site Bindings dialog box, you'll see a list of the site's current bindings.

4. Click Add. In the Add Site Binding dialog box, select HTTPS as the Type.

5. Port 443 is used for SSL by default. As necessary, change the port value in the appropriate text box.

6. On the SSL Certificate list, select the SSL certificate the site should use. Click OK, and then click Close.

The "Configuring Ports, IP Addresses, and Host Names Used by Web Sites" section of Chapter 6, "Configuring Web Sites and Directories," provides a more detailed discussion about site bindings. A site can have multiple SSL identities (meaning that the site can answer on different SSL ports). The SSL port configured in the Web Site tab is the one the site responds to by default. All other SSL ports must be specified in the browser request. For example, if you configure SSL for ports 443, 444, and 445, a request for *https://yoursite/* is handled by port 443 automatically, but you must specify the other ports to use them, such as *https://yoursite:445/*.

Adding the CA Certificate to the Client Browser's Root Store

Most root CA certificates issued by third-party CAs are configured as trusted CAs in Web browsers. However, if you're acting as your own CA or are using a self-signed certificate, client browsers won't recognize and trust your certificate. To get browsers to trust the certificate, the user must install the certificate in the browser's authorities store.

To install the certificate, complete the following steps:

1. Connect to your site by using a secure URL that begins with *https://*.

2. The user's browser displays a security alert stating that there's a problem with the site's security certificate.

3. On the Certificate Error page, click the Continue To This Web Site link. The alert appears because the user hasn't chosen to trust your root CA or you are using a self-signed certificate.

4. When you continue to the site, a Certificate Error option appears to the right of the address field (see Figure 11-5). Click Certificate Error to display a related error dialog box, and then click View Certificates. The Certificate dialog box appears.

5. The General tab information should state that the CA Root certificate isn't trusted. To enable trust, click Install Certificate.

Figure 11-5   Note the certificate error that is being highlighted by Internet Explorer.

6. This starts the Certificate Import Wizard. Click Next.

7. Choose Automatically Select The Certificate Store Based On The Type Of Certificate, and then click Next.

8. Click Finish. The default settings allow the browser to select the certificate store based on the type of certificate.

9. Click OK in response to the successful import message that appears, and then click OK to close the Certificate dialog box. The user shouldn't see the original security alert again.

Confirming that SSL Is Correctly Enabled

Secure connections can be established only when the browser connects to the server by using a secure URL beginning with *https://*. Browsers display a warning if any embedded content (such as images) on a secure Web page are retrieved using an insecure (*http://*) connection. This warning tells users that some of the content on the page is insecure and asks them if they want to continue.

Once you've enabled SSL on your server, you should confirm that SSL is working and that the encryption level is set properly. To confirm that SSL is working in Internet Explorer, complete these steps:

1. Access your Web site by using a secure URL beginning with *https://*. In Internet Explorer 7 or later, the background of address bar turns green and a padlock icon appears to the right of the address bar to indicate that an SSL session has been established. If this does not happen, the SSL session wasn't established.

2. Right-click anywhere on the Web page, and then select Properties. This displays a Properties dialog box, which provides summary information on the Web page.

3. Click Certificates, and then on the Details tab, scroll down to display details concerning the certificates and the level of encryption used.

Resolving SSL Problems

If SSL isn't working, ensure that you've installed the server certificate on the correct Web site and that you've enabled SSL on the site. These steps should resolve a server-based SSL problem.

If the encryption level isn't what you expected, you should check to ensure that the browser supports the encryption level you're using. If a browser supports 256-bit encryption and the encryption level in use according to the browser's Properties dialog box is 128-bit, the problem is the server certificate. The server certificate must be upgraded to 256-bit encryption.

In Internet Explorer, check encryption support by completing the following steps:

1. On the Help menu, select About Internet Explorer.

2. The Cipher Strength field shows the level of encryption supported. You must have 256-bit support to establish a 256-bit session. After viewing the encryption level, click OK.

3. On the Tools menu, select Internet Options. In the Internet Options dialog box, select the Advanced tab.

4. Scroll down through the Advanced options until you see the Security heading. Ensure that Use SSL 3.0 is selected, and then click OK.

Ignoring, Accepting, and Requiring Client Certificates

Client certificates allow users to authenticate themselves through their Web browser. You might want to use client certificates if you have a secure external Web site, such as an extranet. If a Web site accepts or requires client certificates, you can configure client certificate mappings that permit access control to resources based on client certificates. A client certificate mapping can be mapped to a specific Windows account using a one-to-one mapping, or it can be mapped based on rules you specify.

By default, IIS doesn't accept or require client certificates. You can change this behavior. Keep in mind that *accepting* client certificates isn't the same as *requiring* client certificates. When a site requires client certificates, the site is secured for access using SSL only and can't be accessed using standard HTTP. When a site accepts client certificates rather than requiring them, the site can use either HTTP or Hypertext Transfer Protocol Secure (HTTPS) for communications.

To configure client certificate usage, follow these steps:

1. In IIS Manager, select the Web site you want to manage, and then double-click the SSL Settings feature.

2. If you want to require SSL (and preclude the use of insecure communications), select Require SSL. Optionally, you can also select Require 128-Bit SSL if your server has a 128-bit encryption installed and enabled.

3. Under Client Certificates, select the Ignore, Accept, or Require option as necessary, and then click Apply to save your settings.

Note   You can require client certificates only when secure SSL communications are also required. Because of this, you must select the Require SSL check box when you want to require client certificates. If you want to map client certificates to Windows user accounts, enable Active Directory Client Certificate Authentication at the server level.

Requiring SSL for All Communications

In some cases you'll want to create sites that can be accessed using only secure communications. You can do this by requiring SSL and prohibiting the use of insecure communications. To require SSL for communications with a Web site, follow these steps:

1. In IIS Manager, select the Web site you want to manage, and then double-click the SSL Settings feature.

2. If you want to require SSL (and preclude the use of insecure communications), select Require SSL. Optionally, you can also select Require 128-Bit if your server has a 128-bit encryption installed and enabled. Click Apply to save your settings.

Chapter 12

Performance Tuning, Monitoring, and Tracing

Monitoring, performance tuning, and tracing are essential parts of Web administration. You monitor servers to ensure that they're running smoothly and to troubleshoot problems as they occur. You tune the performance of servers to achieve optimal performance based on the current system resources and traffic load. When you have problems that cannot be resolved by performance tuning or diagnosed through standard monitoring, you can use tracing to get detailed diagnostic information about failed requests that allows you to track a request from its start, through individual filter and module notifications, to its end. With the addition of performance statistics, authentication and authorization details, and internal tracing of Microsoft ASP.NET pages, failed request tracing is the definitive power tool for determining the exact cause of request failure whether you are developing or deploying new applications, Web pages, or Web sites.

Monitoring IIS Performance and Activity

Windows Server 2008 includes several tools that you can use to monitor Internet Information Services (IIS). The key tools are the Performance Monitor, Reliability Monitor, Microsoft Windows event logs, and the IIS access logs. You'll often use the results of your monitoring to optimize IIS. Monitoring IIS isn't something you should do haphazardly. You need to have a clear plan—a set of goals that you hope to achieve. Let's look at some reasons that you might want to monitor IIS and the tools you can use to do this.

Why Monitor IIS?

Troubleshooting performance problems is a key reason for monitoring. For example, users might be having problems connecting to the server, and you might want to monitor the server to troubleshoot these problems. Here, your goals would be to track down the problem by using the available monitoring resources and then to solve it.

Another common reason for wanting to monitor IIS is to use the results to improve server performance. Improving server performance can reduce the need for costly additional servers or additional hardware components, such as CPUs and memory. This allows you to squeeze additional processing power out of the server and budget for when you really must purchase new servers and components.

To achieve optimal performance, you must identify performance bottlenecks, maximize throughput, and minimize the time it takes for Web applications to process user requests. You achieve this by:

- Monitoring memory and CPU usage and taking appropriate steps to reduce the load on the server, as necessary. Other processes running on the server might be using memory and CPU resources needed by IIS. Resolve this issue by stopping nonessential services and moving support applications to a different server.

- Resolving hardware issues that might be causing problems. If slow disk drives are delaying file reads, work on improving disk input/output (I/O). If the network cards are running at full capacity, install additional network cards for performing activities such as backups or load balancing.

- Optimizing Web pages and applications running on IIS. You should test Web pages and IIS applications to ensure that the source code performs as expected. Eliminate unnecessary procedures and optimize inefficient processes.

Unfortunately, there are often tradeoffs to be made when it comes to resource usage. For example, as the number of users accessing IIS grows, you might not be able to reduce the network traffic load, but you might be able to improve server performance by optimizing Web pages and IIS applications.

> **Tip** Don't overlook the value of IIS failed request tracing in your optimization efforts for dynamic pages. In a failed request trace, the Performance View shows the exact duration of each step in the request handling process, and other views can also provide important clues about processing delays.

Getting Ready to Monitor

Before you start monitoring IIS, you should establish baseline performance metrics for your server. To do this, measure server performance at various times and under different load conditions. You can then compare the baseline performance with subsequent performance to determine how IIS is performing. Performance metrics that are well above the baseline measurements might indicate areas where the server needs to be optimized or reconfigured.

After you establish the baseline metrics, you should formulate a monitoring plan. A comprehensive monitoring plan involves the following steps:

1. Determine which server resources should be monitored to help you accomplish your goal.

2. Set filters to reduce the amount of information collected.

3. Configure performance counters to measure the resource usage.

4. Log the usage data so that it can be analyzed.

5. Analyze the usage data and replay the data as necessary to find a solution.

These procedures are examined later in this chapter in the "Monitoring IIS Performance and Reliability" section. Although in most cases you should develop a monitoring plan, there are times when you might not want to go through all these steps to monitor IIS. In this case, use the steps that make sense for your situation.

The primary tools you'll use to monitor IIS are:

- **Windows Performance Monitor**   Configure counters to watch resource usage over time. Use the usage information to gauge the performance of IIS and determine areas that can be optimized.

- **Windows Reliability Monitor**   Tracks changes to the system and compares them to changes in system stability, thus giving you a graphical representation of the relationship between changes in the system configuration and changes in system stability.

- **IIS Access logs**   Use information in the access logs to find problems with pages, applications, and IIS. Entries logged with a status code beginning with a 4 or 5 indicate a potential problem. Access logs can be written in several different formats, including IIS log file format, National Center for Supercomputing Applications (NCSA) Common Log File Format, and World Wide Web Consortium (W3C) Extended Log File Format.

- **Windows Event logs**   Use information in the event logs to troubleshoot system-wide problems, including those from the operating system, IIS, and other configured applications. The primary logs you'll want to work with are the System, Security, and Application event logs.

Detecting and Resolving IIS Errors

IIS records errors in three locations: the IIS access logs, the Windows event logs, and the failed request trace logs. In the access logs, you'll find information related to missing resources, failed authentication, and internal server errors. In the event logs, you'll find IIS errors, failed authentication, IIS application errors, and errors related to other applications running on the server. In the failed request trace logs, you'll find detailed diagnostic traces of specific types of failed requests.

Examining the Access Logs

Access logs are created when you enable logging as discussed in Chapter 13, "Tracking User Access and Logging." Every time someone requests a file from a site, an entry goes into the access log, making the access log a running history of resource requests. Because each entry has a status code, you can examine entries to determine the success or failure of a request. Failed requests have a status code beginning with a 4 or 5.

The most common error you'll see is a 404 error, which indicates that a resource wasn't found at the expected location. You can correct this problem by:

- Placing the file in the expected location.

- Renaming the file if the current name is different than expected.

- Modifying the linking file to reflect the file's correct name and location.

If you want to find the access log for a particular site, select the node for the server you want to manage in IIS Manager. If the server you want to use isn't listed, connect to it. In the main pane, the Logging feature is listed under IIS when you group by area. Double-click Logging to open this feature. You should now see the current top-level logging configuration.

The Directory field shows the base directory for this site's access logs. The default base directory is *%SystemDrive%*\Inetpub\Logs\LogFiles. You'll find the site's logs in a subdirectory of the base directory. Typically, subdirectories for sites are named W3SVC*N* where *N* is the index number of the service or a random tracking value. An example of such a subdirectory name is W3CSVC1.

The current log is the file in this subdirectory with the most recent date and time stamp. All other logs are archive files that could be moved to a history directory.

Now that you know where the log files are located for the site, you can search for errors in the log file. Because logs are stored as either American Standard Code of Information Interchange (ASCII) text or Unicode Transformation Format 8 (UTF-8), one way to do this would be to open a log in Microsoft Notepad or another text editor and search for error codes, such as 404. Another way to search for errors would be to use the FIND command from a command-prompt window to search the log files. At an elevated command prompt, you could search for 404 errors in any log file within the current directory by using the following command:

```
find "404" *
```

Once you identify missing files, you can use any of the previously recommended techniques to resolve the problem. You'll learn more about access logs and status codes in Chapter 13.

> **Note** I use the term *elevated command prompt* to refer to a command prompt being run with administrator credentials. To run a command prompt as an administrator, click Start, point to All Programs and then Accessories, right-click Command Prompt, and then select Run As Administrator. When prompted, provide consent for elevation by clicking Continue or providing the appropriate administrator credentials. Then click OK.

Examining the Windows Event Logs

Windows event logs provide historical information that can help you track down problems with services, processes, and applications. The Windows Event Log service controls the events that are tracked. When this service is started, user actions and resource usage events can be tracked through the event logs. Two general types of log files are used:

- **Windows logs**   Logs that the operating system uses to record general system events related to applications, security, setup, and system components

- **Application and service logs**   Logs that specific applications and services use to record application-specific or service-specific events

You access the Windows event logs by completing the following steps:

1. Click Start, point to Administrative Tools, and then select Event Viewer. This starts Event Viewer.

2. As shown in Figure 12-1, Event Viewer displays logs for the local computer by default. If you want to view logs on a remote computer, right-click Event Viewer in the console tree (left pane), and then select Connect To Another Computer. In the Select Computer dialog box, type the name of the computer you want to access, and then click OK.

   > **Tip**   You can connect to another server also by using alternate credentials. To do this, select the Connect As Another User check box, and then click Set User. After you select or type the account name to use in the form *DOMAIN\UserName*, such as CPANLD\WilliamS, type the account password, and then click OK.

3. You can now work with the server's event logs in the following ways:

   ❑ To view all errors and warnings for all logs, expand Custom Views, and then select Administrative Events. In the main pane you should now see a list of all warning and error events for the server.

   ❑ To view all errors and warnings for a specific server role, expand Custom Views, expand ServerRoles, and then select the role to view. In the main pane you should now see a list of all warning and error events for the selected role.

   ❑ To view events in a specific log, expand the Windows Logs node, the Applications And Services Logs node, or both nodes. Select the log you want to view, such as Application or System.

4. Use the information in the Source column to determine which service or process logged a particular event.

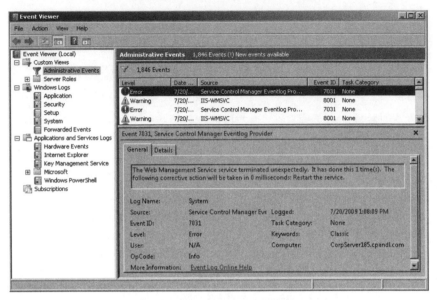

Figure 12-1 Event Viewer displays events according to their source.

Entries in the main pane of Event Viewer provide a quick overview of when, where, and how an event occurred. To obtain detailed information on an event, review the details provided on the General tab in the lower portion of the main window. The event level or keyword precedes the date and time of the event. Event levels include:

- **Information** An informational event, which is generally related to a successful action.

- **Audit Success** An event related to the successful execution of an action.

- **Audit Failure** An event related to the failed execution of an action.

- **Warning** A warning. Details for warnings are often useful in preventing future system problems.

- **Error** An error, such as the failure of a service to start.

  Note Warnings and errors are the two key types of events that you'll want to examine closely. Whenever these types of events occur and you're unsure of the cause, review the detailed event description.

In addition to level, date, and time logged, the summary and detailed event entries provide the following information:

- **Source** The application, service, or component that logged the event

- **Event ID**   Generally a numeric identifier for the specific event, which could be helpful when searching knowledge bases

- **Task Category**   The category of the event, which is almost always set to None but is sometimes used to further describe the related action, such as a process or a service

- **User**   The user account that was logged on when the event occurred, if applicable

- **Computer**   The name of the computer on which the event occurred

- **Description**   In the detailed entries, a text description of the event

- **Data**   In the detailed entries, any data or error code output by the event

The sources you'll want to look for include those summarized in Table 12-1.

Table 12-1   Key Event Sources for Tracking IIS Issues

Event Source	Related System Component
.NET Runtime	Microsoft .NET Framework service
.NET Runtime Optimization Service	Microsoft .NET Framework optimization processes
Active Server Pages (ASP)	Applications and ASP engines
ASP.NET	ASP.NET State Service and other ASP.NET processes
CertificateServices-Client	Authorization and authentication through the Certificate Services client
CertificationAuthority	Certificate Authorities (CAs)
Hostable Web Core	Web Management Service
IISADMIN	IIS Admin Service
IIS-IISManager	Management and configuration processes performed in IIS Manager
IISInfoCtrs	IIS information counters
IIS-W3SVC-PerfCounters	World Wide Web Service performance counters
IIS-W3SVC-WP	World Wide Web Service worker processes
MSDTC	Microsoft Distributed Transaction Coordinator service
MSDTC Client	Client processes when using MS DTC

If you want to see a particular type of event, you can filter the log by completing the following steps:

1. In Event Viewer, select the log you want to work with.

2. In the Actions pane or on the Action menu, click Filter Current Log. This opens the dialog box shown in Figure 12-2.

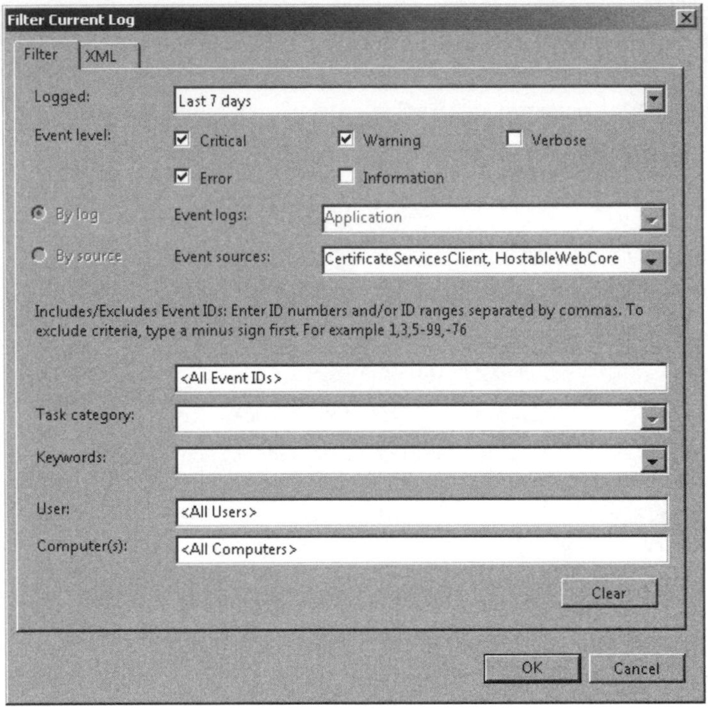

Figure 12-2 You can filter logs so that only specific events are displayed.

3. From the Logged drop-down list, select the included time frame for logged events. You can choose to include events from the Last Hour, Last 12 Hours, Last 24 Hours, Last 7 Days, or Last 30 Days.

4. Select the desired Event Level check boxes to specify the level of events to include. Select Verbose to get additional detail.

5. From the Event Source drop-down list, select the event sources to include, such as .NET Runtime and Active Server Pages, and then click OK.

6. You should now see a filtered list of events. Review these events carefully and take steps to correct any problems that exist. To clear the filter and see all events for the log, in the Actions pane, click Clear Filter.

Examining the Trace Logs

Trace logs allow you to track a failed request from its start, through internal IIS notifications and authentication requests, to its end. Because tracing failed requests can degrade a server's performance, you should enable failed request tracing only when you need to perform detailed diagnostics for troubleshooting. Once you've diagnosed an issue, you should then disable failed request tracing.

Tracing Failed Requests

Failed request tracing is designed to help administrators and developers more easily identify and track failed requests. In previous versions of IIS, you could check for certain HTTP error codes in the IIS logs to identify failed requests, but you could not easily get detailed trace information that would help resolve related issues. With IIS 7.0, request traces can be logged automatically when an error code is generated or when the time taken for a request exceeds a specified duration. For general tracing for debugging or other purposes, you can also configure general tracing on a per-URL basis.

To perform traces, the HTTP Tracing role service must be installed and enabled on the IIS server. Although you can configure the types of failed requests to trace globally for all Web sites and applications on a server, you enable and configure failed request tracing at the site level. Unlike other types of logging, each failed request is stored in a separate file in the logging directory.

Because trace files are named sequentially, starting with FR000001.xml, the file for the most recent failed request is the one with the highest numeric suffix and the most recent date and time stamp. Also in the trace directory is an XSL style sheet (FREB.xsl) that specifies the formatting for trace files when displayed in a Web browser, such as Internet Explorer.

You control the way tracing works by instituting Failed Request Tracing Rules. In IIS Manager, you can view the currently configured trace rules for a server, site, virtual directory, or application by selecting the node for the level you want to manage and then in the main pane, double-clicking Failed Request Tracing Rules. When you are working with failed request tracing rules, as shown in Figure 12-3, rules listed as Local are created at the level you selected. Rules listed as Inherited are created at a higher level.

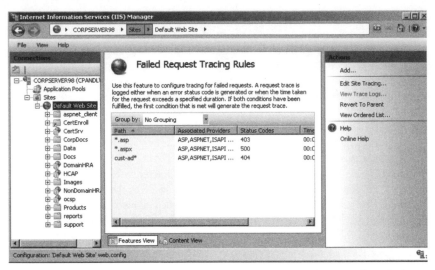

Figure 12-3 You can review the currently configured trace rules by using the Failed Request Tracing feature.

IIS traces a request whenever the trace rule criteria are reached. With each trace rule, you must specify precisely the types of failures to track according to the following criteria:

- **Path** The URL path to trace, which can contain one wildcard at most and must be within the context of the level at which the definition is enabled. For example, you could use the path *.aspx to trace failed requests for ASP.NET pages, or you could use the path page* to trace failed requests for any type of document whose name begins with page, such as page1.asp, paged.aspx, or pages.htm.

- **Condition** The conditions under which a request should be traced, including event severity (Error, Critical Error, or Warning), HTTP status code, and Time Taken. For general tracing, you can also trace information and other non-error events.

- **Trace Provider** The functional area for tracing according to the provider that traces a request, including ASP, ASP.NET, ISAPI extension, and WWW server.

Failed requests can be traced through one or more of the following providers:

- **ASP** Traces the failed request through Active Server Pages (*%Windir%*\System32\Inetsrv\Asp.dll). Use this provider when you want to trace the start and completion of ASP requests.

- **ASP.NET** Traces the failed request through ASP.NET (*%SystemRoot%*\Microsoft.NET\Framework\v2.0.50727\Aspnet_isapi.dll or

%SystemRoot%\Microsoft.NET\Framework\v2.0.50727\Webengine.dll). Use this provider when you want to see transitions into and out of managed code. This includes requests for .aspx pages and any other request processed through managed modules, such as forms-based authentication for static content.

- **ISAPI Extension**   Traces the failed request through ISAPI extension for ASP.NET (*%SystemRoot%*\Microsoft.NET\Framework\v2.0.50727\Aspnet_filter.dll). Use this provider when you want to trace the transition of a request into and out of an ISAPI extension process.

- **WWW Server**   Traces the failed request through the IIS server core. Use this provider when you want to trace requests through IIS worker processes.

When you specify a provider to use, you can set the tracking verbosity as:

- **General**   Trace general information about a request.

- **Critical Errors**   Trace critical errors related to a request.

- **Errors**   Trace standard errors related to a request.

- **Warnings**   Trace warnings related to a request.

- **Information**   Trace information events related to a request.

- **Verbose**   Trace all available information and errors related to a request.

By using ASP.NET, you can specify the area within managed modules to trace as any combination of the following:

- **Infrastructure**   Traces the failed request through ASP.NET infrastructure. Use when you want to trace events that are related primarily to entering and leaving various parts of the ASP.NET infrastructure.

- **Module**   Traces the failed request through HTTP pipeline-related modules, managed modules, or both. Use when you want to trace events that are logged when a request enters and leaves HTTP pipeline and/or managed modules.

- **Page**   Traces page load, trace write, and trace warn events for failed requests. Use when you want to generate trace events that correspond to specific ASP.NET page–related events.

- **AppServices**   Traces the failed request through application services. Use when you want to trace events logged as part of the application services functionality.

By using WWW Server, you can specify the area within the IIS server core to trace as any combination of the following:

- **Authentication**   Traces the failed request through authentication-related modules. Use when you want to trace authentication attempts, including the name of the authenticated user, the authentication method, and the results of the authentication attempt.

- **Security**   Traces the failed request through system security. Use when you want to trace events when requests are rejected by the server for security-related reasons, such as when a client is denied access to a resource because of insufficient permissions.

- **Filter**   Traces the failed request through the IsapiFilterModule, the Request-FilteringModule, or both. Use when you want to determine how long it takes an ISAPI filter to process requests.

- **StaticFile**   Traces the failed request through the StaticFile module. Use when you want to trace how long it takes requests for static files to be completed or to see how filters might be changing requests.

- **CGI**   Traces the failed request through the CgiModule. Use when a request is made for a CGI file and you want to trace execution through the CgiModule.

- **Compression**   Traces the failed request through the StaticCompressionModule or the DynamicCompressionModule. Use when a response is compressed and you want to trace execution through these compression-related modules.

- **Cache**   Traces the failed request through cache-related modules. Use when you want to generate trace events for cache operations associated with a request.

- **RequestNotifications**   Traces the failed request through the RequestMonitor-Module. Use when you want to capture all request notifications from start to completion.

Enabling and Configuring Failed Request Tracing

You can enable and configure failed request tracing for a site by completing the following steps:

1. In IIS Manager, select the node for the server you want to manage. If the server you want to use isn't listed, connect to it.

2. In the main pane, when you group by area, the Failed Request Tracing Rules feature is listed under IIS. Double-click Failed Request Tracing Rules to open this feature. You should now see the currently set rules for failed request tracing (if any). Rules listed as Local, under Entry Type, are set for the site you selected. Rules listed as Inherited are set at the server level.

3. In the Actions pane, click Edit Site Tracing. This displays the Failed Request Tracing Settings dialog box shown in Figure 12-4.

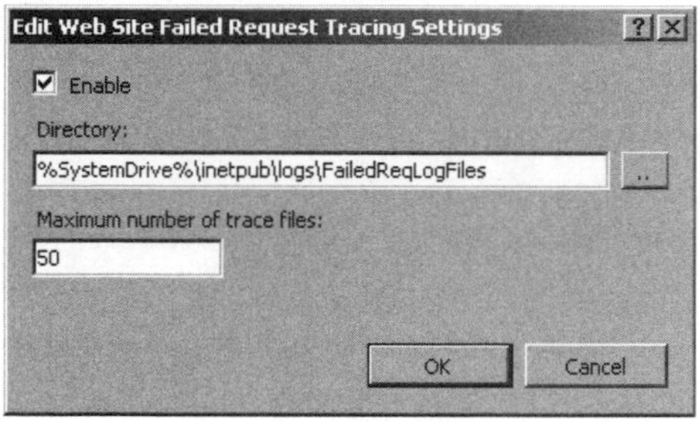

Figure 12-4   You can enable and configure failed request tracing as necessary for advanced diagnostics.

4. If trace logging is currently disabled, all logging options are unavailable and cannot be selected. To enable trace logging select the Enable checkbox in the Failed Request Tracing Settings dialog box.

5. By default, trace log files are located in a subdirectory under *%SystemDrive%* Inetpub\Logs\FailedReqLogfiles. If you want to change the default logging directory, in the Directory field, type the directory path, or click the selection button to look for a directory that you want to use.

6. Unlike other types of logging, each failed request is stored in a separate file in the logging directory. Type a value in the Maximum Number Of Trace Files text box to specify the maximum number of trace files to store at one time, and then click OK to save your settings.

Real World   When the maximum value is reached, IIS deletes an old trace file before creating a new one. The default maximum number of trace files is 50. Although you should rarely perform live tracing on a production server (because doing so could degrade performance considerably), you may need to raise this value on a busy enterprise server to ensure that files are available for the types of failed requests you want to track.

Creating and Managing Trace Rules

You can create a trace rule by completing the following steps:

1. In IIS Manager, access the Failed Request Tracing Rules feature for the server, site, virtual directory, or application you want to manage.

2. In the Actions pane, click Add. This starts the Add Failed Request Tracing Rule Wizard.

3. As shown in Figure 12-5, specify the type of content to trace as one of the following, and then click Next:

- ❑ **All Content (*)**   Configures tracing for all file requests that match the rule criteria.

- ❑ **ASP.NET**   Configures tracing for all ASP.NET file requests that match the rule criteria and have the .aspx file extension.

- ❑ **ASP**   Configures tracing for all ASP file requests that match the rule criteria and have the .asp file extension.

- ❑ **Custom**   Configures tracing based on the value entered, which can contain, at most, one wildcard character. The valid characters are A–Z, a–z, +, –, ., / and the wildcard character (*).

Tip   Trace rules must be unique. You can create only one trace rule for *, *.aspx, and *.asp. You can create only one trace rule for each unique custom trace path.

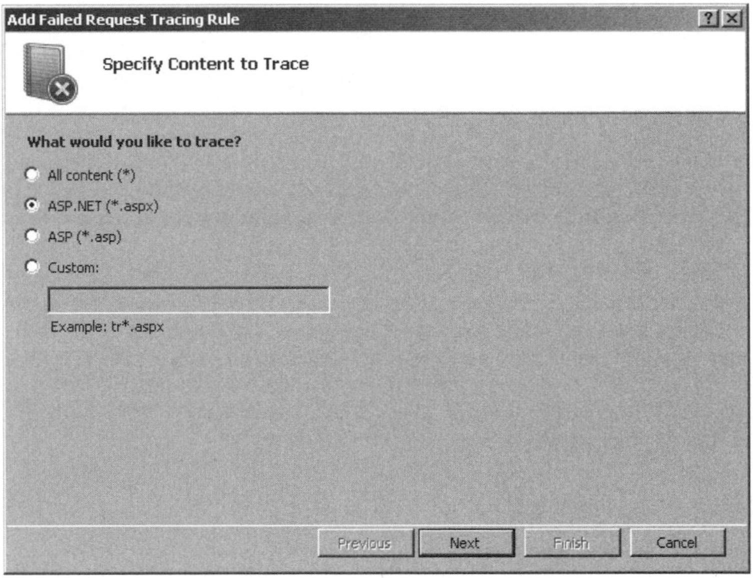

Figure 12-5   Specify the type of content to trace.

4. As shown in Figure 12-6, specify one or more of the following conditions under which IIS should trace a request, and then click Next:

- ❑ **Status Code(s)**   Select the related check box, and then type the HTTP status codes and substatus code combinations to trace. Use a period between an HTTP status code and its optional substatus code. Use a comma to separate multiple entries. A request meets this condition if it causes IIS to generate any one of the listed status codes.

❑ **Time Taken (In Seconds)**   Select the related check box, and then type a Time Taken value in seconds. A request meets this condition if it takes longer to process the response than the specified value. This condition must be selected with another condition.

❑ **Event Severity**   Select the related check box, and then choose a severity level of events to trace. The severity levels you can choose from are Error, Critical Error, and Warning. A request meets this condition if it causes IIS to generate one or more events with the specified severity level. This condition must be selected with another condition.

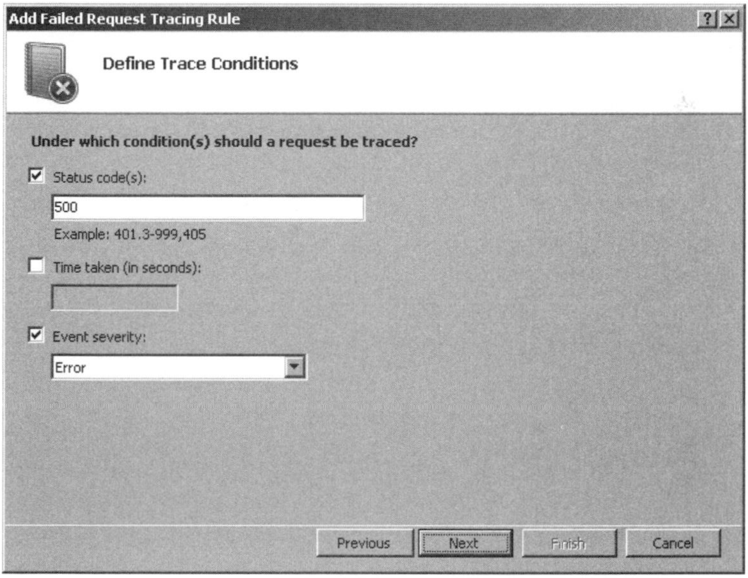

Figure 12-6   Specify the conditions that trigger a trace.

5. As shown in Figure 12-7, specify the providers to trace by selecting or clearing providers.

6. To select a provider, select its check box. Then in the Verbosity drop-down list, you can set the types of related events to trace, or you can elect to trace all related events for that provider. The Verbosity drop-down list is designed so that when you select a level, all preceding levels in the list are included. For example, if you select Errors, General and Critical Errors are also included because they precede General in the list. The default level is Verbose, which as the last level in the list, includes all the others.

The Verbosity drop-down list contains the following levels:

❑ **General**   Includes general informational events that provide context information for the request activity, such as GENERAL_REQUEST_START (which logs the URL and the verb for the request) and GENERAL_REQUEST_END (which logs the bytes sent and bytes received), HTTP status code, and substatus code generated. General includes GENERAL_, FILTER_, and MODULE_ that do not contain warnings or errors. It does not include other notification or informational events, such as those that begin with PRE_BEGIN_, NOTIFY_, or AUTH_.

❑ **Critical Errors**   Includes critical error events that provide information about actions that cause a process to end or that are about to cause a process to end. As a result of critical errors, IIS generally stops processing a request.

❑ **Errors**   Includes general errors that provide information about components that encounter an error when running and cannot continue to process requests. As a result of general errors, IIS usually stops processing a request.

❑ **Warnings**   Includes warning events that provide information about components that encounter a warning when running but can continue to process requests.

❑ **Information**   Includes informational events that provide general information about requests. Information includes all informational events but does not include notification events, such as those that begin with PRE_BEGIN_ or NOTIFY_.

❑ **Verbose**   Includes all events and notifications to provide detailed information about requests from start to finish.

Real World   To get a complete picture of a request from start to finish, you'll need to use the Verbosity level of Verbose. However, as you track additional types of events and notifications, IIS generates more and more information about a request, resulting in increasing resource usage. For example, on a server with most role services enabled, IIS generated 115–175 KB of data for a failed request at a Verbose level. On the other hand, with a Warnings level (which includes General, Critical Errors, Errors, and Warnings) IIS generated trace files of 8–12 KB. And with an Information level (which includes General, Critical Errors, Errors, Warnings, and Information) IIS generated trace files of 29–52 KB.

7. When you select the ASPNET or WWW Server provider in the Areas section, select the check box(es) for the specific areas to track. By default, all areas are selected.

8. Click Finish to create the trace rule.

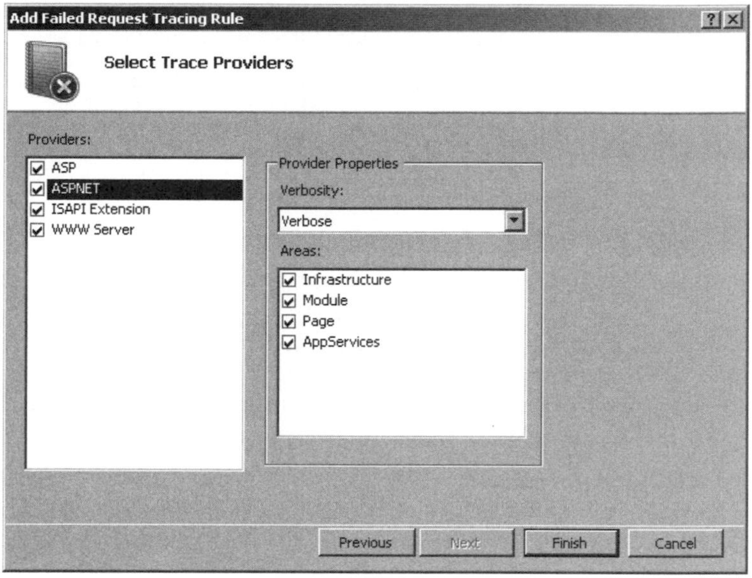

Figure 12-7   Specify the providers to trace.

To edit an existing trace rule, in the main pane, click the rule, and then in the Actions pane, select Edit. To remove a trace rule, in the main pane, select Remove, and then click Yes to confirm that you want to remove the rule. If you remove a rule at a level lower than the one for which it was originally set, you delete the rule only at that level of the configuration hierarchy.

Monitoring IIS Performance and Reliability

Performance tuning is as much an art as it is a science. You often tune performance based on trial and error. You adjust the server, monitor the server's performance over time, and then gauge the success of the updated settings. If things aren't working as expected, you adjust the settings again. In an ideal world, while tuning server performance, you'd have staging or development servers that are similar in configuration to your production servers. Then once you've made adjustments that worked in staging, you could configure these changes on the production servers.

Using the Reliability And Performance Console

The Reliability And Performance Monitor console is the tool of choice for performance tuning. To access a stand-alone console, click Start, point to Administrative Tools, and then click Reliability And Performance Monitor. In Server Manager, you can access this tool as a snap-in under the Diagnostics node. Double-click the Diagnostics node to expand it, then double-click the Reliability And Performance node. With the Reliability

And Performance node selected, you see an overview of resource usage. As shown in Figure 12-8, the resource usage statistics are broken down into four categories:

- **CPU Usage** The summary details show the current CPU utilization and the maximum CPU utilization. If you expand the CPU entry below the graph (by clicking the options button), you'll see a list of currently running executables including name, process ID, description, number of threads used, current CPU utilization, and average CPU utilization.

- **Disk Usage** The summary details show the number of kilobytes per second being read from or written to disk and the highest percentage usage. If you expand the Disk entry below the graph (by clicking the options button), you'll see a list of currently running executables that are performing or have performed I/O operations including name, process ID, description, file being read or written, number of bytes being read per minute, number of bytes being written per minute, I/O priority, and the associated disk response time.

- **Network Usage** The summary details show the current network bandwidth utilization in kilobytes and the percentage of total bandwidth utilization. If you expand the Network entry below the graph (by clicking the options button), you see a list of currently running executables that are transferring or have transferred data on the network, including name, process ID, IP address being contacted, number of bytes being sent per minute, number of bytes received per minute, and total bytes sent or received per minute.

- **Memory Usage** The summary details show the current memory utilization and the number of hard faults occurring per second. If you expand the Memory entry below the graph (by clicking the options button), you'll see a list of currently running executables including name, process ID, hard faults per minute, commit memory in kilobytes, working set memory in kilobytes, shareable memory in kilobytes, and private (non-shareable) memory in kilobytes.

In the Reliability And Performance Monitor console, you'll find two additional tools under Monitoring tools:

- Performance Monitor
- Reliability Monitor

Performance Monitor graphically displays statistics for the set of performance parameters you've selected for display. These performance parameters are referred to as *counters*. When you install IIS on a system, Performance Monitor is updated with a set of counters for tracking IIS performance. You can further update these counters when you install additional services and add-ons for IIS.

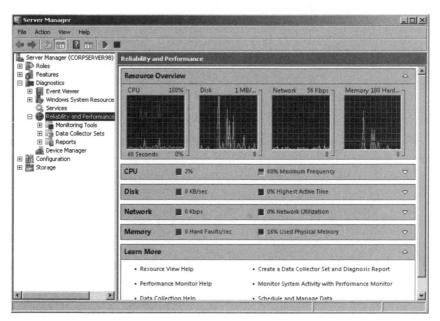

Figure 12-8   Review the resource usage on the server.

As Figure 12 9 shows, Performance Monitor creates a graph depicting the counters you're tracking. The update interval for this graph is configurable but is set to 1 second by default. As you'll see when you work with Performance Monitor, the tracking information is most valuable when you record performance information in a log file so that it can be replayed. Also, you can use Performance Monitor to configure alerts that send messages when certain events occur, such as when an automatic IIS restart is triggered.

The Reliability And Performance Monitor console also includes Reliability Monitor, shown in Figure 12-10. Reliability Monitor tracks changes to the server and compares them to changes in system stability. In this way, you can see a graphical representation of the relationship between changes in the system configuration and changes in system stability. By recording software installation, software removal, application failures, hardware failures, Windows failures, and key events regarding the configuration of the server, you can see a timeline of changes in both the server and its reliability, and then you can use this information to pinpoint changes that are causing problems with stability. For example, if you see a sudden drop in stability, you can click a data point and then expand the related data set, such as Application Failures or Hardware Failures, to find the specific event that caused the drop in stability.

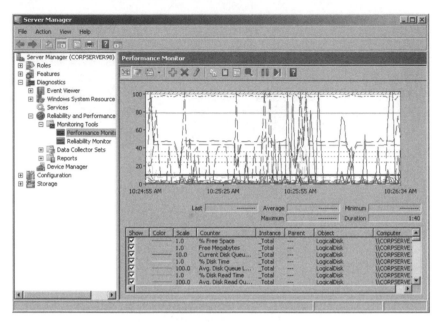

Figure 12-9 Review performance measurements for the server.

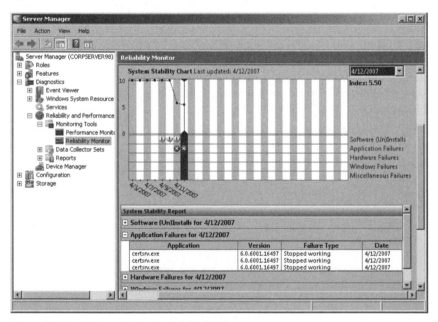

Figure 12-10 Review reliability statistics for the server.

Windows Server 2008 also introduces Data Collector Sets and Reports. Data Collector Sets allow you to specify sets of performance objects and counters that you want to track. Once you've created a Data Collector Set, you can easily start or stop monitoring of the performance objects and counters included in the set. In a way, this makes Data Collector Sets similar to the performance logs used in earlier releases of Windows. However, Data Collector Sets are much more sophisticated. A single data set can be used to generate multiple performance counters and trace logs. You can also:

- Assign access controls to manage who can access collected data.

- Create multiple run schedules and stop conditions for monitoring.

- Use data managers to control the size of collected data and reporting.

- Generate reports based on collected data.

In the Reliability And Performance Monitor console, you can review currently configured Data Collector Sets and reports under the Data Collector Sets and Reports nodes respectively. You'll find data sets and reports that are user-defined and system-defined. User-defined data sets are created by users for general monitoring and performance tuning. System-defined data sets are created by the operating system to aid in automated diagnostics.

Choosing Counters to Monitor

The Performance Monitor tool displays information only for counters you're tracking. IIS counters are related to different IIS services; several hundred IIS counters are available in total. Counters are organized into object groupings. For example, all ASP-related counters are associated with the Active Server Pages performance object. You'll also find object counters for other services. A list of the main IIS-related counter objects follows:

- **ASP.NET** Object counters for general tracking of ASP.NET applications, application requests, and worker processes

- **ASP.NET Applications** Object counters for tracking the ASP.NET application queue and other specific ASP.NET application counters

- **ASP.NET State Service** Object counters for tracking ASP.NET sessions

- **Active Server Pages** Object counters for ASP scripts and applications running on the server

- **HTTP Service, HTTP Service Request Queues, HTTP Service URL Groups** Object counters for URLs, cached URLs, HTTP requests, and other HTTP-related functions of IIS

- **Internet Information Services Global** Object counters for all Internet services (WWW, FTP, SMTP, NNTP, and so on) running on the server

- **Web Service**   Object counters for the World Wide Web Publishing Service

- **Web Service Cache**   Object counters that provide detailed information on the cache used by the Web service, including cache for metadata, files, memory, and Uniform Resource Identifiers (URIs)

The easiest way to learn about these counters is to read the explanations available in the Add Counters dialog box. Start the Performance Monitor tool, then on the toolbar, click the Add button, and then in the Available Counters list, expand an object. Select the Show Description check box, and then scroll through the list of counters for this object.

> **Tip**   Multiple versions of ASP.NET can be installed. As a result, the ASP.NET and ASP Applications counter objects have version-specific instances. Use the counter objects for the specific ASP.NET versions you want to track.

When Performance Monitor is monitoring a particular object, it can track all instances of all counters for that object. Instances are individual occurrences of a particular counter; multiple occurrences can exist. For example, when you track counters for the Web Service object, you often have a choice of tracking all Web site instances or specific Web site instances. Following this, if you configured CorpWeb, CorpProducts, and CorpServices sites, you could use Web Service counters to track a specific Web site instance or multiple Web site instances.

To select which counters you want to monitor, complete the following steps:

1. In the Reliability And Performance Monitor console, expand Monitoring Tools, and then select Performance Monitor.

2. Performance Monitor has several views and view types. Ensure that you are viewing current activity by clicking the View Current Activity button on the toolbar or pressing Ctrl+T. To switch between the view types (Line, Histogram Bar, and Report), click the Change Graph Type button or press Ctrl+G.

3. To add counters, on the toolbar, click Add, or press Ctrl+I. This displays the Add Counters dialog box.

4. In the Select Counters From Computer list box type the Universal Naming Convention (UNC) name of the IIS server you want to work with, such as \\ENGSVR01, or choose <Local computer> to work with the local computer.

> **Note**   You'll need to be at least a member of the Performance Monitor Users group in the domain or the local computer to perform remote monitoring. When you use performance logging, you'll need to be at least a member of the Performance Log Users group in the domain or the local computer to work with performance logs on remote computers.

5. In the Available Counters pane, Performance Objects are listed alphabetically. If you select an object by clicking it, all related counters are selected. If you expand an object entry, you can see all the related counters and can then add individual counters by selecting them, and then clicking Add. For example, you could expand the entry for the Active Server Pages object and then select Requests Failed Total, Requests Not Found, Requests Queued, and Requests Total counters.

6. When you select an object or any of its counters, you see the related instances. Choose All Instances to select all counter instances for monitoring. Or select one or more counter instances to monitor. For example, you could select instances of Anonymous Users/Sec for individual Web sites or for all Web sites.

7. When you've selected an object or a group of counters for an object and the object instances, click Add to add the counters to the graph. Repeat Steps 5 to 7 to add other performance parameters. Click OK when you're finished.

Tip   Don't try to chart too many counters or counter instances at once. You'll make the display too difficult to read, and you'll use system resources—namely, CPU time and memory—that might affect server responsiveness.

Tuning Web Server Performance

Now that you know how to monitor your Web servers, let's look at how you can tune the operating system and hardware performance. I'll examine the following areas:

- Memory usage and caching
- Processor utilization
- Disk I/O
- Network bandwidth and connectivity

Monitoring and Tuning Memory Usage

Memory is often the source of performance problems, and you should always rule out memory problems before examining other areas of the system. One of the key reasons memory can be such a problem has to do with caching. Caching improves performance by returning a processed copy of a requested Web page from cache, resulting in reduced overhead on the server and faster response times. IIS 7.0 supports several levels of caching, including output caching in user mode and output caching in kernel mode. When kernel-mode caching is enabled, cached responses are served from the kernel rather than from IIS user mode, giving IIS an extra boost in performance and increasing the number of requests IIS can process. Improperly configured caching settings, however, can degrade performance either by using too much memory on a server with a relatively small amount of free memory or using too little memory on a server with a relatively large amount of free memory.

The configuration of the HttpCacheModule controls the way output caching works for static files and non-managed code. OutputCacheModule provides output caching for managed code. IIS uses cache in other ways as well. FileCacheModule is used to cache file handles. TokenCacheModule is used to cache security tokens for password-based authentication. UriCacheModule is used to cache URL-specific server state information. In addition to the detailed references for these modules in the appendix, "Comprehensive IIS 7.0 Module and Schema Reference," you'll find more information on server output caching in Chapter 9, "Managing Applications, Application Pools, and Worker Processes."

A server's physical and virtual memory configuration can also present a problem. Adding memory when there's a caching or virtual memory problem on the server won't solve performance problems. Because of this, you should always check for memory, caching, and virtual memory problems at the same time. Table 12-2 provides an overview of counters that you'll want to track to uncover memory, caching, and virtual memory (paging) bottlenecks. The table is organized by issue category.

Table 12-2   Uncovering Memory-Related Bottlenecks

Issue	Counters to Track	Details
Physical and virtual memory usage	Memory \Available Kbytes; Memory \Committed Bytes	Memory\Available Kbytes is the amount of physical memory available to processes running on the server. Memory\Committed Bytes is the amount of committed virtual memory. If the server has very little available memory, you might need to add memory to the system. In general, you want the available memory to be no less than 5 percent of the total physical memory on the server. If the server has a high ratio of committed bytes to total physical memory on the system, you might also need to add memory. In general, you want the committed bytes value to be no more than 75 percent of the total physical memory.

Table 12-2   Uncovering Memory-Related Bottlenecks

Issue	Counters to Track	Details
Memory caching	Memory\Cache Bytes; Internet Information Services Global\Current File Cache Memory Usage; Internet Information Services Global \File Cache Hits %; Internet Information Services Global\File Cache Flushes	Memory\Cache Bytes represents the total size of the file system cache. Internet Information Services Global\Current File Cache Memory Usage represents the current memory used by the IIS file cache. Internet Information Services Global\File Cache Hits % represents the ratio of cache hits to total cache requests and reflects how well the settings for the IIS file cache are working. A site with mostly static files should have a very high cache hit percentage (70–85 percent). Internet Information Services Global\File Cache Flushes tells you how quickly IIS is flushing files out of cache. If flushes are occurring too quickly, you might need to increase the time-to-live value for cached objects (ObjectCacheTTL). If flushes are occurring too slowly, you might be wasting memory and might need to decrease the time-to-live value for cached objects.
Memory page faults	Memory\Page Faults/sec; Memory\Pages Input/sec; Memory\Page Reads/sec	A page fault occurs when a process requests a page in memory and the system can't find it at the requested location. If the requested page is elsewhere in memory, the fault is called a *soft page fault*. If the requested page must be retrieved from disk, the fault is called a *hard page fault*. Most processors can handle large numbers of soft faults. Hard faults, however, can cause significant delays. Page Faults/sec is the overall rate at which the processor handles all types of page faults. Pages Input/sec is the total number of pages read from disk to resolve hard page faults. Page Reads/sec is the total disk reads needed to resolve hard page faults. Pages Input/sec will be greater than or equal to Page Reads/sec and can give you a good idea of your hard page fault rate. If there is a large number of hard page faults, you might need to increase the amount of memory or reduce the cache size on the server. Memory used by IIS can be controlled by modifying cache settings.

Table 12-2   Uncovering Memory-Related Bottlenecks

Issue	Counters to Track	Details
Memory paging	Memory\Pool Paged Bytes; Memory\Pool Nonpaged Bytes	These counters track the number of bytes in the paged and nonpaged pool. The paged pool is an area of system memory for objects that can be written to disk when they aren't used. The nonpaged pool is an area of system memory for objects that can't be written to disk. If the paged pool's size is large relative to the total amount of physical memory on the system, you might need to add memory to the system. If the nonpaged pool's size is large relative to the total amount of virtual memory allocated to the server, you might want to increase the virtual memory size.

Monitoring and Tuning Processor Usage

The CPU does the actual processing of information on your server. As you examine a server's performance, you should focus on the CPUs after memory bottlenecks have been eliminated. If the server's processors are the performance bottleneck, adding memory, drives, or network connections won't overcome the problem. Instead, you might need to upgrade the processors to faster clock speeds or add processors to increase the server's processing capacity. You could also move processor-intensive applications, such as Microsoft SQL Server, to another server.

Before you decide to upgrade or add CPUs, you should rule out problems with memory and caching. If signs still point to a processor problem, you should monitor the performance counters discussed in Table 12-3. Be sure to monitor these counters for each CPU installed on the server.

Table 12-3   Uncovering Processor-Related Bottlenecks

Issue	Counters to Track	Details
Thread queuing	System\Processor Queue Length	This counter displays the number of threads waiting to be executed. These threads are queued in an area shared by all processors on the system. If this counter has a sustained value of 10 or more threads, you'll need to upgrade or add processors.
CPU usage	Processor\% Processor Time	This counter displays the percentage of time the selected CPU is executing a non-idle thread. You should track this counter separately for all processor instances on the server. If the % Processor Time values are high while the network interface and disk I/O throughput rates are relatively low, you'll need to upgrade or add processors.

Table 12-3   Uncovering Processor-Related Bottlenecks

Issue	Counters to Track	Details
ASP performance	Active Server Pages\Request Wait Time; Active Server Pages\Requests Queued; Active Server Pages\Requests Rejected; Active Server Pages\Requests/ sec	These counters indicate the relative performance of IIS when working with ASP. Active Server Pages\Request Wait Time is the number of milliseconds the most recent request was waiting in the queue. Active Server Pages\Requests Queued is the number of requests waiting to be processed. Active Server Pages\Requests Rejected is the total number of requests not executed because there weren't resources to process them. Active Server Pages\Requests/sec is the number of requests executed per second. In general, you don't want to see requests waiting in the queue, and, if requests are queuing, the wait time should be very low. You also don't want to see requests rejected because resources aren't available. Consider and treat these problems relative to the number of requests handled per second. You might notice some variance under peak loads. To resolve these issues you might need to upgrade or add processors.

Real World   In many cases a single server might not be sufficient to handle the network traffic load. If that happens, you might need to scale your site across multiple servers. For example, you could replicate the site to additional servers and then distribute the traffic across these servers by using a load balancer. If you already have a multiple-server Web farm, you could add Web servers.

Monitoring and Tuning Disk I/O

With today's high-speed disks, the disk throughput rate is rarely the cause of a bottleneck. That said, however, accessing memory is much faster than accessing disks. So if the server has to do a lot of disk reads and writes, the server's overall performance can be degraded. To reduce the amount of disk I/O, you want the server to manage memory very efficiently and page to disk only when necessary. You monitor and tune memory usage as discussed previously in the "Monitoring and Tuning Memory Usage" section of this chapter.

Beyond the memory tuning discussion, you can monitor some counters to gauge disk I/O activity. Specifically, you should monitor the counters discussed in Table 12-4.

Table 12-4   Uncovering Drive-Related Bottlenecks

Issue	Counters to Track	Details
Overall drive performance	PhysicalDisk\% Disk Time in conjunction with Processor\% Processor Time and Network Interface\Bytes Total/sec	If the % Disk Time value is high and the processor and network connection values aren't high, the system's hard disk drives might be creating a bottleneck. Be sure to monitor % Disk Time for all hard disk drives on the server.
Disk I/O	PhysicalDisk\Disk Writes /sec; PhysicalDisk\Disk Reads/sec; PhysicalDisk \Avg. Disk Write Queue Length; PhysicalDisk\Avg. Disk Read Queue Length; Physical Disk\Current Disk Queue Length	The number of writes and reads per second tells you how much disk I/O activity there is. The write and read queue lengths tell you how many write or read requests are waiting to be processed. In general, you want there to be very few waiting requests. Keep in mind that the request delays are proportional to the length of the queues minus the number of drives in a redundant array of independent disks (RAID) set.

Note   Counters for physical and logical disks might need to be enabled before they're available. To enable these objects, run the following commands at a command prompt:

- **Diskperf -yd** for physical disks
- **Diskperf -yv** for logical disks

Note   For complete information on Diskperf syntax, switches, and parameters, run **Diskperf -?.**

Monitoring and Tuning Network Bandwidth and Connectivity

No other factor weighs more in a visitor's perceived performance of your Web site than the network that connects your server to the visitor's computer. The delay, or *latency*, between the time a request is made and the time it's received can make all the difference. If there's a high degree of latency, it doesn't matter if you have the fastest server on the planet. The user experiences a delay and perceives that your Web site is slow.

Generally speaking, the latency experienced by the user is beyond your control. It's a function of the type of connection the user has and the route the request takes through the Internet to your server. Your server's total capacity to handle requests and the amount of bandwidth available to your servers are factors under your control, however. Network bandwidth availability is a function of your organization's connection to the Internet. Network capacity is a function of the network cards and interfaces configured on the servers.

A typical network card is equipped to handle a 100-megabit-per-second (Mbps) or 1,000 Mbps (1 Gigabit) connection with fair efficiency, which is much more traffic than the typical site experiences and much more traffic than the typical server can handle. Because of this, your organization's bandwidth availability is typically the limiting factor. If you have a shared T1 for all Internet activity, your servers are sharing the 1.544 Mbps connection with all other Internet traffic. If you have a dedicated T1 for your Web servers, your servers have 1.544 Mbps of bandwidth availability. If you have multiple T1s or a T3, the bandwidth available to your servers could range from 3 Mbps to 45 Mbps.

To put this in perspective, consider that the number of simultaneous connections your network can handle is relative to the speed of the connection, the average size of the data transferred per connection, and the permitted transfer time. For example, if you have a T1, the typical data transfer per connection (for a dial-up connection) is 50 kilobits per second (Kbps), and transfer time allowable is 15 seconds, your connection could handle 30 data transfers per second (1,544 Kbps / 50 Kbps) or 450 simultaneous transfers within 15 seconds (30 data transfers * 15 seconds).

On the other hand, if you have a T3, the typical data transfer per connection is 250 Kbps, and allowable transfer time is 15 seconds, your connection could handle 180 data transfers per second (45,000 Kbps/ 250 Kbps) or 2,700 simultaneous transfers within 15 seconds (180 data transfers * 15 seconds).

Tip   Your network card's capacity can be a limiting factor in some instances. Most servers use 10/100 or 10/100/1000 network cards, which can be configured in many ways. Someone might have configured a card for 10 Mbps, or the card might be configured for half duplex instead of full duplex. If you suspect a capacity problem with a network card, you should always check the configuration. Duplex settings on datacenter network equipment may be a factor as well, so be sure to confirm switch settings with your network administrator.

Real World   A T1 connection is a useful example for many commercial sites. Larger commercial sites are typically co-located at a hosting service and might have a connection speed to the Internet of 100 Mbps or greater. If this is the case for your site, keep in mind that some devices configured on your network might restrict the permitted bandwidth. For example, your company's firewall might be configured so that it allows only 5 Mbps for Web, 2 Mbps for FTP, and 1 Mbps for SMTP.

To determine the throughput and current activity on a server's network cards, you can check the following performance counters:

- Network Interface\Bytes Received/sec
- Network Interface\Bytes Sent/sec
- Network Interface\Bytes Total/sec
- Network Interface\Current Bandwidth

If the total bytes-per-second value is more than 50 percent of the total capacity under average load conditions, your server might have problems under peak load conditions. You might want to ensure that operations that take a lot of network bandwidth, such as backups, are performed on a separate interface card. Keep in mind that you should compare these values in conjunction with PhysicalDisk\% Disk Time and Processor\% Processor Time. If the process time and disk time values are low but the network values are very high, there might be a capacity problem.

IIS provides several ways to restrict bandwidth usage and to improve bandwidth-related performance. These features are as follows:

- **Bandwidth throttling** You can restrict bandwidth usage by enabling bandwidth throttling and limiting the maximum number of allowable connections. Bandwidth throttling restricts the total bandwidth available to a service or to individual sites. Because users will be denied service when the bandwidth limits are exceeded, you should enable these features only when you're sure that this setting is acceptable. Before you restrict bandwidth, you should monitor the network interface object counters discussed earlier in this chapter. If these counters indicate a possible problem, restricting bandwidth is one answer.

- **Connection limitations** Connection limitations restrict the total number of allowable connections to a service. Because users might be denied service when these values are exceeded, you should enable these features only when you're sure that this setting is acceptable. Before you restrict the number of connections to a server, you should monitor the network interface object counters discussed earlier in this chapter. If these counters indicate a possible problem, connection limitation is one answer.

- **HTTP compression** With HTTP compression enabled, the Web server compresses files before sending them to client browsers. File compression reduces the amount of information transferred between the server and the client, which in turn can reduce network bandwidth usage, network capacity, and transfer time. For HTTP compression to work, it must be enabled, and the client browser must support HTTP 1.1. Although most current browsers support HTTP 1.1 and have the feature enabled by default, older browsers might not support HTTP 1.1. Older browsers will still be able to retrieve files from your site, but they won't be taking advantage of HTTP compression. Before you enable compression, you should monitor the current processor usage on the server. HTTP compression adds to the overhead on the server, which means that it will increase overall processor utilization. If your site uses dynamic content extensively and process utilization (% Processor Time) is already high, you might want to upgrade or add processors before enabling HTTP compression.

More Info   For additional details, see the section "Restricting Incoming Connections and Setting Time-Out Values" in Chapter 6, "Configuring Web Sites and Directories," and the following sections in Chapter 7, "Customizing Web Server Content": "Improving Performance with Compression," "Configuring Content Compression for an Entire Server," and "Enabling or Disabling Content Compression for Sites and Directories."

Strategies for Improving IIS Performance

In this section I examine strategies you can use to improve the performance of IIS. The focus of this section is on improving the overall responsiveness of IIS and not the underlying server hardware.

Removing Unnecessary Applications and Services

One of the most obvious ways to improve IIS performance is to remove resource drains on the server. Start by removing applications that might be affecting the performance of IIS, including:

- SQL Server

- Microsoft Exchange Server

- File and print services

- UNIX services

If necessary, move these applications and services to a separate server. This will give IIS more resources to work with. For applications that you can't move, see if there's a way to run the applications only during periods of relatively low activity. For example, if you're running server backups daily, see if you can schedule backups to run late at night when user activity is low.

System services are another area you can examine to see if there are unnecessary resource drains. Every service running on the server uses resources that can be used in other ways. You should stop services that aren't necessary and set them to start manually. Before you stop any service, you should check for dependencies to ensure that your server isn't adversely affected.

If you have dedicated IIS servers, remove roles, roles services, and features that aren't required.

Optimizing Content Usage

Your server's responsiveness is tied directly to the content you're publishing. You can often realize substantial performance benefits by optimizing the way content is used. IIS can handle both static and dynamic content. Although static content is passed directly to the requesting client, dynamic content must be processed before it can be passed to the client. This places a resource burden on the server that you can reduce by using static content.

Note   I'm not advocating replacing all dynamic content with static content. Dynamically generated content is a powerful tool for building highly customized and full-featured sites. However, if there are places where you're using dynamic content for no specific reason, you might want to rethink this strategy.

When you use static content, keep in mind that you should set expire headers whenever possible. Expire headers allow the related files to be stored in the client's cache, and this can greatly improve performance on repeat visits when the original content hasn't changed. For details on setting expire headers, see the "Customizing Web Site Content and HTTP Headers" section in Chapter 7.

With dynamic content, you should limit your use of Common Gateway Interface (CGI) applications. CGI applications require more processor and memory resources than their Internet Server Application Programming Interface (ISAPI), Active Server Pages (ASP), and ASP.NET counterparts. Because of this, you should replace or convert CGI applications with or to ISAPI, ASP, or ASP.NET. An alternate is to install FastCGI–a more robust version of CGI that is available as an add-on module for IIS 7.0.

Whenever you work with ISAPI, ASP, or ASP.NET applications, try to push as much of the processing load onto the client as possible. This reduces the server resource requirements and greatly improves application responsiveness. One example of pushing processing to the client is to use client-side scripting to evaluate form submissions before data is sent to the server. This technique reduces the number of times information is sent between the client and the server; therefore, it can greatly improve the application's overall performance.

To improve content-related performance, you might also want to do the following:

- **Analyze the way content is organized on your hard disk drives.**   In most cases you should keep related content files on the same logical partitions of a disk. Keeping related files together improves IIS file caching.

- **Defragment your drives periodically.**   Over time, drives can become fragmented, and this decreases read/write performance. To correct this, defragment your server's drives periodically. Many defragmentation tools allow you to automate this process so that you can configure a scheduled job to automatically defragment drives without needing administrator intervention.

- **Reduce the size of content files.**   The larger the file size, the more time it takes to send the file to a client. If you can optimize your source Hypertext Markup Language (HTML) or ASP code and reduce the file size, you can increase your Web server's performance and responsiveness. Some of the biggest bandwidth users are multimedia files. Compress image, video, or audio files by using an appropriate compression format whenever possible.

- **Store log files on separate disks from content files.** Logging activity can reduce the responsiveness of a busy server. One way to correct this is to store access logs on a different physical drive from the one storing your site's content files. In this way, disk writes for logging are separate from the disk reads or writes for working with content files, which can greatly improve the overall server responsiveness.

- **Log only essential information**   Trying to log too much information can also slow down a busy server. By using the World Wide Web Consortium (W3C) extended logging format, you can reduce logging overhead by logging only the information that you need in order to generate reports and by removing logging for nonessential information. With any type of logging, you can reduce logging overhead by organizing different types of content appropriately and then disabling logging on directories containing content whose access doesn't need to be logged. For example, you could place all your image files in a directory called Images and then disable logging on this directory.

More Info   Techniques for configuring logging are discussed in Chapter 13. If your organization has large IIS installations running dozens or hundreds of IIS sites per server, you should consider using centralized binary logging, which is also discussed in Chapter 13.

Optimizing ISAPI, ASP, and ASP.NET Applications

Improperly configured and poorly optimized applications can be major resource drains on an IIS server. To get the most from the server, you need to optimize the way applications are configured. Do the following to optimize applications:

- **Enable type library caching.**   IIS can cache type libraries used by applications in memory. This allows frequently used type libraries to be accessed quickly. You can control caching with the *enableTypelibCache* attribute of the *system.webServer/asp/cache* element.

- **Manage application buffering and flushes appropriately.**   Application buffering allows all output from an application to be collected in the buffer before being sent to the client. This cuts down on network traffic and response times. However, users don't receive data until the page is finished executing, which can give the perception that a site isn't very responsive. You can control application buffering by using the *BufferingOn* attribute of the *system.webServer/asp* element.

- **Disable application debugging.**   Application debugging slows IIS performance considerably. You should use debugging only for troubleshooting. Otherwise, you should disable debugging. You can control debugging by using the *appAllowClientDebug* and *appAllowDebug* attributes of the *system.webServer/asp* element.

- **Optimize application performance.** You can configure ASP and ASP.NET applications to shut down idle processes, limit memory leaks and outages, and rapidly detect failures. For more information, see Chapter 9.

- **Manage session configuration appropriately.** As the usage of your server changes, so should the session management configuration. By default, session management is enabled for all applications. If your applications don't use sessions, however, you're wasting system resources. Instead of enabling sessions by default, you should disable sessions by default and then enable sessions for individual applications. You can control sessions with the *allowSessionState*, *keepSessionIdSecure*, *max*, and *timeout* attributes of the *system.webServer/asp/session* element.

- **Set a meaningful session time-out.** The session time-out value is extremely important in determining the amount of resources used in session management. Set this value accurately. Sessions should time out after an appropriate period. Configure session time-out by using the *timeout* attribute of the *system.webServer/asp/session* element.

- **Set appropriate script and connection time-out values.** ASP scripts and user connections should time out at an appropriate interval. By default, ASP scripts time out after 90 seconds and user connections are queued indefinitely (but checked every 3 seconds to make sure they're still valid). Zombie scripts and open connections use resources and can reduce the server's responsiveness. To reduce this drain, set appropriate time-outs based on the way your site is used. You can control script and connection time-outs by using the *scriptTimeout*, *queueConnectionTestTime*, *queueTimeout*, and *requestQueueMax* attributes of the *system.webServer/asp/limits* element.

Optimizing IIS Caching, Queuing, and Pooling

IIS uses many memory-resident caches and queues to manage resources. If you make extensive use of dynamic content or have a heavily trafficked site, you should optimize the way these caches and queues work for your environment. You might want to do the following:

- **Consider changing application pool queue length.** Whenever requests for applications come in, the HTTP listener (Http.sys) picks them up and passes them to an application request queue. To prevent large numbers of requests from queuing up and flooding the server, each application request queue has a default maximum amount of concurrent requests. If this value doesn't meet your needs, you can modify it by using the *queueLength* attribute of the *system.applicationHost/applicationPools* element's *add* collection. In most cases you'll want to set this value to the maximum number of connection requests you want the server to maintain.

■ **Consider changing the maximum processor threads for ASP.**   By default, IIS limits to 25 the maximum number of work threads per processor that IIS can create to handle ASP requests. You can use the *processorThreadMax* attribute of the *system.webServer/asp/limits* element to increase or decrease this value as appropriate.

■ **Consider changing the maximum worker processes for application pools.**   By default, IIS limits to 1 the maximum number of work processes that IIS can create to handle ASP requests for an application pool. If this value doesn't meet your needs, you can modify it by using the *maxProcesses* attribute of the *system.applicationHost/applicationPools* element's *add* collection.

■ **Consider changing the Output Cache settings.**   By default, IIS uses up to 50 percent of the server's available physical memory. This value ensures that IIS works well with other applications that might be running on the server. If the server is dedicated to IIS or has additional memory available, you might want to increase this setting to allow IIS to use more memory. To control IIS file caching, you can use the *maxCacheSize* attribute of the *system.webServer/caching* element.

■ **Consider changing the maximum cached file size.**   By default, IIS caches only files that are 262,144 bytes or less in size. If you have large data files or multimedia files that are accessed frequently, you might want to increase this value to allow IIS to cache larger files. Keep in mind that with file sizes over this size you'll reach a point at which caching won't significantly improve performance. The reason for this is that with small files the overhead of reading from disk rather than the file cache is significant, but with large files the disk read might not be the key factor in determining overall performance. To control the maximum cached file size, you can use the *maxResponseSize* attribute of the *system.webServer/caching* element.

■ **Consider adjusting the Time to Live (TTL) value for cached resources.**   By default, IIS purges from cache any resources that haven't been requested within the last 30 seconds. If you have additional memory on the server, you might want to increase this value so that files aren't removed from cache as quickly. To control the TTL value for cached resources, you can use the *duration* attribute of the *add* collection for the *system.webServer/caching/profiles* element.

> **Tip**   If you have a dedicated server running only IIS, you might want to consider allowing resources to remain in cache until they are overwritten (due to *maxCacheSize* limits). In this case, you would set an unlimited duration by using a value of 00:00:00.

- **Consider modifying the ASP template cache.**   The ASP template cache controls the number of ASP pages that are cached in memory. By default, IIS will cache up to 2,000 files. This typically is enough on a site with lots of ASP content. Template cache entries can reference one or more entries in the ASP Script Engine Cache. To control template caching, you set the *maxDiskTemplateCache-Files* attribute of the *system.webServer/asp/cache* element.

- **Consider modifying the script engine cache.**   The ASP Script Engine Cache is an area of memory directly accessible to the scripting engines used by IIS. As such, the preferred area for IIS to retrieve information from is the script engine cache. By default, the script engine cache can hold up to 250 entries. To control script engine caching, you set the *scriptEngineCacheMax* attribute of the *system.webServer/asp/cache* element.

Chapter 13
Tracking User Access and Logging

One of your primary responsibilities as a Web administrator may be to log access to your company's Internet servers. As you'll see in this chapter, enabling logging on IIS servers isn't very difficult. What is difficult, however, is gathering the correct access information and recording this information in the proper format so that it can be read and analyzed. Software that you use to analyze access logs is called *tracking* software. You'll find many different types of tracking software. Most commercial tracking software produces detailed reports that include tables and graphs that summarize activity for specific periods. For example, you could compile tracking reports daily, weekly, or monthly.

The file format for access logs can be configured in several different ways. You can configure standard logging, Open Database Connectivity (ODBC) logging, and extended logging. With standard logging, you choose a log file format and rely on the format to record the user access information you need. With ODBC logging, you record user access directly to an ODBC-compliant database, such as Microsoft SQL Server 2005. With extended logging, you can customize the logging process and record exactly the information you need to track user access.

Tracking Statistics: The Big Picture

Access logs are created when you enable logging for an IIS server. Every time someone requests a file from your World Wide Web site, an entry goes into the access log, making the access log a running history of every successful and unsuccessful attempt to retrieve information from your site. Because each entry has its own line, entries in the access log can be easily extracted and compiled into reports. From these reports, you can learn many things about those who visit your site. You can do the following:

- Determine the busiest times of the day and week
- Determine which browsers and platforms are used by people who visit your site
- Discover popular and unpopular resources
- Discover sites that refer users to your site
- Learn more about the effectiveness of your advertising
- Learn more about the people who visit your site

- Obtain information about search engine usage and keywords

- Obtain information about the amount of time users spend at the site

IIS 7.0 can be configured to use per-server or per-site logging. With *per-server* logging, IIS tracks requests for all Web sites configured on a server in a single log file. With *per-site* logging, IIS tracks requests for each Web site in separate log files. You'll find that per-server logging is more efficient than per-site logging and can reduce the overhead associated with logging. Because of this, per-server logging is ideal when an IIS server has a large number of sites, such as with Internet service providers (ISPs), and for busy commercial sites, such as those for large organizations. For small and medium installations, you'll find that per-site logging is easier to work with because you'll have separate log files for each site and can use just about any tracking software to review access statistics.

With per-server logging, you can use one of two logging formats:

- **Centralized Binary Logging**   Use centralized binary logging when you want all Web sites running on a server to write log data to a single log file. With centralized binary logging, the log files contain fixed-length and index records that are written in a raw binary format called the Internet Binary Log (IBL) format. Professional software applications and other tools, such as LogParser, can read this format. Because IIS writes the logs in binary format, this logging technique is the most efficient and is recommended for busy commercial sites and ISPs.

- **Centralized World Wide Web Consortium (W3C) Extended Log File Format**   Use the centralized extended format when you want all Web sites running on a server to write log data to a single log file and must customize the tracked information and obtain detailed information. With this format, log entries can become large, and this greatly increases the amount of storage space required. Because recording lengthy entries also can affect the performance of a busy server, this format is not as efficient as centralized binary logging. However, a single centralized extended log is still more efficient than having multiple decentralized extended logs.

With per-site logging, the available formats are:

- **National Center for Supercomputing Applications (NCSA) Common Log File Format**   Use the common log format when your reporting and tracking needs are basic. With this format, log entries are small, so not as much storage space is required for logging.

- **Microsoft Internet Information Services (IIS) Log File Format**   Use the IIS format when you need a bit more information from the logs but don't need to tailor the entries to get detailed information. With this format, log entries are compact, so not as much storage space is required for logging.

- **World Wide Web Consortium (W3C) Extended Log File Format**   Use the extended format when you must customize the tracked information and obtain detailed information. With this format, log entries can become large, and this greatly increases the amount of storage space required. Recording lengthy entries can also affect the performance of a busy server.

- **Custom (ODBC Logging)**   Use the ODBC format when you want to write access information directly to an ODBC-compliant database. With ODBC logging, you'll need tracking software capable of reading from a database. Entries are compact, however, and data can be read much more quickly than from a standard log file. Keep in mind that ODBC logging is more processor-intensive when you write logs directly to a local database instance.

Tip   With NCSA, IIS, and W3C logging, you have two choices for text encoding. You can use standard ANSI encoding or you can use UTF-8 encoding. ANSI encoding is best used with sites and file names that use standard English characters. UTF-8 encoding is best used with sites and file names that use standard English characters in addition to non-English characters. By default, IIS 7.0 uses UTF-8 encoding. Regardless of whether you use per-server or per-site logging, you configure text encoding at the server level, and all text-based log files created on the server use this encoding.

Because an understanding of what is written to log files is important to understanding logging itself, the sections that follow examine the main file formats. I'll start with the most basic format and then work toward the most advanced format. After this discussion, you'll be able to determine what each format has to offer and hopefully better determine when to use each format.

Working with the NCSA Common Log File Format

The NCSA common log file format is the most basic log format. The common log format is a fixed ASCII or UTF-8 format in which each log entry represents a unique file request. You'll use the common log format when your tracking and reporting needs are basic. More specifically, the common log format is a good choice when you need to track only certain items, such as:

- Hits (the number of unique file requests)

- Page views (the number of unique page requests)

- Visits (the number of user sessions in a specified period)

- Other basic access information

With this format, log entries are small, so not as much storage space is required for logging. Each entry in the common log format has only seven fields. These fields are:

- Host

- Identification

- User Authentication

- Time Stamp

- HTTP Request Type

- Status Code

- Transfer Volume

As you'll see, the common log format is easy to understand, which makes it a good stepping-stone to more advanced log file formats. The following listing shows entries in a sample access log that are formatted using the NCSA common log file format. As you can see from the sample, log fields are separated by spaces:

```
192.168.11.15 - ENGSVR01\wrstanek [15/Jan/2009:18:44:57 -0800]
"GET / HTTP/1.1" 200 1970
192.168.11.15 - ENGSVR01\wrstanek [15/Jan/2009:18:45:06 -0800]
"GET /home.gif HTTP/1.1" 200 5032
192.168.11.15 - ENGSVR01\wrstanek [15/Jan/2009:18:45:28 -0800]
"GET /main.htm HTTP/1.1" 200 5432
192.168.11.15 - ENGSVR01\wrstanek [15/Jan/2009:18:45:31 -0800]
"GET /details.gif HTTP/1.1" 200 1211
192.168.11.15 - ENGSVR01\wrstanek [15/Jan/2009:18:45:31 -0800]
"GET /menu.gif HTTP/1.1" 200 6075
192.168.11.15 - ENGSVR01\wrstanek [15/Jan/2009:18:45:31 -0800]
"GET /sidebar.gif HTTP/1.1" 200 9023
192.168.11.15 - ENGSVR01\wrstanek [15/Jan/2009:18:45:31 -0800]
"GET /sun.gif HTTP/1.1" 200 4706
192.168.11.15 - ENGSVR01\wrstanek [15/Jan/2009:18:45:38 -0800]
"GET /moon.gif HTTP/1.1" 200 1984
192.168.11.15 - ENGSVR01\wrstanek [15/Jan/2009:18:45:41 -0800]
"GET /stars.gif HTTP/1.1" 200 2098
```

Most other log file formats are based on the NCSA file format, so it is useful to examine how these fields are used.

Host Field

Host is the first field in the common log format. This field identifies the host computer requesting a file from your Web server. The value in this field is either the IP address of the remote host, such as 192.168.11.15, or the fully qualified domain name of the remote host, such as net48.microsoft.com. The following example shows an HTTP query initiated by a host that was successfully resolved to a domain name:

```
net48.microsoft.com - ENGSVR01\wrstanek [15/Jan/2009:18:44:57 -0800]
"GET / HTTP/1.1" 200 1970
```

IP addresses are the numeric equivalent of fully qualified domain names. You can often use a reverse DNS lookup to determine the actual domain name from the IP address. When you have a domain name or resolve an IP address to an actual name, you can examine the name to learn more about the user accessing your server. Divisions within the domain name are separated by periods. The final division identifies the domain class, which can tell you where the user lives and works.

Domain classes are geographically and demographically organized. Geographically organized domain classes end in a two- or three-letter designator for the state or country in which the user lives. For example, the .ca domain class is for companies in Canada. Demographically organized domain classes tell you the type of company providing network access to the user. Table 13-1 summarizes these domain classes.

Table 13-1   Basic Domain Classes

Domain Name	Description
.com	Commercial; users from commercial organizations
.edu	Education; users from colleges and universities
.gov	U.S. government; users from U.S. government agencies (except military)
.mil	U.S. military; users who work at military installations
.net	Network; users who work at network service providers and other network-related organizations
.org	Nonprofit organizations; users who work for nonprofit organizations

Identification Field

The Identification field is the second field in the common log format. This field is meant to identify users by their user name but in practice is rarely used. Because of this, you will generally see a hyphen (-) in this field, as in the following:

```
net48.microsoft.com - ENGSVR01\wrstanek [15/Jan/2009:18:44:57 -0800]
"GET / HTTP/1.1" 200 1970
```

If you do see a value in this field, keep in mind that the user name is not validated. This means that it could be fictitious and shouldn't be trusted.

User Authentication Field

The User Authentication field is the third field in the common log format. If you have a password-protected area on your Web site, users must authenticate themselves with a user name and password that is registered for this area. After users validate themselves with their user name and password, their user name is entered in the User Authentication field. In unprotected areas of a site, you will usually see a hyphen (-) in this field. In protected areas of a site, you will see the account name of the authenticated user. The account name can be preceded by the name of the domain in which the user is authenticated, as shown in this example:

```
net48.microsoft.com - ENGSVR01\wrstanek [15/Jan/2009:18:44:57 -0800]
"GET / HTTP/1.1" 200 1970
```

Time Stamp Field

The Time Stamp field is the fourth field in the common log format. This field tells you exactly when someone accessed a file on the server. The format for the Time Stamp field is as follows:

DD/MMM/YYYY:HH:MM:SS OFFSET

such as:

15/Jan/2009:18:44:57 -0800

The only designator that probably doesn't make sense is the offset. The offset indicates the difference in the server's time from Greenwich Mean Time (GMT) standard time. In the following example, the offset is −8 hours, meaning that the server time is eight hours behind GMT:

net48.microsoft.com - ENGSVR01\wrstanek **[15/Jan/2009:18:44:57 -0800]**
"GET / HTTP/1.1" 200 1970

HTTP Request Field

The HTTP Request field is the fifth field in the common log format. Use this field to determine the method that the remote client used to request the resource, the resource that the remote client requested, and the HTTP version that the client used to retrieve the resource. In the following example, the HTTP Request field information is bold:

192.168.11.15 - ENGSVR01\wrstanek [15/Jan/2009:18:45:06 -0800]
"GET /home.gif HTTP/1.1" 200 5032

Here, the transfer method is GET, the resource is /Home.gif, and the transfer method is HTTP 1.1. One thing you should note is that resources are specified using relative Uniform Resource Locators (URLs). The server interprets relative URLs. For example, if you request the file *http://www.microsoft.com/home/main.htm,* the server will use the relative URL /Home/Main.htm to log where the file is found. When you see an entry that ends in a slash, keep in mind that this refers to the default document for a directory, which is typically called Index.htm or Default.asp.

Status Code Field

The Status Code field is the sixth field in the common log format. Status codes indicate whether files were transferred correctly, were loaded from cache, were not found, and so on. Generally, status codes are three-digit numbers. As shown in Table 13-2, the first digit indicates the class or category of the status code.

Table 13-2   Status Code Classes

Code Class	Description
1XX	Continue/protocol change
2XX	Success
3XX	Redirection
4XX	Client error/failure
5XX	Server error

Because you'll rarely see a status code beginning with 1, you need to remember only the other four categories. A status code that begins with 2 indicates that the associated file transferred successfully. A status code that begins with 3 indicates that the server performed a redirect. A status code that begins with 4 indicates some type of client error or failure. Last, a status code that begins with 5 tells you that a server error occurred.

Transfer Volume Field

The last field in the common log format is the Transfer Volume field. This field indicates the number of bytes transferred to the client because of the request. In the following example, 4096 bytes (or 4 megabytes) were transferred to the client:

```
net48.microsoft.com - ENGSVR01\wrstanek [15/Jan/2009:18:45:06 -0800]
"GET / HTTP/1.1" 200 4096
```

You'll see a transfer volume only when the status code class indicates success. If another status code class is used in field six, the Transfer Volume field will contain a hyphen (-) or a 0 to indicate that no data was transferred.

Working with the Microsoft IIS Log File Format

Like the common log format, the Microsoft IIS log file format is a fixed ASCII format. This means that the fields in the log are of a fixed type and cannot be changed. It also means that the log is formatted as standard ASCII text and can be read with any standard text editor or compliant application.

The following listing shows entries from a sample log using the IIS log file format. The IIS log entries include common log fields such as the client IP address, authenticated user name, request date and time, HTTP status code, and number of bytes received. IIS log entries also include detailed items such as the Web service name, the server IP address, and the elapsed time. Note that commas separate log fields, and entries are much longer than those in the common log file format.

```
192.14.16.2, -, 04/15/2008, 15:42:25, W3SVC1, ENGSVR01, 192.15.14.81, 0,
594, 3847, 401, 5, GET, /start.asp, -,
192.14.16.2, ENGSVR01\wrstanek, 04/15/2008, 15:42:25, W3SVC1, ENGSVR01,
192.15.14.81, 10, 412, 3406, 404, 0, GET, /localstart.asp, |-
```

```
|0|404_Object_Not_Found,
192.14.16.2, -, 04/15/2008, 15:42:29, W3SVC1, ENGSVR01, 192.15.14.81, 0,
622, 3847, 401, 5, GET, /default.asp, -,
192.14.16.2, ENGSVR01\wrstanek, 04/15/2008, 15:42:29, W3SVC1, ENGSVR01,
192.15.14.81, 10, 426, 0, 200, 0, GET, /default.asp, -,
192.14.16.2, ENGSVR01\wrstanek, 04/15/2008, 15:42:29, W3SVC1, ENGSVR01,
192.15.14.81, 10, 368, 0, 200, 0, GET, /contents.asp, -,
192.14.16.2, -, 04/15/2008, 15:42:29, W3SVC1, ENGSVR01, 192.15.14.81, 0,
732, 3847, 401, 5, GET, /navbar.asp, -,
192.14.16.2, -, 04/15/2008, 15:42:29, W3SVC1, ENGSVR01, 192.15.14.81, 0,
742, 3847, 401, 5, GET, /core.htm, -,
192.14.16.2, ENGSVR01\wrstanek, 04/15/2008, 15:42:29, W3SVC1, ENGSVR01,
192.15.14.81, 20, 481, 0, 200, 0, GET, /navbar.asp, -,
192.14.16.2, ENGSVR01\wrstanek, 04/15/2008, 15:42:29, W3SVC1, ENGSVR01,
192.15.14.81, 91, 486, 6520, 200, 0, GET, /core.htm, -,
```

The fields supported by IIS are summarized in Table 13-3. Note that the listed field order is the general order used by IIS to record fields.

Table 13-3   Fields for the IIS Log File Format

Field Name	Description	Example
Client IP	IP address of the client	192.14.16.2
User Name	Authenticated name of the user	ENGSVR01\wrstanek
Date	Date when the transaction was completed	04/15/2008
Time	Time when the transaction was completed	15:42:29
Service	Name of the Web service logging the transaction	W3SVC1
Computer Name	Name of the computer that made the request	ENGSVR01
Server IP	IP address of the Web server	192.15.14.81
Elapsed Time	Time taken (in milliseconds) for the transaction to be completed	40
Bytes Received	Number of bytes received by the server in the client request	486
Bytes Sent	Number of bytes sent to the client	6520
Status Code	HTTP status code	200
Windows Status Code	Error status code from Microsoft Windows	0
Method Used	HTTP request method	GET
File URI	The requested file	/start.asp
Referrer	The referrer—that is, the location where the user came	http://www.microsoft.com/

Working with the W3C Extended Log File Format

The W3C extended log file format is much different from either of the previously discussed log file formats. With this format, you can customize the tracked information and obtain detailed information. When you customize an extended log file, you select the fields you want the server to log, and the server handles the logging for you. Keep in mind that each additional field you track adds to the size of entries recorded in the access logs, and this can greatly increase the amount of storage space required.

The following listing shows sample entries from an extended log. Note that, as with the common log format, extended log fields are separated with spaces.

```
#Software: Microsoft Internet Information Services 7.0
#Version: 1.0
#Date: 2008-04-05 06:27:58
#Fields: date time c-ip cs-username s-ip s-port cs-method cs-uri-stem cs-
uri-query sc-status cs(User-Agent)
2008-04-05 06:27:58 192.14.16.2 ENGSVR01\wrstanek 192.14.15.81 80 GET
/cust.htm - 304
Mozilla/4.0+(compatible;+MSIE+7.01;+Windows+NT+6.0;+SLCC1;+.NET+CLR+
2.0.50727) 2008-04-05 06:28:00 192.14.16.2 ENGSVR01\wrstanek 192.14.15.81
80 GET /data.htm - 304
Mozilla/4.0+(compatible;+MSIE+7.01;+Windows+NT+6.0;+SLCC1;+.NET+CLR+
2.0.50727) 2008-04-05 06:28:02 192.14.16.2 ENGSVR01\wrstanek 192.14.15.81
80 GET /store.htm - 200
Mozilla/4.0+(compatible;+MSIE+7.01;+Windows+NT+6.0;+SLCC1;+.NET+CLR+
2.0.50727) 2008-04-05 06:28:02 192.14.16.2 ENGSVR01\wrstanek 192.14.15.81
80 GET /prodadd.htm - 200
Mozilla/4.0+(compatible;+MSIE+7.01;+Windows+NT+6.0;+SLCC1;+.NET+CLR+
2.0.50727) 2008-04-05 06:28:05 192.14.16.2 ENGSVR01\wrstanek 192.14.15.81
80 GET /datastop.htm - 200
Mozilla/4.0+(compatible;+MSIE+7.01;+Windows+NT+6.0;+SLCC1;+.NET+CLR+2.0.50727)
```

The first time you look at log entries that use the extended format, you might be a bit confused. The reason for this is that the extended logs are written with server directives in addition to file requests. The good news is that server directives are always preceded by the hash symbol (#), easily allowing you to distinguish them from actual file requests. The key directives you'll see are the directives that identify the server software and the fields being recorded. These directives are summarized in Table 13-4.

Table 13-4   Directives Used with the Extended Log File Format

Directive	Name Description
Date	Identifies the date and time the entries were made in the log
End-Date	Identifies the date and time the log was finished and then archived
Fields	Specifies the fields and the field order used in the log file
Remark	Specifies comments
Software	Identifies the server software that created the log entries
Start-Date	Identifies the date and time the log was started
Version	Identifies the version of the extended log file format used

Most extended log fields have a prefix. The prefix tells you how a particular field is used or how the field was obtained. For example, the *cs* prefix tells you that the field was obtained from a request sent by the client to the server. Field prefixes are summarized in Table 13-5.

Table 13-5   Prefixes Used with the Extended Log Fields

Prefix	Description
c	Identifies a client-related field
s	Identifies a server-related field
r	Identifies a remote server field
cs	Identifies information obtained from a request sent by the client to the server
sc	Identifies information obtained from a request sent by the IIS server to the client
sr	Identifies information obtained from a request sent by the Web server to a remote server (used by proxies)
rs	Identifies information obtained from a request sent by a remote server to the IIS server (used by proxies)
x	Application-specific prefix

All fields recorded in an extended log have a field identifier. This identifier details the type of information a particular field records. To create a named field, the IIS server can combine a field prefix with a field identifier, or it can simply use a field identifier. The most commonly used field names are summarized in Table 13-6. As you examine the table, keep in mind that most of these fields relate directly to the fields we've already discussed for the common and extended log file formats. Again, the key difference is that the extended format can give you information that is much more detailed.

Table 13-6   Field Identifiers Used with the Extended File Format

Field Type	Actual Field Name	Description
Bytes Received	cs-bytes	Number of bytes received by the server.
Bytes Sent	sc-bytes	Number of bytes sent by the server.
Client IP Address	c-ip	IP address of the client that accessed the server.
Cookie	cs(Cookie)	Content of the cookie sent or received (if any).
Date	Date	Date on which the activity occurred.
Method Used	cs-method	HTTP request method.
Protocol Status	sc-status	HTTP status code, such as 404.
Protocol Substatus	sc-substatus	HTTP substatus code, such as 2.
Protocol Version	cs-protocol	Protocol version used by the client.
Referrer	cs(Referer)	Previous site visited by the user. This site provided a link to the current site.
Server IP	s-ip	IP address of the IIS server.
Server Name	s-computername	Name of the IIS server.
Server Port	s-port	Port number through which the client is connected.
Service Name and Instance Number	s-sitename	Internet site and instance number that was running on the server.
Time	Time	Time the activity occurred.
Time Taken	time-taken	Time taken (in milliseconds) for the transaction to be completed.
URI Query	cs-uri-query	Query parameters passed in request (if any).
URI Stem	cs-uri-stem	Requested resource.
User Agent	cs(User-Agent)	Browser type and version used on the client.
User Name	c-username	Name of an authenticated user (if available).
Win32 Status	sc-win32-status	Error status code from Windows.

Real World   When a server is using centralized extended logging, be sure to track the Service Name because this field ensures that the site name and identity is written with each log entry. To ensure proper tracking of errors, you should track both the protocol status and substatus. Protocol Status logs the HTTP status code of the request, such as 404. Protocol Substatus logs the HTTP substatus code of the request, such as 2. When used together, the fields provide the complete status of the request, such as 404.2.

Unlike IIS 6, IIS 7.0 cannot log process accounting information related to HTTP requests. The reason for this is that process accounting applies only to resources used by out-of-process applications. Process accounting does not cover resources used by pooled or in-process applications.

Working with ODBC Logging

You can use the ODBC logging format when you want to write access information directly to an ODBC-compliant database, such as Microsoft Office Access or Microsoft SQL Server. The key advantage of ODBC logging is that access entries are written directly to a database in a format that can be quickly read and interpreted by compliant software. The major disadvantages of ODBC logging are two-fold. First, it requires basic database administration skills to configure and maintain. Second, direct ODBC-logging can use a great deal of system resources, so it could be extremely inefficient.

When using ODBC logging, you must configure a Data Source Name (DSN) that allows IIS to connect to your ODBC database. You must also create a database that can be used for logging. This database must have a table with the appropriate fields for the logging data.

Typically, you'll use the same database for logging information from multiple sites with each site writing to a separate table in the database. For example, if you wanted to log Corporate Web, Support Web, and Sales Web access information in your database, and these services were running on separate sites, you would create three tables in your database, such as the following:

- CorpLog
- SupportLog
- SalesLog

These tables would have the columns and data types for field values summarized in Table 13-7. The columns must be configured exactly as shown in the table. Don't worry; IIS includes an SQL script that you can use to create the necessary table structures. This script is located in the *%SystemRoot%*\System32\Inetsrv directory and is named Logtemp.sql.

Note If you use the Logtemp.sql script, be sure to edit the table name set in the CREATE TABLE statement. The default table name is inetlog. For more information about working with SQL scripts, see *Microsoft SQL Server 2005 Administrator's Pocket Consultant* (Microsoft Press, 2005).

Table 13-7   Table Fields for ODBC Logging

Field Name	Field Type	Description
ClientHost	varchar(255)	IP address of the client that accessed the server
Username	varchar(255)	Name of an authenticated user (if available)
LogTime	datetime	Date and time when the activity occurred
Service	varchar(255)	Internet site and instance number that was running on the server
Machine	varchar(255)	Name of the computer that made the request
ServerIP	varchar(50)	IP address of the IIS server
ProcessingTime	int	Time taken (in milliseconds) for the transaction to be completed
BytesRecvd	int	Number of bytes received by the server
BytesSent	int	Number of bytes sent by the server
ServiceStatus	int	HTTP status code
Win32Status	int	Error status code from Windows
Operation	varchar(255)	HTTP request method
Target	varchar(255)	Requested resource
Parameters	varchar(255)	Query parameters passed in request (if any)

Working with Centralized Binary Logging

You can use centralized binary logging when you want all Web sites running on a server to write log data to a single log file. With centralized binary logging, the log files are written in a raw binary format called the Internet Binary Log (IBL) format. This format can be read by many professional software applications or by using other tools, such as LogParser.

On a large IIS installation where the server is running hundreds or thousands of sites, centralized binary logging can dramatically reduce the overhead associated with logging activities. Two types of records are written to the binary log files:

- **Index**   Act as record headers, similar to the W3C extended log file format, where software, version, date, and field information is provided.

- **Fixed-length**   Provide the detailed information about requests. Each value in each field in the entry is stored with a fixed length.

For more information on centralized binary logging, see the "Configuring Centralized Binary Logging" section later in this chapter.

Understanding Logging

In IIS 7.0, the following role services make it possible for you to use logging:

- **HTTP Logging**   Makes available the standard logging features

- **Custom Logging**   Makes available custom logging features (including features required for ODBC logging)

- **ODBC Logging**   Makes available ODBC logging features

- **Logging Tools**   Makes available additional resources and tools for working with logs

Once the appropriate role services are installed, you can enable and configure IIS logging so that new log entries are generated whenever users access the server. This causes a steady increase in log file size and eventually, in the number of log files. On a busy server, log files can quickly grow to several gigabytes, so therefore, you might need to balance the need to gather information against the need to limit log files to a manageable size.

> **Note**   Keep in mind that log files are stored as ASCII or UTF-8 text files, and if you must, you can split or combine log files as you would with any text file. If your server runs out of disk space when IIS is attempting to add a log entry to a file, IIS logging shuts down and logs a logging error event in the Application log. When disk space is available again, IIS resumes logging file access and writes a start-logging event in the Application log.

When you configure logging, you specify how log files are created and saved. Logs can be created according to a time schedule, such as hourly, daily, weekly, and monthly. Logs can also be set to a fixed file size, such as 100 MB, or they can be allowed to grow to an unlimited file size. The name of a log file indicates its log file format in addition to the time frame or sequence of the log. The various naming formats are summarized in Table 13-8. If a log file uses UTF-8 encoding rather than ASCII, the log file will have a U_ prefix, such as u_ex080305.log for a tracking log in W3C extended log format that has UTF-8 encoding.

Table 13-8   Conventions for Log File Names by Log Format

Format	Log Period	File Name
IIS Log Format	By file size	Inetsv*nn*.log
	Unlimited	Inetsv*nn*.log
	Hourly	In*yymmddhh*.log
	Daily	In*yymmdd*.log
	Weekly	In*yymmww*.log
	Monthly	In*yymm*.log

Table 13-8   Conventions for Log File Names by Log Format

Format	Log Period	File Name
NCSA Common Log Format	By file size	Ncsa*nn*.log
	Unlimited	Ncsa*nn*.log
	Hourly	Nc*yymmddhh*.log
	Daily	Nc*yymmdd*.log
	Weekly	Nc*yymmww*.log
	Monthly	Nc*yymm*.log
W3C Extended Log Format	By file size	Extend*nn*.log
	Unlimited	Extend*nn*.log
	Hourly	Ex*yymmddhh*.log
	Daily	Ex*yymmdd*.log
	Weekly	Ex*yymmww*.log
	Monthly	Ex*yymm*.log
Centralized Binary Log Format	Hourly	Ra*yymmddhh*.ibl
	Daily	Ra*yymmdd*.log
	Weekly	Ra*yymmww*.ibl
	Monthly	Ra*yymm*.ibl

By default, log files are written to the *%SystemDrive%*\Inetpub\Logs\LogFiles directory. You can configure logging to a different directory, such as D:\LogFiles. Regardless of whether you use the default directory location or assign a new directory location for logs, you'll find separate subdirectories for each service that is enabled for logging under the primary directory.

Subdirectories for sites are named W3SVC*N* where *N* is the index number of the service or a random tracking value. The only exception is when you use centralized binary logging or centralized extended logging. Here, Web site logs are stored in the *%SystemDrive%*\Inetpub\Logs\LogFiles\W3SVC directory.

The default server created is number 1. If you create additional sites, an incremental numeric identifier is used. Following this, you could have site directories named W3SVC, W3SVC1, W3SVC2, and so on. To correlate the identifier value to specific Web sites, in IIS Manager, select the Sites node, and then look at the Name and ID columns to determine which identifier belongs to which site.

Configuring Logging

Now that you know how log files are used and created, let's look at how you can enable and configure logging. The sections that follow examine each of the available logging formats. Keep the following in mind:

- When you change logging formats for a server, the format is used the next time you start the World Wide Web Publishing service. If you want the new logging format to be used immediately, you should restart the server process. To do this in IIS Manager, in the left pane, select the server node, and then in the Actions pane, click Restart.

- When you change logging formats for a site, the format is used the next time you start the World Wide Web Publishing service or the selected site. If you want the new logging format to be used immediately, you should restart the site. To do this in IIS Manager, in the left pane, select the site node, and then in the Actions pane, click Restart.

Configuring Per-Server or Per-Site Logging

An IIS server can use either per-server or per-site logging. As discussed previously, with per-server logging, IIS tracks requests for all Web sites configured on a server in a single log file. With per-site logging, IIS tracks requests for each Web site in separate log files.

With NCSA, IIS, and W3C logging, you can use ANSI or UTF-8 text encoding. ANSI supports standard English characters; UTF-8 supports standard English characters and non-English characters. Each IIS server has one text-encoding format, and that format is configured at the server level. All text-based log files created on the server use this encoding.

You can enable logging and configure how IIS logs requests by completing the following steps:

1. In IIS Manager, select the node for the server you want to manage. If the server you want to use isn't listed, connect to it.

2. In the main pane, when you group by area, the Logging feature is listed under IIS. Double-click Logging to open this feature. As shown in Figure 13-1, you should now see the current top-level logging configuration.

3. If logging is currently disabled at the server level, all logging options are dimmed and cannot be selected. To enable logging, in the Actions pane, click Enable.

4. In the One Log File Per drop-down list, select the desired logging technique. If you want the server to use per-server logging, select Server. If you want the server to use per-site logging, select Site.

5. In the Encoding drop-down list, select the desired text encoding for logs formatted with the NSA, IIS, or W3C logging format. Choose either ANSI or UTF8.

6. Click Apply to save your settings.

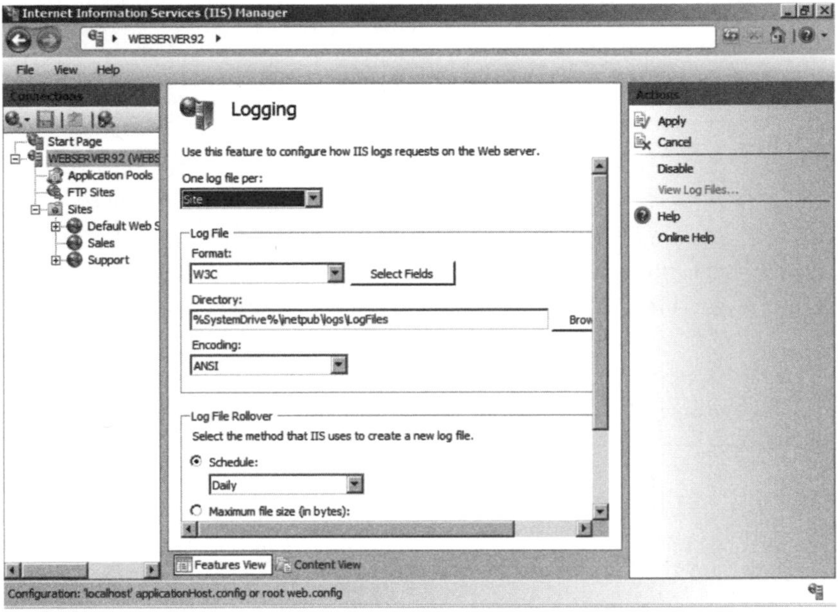

Figure 13-1   Configure how IIS logs requests.

Configuring the NCSA Common Log File Format

The NCSA common log file format is used with per-site logging only. You enable logging and configure the common log file format by completing the following steps:

1. In IIS Manager, navigate to the site you want to manage. In the main pane, when you group by area, the Logging feature is listed under IIS. Double-click Logging to open this feature.

2. If all logging options are dimmed and the server is configured for per site logging, you can click Enable in the Actions pane to enable logging for this site.

3. On the Format list, select NCSA as the log format. By default, log files are located in a subdirectory under *%SystemDrive%*\System32\Inetpub\Logs\Logfiles. If you want to change the default logging directory, type the directory path in the Directory field, or click Browse to look for a directory that you want to use.

4. To configure logging during a specific time period, select Schedule, and then choose one of the following options:

   ❑ **Hourly**   IIS creates a new log each hour.

   ❑ **Daily**   IIS creates a new log daily at midnight.

   ❑ **Weekly**   IIS creates a new log file each Saturday at midnight.

   ❑ **Monthly**   IIS creates a new log file at midnight on the last day of the month.

5. To configure logging using an unlimited file site, select Do Not Create New Log Files. With this option, IIS doesn't end the log file automatically. You must manage the log file.

6. To set a maximum log file size in bytes, select Maximum File Size (In Bytes), and then type the desired maximum file size, such as **1024000**. When the log file reaches this size, a new log file is created.

7. Click Apply to save your settings. The service directory and log file are created automatically, if necessary. If IIS doesn't have Read/Write permission on the logging directory, an error is generated.

Configuring Microsoft IIS Log File Format

The Microsoft IIS log file format is used with per-site logging only. You enable logging and configure the IIS log file format by completing the following steps:

1. In IIS Manager, navigate to the site you want to manage. In the main pane, when you group by area, the Logging feature is listed under IIS. Double-click Logging to open this feature.

2. If all logging options are dimmed and the server is configured for per site logging, you can click Enable in the Actions pane to enable logging for this site.

3. On the Format list, select IIS as the log format. By default, log files are located in a subdirectory under *%SystemDrive%*\System32\Inetpub\Logs\Logfiles. If you want to change the default logging directory, type the directory path in the Directory field, or click Browse to look for a directory that you want to use.

4. To configure logging using a specific time period, select Schedule, and then choose one of the following options:

   ❑ **Hourly**   IIS creates a new log each hour.

   ❑ **Daily**   IIS creates a new log daily at midnight.

   ❑ **Weekly**   IIS creates a new log file each Saturday at midnight.

   ❑ **Monthly**   IIS creates a new log file at midnight on the last day of the month.

5. To configure logging using an unlimited file site, select Do Not Create New Log Files. With this option, IIS doesn't end the log file automatically. You must manage the log file.

6. To set a maximum log file size in bytes, select Maximum File Size (In Bytes), and then type the desired maximum file size, such as **1024000**. When the log file reaches this size, a new log file is created.

7. Click Apply to save your settings. The service directory and log file are created automatically, if necessary. If IIS doesn't have Read/Write permission on the logging directory, an error is generated.

Configuring W3C Extended Log File Format

The W3C extended log file format can be used with per site and per server logging. You enable logging and configure the W3C extended log file format by completing the following steps:

1. In IIS Manager, navigate to the node you want to manage. To configure centralized extended logging for a server, in the left pane, select the server node. To configure extended logging for a site, in the left pane, select the site node.

2. In the main pane, when you group by area, the Logging feature is listed under IIS. Double-click Logging to open this feature. If you selected a site node previously and the Actions pane displays a warning that the server is configured for per server logging, you must manage logging through the server node. If logging is otherwise disabled, you must click Enable in the Actions pane to turn on the logging feature.

3. Using the Format list, select W3C as the log format, and then click Select Fields.

4. In the W3C Logging Fields dialog box, shown in Figure 13-2, select the extended properties that you want to log, and then click OK. The fields you'll want to track in most cases are: Date/Time, Client IP Address, Server IP Address, Service Name, Method, URI Stem, URI Query, Protocol Status, Protocol Substatus, Bytes Sent, Bytes Received, User Agent, Cookie, and Referer.

   Note   The more fields you track, the larger the log entries. Moreover, the larger log entries are, the longer it takes IIS to write them.

5. By default, log files are located in a subdirectory under %SystemDrive%\System32\Inetpub\Logs\Logfiles. If you want to change the default logging directory, type the directory path in the Directory field, or click Browse to look for a directory that you want to use.

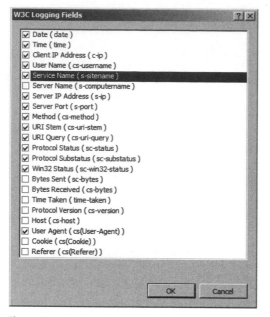

Figure 13-2 Use the extended log format when you need to customize the logging process.

6. To configure logging using a specific time period, select Schedule, and then choose one of the following options:

❑ **Hourly** IIS creates a new log each hour.

❑ **Daily** IIS creates a new log daily at midnight.

❑ **Weekly** IIS creates a new log file each Saturday at midnight.

❑ **Monthly** IIS creates a new log file at midnight on the last day of the month.

7. To configure logging using an unlimited file site, select Do Not Create New Log Files. With this option, IIS doesn't end the log file automatically. You must manage the log file.

8. To set a maximum log file size in bytes, select Maximum File Size (In Bytes), and then type the desired maximum file size, such as **1024000**. When the log file reaches this size, a new log file is created.

9. Click Apply to save your settings. The service directory and log file are created automatically, if necessary. If IIS doesn't have Read/Write permission on the logging directory, an error is generated.

Configuring ODBC Logging

You can configure ODBC Logging as a type of custom logging with per site logging. Use the ODBC format when you want to write access information directly to an ODBC-compliant database. With ODBC logging, you'll need tracking software capable of reading from a database. Entries are compact, however, and data can be read much more quickly than from a standard log file.

To use ODBC logging, you must perform the following tasks:

1. Create a database using ODBC-compliant database software. As long as IIS can connect to the database using an ODBC connection, the database doesn't have to reside on the IIS server. Microsoft Office Access can be used for small to medium-sized sites with moderate traffic. For large or busy sites, use a more robust solution, such as SQL Server 2005.

2. Within the database, create a table for logging access entries. This table must have the field names and data types listed in Table 13-8. You can use the Logtemp.sql script to create this table.

3. Next, create a Data Source Name (DSN) that IIS can use to connect to the database. You'll probably want to use a system DSN to establish the database connection. With SQL Server, you must specify the technique that should be used to verify the authenticity of the login identification (ID). If you use Microsoft Windows NT authentication, the account you specify when configuring IIS must have permission to write to the database. If you use SQL Server authentication, you can specify an SQL Server login ID and password to use.

4. Complete the process by enabling logging for the site and setting the active log format to ODBC logging. When you configure logging, you must specify the DSN name, the table name, and the logon information.

As discussed in the "HttpLoggingModule" section of the appendix, "Comprehensive IIS 7.0 Module and Schema Reference," the configuration schema includes default values for ODBC logging. The default values are InternetDb for the database name, InternetLog for the table name, and InternetAdmin for the user name. When configuring DSNs, the database name is the same as the data source name. You can override these settings by assigning specific values at the appropriate configuration level.

The sections that follow describe how you can use SQL Server 2005 and IIS to configure ODBC logging. These sections assume a fair amount of knowledge of SQL Server 2005 and database administration. If you need more assistance, refer to the *Microsoft SQL Server 2005 Administrator's Pocket Consultant*.

Creating a Logging Database and Table in SQL Server 2005

You can use SQL Server 2005 as your logging server. To do this, you must create a database and configure a logging table. To create a database, complete the following steps:

1. In SQL Server Management Studio, use the Registered Servers view to select the Database Engine server type and the server you want to use.

2. Right-click the Databases folder, and then on the shortcut menu, select New Database. This opens the New Database dialog box.

3. On the General page, in the Database Name box, type **LoggingDB** as the database name.

4. Click OK. SQL Server creates the database.

Next, install the ODBC Logging role service for IIS if this role is not already installed. Then locate the Logtemp.sql script. This script is located in the *%SystemRoot%*\System32\Inetsrv directory on the IIS server. Edit the script so that it sets the table name you want to use for the site's log entries. For example, if you wanted to name the table HTTPLog, you would update the script as shown in the following listing:

```
use LoggingDB
create table HTTPLog (
ClientHost varchar(255),
username varchar(255),
LogTime datetime,
service varchar(255),
machine varchar(255),
serverip varchar(50),
processingtime int,
bytesrecvd int,
bytessent int,
servicestatus int,
win32status int,
operation varchar(255),
target varchar(255),
parameters varchar(255)
)
```

After you update the script, open a Query window in SQL Server Management Studio by selecting New Query on the toolbar. In the Query view, you can access scripts by clicking the Open File button on the toolbar and then typing the location of the script. Alternately, you can copy and paste the script into the newly opened Query view. Run the script by clicking Execute. When the script completes, a new table should be created in the LoggingDB database. If necessary, ensure that you connect to the server running SQL Server using an account with database administrator privileges.

Creating a DSN for SQL Server 2005

Once you create the logging database and the input table, you can configure IIS to connect to the database. IIS connects to the database using a DSN. You must create the DSN on the IIS server.

To create a DSN, complete the following steps:

1. On the Administrative Tools menu, start Data Sources (ODBC).

2. On the System DSN tab, click Add. The Create New Data Source dialog box appears.

3. On the Driver list, select SQL Server, and then click Finish. As shown in Figure 13-3, you should now see the Create A New Data Source To SQL Server dialog box.

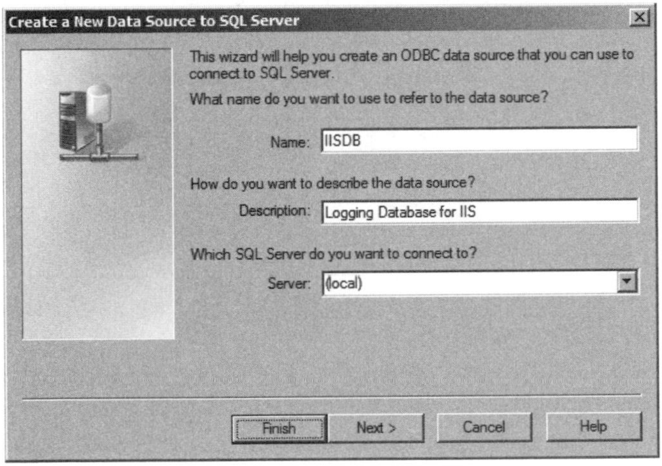

Figure 13-3   Use the Create A New Data Source To SQL Server dialog box to configure the data source.

4. In the Name field, type the name of the DSN, such as **IISDB**.

5. In the Server field, type the name of the SQL Server to which you want to connect, or select (Local) if SQL Server is running on the same hardware as IIS.

6. Next, as shown in Figure 13-4, specify the technique that should be used to verify the authenticity of the login ID. If you use Windows NT authentication, the account you specify when configuring IIS must have permission to write to the logging database. If you use SQL Server authentication, you can specify an SQL Server login ID and password to use.

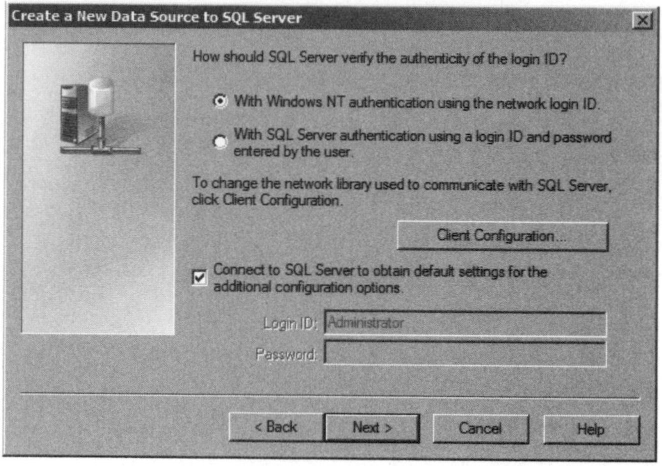

Figure 13-4 Set the authentication method for the DSN connection.

7. Click Next and then click Finish to complete the process. If Windows is unable to establish a connection to the database, you might need to recheck the information you've entered for correctness. You might also need to confirm that the account you are using has the appropriate permissions in the database.

Enabling and Configuring ODBC Logging in IIS

ODBC is a type of custom logging that can be configured only when an IIS server is using per-site logging. To complete the configuration process, you must enable and configure ODBC logging in IIS by following these steps:

1. As necessary, use Server Manager to install and enable the Custom Logging and ODBC Logging role services for the IIS server.

2. In IIS Manager, navigate to the server or site you want to manage. In the main pane, when you group by area, the Logging feature is listed under IIS. Double-click Logging to open this feature.

3. If all logging options are dimmed and the server is configured for per site logging, you can click Enable in the Actions pane to enable logging for this site.

4. On the Format list, select Custom as the log format. No additional logging options can be selected in IIS Manager.

5. Edit the configuration file for the site that should use ODBC logging. Use the attributes of the odbcLogging element, summarized in Table A-17 in the appendix, to configure OBDC logging.

Configuring Centralized Binary Logging

Before you implement centralized binary logging, there are many things you should consider, including how using this format will affect the server and what tools you will use to read the raw binary logs. After planning, you should set up a test installation and determine if it is feasible to switch to centralized binary logging and obtain the information your organization needs from the raw binary log files. Only when you are certain that this format will work for you should you enable binary logging.

When you are ready to implement centralized binary logging, complete the following steps to enable logging and configure the W3C extended log file format:

1. In IIS Manager, select the server you want to manage. In the main pane, double-click Logging to open this feature.

2. If logging is currently disabled at the server level, all logging options are dimmed and cannot be selected. You can enable logging by clicking Enable in the Actions pane.

3. To use per server logging, in the One Log File Per drop-down list, select Server.

4. By default, log files are located in a subdirectory under %SystemDrive%\System32\Inetpub\Logs\Logfiles. If you want to change the default logging directory, type the directory path in the Directory field, or click Browse to look for a directory that you want to use.

5. To configure logging using a specific time period, select Schedule, and then choose one of the following options:

   ❑ **Hourly** IIS creates a new log each hour.

   ❑ **Daily** IIS creates a new log daily at midnight.

   ❑ **Weekly** IIS creates a new log file each Saturday at midnight.

   ❑ **Monthly** IIS creates a new log file at midnight on the last day of the month.

6. To configure logging using an unlimited file site, select Do Not Create New Log Files. With this option, IIS doesn't end the log file automatically. You must manage the log file.

7. To set a maximum log file size in bytes, select Maximum File Size (In Bytes), and then type the desired maximum file size, such as **1024000**. When the log file reaches this size, a new log file is created.

8. Click Apply to save your settings. The service directory and log file are created automatically, if necessary. If IIS doesn't have Read/Write permission on the logging directory, an error is generated.

Disabling Logging

If you don't plan to generate reports from access logs, you might not want to log user access to the sites on a server. In this case, you can disable logging for the server. You can disable logging for the server and all sites by completing the following steps:

1. In IIS Manager, select the node for the server you want to manage. If the server you want to use isn't listed, connect to it.

2. In the main pane, when you group by area, the Logging feature is listed under IIS. Double-click Logging to open this feature.

3. If logging is currently enabled at the server level, logging options are available and can be selected. You can disable logging by clicking Disable in the Actions pane.

You can enable or disable logging for individual sites by completing the following steps:

1. In IIS Manager, select the node for the site you want to manage. In the main pane, when you group by area, the Logging feature is listed under IIS. Double-click Logging to open this feature.

2. If logging is currently enabled for the site and you want to disable it, in the Actions pane, click Disable. If logging is currently disabled for the site and you want to enable it, in the Actions pane, click Enable.

Note   If you've configured per-server logging, you cannot manage or enable logging at the site level. You can, however, disable logging for individual sites.

Chapter 14

IIS Backup and Recovery

When you back up an Internet Information Services (IIS) server, you need to look at the IIS configuration in addition to the system configuration. This means that you must do the following:

- Save the IIS configuration whenever you change the properties of the IIS installation.

- Maintain several configuration backups as an extra precaution.

- Periodically back up the server by using a comprehensive backup procedure, such as the one outlined in this chapter.

Backing up an IIS server by using this technique gives you several recovery options. You can:

- Recover the IIS configuration settings for sites and virtual servers by using the IIS configuration backup you've created.

- Recover a corrupted IIS installation by reinstalling IIS and then recovering the last working IIS configuration.

- Restore the server, its data files, and its IIS configuration by recovering the system from archives.

- Perform a partial server restore to retrieve missing or corrupted files from archives.   '

The sections that follow examine backing up and recovering IIS server configurations and data files.

Backing Up the IIS Configuration

Backing up the IIS configuration is an important part of any Web administrator's job. Before you get started, take a moment to learn the key concepts that'll help you every step of the way.

Understanding IIS Configuration Backups

IIS configuration backups contain metadata that describes the configuration settings used by IIS modules, Web sites, applications, and virtual directories. IIS uses the metadata to restore values for all resource properties on a server. IIS also uses this information to maintain the run state of the server. Therefore, if you save the IIS configuration and then restore the configuration later, the IIS configuration settings are restored and the IIS resources are also returned to their original state.

I recommend that you create an IIS configuration backup every time you make IIS configuration changes and before you make major changes that affect the availability of resources. Because IIS has new configuration architecture, creating and managing IIS configuration backups is fundamentally different than with previous editions of IIS. Throughout this chapter, I'll refer to backups of IIS server configuration and content configuration simply as IIS configuration backups. However, the distinction between server configuration and content configuration is an important one.

Server configuration backups include:

- Automated backups of applicationHost.config created by IIS and stored in the configuration history under *%SystemDrive%*\Inetpub\History by default

- Administrator generated backups of the server's current configuration and running state stored under *%SystemRoot%*\System32\Inetsrv\Backup by default

IIS automatically creates a backup of applicationHost.config when you make configuration changes. This history captures the last 10 configuration changes made on the server in sequentially numbered CFGHISTORY subdirectories of *%SystemDrive%*\Inetpub\History. When you change the configuration, IIS does the following:

1. Deletes the oldest configuration history subdirectory under *%SystemDrive%*\Inetpub\History

2. Creates a new configuration history subdirectory under *%SystemDrive%*\Inetpub\History

3. Writes a copy of applicationHost.config to the newly created subdirectory

As you continue to make configuration changes, IIS does not track every individual change. Instead, after the first configuration change, IIS stores the current configuration every 2 minutes. Thus, if you make a series of changes to the IIS configuration over a period of 10 minutes, IIS would track the configuration changes by creating up to five configuration history files.

As an IIS administrator, you can create backups of an IIS server's current configuration and running state. IIS stores these backups by default in a subdirectory of *%SystemRoot%*\System32\Inetsrv\Backup. Administrator-generated backups generally can include the following configuration files:

- **Administration.config**   Stores the current configuration for delegation and management

- **ApplicationHost.config**   Stores the current configuration and running state of the server plus all applications, application pools, and virtual directories created on the server

- **Mbschema.xml**   Stores the schema for the IIS 6 metabase

- **Metabase.xml**   Stores the IIS 6 metabase

- **Redirection.config**   Stores redirection configuration

Note   IIS 7.0 uses the metabase only for backwards compatibility with FTP services as designed for IIS 6. Metabase files are stored as part of the configuration only when you've installed the IIS metabase compatibility and FTP Server role services.

Content configuration backups include copies of the Web.config files that modify the default configuration for Web site, application, and directory roots. Neither the automated IIS backup process nor the manual administrator backup process creates backup copies of Web.config files. Because of this, you must use a separate backup or copy process to create copies of Web.config files.

Assuming that you've installed the IIS server root under *%SystemDrive%*\Inetpub (per the default configuration), you can quickly obtain a list of all Web.config files used on a server by running the command-line script shown in Listing 14-1.

Listing 14-1   Script for Web.config Files

```
@echo off
@title "Listing IIS web.config files to working.txt"
cls
color 07

echo **************************************************** > working.txt
echo "Listing of web.config files as of:" >> working.txt
date /t >> working.txt
echo **************************************************** >>
working.txt
echo * >> working.txt
for /r %SystemDrive%\inetpub %%B in (web.config) do
(echo %%B >> working.txt)
echo Done...listing contents of working.txt...
echo *
type working.txt
echo *
```

Sample Output
```
****************************************************
"Listing of web.config files as of:"
Fri 12/21/2007
****************************************************
*
C:\inetput\wwwroot\web.config
C:\inetput\wwwroot\Sales\web.config
C:\inetput\wwwroot\Support\web.config
C:\inetput\wwwroot\Reports\web.config
*
```

The heart of this basic script is the following For loop:

```
for /r %SystemDrive%\inetpub %%B in (web.config) do (echo %%B >>
working.txt)
```

This For loop looks recursively in subdirectories of %*SystemDrive*%\Inetpub for instances of files named Web.config and then writes the full path of each file in turn to a text file in the current directory called working.txt. If you created the IIS server root in another location, simply substitute that location for %*SystemDrive*%\Inetpub when running the script. %%B is an iteration variable that tracks the current working value. In this script, %%B tracks an instance of a file path where there's a Web.config file on the server.

The other statements in the script are there for aesthetics. They provide additional details on the command line and in the working file itself. Knowing this, you could also run the For loop at the command prompt by typing the following:

```
for /r %SystemDrive%\inetpub %B in (web.config) do (echo %B >>
working.txt)
```

Note See the syntax change for the iteration variable. You reference iteration variables in scripts by using %% notation and at a command line by using % notation.

IIS configuration backups can help you in many situations. You can:

- **Recover deleted resources** References to all site, application pool, virtual directory, and application instances running on the server are stored with the configuration backup. If you delete a site, application pool, virtual directory, or application, you can restore the necessary resource references by restoring the configuration files.

- **Restore resource properties** All configuration settings of sites, application pools, virtual directories, and applications are stored in the configuration backup. If you change properties, you can recover the previous IIS settings from backup.

- **Recover global settings and module configuration** Global properties and module configuration settings are stored in configuration backups. This means that you can recover default settings for the server and modules from backup.

- **Rebuild a damaged IIS installation** If the IIS installation is corrupted and you can't repair it through normal means, you can rebuild the IIS installation. You do this by uninstalling IIS, reinstalling IIS, and then using the configuration backup to restore the IIS settings. See the "Rebuilding Corrupted IIS Installations" section of this chapter for details.

Backup files created by IIS are simply copies of the original configuration files. This means that you can open them in a standard text editor to view or modify their settings as you would with any of the other configuration files.

Managing the IIS Configuration History

You can manage the way IIS creates automatic backups of configuration changes by running the IIS command-line administration tool's Set Config command and the configHistory section of the applicationHost.config file. The available attributes for this configuration section are:

- **Enabled**   Controls whether configuration history tracking is turned on or off. By default, this attribute is set to True. To turn off configuration history tracking, set this attribute to False.

  Note   Typically, you'd want to turn off the configuration history only when you are doing extensive testing or debugging of applications and don't want any of these changes tracked. When you are finished testing or debugging, you should re-enable configuration history.

- **Path**   Sets the directory to which IIS writes configuration history. The default is *%SystemDrive%\Inetpub\History*.

- **maxHistories**   Sets the maximum number of history files to track. The default is 10.

- **Period**   Sets the interval at which IIS writes configuration history as you continue to make changes. The default interval is every 2 minutes.

Note   You can use maxHistories and Period to optimize history tracking for the way you work with IIS. For example, if you want to maintain more history information and find that you often modify history over extended periods, you may want to increase maxHistories and increase the write period. In this way, IIS will retain more history files and make fewer history files when you modify the running configuration over long periods.

Sample 14-1 provides the syntax and usage for working with configuration history. Note that period values are set in *hh:mm:ss* format where the *h* position is for hours, the *m* position is for minutes, and the *s* position is for seconds.

Sample 14-1   Managing the Configuration History Syntax and Usage

Syntax
```
appcmd set config /section:configHistory
[/enabled: true|false] [/path: "DestPath"]
[/maxHistories: "NumHistories"]
[/period: "HH:MM:SS"
```
Usage to Modify History Tracking
```
appcmd set config /section:configHistory
/maxHistories: "25" /period: "00:05:00"
```
Usage to Disable History Tracking
```
appcmd set config /section:configHistory /enabled:false
```

Viewing IIS Configuration Backups

IIS stores configuration backups by default in the *%SystemDrive%*\Inetpub\History directory. Each subdirectory in this directory contains the files for a specific configuration backup. By using the IIS command-line administration tool, you can list configuration backups by running the List Backup command. Sample 14-2 provides the syntax and usage. As the syntax shows, you can list all backups or a specific backup. You list a specific backup to determine if that specific backup exists. Appcmd doesn't provide other details about a backup, however.

Sample 14-2 List Backup Syntax and Usage

Syntax
```
appcmd list backup [/backup.name:]"BackupName"]
```
Usage
```
appcmd list backup

appcmd list backup "101207_583921"
```

Creating IIS Configuration Backups

Each IIS server has a configuration that must be backed up to ensure that IIS can be recovered in case of problems. You can create backups at the server, site, or virtual directory level.

At the server level, you create a configuration backup of all sites, application pools, applications, and virtual directories on the server by using the IIS command-line administration tool and the Add Backup command. Sample 14-3 provides the syntax and usage. If you do not provide a backup name, AppCmd generates a name using a date time stamp that tracks the year, month, date, and time to the second, such as 20080415T143535.

Sample 14-3 Add Backup Syntax and Usage

Syntax
```
appcmd add backup [/name:"BackupName"]
```
Usage
```
appcmd add backup

appcmd add backup /name:"10-12-08_CurrentSet"
```

After you back up the IIS configuration, you should also back up the content configuration, that is, the individual Web.config files for sites, applications, and virtual directories. Listing 14-1 provides a script for listing each Web.config file on the server.

Removing IIS Configuration Backups

As you create configuration backups, you create more and more configuration backup subdirectories and files on the server. You can delete backups by removing the related subdirectories, which are stored by default under *%SystemDrive%*\Inetpub\History.

By using the IIS command-line administration tool, you can delete individual configuration backups by running the Remove Backup command. Sample 14-4 provides the syntax and usage. As the syntax shows, you must provide the name of the backup configuration to delete.

Sample 14-4   Delete Backup Syntax and Usage

Syntax
```
appcmd delete backup [/backup.name:]"BackupName"
```
Usage
```
appcmd delete backup

appcmd delete backup /backup.name:"10-12-08_CurrentSet"
```

Restoring IIS Server Configurations

You can restore IIS from backup configuration files. When you do this, the previous property settings and state are restored for all sites, application pools, applications, and virtual directories. Recovering the configuration won't repair a corrupted IIS installation. To repair a corrupted installation, follow the technique outlined in the "Rebuilding Corrupted IIS Installations" section of this chapter.

When you restore IIS from a backup configuration, the IIS command-line administration tool stops the server, copies the backup configuration files over the existing configuration files, and then starts the server. IIS then loads the current run state from these files on startup. Stopping and then starting IIS is a precaution to ensure that the full state of the server is reset. If AppCmd did not stop and start the server, some settings that require restart would not be applied until you manually restarted the server process. For example, if the access log settings in the backup configuration are different from those in the running configuration, the restored access log settings are applied only when the server process is restarted.

> **Tip**   Restoring the IIS configuration doesn't' restore content configuration, which may include additional settings that need to be restored. Thus, to restore the configuration fully, you many need to copy the backup Web.config files to their original locations.

By using the IIS command-line administration tool, you can restore a configuration backup by running the Restore Backup command. Sample 14-5 provides the syntax and usage. As the syntax shows, you must provide the name of the backup configuration to restore. Optionally, you can specify whether AppCmd stops the server before restoring the configuration. Because stopping and starting the server causes all server processes to be recycled, this could cause issues with user sessions and applications.

Sample 14-5   Restore Backup Syntax and Usage

```
Syntax
appcmd restore backup [/backup.name:]"BackupName" [/stop:true|false]
Usage
appcmd restore backup "10-12-08_CurrentSet"

appcmd restore backup "10-12-08_CurrentSet" /stop:false
```

Rebuilding Corrupted IIS Installations

A corrupt IIS installation can cause problems with your IIS sites, application pools, applications, and virtual directories. Resources might not run. IIS might not respond to commands. IIS might freeze intermittently. To correct these problems, you might need to rebuild the IIS installation. Rebuilding the IIS installation is a lengthy process that requires a complete outage of the server. The outage can last from 5 to 15 minutes or more.

You rebuild a corrupt IIS installation by completing the following steps:

1. Log on locally to the computer on which you want to rebuild IIS. Make sure to use an account with Administrator privileges.

2. Create a new backup of the server configuration and content configuration by using the techniques discussed previously in this chapter.

3. Start Server Manager by clicking the Server Manager icon on the Quick Launch toolbar or by clicking Start, pointing to Administrative Tools, and then clicking Server Manager.

4. In Server Manager, right-click the Roles node, and then select Remove Roles. This starts the Remove Roles Wizard.

5. On the Remove Server Roles page, Setup selects the currently installed roles. To remove a role, clear the related check box. When you are finished selecting roles to remove, click Next, and then click Remove.

6. In Server Manager, right-click the Roles node, and then select Add Roles. This starts the Add Roles Wizard.

7. On the Select Server Roles page, Setup makes the currently selected roles dimmed so that you cannot select them. To add a role, select it in the Roles list. When you are finished selecting roles to add, click Next, and then click Install.

8. Restore the server configuration by using the IIS command-line administration tool and the Restore Backup command. This restores the IIS server configuration.

9. Restore the content configuration by copying the Web.config files to the appropriate locations.

Backing Up and Recovering Server Files

Windows Server 2008 provides a utility called Windows Server Backup for creating server backups. You use Windows Server Backup to perform common backup and recovery tasks. Other features include startup and recovery options and a facility for making recovery disks.

> **Note**   The focus of this book is on IIS 7.0 administration and not Windows Server administration. A full discussion of backup, recovery, and troubleshooting the operating system is beyond the scope of this book. For additional discussion on these topics, refer to the *Windows Server 2008 Administrator's Pocket Consultant* (Microsoft Press, 2008) or *Windows Server 2008 Inside Out* (Microsoft Press, 2008).

Turning on the Backup Feature

Windows Server Backup is provided as an add-on component for the operating system. In earlier versions of Microsoft Windows, you use the Add/Remove Windows Components application of Add Or Remove Programs to add or remove operating system components. In Windows Server 2008, operating system components are considered Windows features that can be turned on or off rather than added or removed.

To turn on the Backup feature, follow these steps:

1. Start Server Manager by clicking the Server Manager icon on the Quick Launch toolbar or by clicking Start, pointing to Administrative Tools, and then clicking Server Manager.

2. In Server Manager, select the Features node to view a list of installed features. If Windows Server Backup is not listed as an installed feature, click Add Features. This starts the Add Features Wizard.

3. Under Features, select the Windows Server Backup check box.

4. Click Next, and then click Install.

5. When the installation process finishes, click Close to close the Add Features Wizard.

You can now use Windows Server Backup on the server.

Working with Windows Server Backup

Once you've turned on the Windows Server Backup feature, you can access the related utility in several ways, including:

- Click Start, point to Administrative Tools, and then click Windows Server Backup.

- In Server Manager, expand the Storage node, and then select Windows Server Backup.

The first time you use Windows Server Backup, you may want to configure basic performance settings and create a backup schedule. Basic performance settings control whether Windows Server Backup performs full or incremental backups by default. A backup schedule allows you to configure Windows Server Backup to back up the server automatically according to a recurring schedule, such as once daily or twice daily. You also can back up a server manually.

To perform backup and recovery operations, you must have certain permissions and user rights. Members of the Administrators and Backup Operators groups have full authority to back up and restore any type of file, regardless of who owns the file and the permissions set on it. File owners and those that have been given control over files can also back up files, but only those that they own or those for which they have Read, Read And Execute, Modify, or Full Control permissions.

Note Keep in mind that although local accounts can work only with local systems, domain accounts have domain-wide privileges. Therefore, a member of the local administrators group can work with files only on the local system, but a member of the domain administrators group can work with files throughout the domain.

Windows Server Backup can perform two general types of backups:

- Full

- Incremental

With a full (normal) backup, Windows Server Backup backs up all files that have been selected and then clears the archive bit. If a file is later changed, the operating system sets the archive bit to mark the file as needing backup. With full backups, you always have a full set of data, but the backup process takes longer than with incremental backups because you are backing up more data. When you run only full backups, you restore a server by restoring the most recent full backup.

With an incremental backup, Windows Server Backup backs up only files that have changed since the most recent full or incremental backup. Windows Server Backup determines that a file needs to be backed up incrementally based on the file having its archive bit set. With incremental backups, the first backup on the server will always be a full backup and then successive backups will be incremental backups. Because incremental backups back up only files that have changed since the most recent full or incremental backup, incremental backups are usually smaller than full backups and can therefore be created more quickly.

In most cases, you'll want to create full backups of a server at least once a week and then supplement this with daily incremental backups. Restoring a server from incremental backups can be much slower than restoring a server from a full backup. With incremental backups, you restore a server by restoring the most recent full backup and then restoring each incremental backup created since the most recent full backup. For example, you create a full backup on Sunday and incremental backups Monday through Saturday. If the server fails on Friday, prior to creating Friday's incremental backup, you restore the server by applying Sunday's full backup and the incremental backups from Monday, Tuesday, Wednesday, and Thursday.

Although you can back up to shared volumes and DVD media manually, you will need a separate, dedicated hard disk for running scheduled backups. After you configure a disk for scheduled backups, the backup utilities automatically manage the disk usage and reuse the space of older backups when creating new backups. Once you schedule backups, you'll need to check periodically to ensure that backups are being performed as expected and that the backup schedule meets current needs.

Setting Basic Performance Options

By default, Windows Server Backup always performs a full backup of all physical drives on the server. Both internal and external drives are included in the backup as long as the drives are formatted as NTFS.

You can change the default settings so that Windows Backup Server performs incremental backups of all internal drives on the server or selectively performs a full or incremental backup depending on the drive. With full backups, you can perform a full Volume Shadow Copy Service (VSS)–based backup or a copy backup. With full VSS backups, VSS is used to perform block-level (image) backups, which ensures that the backup includes files that are being written to by the operating system or user processes, such as application data. When you perform a copy backup, application data is not included in the backup, and you then also must use a third-party backup utility to back up applications. With scheduled backups, Windows performs copy backups. With manual backups, you can specify whether you want to perform a full VSS or copy backups. Although Windows Server Backup does not currently enable you to specify that you want to perform a full backup weekly or monthly (for instance), and then incremental backups once or twice daily (for instance), this functionality probably will be added in a future service pack.

You can view or change the default options by completing the following steps:

1. In Server Manager, expand the Storage node, and then select Windows Server Backup.

2. In the Actions Pane or on the Action menu, select Configure Performance Settings. The Optimize Backup Performance dialog box appears.

3. Choose an appropriate default backup option. If you choose Custom, you can set the backup options and type for each supported drive. With a custom backup option, you also can exclude drives. However, drives that contain the operating system or applications must always be selected for backup.

4. Click OK to save the default settings.

Scheduling Server Backups

Scheduling a backup allows you to back up a server automatically according to a specified schedule. You create a backup schedule for a server by completing the following steps:

1. In Server Manager, expand the Storage node, and then select Windows Server Backup.

2. In the Actions Pane or on the Action menu, select Backup Schedule. When the Backup Schedule Wizard starts, click Next.

3. You can use the Select Backup Type page to perform either a full server backup, which includes all supported drives, or a custom server backup, in which some drives are excluded from the backup. Note that the size of the full backup is listed. To continue, do one of the following:

   ❏ To perform a full server backup of all supported drives to include both internal and external drives, select Full Server, and then click Next. Drives that are formatted as NTFS are included in the backup set. Drives that are formatted as FAT, FAT32, or another file system are not included in the backup set.

   ❏ To selectively backup drives, select Custom, and then click Next. On the Select Custom Backup Items page, select the check boxes for the drives you want to include and clear the check boxes for drives you want to exclude. You must always include drives that contain the operating system and applications.

4. On the Specify Backup Time page, specify how often you want to run backups. You can schedule backups to run once a day at a specified time or multiple times a day at specified times. Click Next.

   Tip   When scheduling your backups, keep in mind that you typically will want to perform backups during off-peak times because the backup process could result in reduced responsiveness to user requests. Also keep in mind that a full backup of a server can take several hours to complete (as can incremental backups that include many gigabytes of data).

5. On the Select Destination Disk page, select the disk or disks for storing the backup, and then click Next. The Backup Schedule Wizard will check the format of the target disk or disks and reformat the disk or disks as necessary. When

a disk is reformatted, all data on the disk is lost. When selecting target disks, keep the following in mind:

❑ If you choose multiple disks, Windows Server Backup creates multiple copies of the backup. Creating multiple backup copies allows you to store a backup on a disk directly connected to the server in addition to on a remote server or network storage device. Because a network storage device can be in a different physical location, this makes it easier to create and store backups off site to protect against natural disasters. Although being able to create multiple backup copies is a tremendous benefit, keep in mind that each additional backup copy creates an additional burden on the server, and you may need to monitor resource usage carefully during backup creation. In addition, to write backups to different physical locations efficiently, you may need to set up a dedicated backup network.

❑ The list of disks for backups includes both internal and external disks. Any disk connected to the server can be used for storing backups as long as the disk does not have system or application files. Only the most likely disk or disks for storing backups are listed for selection. To list other available disks, click Show All, select a check box for a disk to make it available for use, and then click OK.

❑ When selecting a disk to use for the backup, note the size of the disk in addition to the amount of space used. Note also the Backup Item Size and then Recommended Target Size details. Backup Item Size lists the total size of the backup. Recommended Target Size lists the recommended amount of free space for creating the backup. The recommended amount of free space is more than the required free space to allow Windows Server Backup to create temporary working files and to ensure optimal performance. If a target disk has less free space than the recommended amount, the backup process will be less efficient and slower than usual.

6. If you are writing a backup to an external disk, you see the Label Destination Disk page and are prompted to label the disk so that it is identified as a backup disk. Click Next.

7. On the Confirmation page, review the backup schedule and details, and then click Finish. The server must be turned on at the scheduled run time for automated backups to work.

Backing up a Server

You can use the Backup Wizard to back up a server manually at any time by completing the following steps:

1. In Server Manager, expand the Storage node, and then select Windows Server Backup.

2. In the Actions Pane or on the Action menu, select Backup Once.

3. On the Backup Options page, choose Different Options, and then click Next.

4. On the Specify Backup Type page, you can choose to perform either a full server backup that includes all supported drives or a custom server backup in which some drives are excluded from the backup. To continue, do one of the following, and then click Next:

   ❑ To perform a full server backup of all supported drives to include both internal and external drives, select Full Server, and then click Next. Drives that are formatted as NTFS are included in the backup set. Drives that are formatted as FAT, FAT32, or another file system are not included in the backup set.

   ❑ To selectively back up drives, select Custom, and then click Next. On the Backup Items page, select the check boxes for the drives you want to include and clear the check boxes for drives you want to exclude. You must always include drives that contain the operating system and applications.

5. You can store the backup on a local drive or on a remote shared folder by using the following techniques. To continue, do one of the following, and then click Next:

   ❑ To store the backup on a local drive, select Local Drives, and then click Next. On the Select Backup Location page, on the Backup Location list, choose a backup location. When selecting a disk to use for the backup, note the size of the disk in addition to the amount of space used. Note also the Backup Item Size. The disk you select should have approximately 50 percent more free space than the backup item size. This allows Windows Server Backup to create temporary working files and ensures optimal performance. If a disk doesn't have additional free space, the backup process will be less efficient and slower than usual.

   ❑ To store the backup on a remote shared folder, select Remote Shared Folder, and then click Next. On the Specify Remote Folder page, type the UNC path to the remote shared folder, such as \\BackupServer26 \Backup\WebServer85. The remote shared folder must be configured as an available network location.

6. On the Specify VSS Backup Type page, specify whether you want to perform a copy backup or a VSS full backup. Choose Copy Backup if you are using a separate backup utility to back up application data, such as that from Microsoft SQL Server. Otherwise, choose VSS Full Backup to fully back up the selected volumes, including all application data.

7. On the Confirmation page, review the backup schedule and details, and then click Backup. The Backup Once Wizard will then create a shadow copy of the drives you are backing up. This allows the wizard to back up files that are being written to by the operating system or user processes. Click Backup.

On the Backup Progress page, you'll see the status of the backup and the amount of data transferred. The backup is complete when the backup status reaches 100 percent. If you click Close, the backup will continue to run in the background, and you can review the final backup status for errors or other issues in Server Manager. Simply double-click the backup entry under Messages.

Protecting a Server Against Failure

Backing up a server is one way of protecting a server against failure. Windows Server has a built-in recovery feature that automatically runs if a server fails to start or experiences a fatal system error (also known as a STOP error). For some of these features to work, you may need the original Windows installation disk. Additionally, computer manufacturers increasingly are including recovery features as part of a comprehensive hardware option. These features can also be used to recover the operating system to a bootable state. If these features fail, Windows Server 2008 provides other protection features, including:

- Startup and recovery options
- Recovery disks

The sections that follow discuss how to configure these recovery options.

Configuring Recovery Options

Startup and recovery options control the way Windows Server 2008 starts and handles failures. You can manage startup and recovery options by completing these steps:

1. Click Start, and then click Control Panel. In Control Panel, click System and Maintenance, and then click System.

2. In the System console, in the left pane, click Advanced System Settings. On the Advanced tab, under Startup and Recovery, click Settings. This opens the Startup and Recovery dialog box.

3. If the server has multiple bootable operating systems, you can set the default operating system by selecting one of the operating systems in the Default Operating System drop-down list. These options change the configuration settings that Windows Boot Manager uses.

4. At the startup of a computer with multiple bootable operating systems, Windows Server displays the startup configuration menu for 30 seconds by default. To boot immediately to the default operating system, clear the Time To Display List Of Operating Systems check box. To display the available options for a specific amount of time, select the Time To Display List Of Operating Systems check box, and then set the desired time delay in seconds.

5. When the system is in a recovery mode and is booting, a list of recovery options might appear. To boot immediately using the default recovery option, clear the Time To Display Recovery Options When Needed check box. To display the

available recovery options for a specific amount of time, select the Time To Display Recovery Options When Needed check box, and then set a time delay in seconds.

6. System Failure options control what happens when the system encounters a STOP error. The available options for the System Failure area are as follows:

❑ **Write an Event to the System Log**   Logs the error in the System log, which allows you to review the error later using the Event Viewer.

❑ **Automatically Restart**   Select this check box to have the system attempt to reboot when a fatal system error occurs.

❑ **Write Debugging Information**   Choose the type of debugging information to write to a dump file if a fatal error occurs. You can then use the dump file to diagnose system failures.

❑ **Dump File**   Sets the location for the dump file. The default dump locations are *%SystemRoot%*\Minidump for small memory dumps and *%SystemRoot%*\MEMORY.DMP for all other memory dumps.

❑ **Overwrite Any Existing File**   Ensures that any existing dump files are overwritten if a new STOP error occurs.

7. Click OK to save your settings.

The Windows Recovery Environment includes the following tools:

■ **Windows Complete PC Restore**   Allows you to recover a server's operating system or perform a full system recovery. With an operating system or full system recovery, make sure your backup data is available and that you can log on with an account that has the appropriate permissions. With a full system recovery, keep in mind that existing data that was not included in the original backup will be deleted when you recover the system, including any in-use volumes that were not included in the backup.

■ **Windows Memory Diagnostics Tools**   Allows you to diagnose a problem with the server's physical memory. Three different levels of memory testing can be performed: basic, standard, or exhaustive.

You can also access a command prompt. This command prompt gives you access to the command-line tools available during installation as well as to these additional programs:

■ **On-screen Keyboard (x:\sources\setuposk.exe)**   Allows you to enter keystrokes using the on-screen keyboard.

■ **Rollback wizard (x:\sources\rollback.exe)**   Normally the Rollback wizard starts automatically if Windows Setup encounters a problem during installation.

■ **Startup Repair wizard (x:\sources\recovery\StartRep.exe)**   Normally this tool starts automatically on boot failure if Windows detects an issue with the boot sector, the boot manager, or the boot configuration data (BCD) store.

■ **Startup Recovery Options (x:\sources\recovery\recenv.exe)**   Allows you to start the Startup Recovery Options wizard. If you previously entered the wrong recovery settings, you can provide different options.

You can recover a server's operating system or perform a full system recovery by following these steps:

1. Insert the recovery disc into the CD or DVD drive and turn on the computer. If needed, press the required key to boot from the disc. The Install Windows Wizard should appear.

2. Specify the language settings to use, and then click Next.

3. Click Repair Your Computer. Setup searches the hard disk drives for an existing Windows installation and then displays the results in the System Recovery Options Wizard. If you are recovering the operating system onto separate hardware, the list should be empty and there should be no operating system on the computer. Click Next.

4. On the System Recovery Options page, click Windows Complete PC Restore. This starts the Windows Complete PC Restore Wizard.

Recovering Files and Folders

You can recover files and folders from a backup by completing the following steps:

1. In Server Manager, expand the Storage node, and then select Windows Server Backup.

2. In the Actions Pane or on the Action menu, select Recover. The Recovery Wizard starts.

3. On the Getting Started page, choose This Server.

4. On the Select Backup Date page, note the earliest and latest available backup dates, and then use the calendar view provided to select a date for recovery. Click Next.

   Backup copies are available for dates shown in bold in the calendar view. If there are multiple backup times on a date, select a specific backup from the Time drop-down list. Note the backup target and status of the selected backup. The target disk must be available online to recover files and applications.

5. On the Select Recovery Type page, select Files And Folders to recover specific files and folders from a backup, and then click Next.

6. On the Select Items To Recover page, expand the server, volume, and folder nodes to find the files and folders to recover. You can recover only one folder/file set at a time. When you select a folder by clicking it, the folder and all its related subfolders and files are selected for recovery. Click the folder you want to recover, such as Inetpub, and then click Next.

7. On the Specify Recovery Options page, use the Restore Destination options to choose the restore location and the click Next. The options are:

- ❑ **Original Location**   Restores data to the location from which it was backed up.

- ❑ **Alternate Location**   Restores data to a location that you designate, preserving the existing directory structure. After you select this option, type the folder path to use, or click Browse to select the folder path.

8. Select one of the following options to specify how you want to restore files, and then click Next:

- ❑ **Create Copies So I Have Both Versions Of The File Or Folder**   Select this option if you don't want to copy over existing files. With this option, you'll have copies of the recovered files in the recovery destination and will need to review the files to see which files you want to use. In most cases, you won't want to use this option if you are restoring multiple files to the original location, because this would cause many duplicate files to be created (and you'd probably need to use Windows Explorer to clean up all the duplicates).

- ❑ **Overwrite Existing Files With Recovered Files**   Select this option to replace all existing files on disk with files from the backup and to restore deleted files that do not otherwise exist at the recovery location. This option allows you to recover files and folders to a previous state (the state the files were in when the backup was created). Files that were deleted from the recovery location are also restored.

- ❑ **Don't Recover Any Existing Files And Folders**   Select this option to recover only files that do not exist at the recovery destination. This allows you to recover deleted files without overwriting existing files. If you accidentally removed files from a folder, this is a good option to use to recover only those accidentally removed files.

9. By default, Restore Security Settings is selected. This ensures that the Recovery Wizard restores the original security settings for files and folders. If you don't want to restore the original security settings, clear this check box. The Recovery Wizard will then use the default security settings for the recovery folder. Click Next

10. On the Confirmation page, review the items that will be recovered, and then click Finish. The Recovery Wizard will then recover the selected items. On the Recovery Progress page, you'll see the status of the recovery and the amount of data transferred for each item. Click Recover.

11. The recovery is complete when the recovery status reaches 100 percent. Click Close to finish the wizard.

Comprehensive IIS 7.0 Module and Schema Reference

In IIS 6, the configuration of a Web server is stored in the metabase, which is formatted using Extensible Markup Language (XML). When you create a backup of the metabase in IIS 6, you back up the server configuration into XML files stored in the *%SystemRoot%*\System32\Inetsrv directory. The metabase files are not meant to be edited and instead are managed through the IIS 6 Manager.

Although IIS 7.0 includes IIS 6 metabase support, IIS 7.0 does not use a metabase to store configuration information. Instead, IIS 7.0 uses a distributed configuration system with a single global configuration file, zero or more application-specific configuration files, and XML schema files that define the configuration elements, attributes, and the data that they can contain and provide precise control over exactly how you can configure IIS.

The global configuration file, Application.Host.config, is stored in the *%System-Root%*\System32\Inetsrv\Config directory. This file controls the global configuration of IIS. Application-specific configuration (Web.config) files can be stored in application directories to control the configuration of individual applications. Schema files define the exact set of configuration features and options that you can use within Application.Host.config and Web.config files. On a Web server, schema files are stored in the *%SystemRoot%*\System32\Inetsrv\Config\Schema directory. The three standard schema files are:

- **IIS_schema.xml**   Provides the IIS configuration schema

- **ASPNET_schema.xml**   Provides the Microsoft ASP.NET configuration schema

- **FX_schema.xml**   Provides the Microsoft .NET Framework configuration schema (beyond ASP.NET)

If you want to extend the configuration features and options available in IIS, you can do this by extending the XML schema. You can extend the schema by defining the desired configuration properties and the necessary section container in an XML schema file, placing this file in the *%SystemRoot%*\System32\Inetsrv\Config\Schema directory, and then referencing the new section in the IIS 7.0 global configuration file.

Working with IIS 7.0 Modules

IIS 7.0 features are componentized into more than 40 independent modules. Modules are either IIS 7.0 native modules or IIS 7.0 managed modules.

Introducing the Native Modules

A native module is a Win32 DLL that must be both installed and activated prior to use. The 32 native modules that ship with the IIS 7.0 installation provide the core server functionality. As depicted in Figure A-1, this core functionality can be divided into several broad categories.

- **Application Development**   Modules that provide features for application development and dynamic content

- **Common HTTP**   Modules that provide common features for Hypertext Transfer Protocol (HTTP) and the Web server in general

- **Health and Diagnostics**   Modules that provide features that help administrators track the health of the Web server and diagnose problems if they occur

- **Performance**   Modules that provide features that can be used to improve performance and scale the server

- **Security**   Modules that provide authentication, authorization, and filtering features

Configuration modules can be installed and made available for use:

- During initial setup of IIS

- By editing the Application.Host.config file or Web.config file as appropriate

- Using the graphical administration tool, IIS Manager

- Using the command-line administration tool, Appcmd.exe

Table A-1 provides an overview of specific IIS features, the related configuration modules, and the standard installation technique for each module. As the table shows, you can install most configuration modules by selecting a related feature during initial setup. Some modules are installed automatically as part of the core installation. Others can be installed only manually.

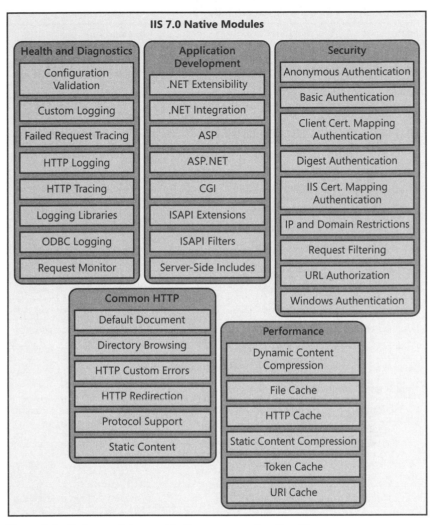

Figure A-1 Native modules provide the core server functionality.

Table A-1   Native Modules Shipped with IIS 7.0

Feature	Related Configuration Module	Installation
Common HTTP Features		
Default Document	DefaultDocumentModule	Installed by feature selection
Directory Browsing	DirectoryListingModule	Installed by feature selection
HTTP Custom Errors	CustomErrorModule	Installed by feature selection
HTTP Redirection	HttpRedirectionModule	Installed by feature selection
Protocol Support	ProtocolSupportModule	Installed automatically as part of the core installation
Static Content	StaticFileModule	Installed by feature selection
Application Development Features		
.NET Extensibility	IsapiModule	Installed by feature selection
ASP	IsapiFilterModule	Installed by feature selection
ASP.NET	IsapiFilterModule	Installed by feature selection
CGI	CgiModule	Installed by feature selection
Fast CGI	FastCgiModule	Installed by feature selection
ISAPI Extensions	IsapiModule	Installed by feature selection
ISAPI Filters	IsapiFilterModule	Installed by feature selection
Server-Side Includes	ServerSideIncludeModule	Installed by feature selection
Health and Diagnostics		
Configuration Validation	ConfigurationValidationModule	Installed automatically as part of the core installation
Custom Logging	CustomLoggingModule	Installed by feature selection
Failed Request Tracing	FailedRequestsTracingModule	Installed by feature selection
HTTP Logging	HttpLoggingModule	Installed by feature selection
HTTP Tracing	TracingModule	Must be manually installed after setup
Logging Tools	CustomLoggingModule	Installed by feature selection
ODBC Logging	CustomLoggingModule	Installed by feature selection
Request Monitor	RequestMonitorModule	Installed by feature selection
Security Features		
Anonymous Authentication	AnonymousAuthentication-Module	Installed automatically as part of the core installation
Basic Authentication	BasicAuthenticationModule	Installed by feature selection

Table A-1   Native Modules Shipped with IIS 7.0

Feature	Related Configuration Module	Installation
Client Certificate Mapping Authentication	CertificateMapping-AuthenticationModule	Installed by feature selection
Digest Authentication	DigestAuthenticationModule	Installed by feature selection
IIS Client Certificate Mapping Authentication	IISCertificateMapping-AuthenticationModule	Installed by feature selection
IP and Domain Restrictions	IpRestrictionModule	Installed by feature selection
Request Filtering	RequestFilteringModule	Installed by feature selection
URL Authorization	UrlAuthorizationModule	Installed by feature selection
Windows Authentication	WindowsAuthenticationModule	Installed by feature selection
Performance Features		
Dynamic Content Compression	DynamicCompressionModule	Installed by feature selection
Static Content Compression	StaticCompressionModule	Installed by feature selection
File Cache	FileCacheModule	Must be manually installed after setup
.NET Integration	ManagedEngine	Must be manually installed after setup
Token Cache	TokenCacheModule	Must be manually installed after setup
URI Cache	UriCacheModule	Must be manually installed after setup

Introducing the Managed Modules

A managed module is a .NET Framework Class Library contained within an assembly. Because managed modules are installed automatically as part of the .NET Framework, they do not need to be installed. However, managed modules do need to be activated for use. Managed modules also require the installation and activation of the ManagedEngine module, which provides the necessary integration functionality between IIS and the .NET Framework.

The IIS 7.0 installation ships with 11 managed modules. As Table A-2 shows, these modules provide the core functionality ASP and ASP.NET applications need for authorization and authentication in addition to utility functions for caching, session management, and URL mapping.

Table A-2   Managed Modules Shipped with IIS 7.0

Feature	.NET Framework Class Library
Security Functions	
Anonymous Identification	System.Web.Security.DefaultAuthenticationModule
File Authorization	System.Web.Security.FileAuthorizationModule
Forms Authentication	System.Web.Security.Forms.AuthenticationModule
Profile Management	System.Web.Profile.ProfileModule
Role Management	System.Web.Security.RoleManagerModule
URL Authorization	System.Web.Security.UrlAuthorizationModule.
Windows Authentication	System.Web.Security.WindowsAuthenticationModule
Utility Functions	
Output Cache	System.Web.Caching.OutputCacheModule
Session Management	System.Web.SessionState.SessionStateModule
URL Mapping	System.Web.UrlMappingsModule

IIS 7.0 Native Module Reference

In the following section, you'll find a reference for the native modules that ship with IIS 7.0. Native modules are used by both administrators and developers.

AnonymousAuthenticationModule

Implements Anonymous authentication

Description   Anonymous authentication is one of several authentication mechanisms available in IIS 7.0. If Anonymous authentication is enabled, any user can access content without being required to provide credentials. The actual component within IIS 7.0 that implements Anonymous authentication is the Anonymous-AuthenticationModule. This module allows Anonymous authentication by creating the necessary *HttpUser* object. The *HttpUser* object is an IIS data structure. The IIS core installation checks to ensure that this object is populated after the authentication phase. See Chapter 10, "Managing Web Server Security," for more information on Anonymous authentication.

> **Note**   At least one authentication module must be configured. Because of this, if you disable Anonymous authentication, you must ensure that another authentication mechanism is enabled. If the *HttpUser* object is not populated as would be the case when there are no configured authentication mechanisms, the IIS server core generates a 401.2 error.

Executable   %Windir%\System32\Inetsrv\Authanon.dll

Dependencies   None

Configuration Element   system.webServer/security/authentication/*anonymous-Authentication*

ApplicationHost.config Usage Examples

```
<anonymousAuthentication enabled="true" userName="IUSR" />

<anonymousAuthentication enabled="true" userName="IUSR" password="[en
c:AesProvider:jAAAAAECAAADZgAAAKQAAJbG5Vze9+qBIwzs3YYUfw4w1FhMxydEPXS
IQN3WjxTI9s7y8a6VsU9h+bMHUsPibqPGbTOZwEovDXWzVGOFg3A/bi7uJAOphgDDP4/
xP18XDwSOrm+22Yyn44lLPbG6d4BGBy7G+b/
O2ywozBFbsdckm7bKyNp1NinWKY9dSzKfa9l2SmYVqvHEQEQjUMXSvg==:enc]" />
```

Element Attributes   Anonymous authentication is controlled through the system.webServer/security/authentication/*anonymousAuthentication* element. Table A-3 summarizes the standard attributes of the *anonymousAuthentication* element.

Table A-3   Standard Attributes of the *anonymousAuthentication* Element

Attribute Name	Attribute Description
defaultLogon-Domain	Sets the optional name of the default domain against which the anonymous users are authenticated. The default logon domain is an empty string.
enabled	Controls whether Anonymous authentication is enabled or disabled. The default is true.
logonMethod	Sets the optional logon method for the anonymous user account as Interactive, Batch, Network, or ClearText. The default is ClearText.
password	Sets the optional password of the account used for anonymous access. This is an optional attribute that must be used only if the account used for anonymous access is assigned a user-managed password. The password is expected to be passed as an encrypted string.
userName	Sets the name of the account used for anonymous access to IIS. You can set this to a specific user or use an empty attribute value (*userName=""*) to use the application pool identity. By default, this value is set to IUSR, the name prefix of the Internet Guest Account created when you installed IIS. The actual account is named in the form: *Prefix_ComputerName*. For example, if the prefix is set as IUSR and the computer name is WebServer81, the account is named IUSR_WebServer81.

BasicAuthenticationModule

Implements Basic authentication

Description   Basic authentication requires a user to provide a valid user name and password to access content. Although all browsers support this authentication mechanism, browsers transmit the password without encryption, making it possible for a password to be compromised. If you want to require basic authentication, you should disable Anonymous authentication. The actual component within IIS 7.0 that implements Basic authentication is the BasicAuthenticationModule. This module implements HTTP Basic authentication described in RFC 2617.

The BasicAuthenticationModule creates the *HttpUser* object used by and validated by IIS after the authentication phase. If the *HttpUser* object is not populated as would be the case when there are no configured authentication mechanisms, the IIS core installation generates a 401.2 error. See Chapter 10 for more information on Basic authentication.

Executable   *%Windir%*\System32\Inetsrv\Authbas.dll

Dependencies   None

Configuration Element   system.webServer/security/authentication/*basicAuthentication*

ApplicationHost.config Usage Example

```
<basicAuthentication enabled="false" realm="Adatum"
defaultLogonDomain="cpandl" />
```

Element Attributes   Basic authentication is controlled through the system.webServer/security/authentication/*basicAuthentication* element. Table A-4 summarizes the standard attributes of the *basicAuthentication* element.

Table A-4   Standard Attributes of the *basicAuthentication* Element

Attribute Name	Attribute Description
defaultLogon-Domain	Sets the name of the default domain against which users are authenticated by default. Any users who do not provide a domain name when they log on are authenticated against this domain. No default logon domain is set.
enabled	Controls whether Basic authentication is enabled or disabled. The default is false.
logonMethod	Sets the optional logon method for the anonymous user account as Interactive, Batch, Network, or ClearText. The default is ClearText.
realm	Sets the optional name of the Domain Name System (DNS) domain or Web address that will use the credentials that have been authenticated against the default domain. No default realm is set.

CertificateMappingAuthenticationModule

Maps client certificates to Active Directory accounts for authentication

Description   Active Directory Client Certificate authentication maps client certificates to Active Directory accounts. When the CertificateMappingAuthentication-Module is enabled, the module performs the necessary Active Directory Certificate mapping for authentication of authorized clients. As with Anonymous and Basic authentication, the CertificateMappingAuthenticationModule also creates the *HttpUser* object used by and validated by IIS after the authentication phase. If the *HttpUser* object is not populated as would be the case when there are no configured authentication mechanisms, the IIS core installation generates a 401.2 error. See Chapter 10 for more information on Active Directory Client Certificate authentication.

Executable   *%Windir%\System32\Inetsrv\Authcert.dll*

Dependencies   For this module to work, the Web server must be a member of an Active Directory domain and be configured to use SSL.

Configuration Element   system.webServer/security/authentication/*clientCertificate-MappingAuthentication*

ApplicationHost.config Usage Examples

```
<clientCertificateMappingAuthentication enabled="false" />

<clientCertificateMappingAuthentication enabled="true" />
```

Element Attributes   Certificate mapping is controlled through the system.webServer/security/authentication/*clientCertificateMappingAuthentication* element. The enabled attribute of the *clientCertificateMappingAuthentication* element controls whether certificate mapping is enabled or disabled.

CgiModule

Implements the Common Gateway Interface (CGI) specification for use with IIS

Description   In IIS 7.0, the Common Gateway Interface (CGI) specification is implemented through the CgiModule. CGI describes how programs specified in Web addresses, also known as *gateway scripts*, pass information to Web servers. Gateway scripts pass information to servers through environment variables that capture user input in forms in addition to information about users submitting information.

The CgiModule has a managed handler that specifies that all files with the .exe extension be handled as CGI programs. The way CGI programs are handled is determined by the *cgi* element defined in the Application.Host.config or Web.config file. If this module is removed, CGI programs stop working.

The *isapiCgiRestriction* element contains the extension restriction list configuration to control which CGI functionality is enabled or disabled on the server. You use the *add* element to specify the full file path to the .exe for the CGI program or the .dll for the ISAPI extension and to specify the allowed status of the application. Optionally, you can also provide a group name for easier management of similar applications and a description of the application.

If you remove this module, IIS will not be able to run CGI programs. See Chapter 8, "Running IIS Applications," for more information on CGI and ISAPI.

Executable   %Windir%\System32\Inetsrv\Cgi.dll

Dependencies   None

Configuration Elements   system.webServer/*cgi*

system.webServer/*isapiCgiRestriction*

ApplicationHost.config Usage Examples

```
<cgi createCGIWithNewConsole="false" createProcessAsUser="true"
timeout="00:15:00" />

<isapiCgiRestriction notListedIsapisAllowed="false"
notListedCgisAllowed="false">
  <clear />
  <add path="c:\Windows\system32\inetsrv\asp.dll" allowed="true"
groupId="ASP" description="Active Server Pages" />
  <add path="c:\Windows\Microsoft.NET\Framework\v2.0.50727\
aspnet_isapi.dll" allowed="true" groupId="ASP.NET v2.0.50727"
description="ASP.NET v2.0.50727" />
  <add path="c:\Windows\system32\msw3prt.dll" allowed="true"
groupId="W3PRT" description="Internet Printing" />
</isapiCgiRestriction>
```

Element Attributes   CGI is controlled through the system.webServer/*cgi* element. Table A-5 summarizes the standard attributes of the *cgi* element. The *isapiCgiRestriction* element contains *add* sub-elements that control which functionality is enabled or disabled on the server. These *add* elements can use the attributes summarized in Table A-6.

Table A-5   Standard Attributes of the *cgi* Element

Attribute Name	Attribute Description
createCGIWith-NewConsole	Indicates whether the gateway script runs in its own console. The default is false. If set to false, gateway scripts run without a console. If set to true, each gateway application creates a new console when it is started.
createProcess-AsUser	Specifies whether a CGI process is created in the system context or in the context of the requesting user. The default is true. If set to false, CGI processes run in the system context. If set to true, CGI processes run in the context of the requesting user.
Timeout	Sets the timeout for gateway scripts. The default is 15 minutes.

Table A-6   Standard Attributes of the *isapiCgiRestriction\add* Element

Attribute Name	Attribute Description
path	Sets the full file path to the .exe for the CGI program or the .dll for the ISAPI extension. No default path is set.
allowed	Indicates whether the application is allowed to run. If set to true, the application can run. If set to false, the application cannot run. The default is false.
groupId	Sets an optional group name for adding the restriction to a group for easier management. No default *groupID* is set.
description	Sets an optional description of the application being added. No default description is set.
notListedIsapi Allowed	Controls whether an ISAPI extension is listed as allowed in IIS Manager. If set to false, the ISAPI extension is not listed as allowed. If set to true, the ISAPI extension is listed as allowed. The default is false.
notListed-CGIAllowed	Controls whether a CGI program is listed as allowed in IIS Manager. If set to false, the CGI program is not listed as allowed. If set to true, the CGI program is listed as allowed. The default is false.

ConfigurationValidationModule

Implements configuration validation and related error reporting

Description   When the ConfigurationValidationModule is enabled, IIS 7.0 validates the configuration of the server and its applications by default. If a server or application is improperly configured, IIS 7.0 generates errors that can help detect and diagnose the problem. If this module is removed, IIS 7.0 will not validate the configuration and also will not report configuration errors.

Executable   *%Windir%\System32\Inetsrv\Validcfg.dll*

Dependencies   None

Configuration Element   system.webServer/*Validation*

ApplicationHost.config Usage Examples

```
<validation validateIntegratedModeConfiguration="false" />

<validation validateIntegratedModeConfiguration="true" />
```

Element Attributes   Configuration validation is controlled through the system.webServer/*Validation* element. By default, the *Validation* element has no content, and its attribute values are taken from the schema. In the schema, the *Validation* element has a single attribute: *validateIntegratedModeConfiguration*. This attribute, set to true by default, controls whether IIS validates the server and application configuration. If you don't want IIS to validate the configuration, set the *validateIntegratedModeConfiguration* attribute to false.

CustomErrorModule

Implements custom error and detailed error notification

Description The CustomErrorModule implements custom error and detailed error notification. When this module is enabled and the server encounters an error, the server can return a customer error page to all clients regardless of location, a detailed error message to all clients regardless of location, or a detailed error for local clients and a custom error page for remote clients. The custom error page displayed is based on the type of HTTP error that occurred. If you remove this module, IIS 7.0 will return minimal error information when HTTP errors occur. See Chapter 7, "Customizing Web Server Content," for more information on custom errors.

Executable *%Windir%*\System32\Inetsrv\Custerr.dll

Dependencies None

Configuration Element system.webServer/*httpErrors*

ApplicationHost.config Usage Examples

```
<httpErrors errorMode="DetailedLocalOnly" defaultPath=""
defaultResponseMode="File">
  <error statusCode="401" prefixLanguageFilePath="%SystemDrive%
\inetpub\custerr" path="401.htm" />
  <error statusCode="404" prefixLanguageFilePath="%SystemDrive%
\inetpub\custerr" path="404.htm" />
  <error statusCode="500" prefixLanguageFilePath="%SystemDrive%
\inetpub\custerr" path="500.htm" />
</httpErrors>
```

Element Attributes Custom errors are controlled through the system.webServer /*httpErrors* element. Table A-7 summarizes the standard attributes of the *httpErrors* element. Table A-8 summarizes the standard attributes of the *error* element.

Table A-7   Standard Attributes of the *httpErrors* Element

Attribute Name	Attribute Description
defaultPath	Sets the default path when the execute URL or redirect mode is used.
defaultResponse Mode	Sets the response mode as File, ExecuteURL, or Redirect. Use the default response mode, File, when you want IIS to serve the client browser a Web document. Use the Redirect mode when you want to redirect users to a local or remote Web address. Use the ExecuteURL mode when you want IIS to execute a specific, relative URL. The resource specified in the URL must be on the current server. The URL itself cannot contain the following characters: ? : @ & = . > < .

Table A-7   Standard Attributes of the *httpErrors* Element

Attribute Name	Attribute Description
detailedMore-InformationLink	Sets the URL used for the More Information link. The default value is *http://go.microsoft.com/fwlink/?LinkID=62293*.
errorMode	Sets the type of error reporting desired. If this attribute is not assigned a value or set to DetailedLocalOnly, local clients see detailed errors and remote clients see custom error pages. Set *errorMode="Detailed"* for detailed error reports only. Set *errorMode="Custom"* for custom error reports only.
existingResponse	Determines how an existing response is handled. The default, Auto, specifies that existing responses are handled automatically with either Replace or Passthrough as appropriate. Use Replace to force IIS to replace the existing response. Use Passthrough to force IIS to pass the existing response through to the client.

Table A-8   Standard Attributes of the *Error* Element

Attribute Name	Attribute Description
Path	Sets the file name of the custom error page within a language-specific subdirectory. No default is set. The path cannot be set to an empty string.
prefixLanguage-FilePath	Sets the full path to the base directory for custom error pages. For each language pack installed, IIS 7.0 looks in a language-specific subdirectory based on the default language of the client browser, such as en-US. No default path is set.
responseMode	Sets the response mode as File, ExecuteURL, or Redirect. Use the default response mode, File, when you want IIS to serve the client browser a Web document for the specific status and substatus code. Use the Redirect mode when you want to redirect users to a local or remote Web address. Use the ExecuteURL mode when you want IIS to execute a specific, relative URL.
statusCode	Indicates the HTTP status code the custom error page should handle. No default value is set for this required field. Valid values are from 400 to 999. For example, if this attribute is set to 404, the custom error page is for HTTP 404 errors.
subStatusCode	Sets the related substatus code. With the default value, -1, IIS does not display or handle the substatus code. Valid values are from -1 to 999.

CustomLoggingModule

Implements custom logging using the Component Object Model (COM)

Description   The CustomLoggingModule implements the ILogPlugin interface. This COM interface is a deprecated feature that allows you to extend IIS logging. Rather than using this module, Microsoft recommends that you create a managed module and subscribe to the RQ_LOG_REQUEST notification.

Executable   *%Windir%\System32\Inetsrv\Logcust.dll*

Dependencies   None

Configuration Element   system.applicationHost/*sites*

ApplicationHost.config Usage Examples

```
<sites>
  <site name="Default Web Site" id="1">
   <application path="/">
    <virtualDirectory path="/"
physicalPath="%SystemDrive%\inetpub\wwwroot" />
   </application>
    . . .
  </site>
  <siteDefaults>
   <logFile logFormat="custom" customLogPluginClsid ="{3a2a4e84-4c21-
4981-ae10-3fda0d9b0f83}" />
    . . .
</sites>
```

Element Attributes   Custom logging is controlled through the system.application-Host/sites/site/*logFile* element. This element has two attributes that determine whether and how custom logging is used: *logFormat* and *customLogPluginClsid*. To turn on custom logging, you must set *logFormat*="Custom" and then use the *customLogPluginClsid* attribute to set the CLSID of the COM object being used for logging.

DefaultDocumentModule

Allows IIS to serve default documents when directory-level URLs are requested

Description   When a user enters a request with a trailing /, such as *http://www.adatum.com/*, IIS can redirect the request to the default document for the Web server or directory. The DefaultDocumentModule determines whether and how default documents are used. When working with default documents, keep the following in mind:

- When a default document is assigned and available, IIS returns the default document whose file name matches one of those listed as acceptable.

- When there are multiple default documents in a directory, IIS returns the default document with the highest precedence.

- When a default document does not exist and directory browsing is enabled, IIS generates a listing of the contents of the specified directory.

If neither the DefaultDocumentModule nor the DirectoryListing Module handle a request for a directory-level URL, an empty response will be returned.

For optimal performance, you should list the default document you use the most first and then reduce the overall list of default documents to only those that are absolutely necessary. See Chapter 7 for more information on default documents.

Executable   *%Windir%*\System32\Inetsrv\Defdoc.dll

Dependencies   None

Configuration Element   system.webServer/*defaultDocument*

ApplicationHost.config Usage Examples

```
<defaultDocument enabled="true">
<files>
<add value="Default.htm" />
<add value="Default.asp" />
<add value="index.htm" />
<add value="index.html" />
<add value="iisstart.htm" />
<add value="default.aspx" />
</files>
</defaultDocument>
```

Element Attributes   You can use the *defaultDocument* element to control whether default documents are used. To configure IIS to stop using default documents, set the *enabled* attribute of the *defaultDocument* element to false. To have IIS use default documents, set the *enabled* attribute of the *defaultDocument* element to true.

You can use the files and *add* elements to control how default documents are used. The *files* element contains *add* elements that define the acceptable default documents. Each acceptable default document must be defined using a separate *add* element. The *value* attribute of the *add* element sets the name of the default document, such as Default.htm. The order of the *add* elements sets the relative priority of the related default documents.

DigestAuthenticationModule

Implements digest authentication as described in RFC 2617

Description   Digest authentication uses a Microsoft Windows domain controller to authenticate user requests for content. Digest authentication can be used through firewalls and proxies. As with other types of authentication, the DigestAuthentication-Module also creates the *HttpUser* object used by and validated by IIS after the authentication phase. If the *HttpUser* object is not populated as would be the case when there are no configured authentication mechanisms, the IIS server core generates a 401.2 error. See Chapter 10 for more information on Digest authentication.

If you want to require Digest authentication, you should disable Anonymous authentication.

Executable   *%Windir%*\System32\Inetsrv\Authmd5.dll

Dependencies IIS must part of an Active Directory domain. The client browser must support HTTP 1.1.

Configuration Element system.webServer/security/authentication/*digestAuthentication*

ApplicationHost.config Usage Examples

```
<digestAuthentication enabled="false" />

<digestAuthentication enabled="true" realm="Adatum" />
```

Element Attributes Digest authentication is controlled through the system.webServer/security/authentication/*digestAuthentication* element. Table A-9 summarizes the standard attributes of the *digestAuthentication* element.

Table A-9   Standard Attributes of the *digestAuthentication* Element

Attribute Name	Attribute Description
enabled	Controls whether digest authentication is enabled or disabled.
realm	Sets the name of the DNS domain or Web address against which the credentials will be authenticated. If this attribute is not set, credentials are authenticated against the user's default (logon) domain.

DirectoryListingModule

Implements directory browsing functionality

Description When a user enters a request with a trailing /, such as *http://www.adatum.com/*, IIS can display a listing of the directory. The DirectoryListingModule in conjunction with the DefaultDocumentModule determines whether and how directory listings are used. When default documents are enabled but there is no current default document, IIS can use this module to generate a listing of the contents of the specified directory. If neither the DefaultDocumentModule nor the DirectoryListing Module handle a request for a directory-level URL, an empty response will be returned. See Chapter 7 for more information on directory browsing.

Executable *%Windir%*\System32\Inetsrv\Dirlist.dll

Dependencies None

Configuration Element system.webServer/*directoryBrowse*

ApplicationHost.config Usage Examples

```
<directoryBrowse enabled="false" />

<directoryBrowse enabled="true" showFlags="LongDate, Extension, Size,
  Time, Date" />
```

Element Attributes Directory browsing is controlled through the system.webServer/*directoryBrowse* element. Table A-10 summarizes the standard attributes of this element.

Table A-10 Standard Attributes of the *directoryBrowse* Element

Attribute Name	Attribute Description
enabled	Controls whether directory browsing is enabled or disabled.
showFlags	Controls the listing details by specifying the desired details in a comma-separated list of values. In addition to file names, IIS can return details about the date, time, long date, file size, and file extension by using the *Date*, *Time*, *LongDate*, *Size*, and *Extension* flags respectively. The default flags are: *Date*, *Time*, *Size*, and *Extension*.

DynamicCompressionModule

Implements in-memory compression of dynamic content

Description Compression squeezes the extra space out of files, resulting in small files and greatly reducing the amount of bandwidth needed to transmit content over a network in most cases. Because compressed files generally are smaller than uncompressed files, users perceive a performance improvement.

IIS supports static compression through the StaticCompressionModule and dynamic compression through the DynamicCompressionModule. With static compression, IIS performs an in-memory compression of static content upon first request and then saves the compressed results to disk for subsequent use. With dynamic content, IIS performs in-memory compression every time dynamic content is requested. IIS must compress dynamic content every time it is requested because dynamic content changes.

Executable *%Windir%*\System32\Inetsrv\Compdyn.dll

Dependencies None

Configuration Elements system.webServer/*httpCompression*

system.webServer/*urlCompression*

ApplicationHost.config Usage Examples

```
<httpCompression directory="%SystemDrive%\inetpub\temp\IIS Temporary
Compressed Files">
 <scheme name="gzip" dll="%Windir%\system32\inetsrv\gzip.dll" />
 <dynamicTypes>
  <add mimeType="text/*" enabled="true" />
  <add mimeType="message/*" enabled="true" />
  <add mimeType="application/x-javascript" enabled="true" />
  <add mimeType="*/*" enabled="false" />
 </dynamicTypes>
```

```
<staticTypes>
<add mimeType="text/*" enabled="true" />
<add mimeType="message/*" enabled="true" />
<add mimeType="application/x-javascript" enabled="true" />
<add mimeType="*/*" enabled="false" />
</staticTypes>
</httpCompression>

<urlCompression doDynamicCompression="true" />
```

Element Attributes Compression is controlled through the system.webServer/*http-Compression* and system.webServer/*urlCompression* elements. The system.webServer /*httpCompression* element controls how IIS uses HTTP compression. The system.web-Server/*urlCompression* element controls per-URL compression. Whereas HTTP compression has many standard configuration settings, URL Compression has no values set by default, which means that the values are taken from the schema.

In a standard configuration, IIS compresses content in the following folder: *%System-Drive%*\Inetpub\Temp\IIS Temporary Compressed Files. By using the directory attribute of the *httpCompression* element, you can specify an alternative directory.

The type of compression IIS uses is set through the *scheme* element. By default, IIS uses GZip compression. The *name* and *dll* attributes of the *scheme* element set the descriptive name of the compression type and the full file path to the DLL that performs the compression.

The *staticTypes* and *dynamicTypes* elements are used to specify how compression can be used. The related *add* elements have *mimeTYPE* attributes that set the Multipurpose Internet Mail Extensions (MIME) type being referenced and enabled attributes that specify the compression status for the identified MIME type. When compression is enabled in a standard configuration, all text- and message-related MIME types for static content are compressed automatically as are scripts written in JavaScript. When dynamic compression is enabled in a standard configuration, the same is true for dynamic content.

When the *doDynamicCompression* attribute of the *urlCompression* element is set to true, compression of dynamic content is enabled. Otherwise, dynamic compression is disabled.

Table A-11 summarizes the standard attributes of the *httpCompression* element. Table A-12 summarizes the standard attributes of the *urlCompression* element.

Table A-11   Standard Attributes of the *httpCompression* Element

Attribute Name	Attribute Description
cacheControlHeader	Sets the maximum time a header can be cached. The default value, max–age=86400, sets the header to expire after 86,400 seconds (24 hours).
Dll	Sets the DLL of the compression utility to use. This value cannot be set to an empty string.
doDiskSpaceLimiting	Controls whether IIS limits the amount of disk space used for caching compressed files. The default value, true, enables disk space limiting.
doDynamic-Compression	Controls whether dynamic compression is used by IIS. The default is true, which means that IIS will try to use dynamic compression if no other restrictions apply.
doStaticCompression	Controls whether static compression is used by IIS. The default is true, which means that IIS will try to use static compression if no other restrictions apply.
dynamicCompression-DisableCpuUsage	Controls whether dynamic compression is disabled when the CPU percent utilization reaches or exceeds a specific level. By default, dynamic compression is disabled when the CPU utilization is 90 percent or higher. The valid range is from 0 to 100.
dynamicCompression-EnableCpuUsage	Controls whether dynamic compression is enabled but throttled when the CPU percent utilization reaches or exceeds a specific level. By default, dynamic compression is enabled when the CPU utilization is 50 percent or higher. The valid range is from 0 to 100.
dynamicCompression-Level	Sets the level of compression used with dynamic content. The default compression level is 0. Compression level can be set from 0 (minimal) to 7 (maximum).
expiresHeaders	Sets the default expiration header. The default value, Wed, 01 Jan 1997 12:00:00 GMT, forces expiration by setting a date earlier than the current date.
maxDiskSpaceUsage	Sets the maximum disk space that can be used for caching compressed files (when disk space limiting is enabled). The default value is 100 MB.
minFileSizeForComp	Sets the minimum file size for compression. Files smaller than the minimum file size are not compressed. The default is 256 bytes.
noCompressionFor-Http10	Controls whether compression is used with HTTP 1.0. The default is true, which means that compression is not used with HTTP 1.0.

Table A-11   Standard Attributes of the *httpCompression* Element

Attribute Name	Attribute Description
noCompression-ForProxies	Controls whether compression is used when transmitting through a proxy. The default is true, which means that compression is not used with proxies.
noCompression-ForRange	Controls whether compression is used for clients on the local network. The default is true, which means that compression is not used with local clients.
sendCacheHeaders	Controls whether IIS sends the cached header to the client. The default value is false.
staticCompression-DisableCpuUsage	Controls whether static compression is disabled when the CPU percent utilization reaches or exceeds a specific level. By default, static compression is disabled when the CPU utilization reaches 100 percent. The valid range is from 0 to 100.
staticCompression-EnableCpuUsage	Controls whether static compression is enabled but throttled when the CPU percent utilization reaches or exceeds a specific level. By default, static compression is enabled when the CPU utilization is 50 percent or higher. The valid range is from 0 to 100.
staticCompressionLevel	Sets the level of compression used with static content. The default compression level is 7. Compression level can be set from 0 (minimal) to 7 (maximum).

Table A-12   Standard Attributes of the *urlCompression* Element

Attribute Name	Attribute Description
doDynamic-Compression	Controls whether dynamic compression is used for per-URL compression. The default is true, which means that IIS will try to use dynamic compression if no other restrictions apply.
doStaticCompression	Controls whether static compression is used for per-URL compression. The default is true, which means that IIS will try to use static compression if no other restrictions apply.
dynamicCompression-BeforeCache	Controls whether IIS performs per-URL compression before caching the file. The default is false, which means that IIS caches a file (as appropriate per the current configuration) and then performs compression.

FailedRequestsTracingModule

Implements tracing of failed requests

Description   Failed request tracing is designed to help administrators and developers more easily identify and track failed requests. In previous versions of IIS, you could check for certain HTTP error codes in the IIS logs to identify failed requests but could not easily get detailed trace information that would help resolve related issues. With IIS 7.0, request traces can be logged automatically when an error code is generated or when the time taken for a request exceeds a specified duration. For general tracing for debugging or other purposes, you can also configure general tracing on a per-URL basis.

You control the way tracing works using Failed Request Tracing Rules. With each rule, you specify:

- The type of content to trace as either all content (*), ASP.NET (*.aspx), ASP (*.asp), or custom.

- The conditions under which a request should be traced, including event severity (Error, Critical Error, or Warning), HTTP status code, and time taken. For general tracing, you can also trace information and other non-error events.

- The provider through which to track the request, including ASP, ASPNET, ISAPI Extension, and WWW Server.

Executable   *%Windir%*\System32\Inetsrv\Iisfreb.dll

Dependencies   None

Configuration Elements   system.webServer/*httpTracing*

system.webServer/*tracing*

ApplicationHost.config Usage Examples

```
<httpTracing>
 <traceUrls>
  <add value="\test.aspx"
 </traceUrls>
</httpTracing>

<tracing>
 <traceFailedRequests>
  <add path="*.aspx">
   <traceAreas>
    <add provider="ASP" verbosity="Verbose" />
    <add provider="ISAPI Extension" verbosity="Verbose" />
    <add provider="WWW Server" areas="Authentication,Security,Filter,
StaticFile,CGI,Compression,Cache,RequestNotifications"
verbosity="Verbose" />
   </traceAreas>
   <failureDefinitions timeTaken="00:00:30" statusCodes="500"
verbosity="Error" />
  </add>
 </traceFailedRequests>

 <traceProviderDefinitions>
  <add name="WWW Server" guid="{3a2a4e84-4c21-4981-ae10-
3fda0d9b0f83}">
```

```
<areas>
<clear />
<add name="Authentication" value="2" />
<add name="Security" value="4" />
<add name="Filter" value="8" />
<add name="StaticFile" value="16" />
<add name="CGI" value="32" />
<add name="Compression" value="64" />
<add name="Cache" value="128" />
<add name="RequestNotifications" value="256" />
</areas>
</add>
<add name="ASP" guid="{06b94d9a-b15e-456e-a4ef-37c984a2cb4b}">
<areas>
<clear />
</areas>
</add>
<add name="ISAPI Extension" guid="{a1c2040e-8840-4c31-ba11-
9871031a19ea}">
<areas>
<clear />
</areas>
</add>
</traceProviderDefinitions>
</tracing>
```

Element Attributes   The system.webServer/*httpTracing* element configures request tracing for whenever a specific URL is accessed. Each URL that you want to trace is specified with the value attribute of an *add* element nested within an *httpTracing\traceUrls* element. The way tracing is handled for a particular file is based on the trace rules you've defined.

In the following example, two URLs are configured for tracing whenever they are accessed:

```
<httpTracing>
 <traceUrls>
  <add value="\test1.aspx">
  <add value="\test2.asp">
 </traceUrls>
</httpTracing>
```

Because you can configure separate tracing rules for .asp and .aspx files, IIS may handle tracing for these files in different ways. Keep in mind that if you've configured tracing rules to track only errors, you won't see the general or information events that may be needed for more general tracing of requests.

The system.webServer/*tracing* element allows you to define tracing rules. Within the system.webServer/*tracing* element, request tracing is implemented through two subelements:

- **traceProviderDefinitions**   Defines the available trace providers

- **traceFailedRequests**   Allows you to define tracing rules

Because you'll rarely, if ever, want to modify the provider definitions, you'll work mostly with the *traceFailedRequests* element. Within this element, you define a type of document to trace using the *path* attribute of the *add* element and then define the related rule within the context of the *add* element. The following snippet of code defines a rule for .aspx files:

```
<add path="*.aspx">
 <traceAreas>
  <add provider="ASP" verbosity="Verbose" />
  <add provider="ISAPI Extension" verbosity="Verbose" />
  <add provider="WWW Server" areas="Authentication,Security,
Filter,StaticFile,CGI,Compression,Cache,RequestNotifications"
verbosity="Verbose" />
 </traceAreas>
 <failureDefinitions timeTaken="00:00:30" statusCodes="500" verbosity
="Error" />
</add>
```

As shown in this example, the *add* element denotes the start and end of the rule:

```
<add path="*.aspx">
...
</add>
```

In this case, the rule applies to all ASP.NET files. ASP.NET files have the .aspx file extension. You could apply a Failed Trace Request Rule to all content by using:

```
<add path="*">
...
</add>
```

You could apply a Failed Trace Request Rule to all ASP files by using:

```
<add path="*.asp">
...
</add>
```

Or you could apply a Failed Trace Request Rule to a custom file type or name by using wildcards as appropriate, such as:

```
<add path="curr*.asp">
...
</add>
```

The *traceAreas* element defines the providers to which the rule applies in addition to how the rule applies to each provider. Failed requests can be traced through one or more of the following providers:

- **ASP**   Traces the failed request through Active Server Pages (*%Windir%*\System32\Inetsrv\Asp.dll)

- **ISAPI Extension**   Traces the failed request through ISAPI extension for ASP.NET (*%Windir%*\Microsoft.NET\Framework\V2.0.50727\Aspnet_isapi.dll)

- **WWW Server**   Traces the failed request through the IIS server core

You specify a provider to use with the *provider* attribute of the *add* element. You then use the *verbosity* attribute to specify the types of information to trace as follows:

- **General**   Trace general information about a request

- **CriticalError**   Trace critical errors related to a request

- **Error**   Trace standard errors related to a request

- **Warning**   Trace warnings related to a request

- **Information**   Trace information events related to a request

- **Verbose**   Trace all available information and errors related to a request

In the following example, tracing for the ASP provider is set to track critical errors:

```
<add provider="ASP" verbosity="CriticalError" />
```

When using WWW Server as the provider, you can specify the area within the IIS server core to trace as any combination of the following:

- **Authentication**   Traces the failed request through authentication-related modules

- **Security**   Traces the failed request through authentication-related modules

- **Filter**   Traces the failed request through the IsapiFilterModule, the Request-FilteringModule, or both

- **StaticFile**   Traces the failed request through the StaticFile module

- **CGI**   Traces the failed request through the CgiModule

- **Compression**   Traces the failed request through the StaticCompressionModule or the DynamicCompressionModule

- **Cache**   Traces the failed request through cache-related modules

- **RequestNotifications**   Traces the failed request through the RequestMonitor-Module

The following examples enables tracing of all areas for the WWW Server:

```
<add provider="WWW Server" areas="Authentication,Security,Filter,
StaticFile,CGI,Compression,Cache,RequestNotifications" verbosity="Verbose" />
```

After you define the trace areas, you must define the type of related failure or events to trace using the attributes of the *failureDefinitions* element. Tracing can be initiated based on two types of events: the time taken to respond as specified with the *timeTaken* attribute and specific status codes as specified with the *statusCodes* attribute. You use the *verbosity* attribute of the *failureDefinitions* element to specify the event severity to track. To see how this works, consider the following example:

```
<failureDefinitions timeTaken="00:00:30" statusCodes="500"
verbosity="Error"/>
```

Here, IIS traces the previously specified file type when the time taken to handle a response is more than 30 seconds or when an HTTP 500 error is generated and tracks events with an Error severity level. The *verbosity* attribute of the *failureDefinitions* element can use the following flags: *Ignore*, *CriticalError*, *Error*, and *Warning*. The default value is *Ignore*.

FastCgiModule

Implements the multithreaded Common Gateway Interface (CGI) specification for use with IIS

Description   See CgiModule.

Executable   *%Windir%*\System32\Inetsrv\Iisfcgi.dll

Dependencies   None

Configuration Elements   system.webServer/fast*Cgi*

system.webServer/*isapiCgiRestriction*

ApplicationHost.config Usage Examples

```
<fastCgi>
 <application fullpath="c:\php\cgi-php.exe"
   maxInstances="10" idleTimeout="120">
 </fastCgi>
```

Element Attributes   FastCGI is controlled through the system.webServer/*fastCgi* /*application* element. Table A-13 summarizes the standard attributes of the *fastCgi/application* element.

Table A-13   Standard Attributes of the *fastCgi/application* Element

Attribute Name	Attribute Description
fullPath	Sets the full file path to the executable for the application to be processed through FastCGI. This value is required and cannot be set to an empty string.
arguments	Sets command-line arguments to pass to the application. This value is a string and must be enclosed in quotation marks.
maxInstances	Sets the maximum number of concurrent instances of the application that can run for multithreading. The default value is 4 instances. The maximum number is 10,000.
idleTimeout	Sets the idle timeout for FastCgi applications in seconds. If the application has not been used and this time elapses, the application instance is deleted. The default value is 300 seconds (5 minutes). The maximum idle time is 604,800 seconds (7 days).
activityTimeout	Sets the activity timeout in seconds. If an active request has been working with longer than this value, it is stopped. The default value is 30 seconds. The maximum activity time is 3,600 seconds (1 hour).
requestTimeout	Sets the request timeout in seconds. If the server has not responded to a request before this time elapses, the request is terminated. The default request timeout is 90 seconds. The maximum request time is 604,800 seconds (7 days).
instance-MaxRequests	Sets the maximum number of requests that each application instance can service. The default is 200 requests. The maximum is 10,000,000.
protocol	Sets the communication protocol for the application. The default value is NamedPipe. Applications can also use TCP IP by setting a value of Tcp.
queueLength	Sets the size of the request queue. If this number of requests are waiting to be processed, additional requests are ignored. The default is 1,000, meaning up to 1,000 requests can be waiting to be processed. The maximum queue size is 100,000,000.
flushNamed-Pipe	Controls whether named pipes are flushed. The default value is false. If set to true, named pipes are flushed when requests are terminated.

FileCacheModule

Caches file handles (*not installed by default*)

Description   The FileCacheModule caches file handles for files opened by the server engine and related server modules. If file handles are not cached, the files have to be opened for every request, which can result in performance loss. In a standard configuration, this module is not added even if you select all available features during installation of IIS.

Executable   *%Windir%*\System32\Inetsrv\Cachfile.dll

Dependencies   None

Configuration Elements   None

HttpCacheModule

Implements output caching and kernel-mode caching

Description   HTTP.sys is the server process that listens for requests made on a Web site. HTTP.sys also performs caching and logging operations on the server. Caching improves performance by returning a processed copy of a requested Web page from cache, resulting in reduced overhead on the server and faster response times. IIS 7.0 supports several levels of caching including output caching in user mode and output caching in kernel mode. When kernel-mode caching is enabled, cached responses are served from the kernel rather than from IIS user mode, giving IIS an extra boost in performance and increasing the number of requests IIS can process.

Executable   *%Windir%*\System32\Inetsrv\Cachhttp.dll

Dependencies   None

Configuration Elements   System.webServer/*asp*

System.webServer/asp/*cache*

System.webServer/*caching*

ApplicationHost.config Usage Examples

```
<asp>
 <cache diskTemplateCacheDirectory="%SystemDrive%\inetpub\temp\ASP
Compiled Templates" />
</asp>

<caching enabled="true" enableKernelCache="true" maxCacheSize="200"
maxResponseSize="262144">
 <profiles>
  <add extension=".axd" policy="CacheForTimePeriod"
duration="00:00:30" />
  <add extension=".aspx" policy="CacheUntilChange"
varyByHeaders="HTTP_ACCEPT" varyByQueryString="Locale" />
 </profiles>
</caching>
```

Element Attributes   Caching is controlled through the System.webServer/asp/*cache* and System.webServer/*caching* elements. As summarized in Table A-14, general caching settings for dynamic files are configured through the attributes of the System.webServer/asp/*cache* element. Table A-15 summarizes the attributes of the System.webServer/*caching* element.

Table A-14 Standard Attributes of the System.webServer/asp/*cache* Element

Attribute Name	Attribute Description
diskTemplate-CacheDirectory	Sets the name of the directory that ASP uses to store compiled ASP templates to disk after overflow of the in-memory cache. This attribute cannot be set to an empty string. The default value is *%SystemDrive%*\Inetpub\Temp\ASP Compiled Templates.
maxDiskTemplate CacheFiles	Sets the maximum number of compiled ASP templates that can be stored on disk. The default value is 2,000. The valid range is from 0 to 2,147,483,647 files.
scriptFile-CacheSize	Sets the maximum number of precompiled script files to cache in memory. The default value is 500 files. The valid range is from 0 to 2,147,483,647 files.
scriptEngine-CacheMax	Sets the maximum number of scripting engines that IIS will keep cached in memory. The default value is 250 cached scripting engines. The valid range is from 0 to 2,147,483,647 files.
enableTypelib-Cache	Determines whether Type Library caching is enabled. The default value, true, enables Type Library caching.

Table A-15 Standard Attributes of the System.webServer/*caching* Element

Attribute Name	Attribute Description
enabled	Controls whether caching is enabled or disabled.
enableKernel-ModeCache	Controls whether output caching in kernel mode is enabled. If set to true, kernel mode caching is enabled. Otherwise, kernel-mode caching is disabled.
maxCacheSize	Sets the maximum size, in megabytes, of the in-memory cache used by IIS. If this attribute is not set or is set to zero, IIS controls the maximum size of the cache.
maxResponseSize	Sets the maximum size, in bytes, of responses that can be stored in the output cache. The default value is 262144 bytes (256 KB). If the response size is large than this value, the response is not stored in the output cache.

The *caching* element can contain a *profiles* element. Within the *profiles* element, you can use *add* elements to define output caching rules. Each rule specifies how specific types of files should be handled. You can cache files until they change or until a specified time interval has elapsed. You also can have multiple cached versions of files based on query string variables or HTTP headers. For example, you may want to allow multiple cached versions of files based on locale. This would allow IIS to store different language versions of a file in cache. The following example ensures that ASP.NET files are cached until they change:

```
<profiles>
  <add extension=".aspx" policy="CacheUntilChange" />
</profiles>
```

To allow multiple language versions of files to be cached, you can use the Locale query string variable as shown in the following example:

```
<profiles>
  <add extension=".aspx" varyByQueryString="Locale" />
</profiles>
```

To allow multiple versions of files to be cached based on HTTP headers, you can specify the type of HTTP header to track. The following example tracks the HTTP_USERAGENT header:

```
<profiles>
  <add extension=".aspx" varyByHeaders="HTTP_USERAGENT" />
</profiles>
```

Table A-16 lists and describes the attributes of the *add* elements used within the *profiles* element.

Table A-16 Standard Attributes of the *profiles/add* Element

Attribute Name	Attribute Description
enabled	Controls whether caching is enabled or disabled.
policy	Sets the overall monitoring policy for cached files. Use *DontCache* to turn off caching. Use *CacheUntilChange* to cache files until they change. Use *CacheForTimePeriod* to cache files for a specified time period.
kernel-CachePolicy	Sets the monitoring policy for cached files when in kernel mode. Use *DontCache* to turn off kernel-mode caching. Use *CacheUntilChange* to cache files in kernel mode until they change. Use *CacheForTimePeriod* to cache files in kernel mode for a specified time period.
duration	Sets the time period for caching files; must be used with *CacheForTimePeriod*. The default value is 00:00:30.
location	Specifies the locations for which caching should be used. The default value is Any. You can also use Client, Server, ServerAndClient, Downstream, and None.
varyBy-QueryString	Allows multiple cached file versions that vary by query string variable, such as Locale.
varyBy-Headers	Allows multiple cached file versions that vary by HTTP header, such as HTTP_ACCEPT.

HttpLoggingModule

Implements standard IIS logging

Description   IIS 7.0 can be configured to use one log file per server or one log file per site. Use per server logging when you want all Web sites running on a server to write log data to a single file. With per server logging, you can use one of two logging formats: centralized binary logging or World Wide Web Consortium (W3C) extended log file format. With centralized binary logging, the log files contain both fixed-length records and index records that are written in a raw binary format called the Internet Binary Log (IBL) format, giving the log file an .ibl extension. Professional software applications or tools in the IIS 7.0 Software Development Kit can read this format.

Use per site logging when you want to track access separately for each site on a server. With per site logging, you can configure access logs in several formats. The standard formats are:

- **National Center for Supercomputer Applications (NCSA) Common Log File Format**   Use the NCSA Common Log File Format when your reporting and tracking needs are basic. With this format, log entries are small, which reduces the amount of storage space required for logging.

- **Microsoft Internet Information Services (IIS) Log File Format**   Use the IIS Log File Format when you need a bit more information from the logs but don't need to tailor the entries to get detailed information. With this format, log entries are compact, which reduces the amount of storage space required for logging.

- **World Wide Web Consortium (W3C) Extended Log File Format**   Use the W3C Extended Log File Format when you need to customize the tracked information and obtain detailed information. With this format, log entries can become large, which greatly increases the amount of storage space required. Recording lengthy entries can also affect the performance of a busy server.

Note   With per site logging, you can also configure custom logging or ODBC logging. Custom logging uses the CustomLoggingModule, which implements the ILogPlugin interface. ODBC logging is a type of custom logging that writes access information directly to an ODBC-compliant database. These advanced logging configurations can be managed only through the ApplicationHost.config file.

With all the standard log file formats, you can specify the log file encoding format as ANSI for standard ASCII text encoding or UTF8 for UTF-8 encoding. You can also specify whether and when log files roll over. For example, you can configure IIS to create new log files every day by configuring daily log file rollover. See Chapter 13, "Tracking User Access and Logging," for more information on logging.

Executable   *%Windir%*\System32\Inetsrv\Loghttp.dll

Dependencies   None

Configuration Elements   system.webServer/*httpLogging* system.webServer/*odbcLogging*

system.applicationHost/*log*

ApplicationHost.config Usage Examples

```
<httpLogging dontLog="false" />

<odbcLogging />

<log logInUTF8="false" centralLogFileMode="CentralW3C">
  <centralBinaryLogFile enabled="true"
  directory="%SystemDrive%\inetpub\logs\LogFiles" period="Weekly"
  localTimeRollover="true" />
  <centralW3CLogFile enabled="true"
  directory="%SystemDrive%\inetpub\logs\LogFiles" period="Hourly"
  localTimeRollover="false" logExtFileFlags="HttpSubStatus, Host,
  ProtocolVersion, Referer, Cookie, UserAgent, ServerPort, TimeTaken,
  BytesRecv, BytesSent, Win32Status, HttpStatus, UriQuery, UriStem,
  Method,
  ServerIP, ComputerName, SiteName, UserName, ClientIP, Time, Date" />
</log>

<sites>
  <site name="Default Web Site" id="1">
  <application path="/">
    <virtualDirectory path="/"
physicalPath="%SystemDrive%\inetpub\wwwroot" />
  </application>
    . . .
  </site>
  <siteDefaults>
  <logFile logFormat="W3C" directory="%SystemDrive%\inetpub\logs\
LogFiles" />
    . . .
</sites>
```

Element Attributes   Logging is controlled through three configuration elements:
system.webServer/*httpLogging*, system.webServer/*odbcLogging*, and system.application-
Host/*log*. The *dontLog* attribute of the *httpLogging* element controls whether HTTP
logging is enabled for the IIS server. With *dontLog*="false", HTTP logging is enabled.
With *dontLog*="true", HTTP logging is disabled.

With the *httpLogging* element, you can configure selective logging using the following
flags for the *selectiveLogging* attribute:

- **LogAll**   Logs both successful and failed access requests. This is the default.

- **LogSuccessful**   Logs only successful access requests.

- **LogError**   Logs only access request failures.

The *odbcLogging* element controls ODBC logging when HTTP logging is disabled. By default it has no content and attribute values are taken from the schema. The default schema values are:

```
<sectionSchema name="system.webServer/odbcLogging">
 <attribute name="dataSource" type="string" defaultValue="InternetDb" />
 <attribute name="tableName" type="string" defaultValue="InternetLog" />
 <attribute name="userName" type="string" defaultValue="InternetAdmin" />
 <attribute name="password" type="string" encrypted="true" />
</sectionSchema>
```

As summarized in Table A-17, the attributes of the *odbcLogging* element control the way ODBC logging is performed.

Table A-17   Standard Attributes of the *odbcLogging* Element

Attribute Name	Attribute Description
dataSource	Sets the Data Source Name (DSN) that IIS can use to connect to the database. Typically, you'll want to use a system DSN.
tableName	Sets the name of the table used to which logging data should be stored within the logging database.
username	Sets the user name of the account you want to use to log on to the database.
password	Sets the password of the account you want to use to log on to the database. The password is expected to be passed as an encrypted string.

Setting the attribute values in ApplicationHost.config overrides the schema default values as shown in the following example:

```
<httpLogging dontLog="true" />
<odbcLogging dataSource="LoggingDB" tableName="WebServer85Log" username=
"IISAdmin" password="[enc:AesProvider:jAAAAAECAAADZgAAAKQAAJbG5Vze9+qBIwzs
3YYUfw4w1FhMxydGFXXSIQN3WjxTI9s7y8a6VsU9h+bMHUsPibqPGbTOZwEovDXWzVGOFg3A
/bi7uJAOphgDDP4/xP18XDwSOrm+22Yyn441LPbG6d4BGBy7G+b/
O2ywozBFbsdckm7bKyNp1NinWKY9dSzKfa912SmYVqvHEQEQjUMXSvg==:enc]" />
```

HttpRedirectionModule

Implements HTTP redirect functionality

Description   You can use HTTP redirection to redirect users from an old site to a new site. In the default configuration for redirection, all requests for files in the old location are mapped automatically to files in the new location you specify. You can change this behavior in several ways. You can:

- Redirect requests to the destination URL without adding any other portions of the original URL. You can use this option to redirect an entire site or directory to one location. For example, you could redirect all requests for any page or resource at *http://www.adatum.com* to *http://www.cpandl.com/wemoved.htm*.

■ Redirect requests for a parent directory to a child directory. For example, you could redirect your home directory (designated by /) to a subdirectory named /Current.

Using status codes, you can indicate to the client browser whether a redirection is a standard redirection (HTTP status code 302), a temporary redirection (HTTP status code 307), or a permanent redirection (HTTP status code 301). Use redirect wildcard characters to redirect particular types of files to a specific file at the destination. For example, you can use redirect wildcard characters to redirect all .htm files to Default.htm and all .asp files to Default.asp. The syntax for wildcard character redirection is:

`*;*.EXT;FILENAME.EXT[;*.EXT;FILENAME.EXT...]`

where *.EXT* is the file extension you want to redirect and *FILENAME.EXT* is the name of the file to use at the destination. As shown, begin the destination URL with an asterisk and a semicolon and separate pairs of wildcard characters and destination URLs with a semicolon. Be sure to account for all document types that users might request directly, such as .htm, .html, .asp, and .aspx documents.

Executable   *%Windir%*\System32\Inetsrv\Redirect.dll

Dependencies   None

Configuration Element   system.webServer/*httpRedirect*

ApplicationHost.config Usage Examples

```
<!-- Redirect requests relative to destination (the default) -->
<httpRedirect enabled="true" destination="http://www.adatum.com/" />

<!-- Redirect all request to the exact destination -->
<httpRedirect enabled="true" destination="http://www.adatum.com/
wemoved.htm" exactDestination="true" />

<!--
 Redirect requests to content in this directory (not subdirectories) -->
<httpRedirect enabled="true" destination="/
Current" childOnly="true" />

<!-- Set a status code for redirection -->
<httpRedirect enabled="true" destination="http://www.adatum.com/"
httpResponseStatus="Permanent" />
```

Element Attributes   The system.webServer/*httpRedirect* element controls HTTP redirection. Table A-18 summarizes the attributes of this element.

Table A-18   Standard Attributes of the *profiles/add* Element

Attribute Name	Attribute Description
enabled	Controls whether redirection is enabled or disabled. If set to true, redirection is enabled and you must provide a destination for redirection. The default is false.
destination	Sets the location to which clients are redirected. This attribute cannot be set to an empty string.
exact-Destination	Controls whether clients are redirected to a relative or absolute location. If set to false, all requests for files in the old location are mapped automatically to files in the new location you specify. If set to true, all requests for any page or resource are redirected to the exact location specified in the destination. The default is false.
childOnly	Controls whether requests for a parent directory are redirected to a child directory. If set to true, requests for a parent directory are redirected to a child directory. If set to false, requests for a parent directory are not redirected to a child directory. The default is false.
httpResponse-Status	Sets the HTTP status code for the redirection. Use Found to indicate a standard redirection (HTTP status code 302). Use Temporary to indicate a temporary redirection (HTTP status code 307). Use Permanent to indicate a permanent redirection (HTTP status code 301).

IISCertificateMappingAuthenticationModule

Implements SSL client certificate mapping

Description   The IISCertificateMappingAuthenticationModule maps SSL client certificates to a Windows account. With this method of authentication, user credentials and mapping rules are stored within the IIS configuration store. At least one authentication module must be configured. When this authentication method is enabled, client certificates can be mapped to Windows accounts in two ways:

- On a one-to-one basis, in which each client must have its own SSL client certificate

- On a many-to-one basis, in which multiple clients can use the same SSL client certificate

This module allows SSL client certificate mapping by creating the necessary *HttpUser* object. The *HttpUser* object is an IIS data structure. The IIS server core checks to ensure that this object is populated after the authentication phase. See Chapter 10 for more information on authentication.

Executable   *%Windir%\System32\Inetsrv\Authmap.dll*

Dependencies   The server must be configured to use SSL and to receive client certificates.

Configuration Element   system.webServer/security/authentication/*iisClient-CertificateMappingAuthentication*

ApplicationHost.config Usage Examples

```
<iisClientCertificateMappingAuthentication enabled="false">
</iisClientCertificateMappingAuthentication>
```

Element Attributes   SSL client certificate authentication is handled through the *iisClientCertificateMappingAuthentication* element. Table A-19 summarizes the standard attributes of this element.

Table A-19   Standard Attributes of the *iisClientCertificateMappingAuthentication* Element

Attribute Name	Attribute Description
defaultLogonDomain	Sets the optional name of the default domain against which the client certificates are authenticated. The default logon domain is an empty string.
enabled	Controls whether client certificate authentication is enabled or disabled. The default is false.
logonMethod	Sets the optional logon method for the related user account as Interactive, Batch, Network, or ClearText. The default is ClearText.
oneToOneCertificate-MappingsEnabled	Controls whether one-to-one certificate mapping is enabled. When client certificate authentication is enabled, the default is true.
manyToOneCertificate-MappingsEnabled	Controls whether many-to-one certificate mapping is enabled. When client certificate authentication is enabled, the default is true.

When SSL client certificate authentication is enabled, certificate mapping relationships, rules, or both must also be defined. With many-to-one certificate mapping, each mapping has a relationship entry and one or more rule definitions in addition to an enabled value that indicates whether the mapping is enabled or disabled. The basic syntax for a many-to-one mapping is as follows:

```
<iisClientCertificateMappingAuthentication enabled="true">
  <manyToOneCertificateMappings>
   <add name="AllClients" description="The default mapping for clients"
enabled="true" permissionMode="Allow" username="authUser"
password="[enc:AesProvider:...:enc]">
    <rules>
     <add certificateField="Subject" certificateSubField=""
```

```
matchCriteria="" compareCaseSensitive="">
  <add certificateField="Issuer" certificateSubField=""
matchCriteria="" compareCaseSensitive="">
  </rules>
  </manyToOneCertificateMappings>
</iisClientCertificateMappingAuthentication>
```

With one-to-one certificate mapping, each mapping has only a relationship entry. The entry specifies the Windows user, the user's encrypted password, and the related certificate as an enabled value that indicates whether the mapping is enabled or disabled. The basic syntax for a one-to-one mapping is as follows:

```
<iisClientCertificateMappingAuthentication enabled="true">
  <oneToOneCertificateMappings>
    <add enabled="true" userName="wrstanek" password="[enc:AesProvider:
...:enc]" certificate="">
  </oneToOneCertificateMappings>
</iisClientCertificateMappingAuthentication>
```

IpRestrictionModule

Implements Internet Protocol (IP) address and domain name restrictions

Description   By default, IIS resources are accessible to all IP addresses, computers, and domains, which presents a security risk that might allow your server to be misused. To control use of resources, you might want to grant or deny access by IP address, network ID, or domain.

Granting access allows a computer to make requests for resources but doesn't necessarily allow users to work with resources. If you require authentication, users still need to authenticate themselves.

Denying access to resources prevents a computer from accessing those resources. Therefore, users of the computer can't access the resources—even if they could have authenticated themselves with a user name and password.

The settings you specify when defining a restriction controls how the restriction is used. For a single computer, provide the exact IP address for the computer, such as 192.168.5.50. For groups of computers, provide the subnet address, such as 192.168.0.0, and the subnet mask, such as 255.255.0.0. For a domain name, provide the fully qualified domain name (FQDN), such as *eng.microsoft.com*.

Executable   *%Windir%*\System32\Inetsrv\Iprestr.dll

Dependencies   Transmission Control Protocol/Internet Protocol (TCP/IP)v4 must be installed on the server.

Configuration Element   system.webServer/security/*ipSecurity*

Applicationhost.config Usage Example

```
<ipSecurity allowUnlisted="true" />
```

Element Attributes   The system.webServer/security/*ipSecurity* element controls IP address and domain name restrictions. Table A-20 summarizes the standard attributes of the *ipSecurity* element. The *ipSecurity* element can contain *add* elements, which define the restrictions you want to use. The attributes of the *ipSecurity/add* element are summarized in Table A-21.

Table A-20   Standard Attributes of the *ipSecurity* Element

Attribute Name	Attribute Description
enable-ReverseDNS	Controls whether IIS can perform reverse DNS lookups. This is useful when you are restricting by domain and the computer has only an IP address set. The default is false, which means that reverse lookups are not used.
allowUnlisted	Determines whether IP addresses not specifically listed as allowed are granted access to server resources. The default value is true, which means that all IP addresses are granted access.

Table A-21   Standard Attributes of the *ipSecurity/add* Element

Attribute Name	Attribute Description
ipAddress	Sets the IP address of the computer or network for which you want to grant or deny access.
subnetMask	Sets the subnet mask of the computer or network for which you want to grant or deny access. The default value is 255.255.255.255.
domainName	Sets the domain name for which you want to grant or deny access.
allowed	Controls whether a computer, network, or domain is granted or denied access. If set to true, IIS grants access. If set to false, IIS denies access. The default is false.

Examples of configuring grant and deny restrictions follow:

Allow unrestricted access

```
<ipSecurity allowUnlisted="true" />
```

Restrict access to a specific grant list

```
<ipSecurity allowUnlisted="false">
 <add ipAddress="192.168.5.53" allowed="true">
 <add ipAddress="192.168.5.62" allowed="true">
</ipSecurity>
```

Allow open access except for specific computers

```
<ipSecurity allowUnlisted="true">
 <add ipAddress="192.168.5.53 allowed="false">
 <add ipAddress="192.168.5.62 allowed="false">
</ipSecurity>
```

Allow open access except for specific networks

```
<ipSecurity allowUnlisted="true">
 <add ipAddress="192.168.10.0 subnetMask="255.255.0.0" allowed="false">
 <add ipAddress="192.168.11.0 subnetMask="255.255.0.0" allowed="false">
</ipSecurity>
```

Allow open access except for specific domains

```
<ipSecurity allowUnlisted="true">
 <add domain="eng.microsoft.com" allowed="false">
</ipSecurity>
```

IsapiFilterModule

Implements ISAPI filter functionality

Description   IIS uses ISAPI filters to provide additional functionality. If you selected ASP.NET during initial configuration, an ASP.NET filter is configured to provide this functionality. Each version of ASP.NET installed on the Web server must have a filter definition that identifies the version and path to the related filter. After you install new versions of ASP.NET, you can add definitions for the related filter. If you remove this module, IIS will not be able to load ISAPI filters, and applications might stop working, which could expose sensitive content.

Executable   *%Windir%*\System32\Inetsrv\Filter.dll

Dependencies   None

Configuration Element   system.webServer/*isapiFilters*

ApplicationHost.config Usage Examples

```
<isapiFilters>
 <filter name="ASP.Net_2.0.50727.0"
path="%windir%\Microsoft.NET\Framework\v2.0.50727\aspnet_filter.dll"
enableCache="true"
preCondition="bitness32" />
</isapiFilters>
```

Element Attributes   The system.webServer/*isapiFilters* element determines which filters are available. Each filter you want to use must have a corresponding *filter* element. Table A-22 summarizes the standard attributes of the filter element.

Table A-22   Standard Attributes of the *isapiFilters* Element

Attribute Name	Attribute Description
Name	Sets the unique name of the filter.
Path	Sets the full file path to the DLL for the filter.
Enabled	Controls the availability of the filter. If set to true, the filter is available. If set to false, the filter is not available. The default is true.
enableCache	Determines whether the filter can use the caching features of IIS. If set to true, the filter can use caching. If set to false, the filter cannot use caching. The default is false.
precondition	Sets any necessary prerequisites for the filter.

IsapiModule

Implements ISAPI Extension functionality

Description   The IsapiModule makes it possible to use ISAPI Extension functionality. In the IIS core installation, several components rely on handlers that are based on ISAPI extensions, including ASP and ASP.NET. The IsapiModule has a managed handler that specifies that all files with the .dll extension are handled as ISAPI extensions. If you remove this module, ISAPI Extensions mapped in the <handlers> section or explicitly called as ISAPI Extensions will no longer work.

This module is used with the system.webServer/*isapiCgiRestriction* element. See the "CgiModule" section of this appendix for more information.

Executable   %Windir%\System32\Inetsrv\Isapi.dll

Dependencies   None

Configuration Elements   system.webServer/*isapiCgiRestriction*

system.webServer/*handlers*

ApplicationHost.config Usage Examples

```
<!-- related handler definitions -->
<add name="ASPClassic" path="*.asp" verb="GET,HEAD,POST"
modules="IsapiModule" scriptProcessor="%windir%\system32\inetsrv
\asp.dll" resourceType="File" />
<add name="SecurityCertificate" path="*.cer" verb="GET,HEAD,POST"
modules="IsapiModule" scriptProcessor="%windir%\system32\inetsrv
\asp.dll" resourceType="File" />
<add name="AXD-ISAPI-2.0" path="*.axd" verb="GET,HEAD,POST,DEBUG"
```

```
modules="IsapiModule" scriptProcessor="%windir%\Microsoft.NET
\Framework\v2.0.50727\aspnet_isapi.dll" preCondition="classicMode,
runtimeVersionv2.0,bitness32" responseBufferLimit="0" />
<add name="PageHandlerFactory-ISAPI-2.0" path="*.aspx"
verb="GET,HEAD,POST,DEBUG" modules="IsapiModule"
scriptProcessor="%windir%\Microsoft.NET\Framework\v2.0.50727\aspnet_
isapi.dll" preCondition="classicMode,runtimeVersionv2.0,bitness32"
responseBufferLimit="0" />
<add name="SimpleHandlerFactory-ISAPI-2.0" path="*.ashx" verb="GET,
HEAD,POST,DEBUG" modules="IsapiModule" scriptProcessor="%windir%
\Microsoft.NET\Framework\v2.0.50727\aspnet_isapi.dll" preCondition="
classicMode,runtimeVersionv2.0,bitness32" responseBufferLimit="0" />
<add name="WebServiceHandlerFactory-ISAPI-2.0" path="*.asmx"
verb="GET,HEAD,POST,DEBUG" modules="IsapiModule"
scriptProcessor="%windir%\Microsoft.NET\Framework\v2.0.50727\aspnet_
isapi.dll" preCondition="classicMode,runtimeVersionv2.0,bitness32"
responseBufferLimit="0" />
<add name="HttpRemotingHandlerFactory-rem-ISAPI-2.0" path="*.rem"
verb="GET,HEAD,POST,DEBUG" modules="IsapiModule"
scriptProcessor="%windir%\Microsoft.NET\Framework\v2.0.50727
\aspnet_isapi.dll" preCondition="classicMode,runtimeVersionv2.0,
bitness32" responseBufferLimit="0" />
<add name="HttpRemotingHandlerFactory-soap-ISAPI-2.0" path="*.soap"
verb="GET,HEAD,POST,DEBUG" modules="IsapiModule"
scriptProcessor="%windir%\Microsoft.NET\Framework\v2.0.50727
\aspnet_isapi.dll" preCondition="classicMode,runtimeVersionv2.0,
bitness32" responseBufferLimit="0" />
<add name="ISAPI-dll" path="*.dll" verb="*" modules="IsapiModule"
resourceType="File" requireAccess="Execute" allowPathInfo="true" />
```

Element Attributes   See the "CgiModule" section of this appendix for details.

ManagedEngine

Implements ASP.NET integration (*not installed by default*)

Description   ManagedEngine provides the necessary functionality for IIS integration with the ASP.NET runtime engine. If you remove this module, ASP.NET integration will be disabled. As a result, none of the managed modules declared in the <modules> section or ASP.NET handlers declared in the <handlers> section will be called when the application pool runs in Integrated mode. In a standard configuration, this module is not added even if you select all available features during installation of IIS.

Executable   %Windir%\Microsoft.NET\Framework*Version*\Webengine.dll

Dependencies   None

Configuration Elements   None

ApplicationHost.config Usage Examples

```
<!-- globalModules installation definition -->
<add name="ManagedEngine" image="%windir%\Microsoft.NET\Framework
\v2.0.50727\webengine.dll" preCondition="integratedMode,runtime
Versionv2.0,bitness32" />

<!-- modules activation definition -->
<add name="ManagedEngine" preCondition="integratedMode,
runtimeVersionv2.0,bitness32" />
```

ProtocolSupportModule

Implements keep-alive support, custom headers, and redirect headers

Description   The ProtocolSupportModule makes it possible for IIS to use the TRACE and OPTIONS verbs in HTTP headers. These features are used with HTTP keep-alive, custom headers, and redirect headers. If you remove this module, IIS will return a "405 Method not allowed" error message any time you attempt to use these features.

Executable   %Windir%\System32\Inetsrv\Protsup.dll

Dependencies   None

Configuration Element   system.webServer/*httpProtocol*

ApplicationHost.config Usage Examples

```
<httpProtocol>
 <customHeaders>
  <clear />
   <add name="X-Powered-By" value="ASP.NET" />
 </customHeaders>
 <redirectHeaders>
  <clear />
 </redirectHeaders>
</httpProtocol>
```

Element Attributes   The *httpProtocol* element controls the use of keep-alive support, custom headers, and redirect headers. The basic syntax for working with these features follows:

```
<httpProtocol>
 <customHeaders>
 . . .
 </customHeaders>
 <redirectHeaders>
 . . .
 </redirectHeaders>
</httpProtocol>
```

Generally, you set either a custom header or a redirect header, but not both. Before using these features, you should clear out the current values by using an empty clear element, such as:

```
<redirectHeaders>
 <clear />
</redirectHeaders>
```

Using the *add* element, you can then define the necessary custom header or redirect header. The *add* element has two basic attributes: *name* and *value*. As shown in the following example, the *name* attribute sets the type of header, and the *value* attribute sets the contents of the header:

```
<customHeaders>
 <clear />
 <add name="X-Powered-By" value="ASP.NET" />
</customHeaders>
```

RequestFilteringModule

Implements request filtering

Description   The RequestFilteringModule is designed to reject suspicious requests by scanning URLs sent to the server and filtering out unwanted requests. You can filter requests in several ways. You can:

- Specify that only requests with specified file extensions be allowed

- Specify that all requests except specified file extensions be allowed

- Specify that certain code segments are hidden so that they cannot be accessed in clients

By default, IIS is configured to block requests for file extensions that could be misused and also blocks browsing of critical code segments. If you uninstall or disable the RequestFilteringModule, you will reduce the overall security of the server and may open the server to attack.

Executable   *%Windir%*\System32\Inetsrv\Modrqflt.dll

Dependencies   None

Configuration Element   system.webServer/security/*requestFiltering*

ApplicationHost.config Usage Examples

```
<requestFiltering>
 <fileExtensions allowUnlisted="true" applyToWebDAV="true">
  <add fileExtension=".asax" allowed="false" />
```

```
    <add fileExtension=".ascx" allowed="false" />
    …
    </fileExtensions>
    <verbs allowUnlisted="true" applyToWebDAV="true"/>
    <hiddenSegments applyToWebDAV="true">
     <add segment="web.config" />
     <add segment="bin" />
     <add segment="App_code" />
     <add segment="App_GlobalResources" />
     <add segment="App_LocalResources" />
     <add segment="App_WebReferences" />
     <add segment="App_Data" />
     <add segment="App_Browsers" />
    </hiddenSegments>
    </requestFiltering>
```

Element Attributes   Within the *requestFiltering* element, you can use the *fileExtensions* element to define file extensions that are either allowed or blocked and the *hiddenSegments* element to define segments that should be hidden from clients.

To allow all requests except specified file extensions, you use the following basic syntax:

```
<fileExtensions allowUnlisted="true" applyToWebDAV="true">
  <add fileExtension=".asax" allowed="false" />
  . . .
</fileExtensions>
```

Here the *allowUnlisted* attribute of the *fileExtensions* element is set to true to allow all file requests by default. The *add* element is then used to define exceptions to this rule. The *fileExtension* attribute of the *add* element sets the file extension for the exception. The *allowed* attribute specifies whether requests for files with the extension are allowed or blocked. If allowed="true", requests for files with the extension are allowed. If allowed= "false", requests for files with the extension are blocked.

To specify that only requests with specified file extensions be allowed, you use the following basic syntax:

```
<fileExtensions allowUnlisted="true" applyToWebDAV="true">
  <add fileExtension=".asax" allowed="true" />
  . . .
</fileExtensions>
```

Here the *allowUnlisted* attribute of the *fileExtensions* element is set to false to block all file requests by default. The *add* element is then used to define exceptions to this rule as discussed previously.

To specify that certain segments are hidden so that they cannot be accessed in clients, you use the following basic syntax:

```
<hiddenSegments applyToWebDAV="true">
  <add segment="bin" />
  . . .
</hiddenSegments>
```

Here, the *segment* attribute of the *add* element is used to specify a code segment that is hidden.

RequestMonitorModule

Implements a run-time interface for making queries

Description   The RequestMonitorModule implements the IIS 7.0 Run-Time State and Control Interface (RSCA). RSCA makes it possible for applications and clients to query for run-time information, such as details on currently executing requests, the run state of a Web site, or the currently executing application domains. If you remove this module, applications and clients won't be able to query the run-time environment.

Executable   *%Windir%*\System32\Inetsrv\Iisreqs.dll

Dependencies   None

Configuration Elements   None

ApplicationHost.config Usage Examples

```
<!-- globalModules installation definition -->
<add name="RequestMonitorModule" image="%windir%\System32\inetsrv
\iisreqs.dll" />

<!-- modules activation definition -->
<add name="RequestMonitorModule" />
```

ServerSideIncludeModule

Implements Server-Side Includes (SSI)

Description   When you install and activate the ServerSideIncludeModule, IIS can use Server-Side Includes (SSI). This module has managed handlers that specify that it is executed only for files with the .stm, .shtm, and .shtml extensions. If you remove this module, .stm, .shtm and .shtml files will be handled by the static file module.

Note   In the Application.Host.config file you define MIME types the server can handle using *mimeMap* elements. The Application.Host.config file does not have *mimeMap* definitions for the extensions used for Server-Side Includes (SSI). This is as designed, and you should not change this. If you create *mimeMap* definitions for the .stm, .shtm, and .shtml extensions, files with these extensions will be served as text (rather than content that needs to be executed to process the Server-Side Includes (SSI).

Executable   %Windir%\System32\Inetsrv\Iis_ssi.dll

Dependencies   None

Configuration Element   system.webServer/*serverSideInclude*

ApplicationHost.config Usage Examples

```
<!-- related handler definitions -->
<add name="SSINC-stm" path="*.stm" verb="GET,POST"
modules="ServerSideIncludeModule" resourceType="File" />
<add name="SSINC-shtm" path="*.shtm" verb="GET,POST"
modules="ServerSideIncludeModule" resourceType="File" />
<add name="SSINC-shtml" path="*.shtml" verb="GET,POST"
modules="ServerSideIncludeModule" resourceType="File" />


<!-- element usage examples -->
<serverSideInclude ssiExecDisable="false" />
```

Element Attributes   The *ssiExecDisable* attribute of the *serverSideInclude* element can be used to enable or disable Server-Side Includes (SSI) without having to uninstall or remove the ServerSideIncludeModule. To disable Server-Side Includes (SSI) globally by default, you can set this attribute as shown in this example:

```
<serverSideInclude ssiExecDisable="true" />
```

To enable Server-Side Includes (SSI) globally by default, you can set this attribute as shown in this example:

```
<serverSideInclude ssiExecDisable="false" />
```

You can edit an application's Web.config file to override the default setting.

StaticCompressionModule

Implements compression of static content

Description   You can use the StaticCompressionModule to enable compression of static content. This module uses both in-memory as well as persistent in-the-file-system compression to reduce the size of files sent to client browsers, decreasing transmission time and improving performance. If you remove this module, compression of static content is disabled and uncompressed content is sent to client browsers.

See the "DynamicCompressionModule" section of this appendix for specific details on how compression can be configured.

Executable *%Windir%*\System32\Inetsrv\Compstat.dll

Dependencies None

Configuration Elements system.webServer/*httpCompression*

system.webServer/*urlCompression*

ApplicationHost.config Usage Examples

```
<!-- globalModules installation definition -->
<add name="StaticCompressionModule"
image="%windir%\System32\inetsrv\compstat.dll" />

<!-- modules activation definition -->
<add name="StaticCompressionModule" />
```

StaticFileModule

Implements static file handling

Description Sends out static files with the file extension .html, .jpg, and many others. The list of file extensions is determined by the *staticContent/mimeMap* configuration collection. Potential issues when removing this module include static files no longer being served and requests for files return a "200 - OK" message with an empty entity body.

Executable *%Windir%*\System32\Inetsrv\Static.dll

Dependencies None

Configuration Element system.webServer/*staticContent*

ApplicationHost.config Usage Examples

```
<staticContent lockAttributes="isDocFooterFileName">
<mimeMap fileExtension=".323" mimeType="text/h323" />
. . .
<mimeMap fileExtension=".zip" mimeType="application
/x-zip-compressed" />
</staticContent>
```

TokenCacheModule

Implements security token caching for password-based authentication schemes (*not installed by default*)

Description The TokenCacheModule caches Windows security tokens for password-based authentication schemes, including Anonymous authentication, Basic authentication, and Digest authentication. Once IIS has cached a user's security token, the cached security token can be used for subsequent requests by that user. If you disable or remove this module, a user must be logged on for every request, which can result in multiple logon user calls, which could substantially reduce overall performance.

Executable   %Windir%\System32\Inetsrv\Cachtokn.dll

Dependencies   None

Configuration Elements   None

ApplicationHost.config Usage Examples

```
<!-- globalModules installation definition -->
<add name="TokenCacheModule"
image="%windir%\System32\inetsrv\cachtokn.dll"

<!-- modules activation definition -->
<add name="TokenCacheModule" />
```

TracingModule

Implements event tracing and trace warning (*not installed by default*)

Description   The TracingModule implements event tracing and trace warning. If you remove or disable this module, event tracing and warning won't work. For details on how tracing can be configured, see the "FailedRequestsTracingModule" section in this appendix.

Executable   %Windir%\System32\Inetsrv\Iisetw.dll

Dependencies   None

Configuration Element   system.webServer/*httpTracing*

ApplicationHost.config Usage Examples

```
<!-- globalModules installation definition -->
<add name="TracingModule"
image="%windir%\System32\inetsrv\iisetw.dll" />

<!-- modules activation definition -->
<add name="TracingModule" />
```

UriCacheModule

Implements a generic cache for URL-specific server state (*not installed by default*)

Description   The UriCacheModule implements a generic cache for URL-specific server state, such as configuration details. With this module, the server will read configuration information only for the first request for a particular URL. For subsequent requests, the server will use the cached information as long as the configuration does not change. If you remove or disable this module, the server must retrieve the state information for every request, which could reduce the overall performance of the server.

Executable   *%Windir%*\System32\Inetsrv\Cachuri.dll

Dependencies   None

Configuration Elements   None

ApplicationHost.config Usage Examples

```
<!-- globalModules installation definition -->
<add name="UriCacheModule"
image="%windir%\System32\inetsrv\cachuri.dll" />

<!-- modules activation definition -->
<add name="UriCacheModule" />
```

UrlAuthorizationModule

Implements authorization based on configuration rules

Description   The UrlAuthorizationModule implements authorization based on configuration rules. When you enable and configure the features of this module, you can require logon and allow or deny access to specific URLs based on user names, .NET roles, and HTTP request method. If you remove or disable this module, managed URLs will no longer be protected.

Executable   *%Windir%*\System32\Inetsrv\Urlauthz.dll

Dependencies   None

Configuration Element   system.webServer/security/*authorization*

ApplicationHost.config Usage Examples

```
<authorization>
  <add accessType="Allow" users="*" />
</authorization>
```

Element Attributes   The system.webServer/security/*authorization* element is used to allow or deny access to managed URLs. The attributes of the related *add* element are summarized in Table A-23.

Table A-23   Standard Attributes of the *authorization/add* Element

Attribute Name	Attribute Description
accessType	Sets the access type for the specified user, role, or HTTP request. If set to Allow, the specified user, role, or HTTP request is granted access. If set to Deny, the specified user, role, or HTTP request is denied access.
bypassLogin-Pages	Controls whether a user can bypass the logon page. If set to true, IIS can use the user's current credentials for logon and will allow the user to bypass any logon page. If set to false, IIS will require the user to log on through an applicable logon page.
roles	Sets the name of the .NET role or roles to which the authorization rule applies. If set to *, the rule applies to all .NET roles.
users	Sets the name of the user or users to which the authorization rule applies. If set to *, the rule applies to all users.
verbs	Sets the name of the HTTP request method to which the authorization rule applies, such as GET, HEAD, or POST. If set to *, the rule applies to all HTTP request methods.

WindowsAuthenticationModule

Implements Windows authentication using NTLM, Kerberos, or both

Description   The WindowsAuthenticationModule implements Windows authentication by using NTLM, Kerberos, or both. At least one authentication module has to be configured. As necessary, the WindowsAuthenticationModule creates the *HttpUser* object used by and validated by IIS after the authentication phase. If the *HttpUser* object is not populated as would be the case when there are no configured authentication mechanisms, the IIS server core generates a 401.2 error. See Chapter 10 for more information on Windows authentication.

Executable   *%Windir%\System32\Inetsrv\Authsspi.dll*

Dependencies   None

Configuration Element   system.webServer/security/authentication/*windowsAuthentication*

ApplicationHost.config Usage Examples

```
<windowsAuthentication enabled="true">
 <providers>
  <add value="Negotiate" />
  <add value="NTLM" />
 </providers>
</windowsAuthentication>
```

Element Attributes   The *enabled* attribute of the *windowsAuthentication* element can be used to enable or disable Windows authentication without having to uninstall or remove the WindowsAuthenticationModule. To disable Windows authentication globally by default, you can set this attribute as shown in this example:

`<windowsAuthentication enabled="false">`

To enable Windows authentication globally by default, you can set this attribute as shown in this example:

`<windowsAuthentication enabled="true">`

Within the *providers* element, the attributes of the related *add* element control the permitted authentication mechanisms. You can permit NTLM, Negotiate (Kerberos), or both, as shown in the following example:

```
<providers>
 <add value="Negotiate" />
 <add value="NTLM" />
</providers>
```

Because Negotiate (Kerberos) is more secure, it is the mechanism you want to try first. So always list it first when you allow both NTLM and Kerberos.

IIS 7.0 Managed Module Reference

In the following section, you'll find a reference for the managed modules that ship with IIS 7.0. Managed modules are used primarily by application developers.

AnonymousIdentificationModule

Manages anonymous identifiers for ASP.NET applications

.NET Framework Class Library   System.Web.Security.AnonymousIdentification-Module

ApplicationHost.config Usage Examples

```
<!-- modules activation definition -->
<add name="AnonymousIdentification" type="System.Web.Security
.AnonymousIdentificationModule" preCondition="managedHandler" />
```

Microsoft Visual Basic Usage

```
Public NotInheritable Class AnonymousIdentificationModule
    Implements IHttpModule
Dim instance As AnonymousIdentificationModule
```

C# Usage

```
public sealed class AnonymousIdentificationModule : IHttpModule
```

Dependencies   The ManagedEngine module must be installed.

Configuration Elements   None

DefaultAuthenticationModule

Ensures that an authentication object is provided in the current context

.NET Framework Class Library   System.Web.Security.DefaultAuthenticationModule

ApplicationHost.config Usage Examples

```
<!-- modules activation definition -->
<add name="DefaultAuthentication" type="System.Web.Security.Default
AuthenticationModule" preCondition="managedHandler" />
```

Visual Basic Usage

```
Public NotInheritable Class DefaultAuthenticationModule
    Implements IHttpModule
Dim instance As DefaultAuthenticationModule
```

C# Usage

```
public sealed class DefaultAuthenticationModule : IHttpModule
```

Dependencies   The ManagedEngine module must be installed.

Configuration Element   system.web/*authentication*

FileAuthorizationModule

Verifies that a user has permission to access the requested file

.NET Framework Class Library   System.Web.Security.FileAuthorizationModule

ApplicationHost.config Usage Examples

```
<!-- modules activation definition -->
<add name="FileAuthorization" type="System.Web.Security.File
AuthorizationModule" preCondition="managedHandler" />
```

Visual Basic Usage

```
Public NotInheritable Class FileAuthorizationModule
    Implements IHttpModule
Dim instance As FileAuthorizationModule
```

C# Usage

```
public sealed class FileAuthorizationModule : IHttpModule
```

Dependencies   The ManagedEngine module must be installed.

Configuration Elements   None

FormsAuthenticationModule

Allows you to manage client registration and authentication at the application level instead of relying on the authentication mechanisms in IIS 7.0

.NET Framework Class Library   System.Web.Security.Forms.AuthenticationModule

ApplicationHost.config Usage Examples

```
<!-- modules activation definition -->
<add name="FormsAuthentication" type="System.Web.Security.
FormsAuthenticationModule" preCondition="managedHandler" />
```

Visual Basic Usage

```
Public NotInheritable Class FormsAuthenticationModule
    Implements IHttpModule
Dim instance As FormsAuthenticationModule
```

C# Usage

```
public sealed class FormsAuthenticationModule : IHttpModule
```

Dependencies   The ManagedEngine module must be installed.

Configuration Element   system.web/*authentication*

Library Settings   Table A-24 summarizes the standard settings used with forms-based authentication.

Table A-24   Settings Used with Forms Authentication

Setting Name	Setting Description
Authentication cookie time-out	Sets the time interval, in minutes, after which the cookie expires. The default value is 30 minutes. If sliding expiration is allowed, the *time-out* attribute is a sliding value, expiring at the specified number of minutes after the time the last request was received. Persistent cookies do not time out.
Extend cookie expiration on every request	Specifies whether sliding expiration is enabled. If sliding expiration is allowed, the time-out attribute is a sliding value, expiring at the specified number of minutes after the time the last request was received. By default, this is enabled.
Login URL	Sets the URL to which the request is redirected for logon if no valid authentication cookie is found. The default value is login.aspx.
Mode	Specifies where to store the Forms authentication ticket. The options are: ■ **Don't use cookies.** Cookies are not used. ■ **Use cookies.** Cookies are always used, regardless of device. ■ **Auto-detect.** Cookies are used if the device profile supports cookies. Otherwise, no cookies are used. ASP.NET checks to determine whether cookies are enabled. ■ **Use device profile.** Cookies are used if the device profile supports cookies. Otherwise, no cookies are used. ASP.NET does not check to determine if cookies are enabled. This is the default setting for IIS 7.0.
Name	Sets the name of the Forms authentication cookie. The default name is .ASPXAUTH.
Protection Mode	Specifies the type of protection, if any, to use for cookies. The options are: ■ **Encryption and validation.** Specifies that both data validation and encryption are used to help protect the cookie. This is the default and recommended value. ■ **None.** Specifies that both encryption and validation are disabled. ■ **Encryption.** Specifies that the cookie is encrypted using Triple-DES or DES, but data validation is not performed on the cookie. ■ **Validation.** Specifies that a validation scheme verifies that the contents of a cookie have not been changed in transit.
Requires SSL	Specifies whether an SSL connection is required in order to transmit the authentication cookie. By default, this setting is disabled.

OutputCacheModule

Implements output Caching functionality in managed code for a scalable and fast native alternative

.NET Framework Class Library System.Web.Caching.OutputCacheModule

ApplicationHost.config Usage Examples

```
<!-- modules activation definition -->
<add name="OutputCache" type="System.Web.Caching.OutputCacheModule"
preCondition="managedHandler" />
```

Dependencies The ManagedEngine module must be installed. Potential issues when removing this module include managed content no longer being able to store content in the managed output cache.

Configuration Element system.web/caching/*outputCache*

ProfileModule

Manages the creation of user profiles and profile events

.NET Framework Class Library System.Web.Profile.ProfileModule

ApplicationHost.config Usage Examples

```
<!-- modules activation definition -->
<add name="Profile" type="System.Web.Profile.ProfileModule"
preCondition="managedHandler" />
```

Visual Basic Usage

```
Public NotInheritable Class ProfileModule
    Implements IHttpModule
Dim instance As ProfileModule
```

C# Usage

```
public sealed class ProfileModule : IHttpModule
```

Dependencies The ManagedEngine module must be installed.

Configuration Elements None

RoleManagerModule

Manages the .NET role–based security information for the current HTTP request, including role membership

.NET Framework Class Library System.Web.Security.RoleManagerModule

ApplicationHost.config Usage Examples

```
<!-- modules activation definition -->
<add name="RoleManager" type="System.Web.Security.RoleManagerModule"
preCondition="managedHandler" />
```

Visual Basic Usage

```
Public NotInheritable Class RoleManagerModule
    Implements IHttpModule
Dim instance As RoleManagerModule
```

C# Usage

```
public sealed class RoleManagerModule : IHttpModule
```

Dependencies   The ManagedEngine module must be installed.

Configuration Elements   None

SessionStateModule

Manages session state services for ASP.NET applications

.NET Framework Class Library   System.Web.SessionState.SessionStateModule

ApplicationHost.config Usage Examples

```
<!-- modules activation definition -->
<add name="Session" type="System.Web.SessionState.SessionStateModule"
 preCondition="managedHandler" />
```

Visual Basic Usage

```
Public NotInheritable Class SessionStateModule
    Implements IHttpModule
Dim instance As SessionStateModule
```

C# Usage

```
public sealed class SessionStateModule : IHttpModule
```

Dependencies   The ManagedEngine module must be installed.

Configuration Element   system.web/*sessionState*

UrlAuthorizationModule

Verifies that a user has permission to access the requested URL. This implementation in managed code provides a scalable and fast native alternative to the like-named native module.

.NET Framework Class Library   System.Web.Security.UrlAuthorizationModule

ApplicationHost.config Usage Examples

```
<!-- modules activation definition -->
<add name="UrlAuthorization" type="System.Web.Security.Url
AuthorizationModule" preCondition="managedHandler" />
```

Visual Basic Usage

```
Public NotInheritable Class UrlAuthorizationModule
    Implements IHttpModule
Dim instance As UrlAuthorizationModule
```

C# Usage

```
public sealed class UrlAuthorizationModule : IHttpModule
```

Dependencies   The ManagedEngine module must be installed.

Configuration Elements   system.web/*authorization*

UrlMappingsModule

Implements a URL mapping functionality for ASP.NET applications

.NET Framework Class Library   System.Web.UrlMappingsModule

ApplicationHost.config Usage Examples

```
<!-- modules activation definition -->
<add name="UrlMappingsModule" type="System.Web.UrlMappingsModule"
preCondition="managedHandler" />
```

Dependencies   The ManagedEngine module must be installed.

Configuration Elements   None

WindowsAuthenticationModule

Allows Windows authentication to be used to set the identity of a user for an ASP.NET application. With Windows authentication, you can use the existing Windows domain security to authenticate client connelctions. Windows authentication works only in intranet environments. Because of this, clients must access the internal network to use this authentication mechanism.

.NET Framework Class Library   System.Web.Security.WindowsAuthenticationModule

ApplicationHost.config Usage Examples

```
<!-- modules activation definition -->
<add name="WindowsAuthentication" type="System.Web.Security.Windows
AuthenticationModule" preCondition="managedHandler" />
```

Visual Basic Usage

```
Public NotInheritable Class WindowsAuthenticationModule
    Implements IHttpModule
Dim instance As WindowsAuthenticationModule
```

C# Usage

```
public sealed class WindowsAuthenticationModule : IHttpModule
```

Dependencies   The ManagedEngine module must be installed. Both the client and server must be in an internal domain.

Configuration Element   system.web/*authentication*

Index

Symbols

& (ampersand), in URL, 61
* (asterisk)
  in cmdlets, 91
  in URL, 60
@ (at symbol)
  in e-mail addresses, 231
  in URL, 61
{ } (braces), in URL, 61
[ ] (brackets)
  in set site command, 154
  in URL, 61
^ (caret), in URL, 61
: (colon), in URL, 59, 60, 61
$ (dollar sign)
  preceding redirect variables, 178
  in URL, 60
= (equal sign), in URL, 61
! (exclamation point)
  redirect variable, 178
  in URL, 60
- (hyphen)
  preceding cmdlet parameter, 91
  in URL, 60
#include directive, 183
( ) (parentheses), in URL, 60
% (percent sign), in URL, 61
. (period), in URL, 59, 60
+ (plus sign), in URL, 60, 61
? (question mark), in URL, 61
' (single quote), in URL, 60
/ (slash), in URL, 61
// (double slash), in URL, 59, 61
~ (tilde), in URL, 61
_ (underscore), in URL, 60

A

access control, 63–64. See also
  authentication
  based on domain name. See domain
    restrictions
  based on IP address. See IP restrictions

access logs, 351–352, 385–387
  analyzing, tracking software for, 385
  centralized binary logging, 386, 397
    configuring, 409
    naming conventions for, 399
  centralized W3C extended log file
    format, 386
    configuring, 400–401
  disabling, 410
  enabling, 400
  format of
    changing, 400
    choosing, 385
    list of, 386–387
  IIS log file format, 386, 391–392,
    402–403, 458
    configuring, 402–403
    naming conventions for, 398
  location of, 352, 399
  NCSA common log file format. See NCSA
    common log file format
  ODBC logging. See ODBC logging
  per-server logging, 386, 400
  per-site logging, 386, 400
  searching, 352
  text encoding for, 352, 387, 400
  uses of, 385
  W3C extended log file format, 387,
    393–396, 458
    configuring, 403–404
    naming conventions for, 399
access permissions, 64, 173, 296. See also
  group policies
  assigning, guidelines for, 297
  inherited, 298
  list of, 296
  module for, 434, 479
  setting, 298–299
  special permissions, 296
  users and groups allowed to
    configure, 296
  viewing, 297

multiple host headers for, 138–140
multiple port numbers for, 138
naming conventions for, 136
for private networks, 135
for public networks, 136
for server, determining, 140
types of, 135
IP restrictions
availability of, by server role, 30, 39
configuration levels of, 109
module for, 433, 464–466
with Web servers, 44
ipal cmdlet alias, 92
ipcsv cmdlet alias, 92
IpRestrictionModule module,
433, 464–466
IPv4 address restrictions, 315–318
ISAPI applications, 69, 209–210, 380,
381–382
ISAPI extensions, 210
availability of, by server role, 28, 38
HTTP request types used with, 210
module for, 432, 467–468
restrictions, configuring, 109, 210–213
with Web servers, 42
ISAPI filters, 209, 213
availability of, by server role, 28, 38
for compression (in previous
versions), 189
configuration levels of, 109
configuring, 213–214
global filters, 210
local (site) filters, 210
module for, 432, 466–467
with Web servers, 43
when to use, 210
IsapiCgiRestriction section, 213
IsapiFilterModule module, 69, 432, 466–467
IsapiModule module, 69, 432, 467–468
isUniqueKey attribute, 7
IUSR_ComputerName account, 292, 295

J
jump pages, 207

K
keep-alive support, HTTP, 158–159,
469–470
Kerberos policies, 303

key/value pairs stored by ASP.NET,
233–234
keys, SSL encryption, 323
kill cmdlet alias, 93

L
latency, 376
libraries, on SharePoint sites, 46
list app command, AppCmd, 103, 254
list apppool command, AppCmd, 102, 268
list backup command, AppCmd, 105, 416
LIST command, 22
list config command, AppCmd, 98, 113–114
List Folder Contents permission, 296
list module command, AppCmd, 100
list request command, AppCmd, 105, 269
list site command, AppCmd, 101, 142–151
list trace command, AppCmd, 106
list vdir command, AppCmd, 104, 164
list wp command, AppCmd, 105, 269
lists, on SharePoint sites, 46
local-level accounts, 292
local service account, 292
local service domain, 232
local system account, 292, 293, 296
location
getting, 90
pushing to stack, 90
setting, 90
location locking, 112
lock config command, AppCmd, 99, 116
locking, location, 112
locking of configuration values
compared to location locking, 112
inheritance of, 107
limitations of, 113
overriding, 111, 112–113
specifying, 99, 116
unlocking, 99, 116
logEventOnRecycle attribute, 7
logging, 398–399
access logs. *See* access logs
availability of, by server role, 29, 39
configuration levels of, 109
custom, 398
availability of, by server role, 29, 39
module for, 432, 441–442
with Web servers, 43
data from Windows log files, getting, 90

About the Author

William R. Stanek (*http://www.williamstanek.com/*) has over 20 years of hands-on experience with advanced programming and development. He is a leading technology expert, an award-winning author, and an excellent and popular instructional trainer. Over the years, his practical advice has helped millions of technical professionals all over the world. He has written more than 65 books, including *Microsoft Exchange Server 2007 Administrator's Pocket Consultant, Windows Vista Administrator's Pocket Consultant, Windows Server 2008 Administrator's Pocket Consultant,* and *Windows Server 2008 Inside Out.*

Stanek has been involved in the commercial Internet community since 1991. His core business and technology experience comes from over 11 years of military service. He has substantial experience in developing server technology, encryption, and Internet solutions. He has written many technical white papers and training courses on a wide variety of topics. He frequently serves as a subject matter expert and consultant.

Stanek has an MS degree with distinction in information systems and a BS degree (magna cum laude) in computer science. He is proud to have served in the Persian Gulf War as a combat crewmember on an electronic warfare aircraft. He flew on numerous combat missions into Iraq and was awarded nine medals for his wartime service, including the Air Force Distinguished Flying Cross, one of the highest flying honors one can receive in the U.S. military. Currently, he resides in the Pacific Northwest with his wife and children.